ARBITRATION AND COLLECTIVE BARGAINING:
Conflict Resolution in Labor Relations

McGRAW-HILL SERIES IN MANAGEMENT

KEITH DAVIS, *Consulting Editor*

ARBITRATION AND COLLECTIVE BARGAINING:

CONFLICT RESOLUTION IN LABOR RELATIONS

PAUL PRASOW
Institute of Industrial Relations and
Graduate School of Business Administration
University of California, Los Angeles

EDWARD PETERS
Formerly Presiding Conciliator
California State Conciliation Service
Southern Area

McGraw-Hill Book Company

New York   St. Louis   San Francisco   London
Sydney   Toronto   Mexico   Panama

**Arbitration and
Collective Bargaining:
Conflict Resolution in Labor Relations**

**Copyright © 1970 by McGraw-Hill, Inc. All rights reserved.
Printed in the United States of America. No part of this
publication may be reproduced, stored in a retrieval system,
or transmitted, in any form or by any means, electronic,
mechanical, photocopying, recording, or otherwise, without
the prior written permission of the publisher.**

Library of Congress Catalog Card Number 78–89791

50673

1 2 3 4 5 6 7 8 9 0   M A M M   7 6 5 4 3 2 1 0 6 9

This book was set in Baskerville by
Monotype Composition Company,
Inc., and printed on permanent paper
and bound by The Maple Press Company. The designers were Merrill
Haber and John Condon. The
editors were Gerald C. Spencer and
Cynthia Newby. Stuart Levine
supervised the production.

This book is dedicated to
the memory of the four deceased
past presidents of the
National Academy of Arbitrators
Pioneers in the development
of the modern system of labor
arbitration in the United States

David A. Wolff	Pres	1952
Edgar L. Warren	Pres	1953
Saul Wallen	Pres	1954
Aaron Horvitz	Pres	1955

It is the part of equity to make allowances for human weaknesses; to look not to the law but to the legislator; not to the letter of the law but to the purpose of the lawgiver; not to the action alone of the accused, but to the inherent motivation of his action; not to the isolated part but to the whole; not to the character of a man as he appears at the moment but to his habitual or life mode of behavior; for him to remember the good he has received rather than the evil, and the benefits given to him rather than those he has himself given; to endure a wrong with patience; to be disposed to reach a decision through discussion rather than by direct action; to prefer to engage in arbitration rather than litigation in court, for the arbitrator looks to what is reasonable but the judge is concerned with the interpretation of the law. For this reason the arbitrator was conceived so that equity might thrive.

Aristotle, *Rhetoric*: translator Barbara E. Killian.

Foreword

In an address before the National Academy of Arbitrators on January 30, 1959, Archibald Cox, Boylston Professor of Law at Harvard, observed that "we have not labored at the administration of collective agreements for almost two decades without arriving at some generalizations upon which the unbiased can agree even though partisan interests preclude unanimity." He then urged those intimately familiar with the arbitration process to distill "generalizations from the amorphous mass of arbitration opinions" in order that "the industrial jurisprudence which they have been developing might give wisdom and vitality to conventional law."

At the time Professor Cox gave his talk, the authors of this book were beginning to explore the nature of this emerging industrial jurisprudence. As their investigation proceeded, they began to formulate a philosophy of grievance arbitration and endeavored to translate this industrial jurisprudence "into a body of common law governing judicial interpretation and enforcement of collective agreements." This text represents the fruition of their efforts. How well they have succeeded is a matter of judgment for each reader.

The book is about labor arbitration in particular and collective bargaining in general. The authors believe that a study of arbitral concepts and issues is an effective means of illuminating the dynamics of the larger institution of which arbitration is a part. Collective bargaining comprises much more than the periodic and sometimes dramatic negotiations which occur every few years. Collective bargaining is a continuous process, the very heart of which consists of the countless day-to-day adjustments and accommodations made by the parties during the life of their collective agreement.

The approach throughout the book is analytic and philosophical. The major emphasis is on concept rather than technique. The authors seek to provide a theoretical basis for understanding the arbitration process. Criteria are analyzed and illustrated through the use of significant arbitral opinions. The authors' intention was not to examine the awards of the arbitrators, but to analyze the reasoning behind their awards and to suggest fundamental criteria on which arbitrators were in general agreement, as well as areas where there was some disagreement, such as the issue of clear language versus past practice.

The book combines a theoretical framework with an empirical analysis reflecting the long experience of each author as teacher and practitioner, one as an impartial arbitrator and the other as a professional mediator. Although this volume is not a casebook, the authors use case material to trace the development of judicial arbitration and to analyze the unfolding of arbitral principles. In their words, the central theme of their book is "a study of arbitral criteria and concepts which are at the core of the decision-making process."

Paul Prasow is Associate Director and Research Economist at the Institute of Industrial Relations, UCLA, and Senior Lecturer in the Graduate School of Business. He is currently Vice President of the National Academy of Arbitrators and has served as an arbitrator for over twenty-five years in many hundreds of labor-management disputes involving a wide range of issues. He has written a number of articles on industrial relations and is coauthor of *The Management of Personnel and Labor Relations* (1950). Edward Peters has served as a mediator for almost a quarter of a century and has helped settle literally thousands of labor disputes. Until his retirement in 1967, Mr. Peters was Presiding Conciliator of the California State Conciliation Service, Southern Area. He is the author of two books, *Conciliation in Action* (1952) and *Strategy and Tactics in Labor Negotiations* (1955). He has also published many articles on mediation and collective bargaining.

BENJAMIN AARON, Professor of Law and Director
Institute of Industrial Relations
University of California, Los Angeles

Preface

The authors submit this work in the fond hope that it represents a significant breakthrough in the treatment of essential arbitral concepts and criteria, or at least that it will provide a foundation for social science scholars who would pursue this worthy objective.

The book focuses on the decision-making function of the arbitrator and on the dynamics of the arbitration process as an integral part of the larger institution of collective bargaining in the United States. It seeks to throw light on those fundamental questions which face any adjudicator, arbitrator, or judge, whose pervasive influence is felt by the parties in crucial areas of their bargaining relationships. Such questions, marvelously formulated by Justice Cardozo in his classic study *The Nature of the Judicial Process*,[1] are pertinent to the arbitral process:

> What is it that I do when I decide a case? To what sources of information do I appeal for guidance? In what proportions do I permit them to

[1] Yale University Press, New Haven, 1921, p. 10.

> contribute to the result? In what proportions ought they to contribute? If a precedent is applicable, when do I refuse to follow it? If no precedent is applicable, how do I reach the rule that will make a precedent for the future? If I am seeking logical consistency, the symmetry of the legal structure, how far shall I seek it? At what point shall the quest be halted by some discrepant custom, by some consideration of the social welfare, by my own or the common standards of justice and morals? Into that strange compound which is brewed daily in the caldron of the courts, all these ingredients enter in varying proportions.

This book on peaceful resolution of conflicts through arbitration and collective bargaining should be of value to students and practitioners alike, as well as to those engaged in the judicial process. We believe that a systematic analysis of the "common law" of labor arbitration should be of particular interest to faculty and students of industrial relations in courses offered in law schools, schools of business administration, schools of industrial relations, or departments of economics, political science, and sociology. Behavioral scientists engaged in research on conflict resolution in union-management relations will find the material of value.

The subject matter has been presented in a manner which we hope will be of maximum usefulness to active participants in the arbitral process, either as protagonists or as adjudicators. A particular focus in this regard is to meet the needs of personnel and industrial relations executives, line management, union and employee association representatives, attorneys representing either party, arbitrators, judges, and public officials whose responsibilities encompass labor-management relations.

Although this is not a casebook, a substantial part of the material is taken from actual arbitration opinions and awards. We drew freely from our own experience as teachers and practitioners, as well as from the experiences of a number of arbitrators with whom we could discuss matters intimately. We also interviewed some of the parties to the arbitrations analyzed in the book. In several instances the cases treated have been altered to preserve the anonymity of persons, places, and organizations, thus allowing greater latitude for discussion and analysis.

Much of the material of this study was organized in classrooms over a period of years, tested in mid-term and final examinations given to practitioners and undergraduate and graduate students. Throughout our teaching we continued to revise and adapt the material for maximum learning effectiveness. Not only older students with experience in industry, but undergraduate and graduate students, who viewed the subject matter with an "eye of innocence," at times raised disconcerting questions which caused us to reexamine and modify some of our most cherished premises. After a number of years of constant reshaping of these courses to respond to the needs of our students and to grapple with the day-to-day problems of the practitioners among them, it became clear that a book was emerging that would provide a theoretical framework upon which to build. It became possible to unify many facets of arbitration and collective bargaining into a coherent significant structure, a synthesis of theory and practice in which the whole was greater than the sum of its constituent parts.

The authors have tried to develop a rationale of judicial arbitration; to identify and codify the standards which shape arbitral opinions; to raise to a conscious level the submerged aspects of decision making which are normally considered matters of intuition; to illuminate the subtleties of arbitral decision making; and to specify the sources of information to which arbitrators turn for guidance.

Chapter 1 examines the essence of the collective-bargaining relationship in this country as contrasted with that prevailing in other industrially advanced nations. It shows historically how the collective agreement in the United States has changed from a brief series of broad general statements to the detailed legally enforceable document of today. It traces the development of judicial arbitration from the earlier process of consensus arbitration which predominated prior to World War II.

Chapter 2 focuses on the nature and scope of the arbitrator's authority in interpreting a written agreement. It stresses the critical nature of the submission agreement in limiting the arbitrator's authority and defining precisely the issues to be decided. Also stressed is the role of the record made by the parties at the arbitral hearings.

Chapter 3 seeks to cast additional light on the entire concept of management's rights and obligations in the context of the bargaining relationship. The reserved rights theory of management is considered as a basic frame of reference, incorporating within it the doctrine of employer implied obligations.

To our knowledge Chapter 4 constitutes the first systematic treatment of semantic principles as applied to arbitration and collective bargaining. It serves as the basis for Chapter 5 and illustrates the progression from a philosophical discussion of semantic and linguistic principles involved in contract language to specific case studies demonstrating how these principles are utilized in actual arbitral situations.

Chapters 6 and 7 present an extensive treatment of the nature and role of past practice on contract administration and enforcement. Chapter 8 analyzes two methods of dealing with ambiguity in the written instrument. In one method the issue is disposed of substantively and the ambiguity is resolved by a single conclusive determination. In the second, the ambiguity is treated on a case-by-case basis by an established mode of procedure which involves recurrent negotiations on individual claims during the life of the agreement.

Chapter 9 is an in-depth analysis of the importance of precontract negotiations and their influence on the resolution of subsequent questions of interpretation and application. Chapter 10 is a pragmatic adaptation of the legal rules of evidence and burden-of-proof concepts as they have been applied in the quasi-judicial arbitration process.

Chapter 11 analyzes the essential criteria developed by arbitrators to review managerial decisions affecting an employee's status. Cases involving discipline, discharge, and promotion are included to illustrate the three most common tests used by arbitrators to determine whether managerial discretion has been exercised reasonably.

Chapter 12 presents an analysis of collective negotiations in the public sector, including some significant comparisons with bargaining in the private sector. The section examines some legal and philosophical concepts of governmental sovereignty and the settlement of public employee disputes in the light of recently emerging patterns.

Chapter 13 focuses primarily on development of the federal substantive law on labor arbitration. Included is a discussion of the Steelworkers Trilogy of 1960 and a review of later key high court decisions affecting the legal status of arbitration. Reference is also made to the jurisdiction of state courts in this area of labor-management relations.

Chapter 14 goes to the heart of the institutional roles of the parties in collective bargaining. It emphasizes a theme recurrent throughout the entire work, namely, that the employer acts and the union reacts—that management exercises the right of administrative initiative and the union is free to challenge its decisions. The Torrington Case is ideally suited to illustrate fundamental premises of the nature of collective bargaining which are not infrequently lost sight of by the parties.

The book concludes with a colloquy between the authors which seeks to illuminate some of those tangible and intangible forces that contribute to the development and acceptability of an arbitrator—typical of the few hundred persons who do most of the labor arbitration in the United States.

PAUL PRASOW
EDWARD PETERS

Acknowledgments

First and foremost to be acknowledged is our indebtedness to the Institute of Industrial Relations of the University of California at Los Angeles for providing a climate conducive to independent scholarly research and for furnishing valuable economic support, research assistance, editorial service, and stenographic help.

The Institute's reading committee, consisting of Irving Bernstein, Frederic Meyers, and David Ziskind, offered many helpful and provocative suggestions. In addition, our deep appreciation goes to others who read all or portions of the manuscript and offered valuable comment and criticism based on their own expert knowledge. These include Benjamin Aaron, Morrison Handsaker, Edgar A. Jones, Jr., Thomas Kennedy, and Ralph T. Seward.

The following arbitrators have generously furnished us with one or more of their pertinent arbitration opinions and awards: Irving Bernstein, Howard S. Block, Morrison Handsaker, Adolph M. Koven, Edgar A. Jones, Jr., Thomas Kennedy, Wayne McNaughton, Harry Platt, Harold

Somers, and Arthur Stark. Particularly noteworthy in this regard are Howard S. Block and Adolph M. Koven, who uninhibitedly shared with us their doubts, vacillations, and insights born of adversary pressures, those intangible aspects of decision making which seldom find their way into written arbitral opinions and awards.

The research resources of the Institute greatly facilitated the development and progress of our writing. We should like to acknowledge the skilled editorial judgment of Felicitas Hinman, the Institute's editor, whose suggestions on style and form were most helpful. Hazelle Van Gorder, the Institute's administrative services officer, eased our burdens considerably by managing many administrative aspects associated with this project.

The staff of the Social Sciences Materials Service of the UCLA Graduate Research Library has been especially cooperative. Our thanks in particular go to Edwin H. Kaye, Ann Mitchell, and Elizabeth Smith. A number of graduate research assistants participated in various phases of the research. Deserving of special mention are Alan Mendelsohn and Sharon Nickel, who worked diligently on the bibliography and index.

Our thanks to June Jensen, who gave so generously of her time and energy, interest, and proficient stenographic and clerical assistance throughout the difficult and protracted period of drafting the manuscript. We were fortunate, indeed, that her successor, Helen Mills, carried on with the same enthusiastic interest and cooperation the arduous tasks of the final draft of the manuscript.

Ron Prizeman, who did graduate work at UCLA and is now an industrial engineer in his native England, provided us with relevant material from British publications which widened our perspective of the subject matter and helped crystallize our approach to the opening chapter of the work.

Our present study owes much, of course, to the trail-blazing efforts of such early giants in labor arbitration as George W. Taylor, William Leiserson, Harry Shulman, William H. Davis, and Wayne Morse. They have profoundly influenced our thinking on significant aspects of this subject. Paul Prasow takes this opportunity to express his own indebtedness to George W. Taylor, who, as professor, arbitrator, and mediator, served also as an inspiration to countless other admirers.

Our appreciation to Cynthia Newby, of McGraw-Hill, for an expert job of supervising the editing of the manuscript. Our thanks to Gerald C. Spencer, editor-in-chief of McGraw-Hill's business, economics, and engineering books, for his warm support and personal attention throughout various stages of the manuscript.

To our wives, Dorothy Prasow and Rena Peters, we owe the greatest debt of all as alter egos and morale builders.

Our thanks are due to the following publishers for permission to reprint copyrighted material:

Benjamin Aaron, "Judicial Intervention in Labor Arbitration," reprinted with permission of the *Stanford Law Review,* copyright © 1967 by the Board of Trustees of the Leland Stanford Junior University.

Edgar A. Jones, Jr., "The Name of the Game Is Decision—Some Reflections on 'Arbitrability' and 'Authority' in Labor Arbitration," reprinted with permission of the *Texas Law Review,* copyright © 1968.

Paul Prasow and Edward Peters, "The Development of Judicial Arbitration in Labor-Management Disputes," reprinted with permission of the *California Management Review,* copyright © 1967 by the Regents of the University of California.

Paul Prasow and Edward Peters, "New Perspectives on Management's Reserved Rights," reprinted with permission of *Labor Law Journal,* copyright © 1967 by Commerce Clearing House, Inc.

Paul Prasow and Edward Peters, "The Semantic Aspects of Collective Bargaining," reprinted with permission of *ETC,* copyright © 1968 by the International Society for General Semantics.

The views expressed in this book are, of course, the authors' and do not necessarily reflect those of the Institute of Industrial Relations or of the University of California.

PAUL PRASOW
EDWARD PETERS

Contents

ARBITRATION AND COLLECTIVE BARGAINING:
Conflict Resolution in Labor Relations

Chapter 1

The collective bargaining agreement

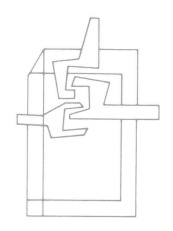

■ An examination question sometimes posed to labor relations students is: "More than twice as many unfair labor practice charges are filed with the National Labor Relations Board by unions against employers as are filed by employers against unions. What is the reason for this disparity?"

Certainly unions are not twice as virtuous as employers. The correct answer lays bare the essence of the collective-bargaining relationship—that the employer *acts* and the union *reacts*. The employer does not go to the NLRB and ask permission to make changes affecting wages, hours, and working conditions. He is much more likely to call his attorney, who might advise him as follows: "If you do it *this* way, you could be on thin ice with the Labor Board; if you do it *that* way, you will be on solid footing." It is then up to the employer to decide which way to proceed on his own. If he anticipates opposition, especially from a strong or militant union, he may consult with the union representatives and attempt to win them over.

However, assuming the union withholds its acquiescence, even objects strenuously, the employer, if he wants to inaugurate the proposed changes, is free to do so unilaterally. The burden then shifts to the union to file charges with the NLRB or, if there is a binding contract, to invoke the grievance and arbitration provisions. If the collective agreement is open for modification, the union might even resort to economic sanctions such as strikes, picketing, and boycotts. It cannot be overstressed, however, that it is the union which is the moving party, the union which attempts to alter the status quo—the status quo, as defined by Webster, being "the existing state of affairs at the time in question."

Another examination question illustrates the same point: "How would you answer an employer who says: 'All through these contract negotiations I have made one concession after another and the union has not offered me a single thing in return. Is *this* what you call collective bargaining?'" To answer his question one must first consider what a union can really offer the employer in exchange for improvements in wages, hours, and working conditions. Can it give up old benefits secured in past negotiations for new, improved benefits? Obviously not. Such an arrangement would transform collective bargaining into a process where the employer takes back with one hand the equivalent of what he has offered with the other.

Assuming that the employer is not trying to revamp or rescind an old established working condition,[1] there are basically only two things the union can offer. It can give up all or part of its other negotiating demands; and above all, the union, for the duration of the current contract term, can give up its right to strike. And that, stripped of pretexts and platitudes, is the fundamental bargain struck by the parties. The union signs away its right to strike for a fixed period of time in exchange for a contract guaranteeing acceptable minimum rates of pay and working conditions.[2]

AN AMERICAN PHENOMENON

This bald exposition of the inner dynamics of collective bargaining is no more complete as a description of the labor-management relationship than "skeleton" is as a description of a human organism. It is intended only to

[1] The 1960 agreement between the West Coast Longshoremen's Union and the Pacific Maritime Association is a case in point. The longshoremen yielded long-established working rules governing size of gangs and severely restricting laborsaving methods and equipment in cargo handling in exchange for a mechanization fund of 5 million dollars annually for 5½ years.

[2] On this point, Morrison Handsaker observes that the union signs away its right to strike only if the arbitration clause and the no-strike clause are unlimited. In a considerable number of cases certain types of grievances are (unwisely in his view) excluded from the arbitration process and therefore also from the application of the no-strike clause. Disputes over production standards in the auto industry constitute one well-known example of the limited arbitration clause and the limited no-strike clause.

lay bare the essential nature and reality of the ultimate agreement. To restate that reality: The employer establishes a status quo, a set of conditions, *with* or *without* the consent of the union. The union as the moving party attempts to alter those conditions. If there is a binding contract prohibiting strikes and lockouts (as provided in approximately 95 percent of contracts in the United States),[3] the ultimate recourse of the union is to arbitration. If there is no binding contract, the union may resort to some form of economic action, including strikes and picketing. It is to be expected that this classic stance of the parties should result in contrary views of the written agreement—views which are not static, but are, it may be argued, in a gradual transition moving toward each other.

The written labor contract as we know it today is a peculiarly American phenomenon. It had its origin in the vast upheavals of the late 1930s, when nonunion mass-production industries such as rubber, automobile, and steel were decisively breached by the CIO. Prior to the big breakthrough, labor agreements, with few exceptions (principally in the railroad and printing industries), were skeletal or generalized agreements where working conditions or rules were left to more informal arrangements. Thus pre-New Deal labor contracts approximated the Western European concept of the collective agreement as a statement of general principles and purposes, depending for enforcement on the good faith of the parties or job action by workers rather than on their present status as legally enforceable documents.

Although in those days American and European collective agreements were quite similar, their resemblances were based on fundamentally, even diametrically, opposed considerations. In the United States the pre-New Deal labor movement was inordinately weak. It entered the twentieth century with little more than 750,000 members, comprising 3 percent of the civilian labor force. Two decades of steady growth brought union membership in 1920 to a peak of 5 million, comprising 12 percent of the civilian labor force. Then postwar reaction, coupled with the relative prosperity of the 1920s and followed by the Great Depression, set the labor movement back numerically below the year of our entrance into World War I. By 1933, total union membership had declined to 3 million, comprising less than 6 percent of the civilian labor force. For all but one year of the pre-New Deal period, at least 90 percent of the civilian labor force remained unorganized.[4] Included among the nine out of ten workers quartered out-

---

[3] *Major Collective Bargaining Agreements: Arbitration Procedures,* U.S. Bureau of Labor Statistics Bulletin 1425–6, 1966, p. 5.

[4] These statistics are from Irving Bernstein's study of labor-union membership as reported in "The Growth of American Unions," *The American Economic Review,* June, 1954, pp. 301–318.

side the house of labor were such entire industries as automobile, steel, ocean transport, and oil, where unions had barely penetrated or had been all but wiped out in the 1920s.

Under such general conditions, neither party was much inclined to limit its flexibility by detailed collective agreements. Management wanted the freedom to operate with virtually no hindrance from the union, and the union wanted to be in a position to seize every opportunity to win gains for its members.

EUROPEAN LABOR UNIONS

In contrast, the trend in Western Europe toward broad general and legally unenforceable agreements stemmed from the strength and militancy, or more accurately the socialist and syndicalist philosophies, of the labor movement. European unions are class conscious, closely linked to class-based political parties having announced ideals of reorganizing the social order by varying degrees of nationalization of the means of production and exchange. Although their role as bargaining agents should not be underestimated, the main thrust of the European labor movement is political, with widespread economic action on occasion resorted to in support of political and social goals. As noted by David Granick:

> Not only in their political emphasis, but also in their collective bargaining procedures, European trade unions maintain a national rather than an individual company orientation. Viewing themselves as representatives of a class, they are concerned with raising all workers to new levels. Thus their negotiations conducted in terms of large and heterogeneous industry groups, are geared to winning a level of wages which is applicable to firms of all types; the profitable and the unprofitable, the expanding and the contracting, those which are situated in local areas of excess labor and those which are desperately short of workers.[5]

The subordination of the union's role as bargaining agent to broad goals of reforming the social order is nowhere better illustrated than in the French disinterest in seniority systems for governing layoffs and recall. As Granick describes it:

> Thus the major trade union confederation of France normally refuses to have any truck with layoff procedure. Dismissals of any type should be fought. The result, of course, is not the absence of plant layoffs in times of seasonal or cyclical reduction of demand. Rather, it is the

---

[5] David Granick, *The European Executive*, Anchor Books, Doubleday & Company, Inc., Garden City, N.Y., 1962, pp. 174–175. Copyright © 1962 by David Granick. Reprinted by permission of Doubleday & Company, Inc.

complete preservation in the hands of management of the decision making power, as to which workers should be dismissed. Nevertheless, the ideological purity of the trade unions is preserved, and they are not placed in the position of doing the dirty work of the employers.[6]

To complete the picture, however, it must be noted that the right to continued employment in France is given legal recognition for all employees, whether union or nonunion. In this connection Frederic Meyers notes:

Damages are still, generally, the only sanction, and, for industrial workers, damage awards are still typically small.[7]

Further illumination on the sharply contrasting collective-bargaining systems of the United States and Western Europe is provided by Margaret K. Chandler:

In the United States, labor-management consensus regarding common values has been combined with some fairly effective labor challenges to management rights; in France, the opposite situation has prevailed. Class divisions run deep. For management and workers, there is little sharing of values, but this lack of consensus is not reflected in effective worker opposition at the plant level. Workers may have resented the "capitalist" who operates the business and questioned his right to function in this role at all, but nevertheless management could make transfers, introduce automation, or contract-out without interference from the unions.[8]

American trade unions, by contrast, have made wages, hours, and working conditions, such as seniority protection, their principal activity. "Business unionism," as it is termed, approvingly by some and disparagingly by others, is job conscious rather than class conscious. The United States labor movement has few ultimate goals beyond higher wages, shorter hours, and better working conditions. The emphasis is on Gompers's classic statement, "More, more, more—now." American unions favor the preservation of the key institutions of capitalism, provided that the worst abuses are mitigated through collective bargaining and legislation.

W. H. McPherson further summarizes the basic contrast between the Western European system and our own in the following excerpt:

Grievances are raised much less frequently in most European countries than in the United States. One reason for this difference is that

---

[6] *Ibid.,* p. 178.

[7] Frederic Meyers, "Job Protection in France and Britain," *Labor Law Journal,* vol. 13, no. 7, CCH (Commerce Clearing House), Inc., Chicago, July, 1962, p. 574. In Japan also the employment relationship of those who have gained the status of permanent employees is guaranteed by law and they cannot be laid off or discharged so long as the firm remains in business.

[8] Margaret K. Chandler, *Management Rights and Union Interests,* McGraw-Hill Book Company, New York, 1964, p. 20.

> European agreements place fewer limitations on the rights of management. Many subjects that are covered by American agreements usually remain within the realm of the prerogatives of European management. For example, an issue is seldom raised regarding job assignment, subcontracting, promotion, transfer, or the assignment of overtime.[9]

This observation applies even to the Federal Republic of Germany, whose labor movement is almost as large as that of the United Kingdom. Through a system of "codetermination," as it is called, the labor movement of West Germany has a voice and influence in the management of industry unmatched in any other country, yet it is ineffective on the job level. This is best summarized by E. J. Forsythe in the following:

> The prevalent form of worker representation at the shop level is not the union but the works council (Betriebsrat). Crucial fact is that the German labor union does not have a formal existence within the plant—a fact the unions are trying to correct.
>
> Works council legislation provides a framework of consultation and negotiation on various questions and is designed to preserve industrial peace. It can be argued that it reflects the desire on the part of employers to keep trade unions out of the plants.[10]

HISTORICAL BACKGROUND

It is not difficult in retrospect to discern the key factors which transformed the collective agreement in the United States from a brief, general statement of terms to the detailed, legally enforceable document of today. First was the growth of the labor movement from a low of 3 million in 1933 to 8½ million at the time of the Pearl Harbor attack in December, 1941, and its continued growth through the war years to a membership of almost 13 million by 1946.[11] Lacking class consciousness, the energies of the emerging mass labor movement were directed, not toward radical reorganization of the social order, but to the improvement of wages, hours, and conditions on the job level. Although political and legislative activities have been greatly stepped up, they remain supplementary features of the 18-million-member labor movement of today. The focus of activity is still collective bargaining at the workplace.

Second, as American labor unions became stronger, they were able to penetrate deeply into many areas previously considered the exclusive respon-

---

[9] W. H. McPherson, "Grievance Settlement in Western Europe," *Proceedings of the Fifteenth Annual Meeting, Industrial Relations Research Association,* Madison, Wis., 1963, pp. 26–27.

[10] E. J. Forsythe, "Collective Bargaining in Western Europe," *Labor Law Journal,* vol. 14, no. 11, CCH, Inc., November, 1963, p. 931.

[11] Bernstein, *op. cit.,* p. 304.

sibility of management. In attempting to erect a barrier against union encroachment into managerial prerogatives not agreed to, employers began to spell out in the contract, as unambiguously as possible, those areas which they had reluctantly agreed to share with the union. As unions countered with their own qualifying language, contracts became increasingly more detailed. Additional provisions crept into the agreements as unions pressed for language to consolidate gains acquired by developing practices at the job level. In this gradual process of accretion, the parties were manifesting the American predisposition to legislate or legalize solutions to problems. Martin Mayer has pointed out that "the United States was the first nation in history to organize its governmental apparatus by a written constitution, which fairly quickly came to be regarded as the true source of all authority."[12] Mayer also notes that the United States has four times the population of Great Britain, but twelve times as many lawyers.[13]

A third important factor which strengthened the role of the written, detailed, binding agreement was the decision of the NLRB, later upheld by the U.S. Supreme Court, making it an unfair labor practice for an employer to refuse to sign and put a negotiated agreement into writing.[14] Subsequently, this principle was incorporated by statute in the Taft-Hartley Act of 1947.

A fourth factor in shaping the labor agreement of today was the direction taken by the newly organized industrial unions in the mass-production industries during the late 1930s. Even before Pearl Harbor, most of them had begun to sign no-strike, no-lockout provisions with binding arbitration of grievances for the contract term. The CIO unions thus demonstrated that job consciousness, rather than class consciousness, was not peculiar to skilled craft unions, but was characteristic of all American unions, even those whose leaders might have a contrary philosophy. It must be stressed that the no-strike provision with mandatory arbitration of grievances and disputes over interpretation was a necessary precondition for the supremacy of the written, binding contract.

Regarding the above observation that the United States was the first nation in history to organize its government by a written constitution, the following paragraphs by C. Herman Pritchett are exceptionally informative:

> Until the eighteenth century, the term "constitution" usually meant the general system of laws, institutions, and customs pertaining to the government of a country. The French and American Revolutions, however, brought a new concept of constitution into existence. The con-

[12] Martin Mayer, "Justice, the Law, and the Lawyer," *The Saturday Evening Post,* Feb. 26, 1966, p. 37.
[13] *Ibid.,* p. 36.
[14] *H. J. Heinz Co. v. NLRB,* 311 U.S. 514 (1941).

stitutional system was no longer to be the product of evolutionary processes. It was not to be deduced from a nation's history or practice. Rather, a constitution was a formal, written instrument, a "social contract" drafted by a representative assembly and ratified by a special procedure for determining public assent. A constitution was the act of a people constituting a government. The constitution brought the government into existence and was its source of authority. The government was the creature of the constitution.

To one accustomed to the older developmental view of constitutions, this was a disturbing departure. The Englishman Arthur Young, writing in 1792, spoke with contempt of the French and American idea of a constitution—"a new term they have adopted, and which they use as if a constitution was a pudding to be made by a recipe." To an Englishman it was obvious that a constitution could not be made; it had to grow.

Actually, of course, constitutions can combine both qualities. The Constitution of the United States was made in the summer of 1787, but it incorporated a tremendous amount of political experience from the past, and has been growing ever since. English experience has demonstrated that a democratic political system can develop and individual liberties be protected as well with a traditional unwritten constitution as with the newfangled recipe type of constitution. We have even come to see that there may be actually little difference between written and unwritten constitutions—the written one is constantly being reinterpreted and revised by practice and unwritten custom, while the principles of the unwritten constitution are constantly being reduced to writing in statutes, judicial decisions, and constitutional commentaries.[15]

NATIONAL WAR LABOR BOARD

One more key element accelerating the trend toward the written agreement of today was the activity of the National War Labor Board during World War II, when most American unions had voluntarily given up their right to strike. Functioning in effect as a tripartite arbitration board of disputes over unresolved contract terms, the War Labor Board laid a foundation for arbitration, American style, by pioneering many of the criteria applied by arbitrators today. A tremendous stimulus in the use of grievance arbitration was given by the WLB through its policy of ordering the adoption of contract clauses providing for arbitration of disputes over interpretation or application of the agreement. Undoubtedly this policy was the major impetus for the widely accepted practice of making arbitration the terminal point of the grievance procedure.

[15] C. Herman Pritchett, *The American Constitutional System,* McGraw-Hill Book Company, New York, 1963, pp. 2–3.

R. W. Fleming has well summarized the War Labor Board's contribution to arbitration as follows:

> In retrospect it is clear that World War II did three things insofar as voluntary arbitration is concerned. First of all, it encouraged widespread adoption of arbitration techniques. Second, it sharpened the distinction between arbitration over "rights" and "interests." ["Interests" disputes are concerned with the negotiation or modification of the terms of a collective agreement. They are unresolved issues in contract negotiations. "Rights" disputes arise during the term of a written binding agreement and involve the interpretation and application of that agreement. The vast majority of arbitrations are over "rights" rather than "interests."] Henceforth, it would be clear that the commitment of the parties was to grievance arbitration, not to arbitration of the terms of a new agreement or to substantive issues not covered by the contract. Finally, the War Labor Board served as a training ground for the men who subsequently served as arbitrators. This cadre has ever since constituted the hard core of the arbitration profession. Without the understanding which they brought to the job it is possible that grievance arbitration would have been less readily accepted.[16]

One does not have to reflect long to realize that when contracts constitute merely brief statements of general principles, arbitration is bound to be a fundamentally different kind of proceeding than when contracts treat working conditions in considerable detail providing numerous specific guideposts for decision making. Pre-New Deal labor unions, with some notable exceptions, did not usually engage in arbitration of grievances. Even as late as 1940, arbitration was not a customary terminal point of grievance procedures. Pullman and Tripp observe:

> By and large, within the newly organized mass production industries at the turn of the decade (1940) arbitration either was not mentioned at all in the contracts, or it was provided for on an *ad hoc* basis. The conclusion to be drawn is that it was visualized as a somewhat remote possibility.[17]

THE IMPARTIAL CHAIRMAN

Understandably, the focus of pre-New Deal arbitration was on the spirit rather than upon the letter of the contract. Contract provisions were so broadly phrased, so general in scope, that on specific grievances they served

---

[16] R. W. Fleming, *The Labor Arbitration Process,* The University of Illinois Press, Urbana, Ill., 1965, p. 19.

[17] Doris E. Pullman and L. Reed Tripp, "Collective Bargaining Developments," in Milton Derber and Edwin Young (eds.), *Labor and the New Deal,* The University of Wisconsin Press, Madison, Wis., 1957, p. 354.

as little more than a sounding board for the parties to air their conflicting claims. As often as not, the only role played by the contract was its use by the parties, usually the union, to invoke arbitration. Consequently, early arbitration, especially in the needle trades, was equated with humanitarianism, scorned by voluntarists and ideologists alike. However, in such industries as railway transportation and coal mining, arbitration more closely resembled the present system.

While the arbitrator, or "impartial chairman," as he was often called, was vested with power to make binding decisions, his continued survival depended on his ability to forge a consensus by gaining the concurrence of the contending parties directly or through their representatives sitting on a board with him as partisan arbitrators. Hence he was popularly regarded, with more than a little accuracy, as a mediator with a club, a diplomat whose persuasive powers were reinforced by the ability to indicate that he who rejected a solution offering him part of the loaf might end up with no bread at all.

George W. Taylor has aptly described the role of the impartial chairman (invariably a consensus arbitrator) as follows:

> An impartial chairman, then, is first of all a mediator. But he is a very special kind of mediator. He has a reserve power to decide the case either by effectuating his own judgment or by joining with one of the partisan board members to make a majority decision, depending upon the procedure designated by the agreement. A new reason for labor and management to agree is introduced—to avoid a decision. By bringing in a fresh viewpoint, moreover, the impartial chairman may be able to assist the parties in working out their problem in a mutually satisfactory manner. To me, such a result has always seemed to be highly preferable to a decision that is unacceptable to either of the parties. What's wrong per se about an agreement when agreeing is the essence of collective bargaining?[18]

Another classic description of the consensus arbitrator is provided by William Leiserson:

> His method was primarily that of a court of equity rather than a court of law; but though acting as a judge, he functioned as the administrator of the law as much as its interpreter. . . . He would not decide cases merely on the merits of the briefs or arguments of the parties, for it would not help the industry or either party to have the other party lose a case if it was right but happened to present its case poorly or had its arguments wrong. He would make investigations on his own initiative, get all the facts in the situation, and then decide on the basis of those

---

[18] George W. Taylor, "Effectuating the Labor Contract through Arbitration," *The Profession of Labor Arbitration,* BNA (Bureau of National Affairs), Inc., Washington, D.C. 1957, p. 20.

facts regardless of what might have been presented or omitted in the argument of the case. In making these investigations he often consulted each party separately and in confidence. He found it necessary to do this to get the real truth in industrial cases, which as in ordinary law cases are often hidden by the trial.[19]

Charles Killingsworth and Saul Wallen have written an insightful paper on the development of arbitration systems in the United States which succinctly defines the impartial chairmanship in a statement which could encompass most of the pioneer arbitrators. Consensus arbitration is defined as "a system for resolving all problems that arise during the life of a contract, utilizing a technique of continuous negotiation, and centering on a mediator who is vested with the reserved power to render a final and binding decision."[20] Which explains the lingering confusion of those who have not kept up with developments of the past two decades and still regard "mediation" and "arbitration" as loosely interchangeable terms for one and the same process. They cling to the so-called "humanitarian" approach to arbitration, unaware that it has gone the way of the buffalo.

Labor mediation today, it cannot be overstressed, is in essence a voluntary process which leaves the parties free to make their own decisions, as contrasted to arbitration, which is a judicial process, the arbitrator making an award binding upon the parties. With few exceptions, notably the garment industry, arbitration has lost its hybrid character, having divested itself of mediation as an integral part of the process. Most arbitrations today are conducted by a single arbitrator who has been selected on an ad hoc basis.[21] The arbitrator who would venture beyond a tactful and mild suggestion that the parties attempt mediation of the issue before him would leave himself open to a stinging rebuke. He is there to "call it," not to probe for a consensus solution.

THE JUDICIAL APPROACH

The judicial approach to arbitration, as contrasted with consensus arbitration, received its greatest impetus from the War Labor Board and emerged full-blown after World War II. Its principal difference from consensus

[19] William M. Leiserson, "Constitutional Government in American Industries," *American Economic Review Supplement,* March, 1922, p. 65.
[20] Charles C. Killingsworth and Saul Wallen, "Constraint and Variety in Arbitration Systems," *Labor Arbitration—Perspectives and Problems: Proceedings of the Seventeenth Annual Meeting, National Academy of Arbitrators,* BNA, Inc., 1964, p. 60.
[21] Morrison Handsaker notes that there are major industries, such as basic steel and automobiles, which maintain permanent umpireships. There is also a decreasing number of arbitrations handled by tripartite boards.

arbitration is that the arbitrator can no longer decide any and all disagreements between the employer and the union that arise during the life of the contract. He can rule only on alleged violations of the collective agreement. His authority is confined to the interpretation and application of that agreement. No longer can he function as a freewheeling agent of the parties with the authority to initiate his own investigations, import evidence from whatever source he deems pertinent, and render a Solomon-like verdict based on his own notions of right and wrong. In the language of the U.S. Supreme Court:

> An arbitrator is confined to interpretation and application of the collective bargaining agreement; he does not sit to dispense his own brand of industrial justice. He may of course look for guidance from many sources, yet his award is legitimate only so long as it draws its essence from the collective bargaining agreement. When the arbitrator's words manifest an infidelity to this obligation, courts have no choice but to refuse enforcement of the award.[22]

The arbitrator must render the mutual intent of the parties, whether or not he approves of that intent. He must ascertain that intent, not through his own independent investigation, but from the record made by the parties themselves, as presented to him at a formal arbitration hearing. The parties must be given full opportunity to testify, to present evidence, and to cross-examine those who testify and present evidence against them. The arbitrator must base his decision on that record, and only within narrow limits can he take judicial notice of facts not introduced into the record. Whatever the record, all roads must lead to a single basic objective—the interpretation and application of the collective agreement. The arbitrator must be bound by the agreement and may not reform it by adding to or subtracting from its written provisions.

THREE REASONS FOR CHANGE

The transformation from consensus arbitration to judicial arbitration was an inevitable result of three developments, two of which have already been mentioned here. First was the conquest of the nonunion mass-production industries by the labor movement in the New Deal period and its unprecedented growth thereafter. Second was the focus of Big Labor on "pork chops" trade unionism and its effective penetration into areas where managerial discretion, previously unchallenged, had been supreme. As management tried to limit union incursions into these sacrosanct domains

---

[22] *United Steelworkers v. Enterprise Wheel & Car Corp.*, 363 U.S. 593, 597 (1960).

and unions tried to write in improvements gained informally by pressures on the job level, the contract became increasingly more detailed and specific on such matters as job rates, transfers, promotions, layoffs, and other working conditions.

Third were landmark arbitrations of such eminent pioneers as the late Dean Harry Shulman of the Yale Law School and Wayne Morse, who shifted their emphasis from the mere attainment of a consensus to the writing of opinions which enunciated guideposts for the parties in their day-to-day labor relations. The guideposts evolved by influential consensus arbitrators provided the minimum uniformity of contract interpretation necessary for the transition to judicial arbitration. By the end of World War II, the more important opinions of these arbitrators were being systematically collected and published in topically indexed volumes, first by the Bureau of National Affairs (BNA) and subsequently by Commerce Clearing House (CCH) and Prentice-Hall. As the number of these volumes increased, a "common law" (judge made) of arbitration became firmly established.[23]

The analogy between a body of accepted arbitration criteria and common law is heightened when the collective agreement is likened to statutory law. The analogy becomes even more pertinent when we consider how much arbitration criteria are imported from contract law and applied on a quasi-judicial basis.[24] The quasi-judicial character of the process must be maintained if its usefulness is to be preserved. If arbitration were to lose its present flexibility by aping courtroom proceedings and obliterating the distinction between the two, then arbitration would lose its reason for existence. Flexibility, however, becomes license when the arbitrator imposes his own subjective notions of justice on the parties rather than seeking to ascertain their mutual intent.

The following excerpts from an address by Donald B. Straus, president of the American Arbitration Association, provide an excellent summary of modern arbitration:

> Today, labor contracts are lengthy documents, with every conceivable situation covered, and with a long background of both legislative and judicial battles over the language. Even the arbitration clause itself is

[23] According to Irving Bernstein, the main reasons for the transformation from consensus to judicial arbitration are (1) big industry's desire to contain the union, (2) the "legalization" of collective bargaining with the Wagner Act, (3) the impact of such pioneers as Shulman and Morse, and (4) the growing complexity of the issues, especially nonwage dollar benefits.

[24] It must be stressed that the term "common law" is used for analogy and not in a strict legal sense. Morrison Handsaker has wisely cautioned that "this statement about common law could be misunderstood. There is no doctrine of *stare decisis* in arbitration. Published awards are important and have an impact but a reader [should not] infer that they create binding precedents, as the real common law does."

apt to run many pages, attempting to define both the duties and the limitations of the arbitrator's function. . . .

Both the critics and the boosters of arbitration share the fault of generalizing about this process when it has, in fact, become a highly specialized tool. In the beginning was the need for a man of good reputation to use his wisdom and integrity to get two unruly and unsophisticated parties together. Today it is highly sophisticated—as a peacemaking and as a war-making device—with many different applications and uses. In the performance of their duties, arbitrators a decade or so ago needed only to exercise their Solomon-like instincts. Today, they must be professionally trained specialists, ready to apply their training to the peculiar circumstances established over a long history of collective bargaining by the parties.[25]

CORPS OF SPECIALISTS

The development of established arbitration criteria for interpreting collective agreements gave rise to a corps of specialists representing the parties, who accelerated the trend in the direction of judicial arbitration. These specialists came to rely on the predictability of the emerging common law of arbitration. Their laboriously acquired expertise was wasted on consensus arbitrators; therefore they sought arbitrators who would adhere to judicial standards which could be researched in preparation of their positions. A process of "natural selection" has all but eliminated the "human relations" consensus arbitrators as well as the eager, untrained humanitarians whose principal qualifications for deciding issues were their sterling characters and warm feeling for people.

In stressing the point that arbitrators today are not chosen by caprice, Straus noted:

They are checked upon, cross-referenced and indexed by trade associations, union research departments, law firms, individual industrial relations directors and union business agents. There are even several firms which make a specialty of providing information about individual arbitrators and their performance as reported by companies that have used them before—a sort of private FBI whose dossiers are available for a fee. Opinions about their intelligence, performance, character and adherence to evidence and contract terms are solicited from many sources before they become the selection of both parties, at least in any case of significance to the parties.[26]

This narrowing down of eligibility has reached the point where in a major industrial center such as Los Angeles and its environs it is safe to say

25 Donald B. Straus, "Labor Arbitration and Its Critics," *The Arbitration Journal,* vol. 20, no. 4, 1965, pp. 197–198.
26 *Ibid.,* p. 206.

that between fifteen and twenty arbitrators do at least 90 percent of the arbitrating. An informal check of top members of the National Academy of Arbitrators suggests that in the entire nation three hundred arbitrators at most handle 90 percent of the cases. In the final analysis, there is only one indispensable qualification for becoming an arbitrator—the acceptance by *both* contending parties. And it is this hurdle which keeps the total number of active arbitrators down to a relative handful.

The director of one agency which furnishes arbitration lists gives a graphic account of the "supply and demand" situation in this field of private jurisprudence. He reports:

> New blood, they say, give us new blood. So now and then, when we submit a panel of arbitrators, we slip in the name of a promising young man, a comer, and who are the ones we hear from? You're so right. Those who complain the most that we make up panels by shuffling around the same little group of people. We tried to get a line on him, they'll say, and he's indexed for a mere handful of cases; he's still wet behind the ears and I had to use up a valuable challenge to knock him off. What are you trying to do to us?

A TYPICAL CASE

A would-be arbitrator, it seems, has the same problem of acquiring practical experience as a would-be surgeon. No one wants to be operated on by an apprentice. Perhaps the following account of a typical arbitration case will present a more vivid picture of arbitration as it exists today.

The language of the agreement, let us say, is ambiguous in respect to the issues between the parties. A decade or so ago, telephones would have been ringing all over town, both sides checking out each others' nominations in an anxious search for the "right" arbitrator. Score keeping would have been the order of the day. The union would have been on the lookout for a "liberal," a humanitarian who would lean to the underdog. Management would have been trying to get acceptance of a "no-nonsense man," not a do-gooder, but a sound thinker of unquestioned integrity who would respect and uphold the employer's right to manage, to prosper, to provide jobs for everyone with a minimum of interference from the union. In this morass, both parties would have stumbled, vaguely sensing the need for a trained arbitrator but themselves lacking the expertise to deal with a professional in the unlikely event they found one.

Today the parties begin their search with the knowledge that when contract language is ambiguous, a valid past practice of the company is one of the primary guideposts for ascertaining their common intent. Let us assume that a practice does exist which seems to support the company's interpretation (perhaps because management keeps better records of past practices than do employees). The union knows it cannot prepare its case by ignoring this criterion of past practice; it knows that if the company can establish, beyond reasonable doubt, its version of this criterion, the company will carry the day. The union will counter, perhaps, with testimony and arguments that the alleged past practice is fragmentary, inconsistent, and invalid, because it was not known to the union, and so on. Casebooks will be pulled off shelves, summary indexes skimmed for arbitrations similar to the one pending (cases are often similar but rarely identical), not just to cite arbitration verdicts, but to follow the reasoning which led to the verdicts and to extract guideposts which can be offered in support of a position.

However, one frail reed the parties will not lean on for support is so-called "horse sense." Blinding revelations of right and wrong carry little or no weight in the proceeding. One does not submit the Ten Commandments or the Golden Rule into the record and say, "I rest my case." The beckoning star which guides the wise men of arbitration is the mutual intent of the parties, often obscured by the ambiguities of the contract language pertinent to the dispute.

Consensus arbitration still plays a useful role in a number of industries which retain an impartial chairman or umpire. The most prominent of these are the men's and women's clothing industries, which have had a half century of experience with consensus arbitration. However, the great bulk of arbitrations today are judicial in nature. The awards which emanate from these proceedings are rooted primarily in the provisions of the collective agreement and in the practices of the workplace.

SUMMARY

The powers of the arbitrator prior to World War II were loose and ill defined, largely because the collective agreement was so broadly phrased (at least on noneconomic items) and its general terms so vague as to be well-nigh unenforceable. Hence *consensus arbitration* prevailed. The unprecedented growth in the 1930s and 1940s of a labor movement oriented to the improvement of conditions on the job rather than to the abolition of the existing social order radically transformed the written agreement, making it the focus of collective bargaining. This development was so accelerated by the activities of the National War Labor Board that at the end of World War II *judicial arbitration* was greatly in the ascendancy over consensus arbitration.

Chapter 2

The submission agreement and the record

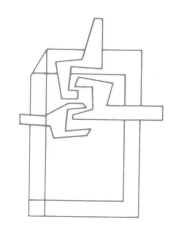

RESTRICTIONS ON ARBITRAL POWERS

■ Because the judicial arbitrator is asked to render the mutual intent of the parties rather than impose upon them his own subjective notions of right and wrong, his powers are restricted in a number of important respects. His decision cannot contradict or go beyond (1) the written agreement, (2) the record developed by the parties at the hearing, and (3) the submission agreement. Even novices understand the importance of the written agreement. Many of them, however, are slow to grasp the fact that the arbitrator also rules on the record made at the arbitration hearing—until their wits are sharpened by a succession of adverse decisions. But one of the most common mistakes of those who lack expertise is their neglect of the importance of the submission agreement, their failure to understand that this document can compel an arbitral decision which is contrary to the weight of evidence in the record and contrary even to the obvious merits of the case.

SUBMISSION AGREEMENT DEFINES
ARBITRAL AUTHORITY

The basic purpose of the submission agreement is to specify in writing the disputed issue, to formulate it as a question or questions to be posed before the arbitrator. The parties seek an answer to *these questions* and no others. Regardless of how freely the arbitrator may express himself in his opinion, only his award is legally binding upon the parties and enforceable by the courts. The award is couched in language to answer precisely the questions in the submission agreement; the opinion usually comes first, is separate and distinct from the award, and has no binding effect on the parties. The submission agreement defines the authority of the arbitrator. Not only does it set forth the issue to be arbitrated in precise language, but it may also contain procedural provisions governing the hearings and placing restrictions on other matters.

The courts will not vacate an arbitrator's award because of mistakes of fact or of law. Since the year 1960, when the U.S. Supreme Court issued three famous decisions popularly referred to as the Steelworkers Trilogy,[1] the grounds upon which the courts can vacate an arbitrator's award are few indeed. The most common ground, under state and federal law, for overturning an arbitrator's verdict is that he exceeded the authority prescribed for him in the submission agreement or in the collective agreement. The arbitrator's award becomes vulnerable if he decides matters not presented to him in the submission; hence both parties strive for formulation of the issue which will weight the argument in their favor. It is not unheard of for an inexperienced person to agree on language which forfeits his claim on the very face of the submission agreement.

IMPACT OF ARBITRATION SUBMISSION AGREEMENT
ON DETERMINING OUTCOME OF CASE

The case of Joseph T., an employee of Falcon Engineering Corporation, illustrates one such instance. Joseph T. was classified as a Jig and Fixture Leader while working on a long-term project which was completed on Friday, March 4, the end of the regular workweek. No new project was scheduled for tooling on the Monday following, so Joseph T. was reassigned temporarily to the rework department in the classification of Tool Engineer.

---

[1] *United Steelworkers v. Warrior & Gulf Navigation Co.,* 363 U.S. 574 (1960); *United Steelworkers v. Enterprise Wheel & Car Corp.,* 363 U.S. 593 (1960); *United Steelworkers v. American Mfg. Co.,* 363 U.S. 564 (1960).

By Monday, March 14, the beginning of the next regular workweek, there being no new tooling project in the offing, the temporary transfer was converted to a permanent one. Unexpectedly an order came in, a sizable one, and on Monday, March 28, the company began a new tooling-up project, reviving the defunct Jig and Fixture Leader Classification. When other employees were moved into the classification and Joseph T. was passed by, he hit the ceiling.

The union filed a written grievance on his behalf, stating his claim as follows:

> On March 7th, just three weeks ago, Joseph T. was temporarily transferred from Jig and Fixture Leader to Tool Engineer. On March 14th, without his consent, the transfer was made permanent. On Monday, March 28th, the Jig and Fixture Leader Classification was reactivated. Joseph T. asks that he be transferred back to his old job.

At the first meeting on the grievance, the union pointed to contract language which read:

> The employer may in his discretion transfer employees between jobs, shifts, and departments. Such transfers will take into consideration seniority and the wishes of the employee involved.

The company replied that the need for Joseph T. as Tool Engineer had far outweighed his personal preference and seniority. In subsequent meetings, the union shifted its ground to a challenge of management's action on March 14, the date it converted Joseph T.'s transfer from a temporary to a permanent one. Management may have been acting in good faith, the union argued, but its decision was based on an assumption which turned out to be wrong, and the grievant should not have to suffer for that mistake. The union was so carried away by this argument that it allowed the following formulation of the issue to be written into the submission:

> Was the Company's action in not retaining Joseph T. in the Jig and Fixture Leader Classification on March 14, 1966, in violation of the agreement?

The union's exclusive focus on the date of March 14 was a fatal error. The arbitrator was unable to review the company's action on March 28 in failing to transfer Joseph T. back to the Jig and Fixture Leader Classification, the first day the classification was revived and the first day that his personal preference and seniority would be relevant. He could only review management's action on March 14, a day when the Jig and Fixture Leader job did not exist. Since the company had acted in good faith on that date, as the union readily acknowledged, based on the facts as they were that day, the arbitrator had no choice but to sustain management's action in making Joseph T.'s transfer a permanent one. Had the arbitrator been given authority to review management's action on March 28, in all likelihood (a he indicated in his dicta) he would have ruled that Joseph T.'s seniority and personal preference, as set forth in the contract, had not been given sufficien weight.

The case of Joseph T. also illustrates a fundamental difference in the relationship of the respective parties to the submission. The following examination question has been used in arbitration classes to probe thi difference:

> Here are two alternative statements of the issue as proposed for th submission agreement:
> 1 Did the Company violate Article V, Section 3, in denying John Do one week's vacation pay?
> 2 Was the Company justified in denying John Doe one week's vacatio pay?
> Which of the two statements of the issue would ordinarily be to th advantage of the union?

The correct answer, so cogently demonstrated by the case of Joseph T., i statement 2. The union is the moving party. It challenges a specific act o management, an accomplished fact. Management is, metaphorically speak ing, a moving target trying to keep the basis on which it may be reversed a narrow as possible. The union, as a rule, wants the question in the submis sion phrased as broadly as possible. Joseph T. would probably have won the case if the question before the arbitrator had been phrased broadl enough to encompass the key date of March 28.

The processes by which a person may be drawn into a disadvantageou formulation in the submission are illuminated by the following dialogu between two blue-collar workers. Mike: "The man I'm voting for is shoo-in. I understand the betting is 3 to 1 in his favor over your candidate. Ike: "Don't kid yourself. My candidate may be rated an underdog, bu believe me, there's gonna be a big upset on election day. Everywhere listen people say they're voting for my candidate." The argument the becomes heated. Mike reaches for his wallet, "Ten bucks say my candidat wins it going away." Ike's face turns several shades. "You've got yourself bet," he says, reaching for his wallet. He knows he should be demandin 3 to 1 odds, but he won't do it. He is so carried away by his partisanshi that to ask for odds might suggest self-doubts about his choice. He has aire his opinions so vehemently that he can't bear to modify them now. H pride won't let him, so he is drawn into what the shop calls a "sucker bet. Let no one who allows pride and emotion to influence his approach to submission think he is immune from a sucker bet.

PARTIES' FORMULATION OF ISSUE TO BE
DECIDED BY ARBITRATOR IS CRUCIAL

Consider the following incident at the Copleston Machine Works. During lunch break two supervisors swooped down on a crap game in the shipping and receiving department. Caught dead to rights were one employee rolling the dice and another who had instinctively grabbed up the money strewn on the floor. The company made good its threat to treat gambling on company property at any time as a Class A offense and promptly fired not only the two employees caught in the act but also three other employees who had been huddled over the dice thrower at the moment of the raid. The latter three employees protested that they were spectators, not participants in the game. To a superficial or biased eye, the union argued, these three seemed to have been involved, but in truth they were only watching. The union became so enamored with this defense that it readily accepted a formulation in the submission which read:

> Were John Doe, Richard Roe, and Jack Moe guilty of gambling on company property during their lunch period on July 1, 1966?

The union based its entire case on disproving the company's contention that the proximity of the grievants to the game had inescapably involved them as participants. Granted that this was the fundamental question to be decided, and granted that even sucker bets are occasionally won, here are just a few considerations advantageous to the grievant which were removed from the arbitrator's authority by the phrasing of the question:

1 Excessive penalty. Discharge may have been an unduly harsh measure for an employee with a good past record and five or more years of service with the company.
2 The ban on gambling was announced through company supervisors months earlier. The practice prior to the announcement had been uneven. Some supervisors had stopped card games, and some had looked the other way. The rule against gambling had never been posted, and there was no clear proof that the grievants were aware of it.
3 The summary discharge of five employees was in the nature of a sudden crackdown, a shooting from the hip. Other employees caught gambling after the ban had been announced had been let off with a warning.
4 A foreman in an adjacent department had sold tickets for a baseball pool to the grievants as well as to other employees.
5 By agreeing to limit the arbitrator's authority to a bare determination of whether the grievants were gambling or not, the union forfeited the right to challenge the reasonableness of a company rule which made gambling cause for dismissal on the first offense regardless of the past record of the accused.

How then, it may be asked, should the question have been phrased to assure an adequate defense of the aggrieved employees? Obviously, the union should have challenged the company's action as a whole rather than have singled out only one aspect as vulnerable.

Most collective agreements provide for the right of management to discipline and discharge for just cause. "Just cause" is an exceedingly broad phrase, the subject of volumes of printed arbitration decisions encompassing a common law of arbitration criteria which have become firmly established. To invoke the application of these criteria, the union should have insisted that the question in the submission agreement be along the following lines. "Were the grievants, John Doe, Richard Roe, and Jack Moe, dismissed on July 1, 1966, for just cause?" Or, "Was the company in violation of the agreement when John Doe, Richard Roe, and Jack Moe were dismissed on July 1, 1966?"

Still another example of how strictly the arbitrator's authority is circumscribed by the submission agreement is the case of Rheem Manufacturing Company and the Stove Mounters' Union, where the arbitrator's award was challenged in the court because he did *not* go beyond the following question in the submission: "Is the Company required to pay 10 days vacation pay to John J. Silva . . . ?"

John J. Silva had been given slightly under five days pro-rata vacation by the company. The union contended that he was entitled to ten days. The chairman of the arbitration board cast a majority vote sustaining the company, while making it clear that had he been given the authority, he would have awarded approximately six and a half days pro-rata vacation instead of the five days granted by the company. Quoting from his opinion:

> The wording of the Submission Agreement is important in that it restricts the Board to a yes-or-no answer. It is fundamental that the powers of an arbitration board are created and limited by the submission agreement; and to make assurance doubly sure, the parties have directed that "the arbitrators shall confine their decision to the issues set forth above." The Union contends that Mr. Silva should have received a full 10 days' pay. The Company argues that it was not contractually required to pay him anything, but made a pro-rata allowance until November 9, 1956, for equitable reasons. As it will appear, there reason to believe that his pro-rata allowance should have been computed to December 31, 1956. But the parties have framed the issue in such a fashion as to preclude a decision in such terms. We must decide whether Mr. Silva was entitled to ten days, or was not entitled to ten days: and nothing more.[2]

Needless to say, the California Appeals Court upheld the award.

[2] *Stove Mounters' Union v. Rheem Mfg. Co.*, California District Court of Appeals, First District, 32 LA 266–267 (1960).

RESOLVING DEADLOCKS IN DEFINING THE ISSUE

It may be asked, since so much rides on the submission, how is it ever possible for the parties to agree on the formulation of the question to go before the arbitrator? In the very nature of the situation there are persuasive considerations for bringing about an accord on the question to be arbitrated. One of the most important of these arises from the reluctance of either party to reject a formulation which calls for an interpretation of the agreement in all its provisions pertinent to the issue in dispute. After all, the contract is the framework which the parties themselves have chosen to stabilize their relationship.

Nevertheless, a large number of cases come before arbitrators without a submission agreement. Many parties, through suggestions and tactful prodding by the arbitrator, are able to agree on a formulation at the start of the hearing before testimony is taken. Others become receptive to a phrasing of the issue by the arbitrator when the hearing is well under way. In some cases the impasse is resolved by asking the arbitrator to phrase the issue for the parties. A last resort in many cases is for the parties to formulate their own respective versions of the issue and allow the arbitrator to decide between the two. If none of these alternatives is acceptable, then the parties and the arbitrator proceed at their own risk. Sometimes the arbitrator can arrive at an acceptable formulation of the issue after the hearing is completed, and he is then able to review the record of the case, which usually includes testimony of witnesses and pertinent documents such as the minutes of grievance meetings and correspondence between the parties. Also the briefs submitted by the parties are often more illuminating than a verbatim transcript of the hearing.

CONFLICT BETWEEN LANGUAGE OF SUBMISSION AGREEMENT AND CONTRACT PROVISIONS

The point has been stressed repeatedly that the authority of the arbitrator is defined by both the submission agreement and the collective agreement. But what happens when the submission and the collective agreement are in real or apparent conflict with each other? There is the award, for example, of an arbitrator who was authorized by the submission to decide the remedy if he found that the grievant had been unjustly discharged. The arbitrator reversed the action of the company ruling that while the employee was not blameless, the extreme penalty of discharge was not justified. The appropriate remedy, he declared, was reinstatement but without back pay. The award was in conformity with the authority given him by the submission—but not with the collective agreement. In granting the union's motion to modify the arbitrator's award by bringing it in conformity with the collective agreement, Justice Conlon of the New York Supreme Court tersely set forth his complete opinion as follows:

> The fact that the submission authorized the arbitrator, if he found the discharge unjustified to decide what the remedy should be, did not empower him to disregard the contractual provision that an employee found to have been wrongfully discharged "shall be reinstated with back pay for time lost."
>
> The motion to modify the award is granted, and the crossmotion is also granted, but only to the extent of confirming the award as modified. Settle order.[3]

IMPORTANCE OF THE RECORD

The arbitrator's authority is legally defined not only by the submission and the collective agreement; there is a third limitation to his decision-making powers. While it is not a matter of law, there is a fundamental standard of judicial arbitration upon which his future acceptability as an arbitrator depends. As stated by Arthur M. Ross:

> The arbitrator's decision is based on the record. It is not based on his expert knowledge, even if he has a little. It is not based on any independent studies made on his own initiative when the hearing is concluded. It is not based upon his theories of sound human relations o good personnel administration. It is based upon the record which he receives. And if the party doesn't produce the evidence, he won't get the decision.
>
> As a matter of fact, the submission agreement often recites that the arbitrator's decision must be based upon the record. This goes without saying, even if not specified by the parties. It is true that participants normally select an arbitrator who has some expert knowledge of industrial relations. However, their reason for doing so should not be misconceived. They don't select an expect because they want him to resor to his own knowledge as a substitute for evidence. They select him because he is qualified to evaluate the evidence which they themselves produce.[4]

---

[3] *O'Rourke v. Hickey Co.*, New York Supreme Court, 31 LA 765 (1959).
[4] Arthur M. Ross, "What the Arbitrator Needs from the Parties," in *Preparing and Presenting Arbitration Cases*, University of California, Institute of Industrial Relations Berkeley, Calif., 1954, p. 3.

THE PARTIES ARE RESPONSIBLE
FOR MAKING THE RECORD

Although arbitration today is an adversary proceeding, most arbitrators take a very broad view of what evidence should be accepted into the record. The decision, for example, in the case of Lorenzo C. hinged on the testimony of Foreman Wilkens. Lorenzo had been discharged for leaving the job an hour before the end of his shift without permission of his supervisor. The offense did not in itself warrant such a drastic penalty. The company had made up its mind to dismiss him when four written reprimands for other offenses were found in his personnel file, all issued during the previous eighteen months. Lorenzo stoutly denied any knowledge of three of the reprimands and could recollect only vaguely the fourth. The plant manager was grilled on the witness stand and had to admit embarrassedly that record keeping on reprimands was somewhat on the sloppy side. When the hearing recessed for lunch, the union business agent whispered audibly to Lorenzo, "It's in the bag." He was a capable union official and no stranger to arbitration proceedings, but this was the first one he was handling by himself, and Lorenzo's reinstatement would have been a considerable feather in his cap.

When the hearing resumed at 2 P.M., the company put K. T. Wilkens on the stand. K. T. had been promoted just six months before from a working leadman in Lorenzo's department to foreman. He had also been chief steward during the period when Lorenzo had had three of the reprimands placed in his record. K. T. stated flatly that Lorenzo had seen the three reprimands at the time they were issued. Not only that, K. T. said, Lorenzo had been spared other reprimands because he, as chief steward, had been able to talk the management out of them. The union corner of the hearing room buzzed with indignation. Epithets could be heard in emotional undertones, the milder of them being "renegade" and "rat-fink."

The business agent came forward for cross-examination and glowered at Wilkens, trying to collect himself. Twice he began a question, then halted in midsentence. He looked at the arbitrator and shook his head wordlessly. Then he turned his back on the witness deliberately and returned to his seat.

Wilkens' testimony was crucial, and the arbitrator said so in his written opinion upholding the discharge. After the award was published, the arbitrator was asked by one of his intimates, "How come?"

"How come what?"

"How come you accepted K. T. Wilkens' testimony into the record?"

"I had no choice," said the arbitrator. "I suppose you think it should have been stricken as privileged information."

"Definitely. Arbitration is, after all, an adversary proceeding. For K. T. to give evidence against Lorenzo, obtained by representing Lorenzo when he was his chief steward, can hardly be called cricket. It's no different, in my opinion, than if the union had retained a management consultant to give confidential information about his client obtained by representing the client in an earlier proceeding against the union."

The arbitrator smiled. "But you yourself," he said, "just pointed out that arbitration is an adversary proceeding. It was up to the union to lodge a protest. It was not for me to move that K. T.'s testimony be stricken from the record. That would've been highly improper—trying the union's case for them."

"Hmmmm. Now that I think of it, you're probably right. Ironic, isn't it?"

"And how!" the arbitrator exclaimed. "They blew their tops, cussed him out properly—but strictly among themselves. Not even one remark of theirs found its way into the record. You know something? I don't even think they know yet there is such a thing as a record in an arbitration proceeding."

One last case demonstrates that being right is not enough, even when the arbitrator is convinced you are right. The record must show that you are right or the decision will go the other way.

Expert Testimony Should Be Countered by Experts Not by Laymen

Mary G. was a drill-press operator in a large metal-fabricating plant. For some time she had been socializing with her foreman after work hours. The relationship was clearly not a platonic one and, as is usual in such circumstances, it became known to her coworkers before the company got wind of it. When the company did find out, the foreman was abruptly terminated. A month later, Mary G. was terminated on the recommendation of the company doctor, who declared she was "accident prone." As a wag in her department put it, "Prone she may have been, but her dismissal was no accident." Even those who shared the company's implacable attitude toward transgressions between employees and supervisors were disturbed by the charge.

"Accident prone!" The business agent shook his head, "I don't like it, and neither does anyone else on the grievance committee. It's a bad precedent if we let them get away with it."

At the arbitration hearing, the company produced as evidence a copy of the grievant's accident record taken from her personnel file. Thirty-three accidents in less than two years, twenty-two of them in the final six months of her employment, appeared at first glance to give the company an iron clad case. A close analysis of the record by the union, coupled with a stringent cross-examination of department supervisors, placed the formidable list of accidents in a new perspective. All of them were minor in nature, several amounting to no more than the removal of a cinder from Mary's eye.

"Faulty goggles," Mary testified. "I just couldn't find a pair that fit right. So in two days I went eight times to a first-aid station and had a cinder removed from my eye. For this they chalked up eight accidents against me. I could have had somebody around take them out with a dampened Kleenex tissue. But like an idiot"—she paused to control her indignation—"I believed the safety posters and went to a first-aid station."

The key company witness was the doctor, who admitted under cross-examination that the term "accident prone" was psychological in origin rather than medical in the strict sense of the word. On redirect examination, he explained that he had taken courses in psychology and related subjects at the largest university in the area and felt qualified to diagnose Mary G. as accident prone.

The union's heavy gun was an attorney who had been retained because of his reputation as an expert on industrial accidents. On the witness stand, drawing on his many years of experience in the litigation of industrial accidents, he challenged the company doctor's diagnosis and vehemently affirmed his own expert opinion that Mary G. was not accident prone.

The union followed up his testimony by submitting a notarized statement from a medical doctor on the staff of an industrial hospital who had interviewed and examined Mary G., declaring he had evaluated her accident record and had arrived at precisely the same conclusion as the union's attorney.

The arbitrator refrained from a personal evaluation of the record of accidents placed in evidence by the company. He confined his dicta to weighing the testimony of the witnesses and then ruled in favor of the company.

"What else could I do?" he said afterward to his intimates. "Maybe the company was out to get her. It's quite possible—even probable—but the union had no effective defense against the company doctor. He's a medical man, and on the witness stand he gave a psychiatric diagnosis. Who am I to contradict him? I'm a layman, not a medical man, let alone an accredited psychologist. And I don't think a lawyer, even a specialist in industrial accidents, is any more qualified to rebut psychiatric testimony than I am. Why didn't the union put a medical man on the stand instead of submitting an affidavit from one? Under the circumstances, the affidavit wasn't worth the paper it was written on. The union should've put a medical doctor on the stand whose testimony would be subject to cross-examination. Then I could've said: 'Well, it seems that qualified experts are unable to agree on whether this woman is accident prone. Therefore I, the arbitrator will decide.' By failing to put a doctor on the stand, the union left it solely up to me to override medical testimony. That I will never do—not if I can help it."

The arbitrator pondered the matter for a long moment. "Many years ago," he said, "I worked for a man who taught me, 'Never fight a newspaper except with another newspaper' "—he shook his head ruefully—"and that principle could be extended to say, 'Never fight a doctor except with another doctor.' I'll go even further. If you can help it, don't challenge a bona fide expert except with another expert."

SUMMARY

Although the collective agreement may provide for arbitration as the final step in the grievance procedure, it does not generally define the arbitrator's authority in a specific case. The submission agreement is the instrument to define precisely the issues to be decided in a given dispute and to state the limits of the arbitrator's authority. Failure to formulate the submission agreement properly may prevent determination of the actual controversy. The arbitrator's ruling may not exceed the terms of the submission. If it should, a state or federal court may be asked to set aside that portion of the award which goes beyond the submission agreement.

The arbitrator's decision is also based on the record, which normally includes relevant provisions of the collective agreement. Although the arbitrator may initiate requests for information or exclude certain kinds of evidence, the burden for making the record rests primarily with the parties.

Chapter 3

Management's reserved rights and obligations

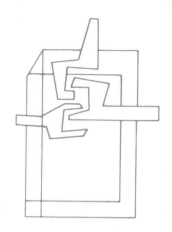

■ The arbitrator's decision was an unpopular one—with the loser, of course —and the loser in this case was the union. The award went to a major oil company on a matter of work assignments. The controversy involved a number of huge cooling towers in the refinery. Each of the towers was secured by a crisscross of guy wires running to five cement-filled iron casings (called "deadmen") spaced around the tower and sunk deep into the ground. The bulk of the refinery employees were organized into an industrial union which jealously guarded its jurisdiction against inroads by craft unions representing various skilled trades.

ISSUE

At issue was the assignment of electricians to dig postholes, install deadmen, and string a complete new set of guy wires around a tower. Three employees, with an average seniority of ten years, testified for the contending union that they and other operator-mechanics had on several past occasions replaced worn-out guy wires, and were quite capable of doing the work in question.

On cross-examination, they admitted that they had never strung a complete set of guy wires around a tower starting from scratch with newly installed deadmen. They insisted, nonetheless, that such work did not require highly specialized skills and that their experience in replacing worn-out guy wires one at a time was sufficient.

The company counsel put the refinery superintendent on the stand and elicited from him the following testimony:

> **Q.** Well, do you feel that an operator-mechanic in the refinery would have this type of skill to set up these new groups of guy wires?
>
> **A.** We didn't feel there was anybody available in our plant to do it. That is correct.
>
> **Q.** And is that why you gave it to the electricians?
>
> **A.** That is correct.
>
> **Q.** And do the electricians do this all the time?
>
> **A.** They string guy lines to power poles all the time.
>
> **Q.** I assume that in putting up a new set of guy wires, if you put too much stress, you would pull your whole operation, or your whole cooling tower out of whack, isn't that correct?
>
> **A.** That is correct, especially an old piece of equipment of this kind, an old structure, I should say.

"The union is sure unhappy," the arbitrator later told a friend, "but in light of that testimony, how else could I have ruled? In its posthearing brief, all the union did was deride the refinery superintendent and the other company witnesses who had testified that the work required special skills. The only rebuttal the union offered was the flat statement that any roustabout could do the work. Neither side produced supporting proof for their statements. It was a plain case of choosing one over the other. So I chose management's; what else could I do?"

The friend said, "You could've chosen the opinion you believed—the union's if you didn't believe management's."

"Oh, no," the arbitrator said vehemently. "In a case of this kind, I had to put the burden of proof on the union. Even if I believed them—and in truth I didn't know who to believe—but if I had believed the union, I still wouldn't have ruled for them without very strong supporting proof. It would've had to be a proof so strong, so compelling, as to remove the faintest shadow of a doubt in my mind."

"Why, may I ask? Why not accept the union's unsupported testimony if you believed it over the management's unsupported testimony? You have that privilege."

"Yes," said the arbitrator, "I also have the privilege of committing hari-kari. Just picture me telling the parties: 'The union is right. Any roustabout, any helper can string a whole new set of guy wires.' So the company abides by my award and assigns the work to an unskilled crew. Then one night there is a big windstorm, a gale perhaps, and the guy wires are not installed properly. Can't you just see one of those cooling towers beginning to topple—$150,000 I believe it costs—and it keeps on toppling—going, going, gone—$150,000! And can't you just see the embarrassed look on the faces of the union witnesses: 'Yeah, gee whiz, I guess we were wrong after all.' "

The arbitrator added: "One side has an opinion, just that and nothing more. The other side also has an opinion—plus"—he paused meaningfully —"plus an investment of $150,000 in each of the cooling towers. In short, they manage the establishment. They have the ultimate responsibility. On whom would *you* put the burden of proof?"

JUDICIAL ARBITRATION

And it is this truism—that management must have the ultimate power to operate the business, to manage, a right recognized not only by arbitrators but by most union members and their leaders—that inhibits unions' acceptance of judicial arbitration. The deep-seated ambivalence of unions toward the arbitration process is perpetuated by the very fact that there are fundamental problems of operating the business which logically require most doubts to be resolved in favor of those who manage, although management actions in these areas can camouflage injustice. Even as judicial arbitration gains in ascendancy, union representatives look back lingeringly at consensus arbitration, trying to allay their fears by advocating mutually contradictory aspects of both systems which present short-term advantages.

RESERVED-RIGHTS THEORY

The very heart of the conflict between the parties is the application of what has become best known as the "theory of management reserved rights." The reserved-rights doctrine is the basic frame of reference for interpreting the collective agreement, accepted even by those who are quick to challenge it whenever it is enunciated as a full-blown theory.

Stated in an unqualified simplistic form, the reserved-rights theory holds that management's authority is supreme in all matters except those it has expressly conceded in the collective agreement and in all areas except those where its authority is restricted by law. Put another way, management does not look to the collective agreement to ascertain its rights; it looks to the agreement to find out which and how many of its rights and powers it has conceded outright or agreed to share with the union. The reserved-rights theory is somewhat analogous to the Tenth Amendment of the United States Constitution.[1]

Not a few proponents of the reserved-rights doctrine would challenge the union's right to arbitrate any issue on which the collective agreement is silent. Some would go so far as to deny arbitration on any issue which is not clearly and unambiguously covered by the agreement. As one union negotiator observed, "With those restrictions we wouldn't need arbitrators; just call in an English teacher."

If the reserved-rights doctrine were applied as narrowly and inflexibly as demanded by its more ardent advocates, the doctrine would rapidly become obsolete. Few unions possessing minimal strength would sign an agreement restricting arbitration to issues which are covered by specific language in the written instrument. In an article which included a discussion of the arbitrator's acceptability to the parties, R. W. Fleming cast a revealing light on why the process would become obsolete if arbitrators were to take a simplistic view of the reserved-rights theory:

> They [the arbitrators] remember that grievance arbitration was often imposed upon the parties by War Labor Board decree and that its survival in a peacetime economy depended in large measure on acceptance by the parties. They know from intimate experience that arbitration is the substitute for the strike and the lockout, and that the parties can return to a show of strength at any time that the process of arbitration becomes unacceptable to them. Finally, they have had indelibly impressed upon their minds the fact that, unlike the situation in the typical court case, the parties must continue to live together after the decision. Added to all this may be a factor of survival for the arbitrator, for in the absence of any tenure his continuation is clearly dependent upon making decisions which are acceptable to the parties.[2]

The reserved-rights doctrine is a valid and necessary frame of reference for contract interpretation, but the notion that it admits of no qualification stems from a failure to grasp the true nature of the collective agreement. Years ago, back in 1949, Harry Shulman wrote:

> The agreement is negotiated and drafted by representatives on both sides for acceptance by numerous people. It must be satisfactory not to one person, but to a multitude. The multitude will contain a variety

---

[1] "ARTICLE X. The powers not delegated to the United States by the Constitution, nor prohibited by it to the States, are reserved to the States respectively, or to the people."
[2] R. W. Fleming, "Reflections on the Nature of Labor Arbitration," *Michigan Law Review*, vol. 61, no. 7, May, 1963, p. 1269.

of objections to different provisions. What will pass one person or group will be harped on by another. To each the whole may be acceptable except for the one detail, none would reject the agreement because of that alone. But the aggregation of the diverse objections to the different details may create the impression of total inadequacy and unacceptability. . . .

. . . The vagueness which to the interpreter shows no "meeting of minds" may be the very factor which made agreement possible. I am not speaking now of more or less unintended vagueness in setting down general rules without exploration of all the particulars. I am speaking rather of the purposeful vagueness which the parties embrace when they know that they cannot agree on more precise statement and prefer to take a chance on future application rather than break up in total disagreement.

Many illustrations can be cited. Negotiators can readily agree that the employer should have the power to discipline for cause. But they would probably negotiate for years without reaching agreement on all matters that should or should not constitute proper cause and what specific penalties should be appropriate in the diverse circumstances.

Negotiators can generally agree that "merit and ability" should be a factor, perhaps the paramount factor, in promotions. But they are likely to leave the agreement with quite different notions of what is meant by "merit" and by "ability" and how the factors are to be established.[3]

The unique character of the evolving collective agreement as contrasted to a commercial contract has been pointed out by numerous other authorities, not the least of them Archibald Cox. In a landmark decision, part of the 1960 Steelworkers Trilogy, the U.S. Supreme Court prefaced its own viewpoint on the collective agreement by quoting with obvious approval the following extract from his writings:

It is not unqualifiedly true that a collective-bargaining agreement is simply a document by which the union and employees have imposed upon management limited, express restrictions of its otherwise absolute right to manage the enterprise, so that an employee's claim must fail unless he can point to a specific contract provision upon which the claim is founded. There are too many people, too many problems, too many unforeseeable contingencies to make the words of the contract the exclusive source of rights and duties. One cannot reduce all the rules governing a community like an industrial plant to fifteen or even fifty pages. Within the sphere of collective bargaining, the institutional characteristics and the governmental nature of the collective-bargaining process demand a common law of the shop which implements and furnishes the context of the agreement. We must assume that intelli-

---

[3] Harry Shulman, "The Role of Arbitration in the Collective Bargaining Process," in *Collective Bargaining and Arbitration,* University of California, Institute of Industrial Relations, Los Angeles and Berkeley, Calif., 1949, pp. 21–22.

gent negotiators acknowledged so plain a need unless they stated a contrary rule in plain words.[4]

To summarize, the collective agreement is often specific, the language clearly and unambiguously defining the rights and duties of the parties. In other areas the agreement is couched in broad, general terms. Whenever a question arises as to the application of these broadly phrased provisions, management exercises its inherent right of administrative initiative or, to put it more concretely, its reserved right to make initial decisions and to require that these decisions be complied with promptly except where certain hazards are involved. On its part, the union has the right to protest these administrative decisions, to challenge the status quo established by management, and to seek redress through the grievance and arbitration machinery. It is understood, of course, that if the union's position is ultimately upheld, management will make appropriate adjustments retroactively.

The question now arises, when the agreement is quite broadly phrased in respect to an issue, or perhaps silent, and the reserved-rights doctrine cannot be applied so narrowly as to exclude arbitration, does this mean that the issue is automatically subject to the freewheeling methods of consensus arbitration?

Emphatically no!

GAP OF AMBIGUITY

Let us consider the first kind of grievance dispute, where the agreement is so general or so vague as to serve only as a means of invoking the arbitration process. How then does the arbitrator set about filling the "gap of ambiguity," as it is often called? By imposing his own notions of industrial justice? Again, emphatically no!

A complete area of managerial authority is defined in the following short sentence: "Management may discipline and discharge employees for *just cause*." Whatever restriction there is on the exercise of this vast range of managerial discretion is compressed into the two short words "just cause," a deceptively simple phrase which has brought to an abrupt end the careers of uncounted numbers of aspiring arbitrators. For the surviving arbitrators in the United States are the few hundred individuals who display a proficiency, both inherent and acquired, in the application of established standards for reviewing shop discipline. These standards, having their roots in the pre-

[4] Archibald Cox, "Reflections upon Labor Arbitration," *Harvard Law Review*, vol. 72, 1959, pp. 1498–1499; as quoted by the U.S. Supreme Court in *United Steelworkers v. Warrior & Gulf Navigation Co.*, 363 U.S. 574 (1960).

epts of enlightened management, were evolved out of a huge number of arlier cases, many of them published in full text. The published criteria ave become so widely accepted as to attain the status of a common law for valuating "just cause." This arbitral body of common law reaffirms man-gement's inherent right to discipline and discharge for just cause, but nplicit in this right is the corollary obligation to be fair and reasonable, to 1ake decisions affecting an employee's status and security which are neither rbitrary, capricious, nor discriminatory.

Lest plant discipline and discharge be considered an exceptional area of ontract administration, consider the following two provisions found in one orm or another in several thousand collective agreements:

1 Section 7. Overtime shall be distributed as *equitably as possible*, and, *in so far as practicable*, among those employees with the greatest seniority in the classification and in the department that is scheduled to work overtime.

2 Section 11. Promotions shall be granted on the basis of seniority, but *due consideration* shall be given to *merit and ability* of eligible employees; the company will promote from within *whenever possible* before hiring new employees.

he italicized phrases are intentionally generalized language in the same 1tegory as "just cause." The parties write them into the agreement know-1g full well that issues may arise and probably will arise which will produce onflicting interpretations and contrary understandings of such expressions ; "equitably as possible" and "in so far as practicable." Nor will these sues in most cases be referred to consensus arbitrators to be disposed of by 1eir Solomon-like wisdom. The parties will, on the contrary, turn to judi-al arbitrators and rely on their proficiency in the application of widely ccepted standards of a common law which have evolved about each of these hrases. The examples given by no means exhaust the list of phrases which ·e heavily dependent for their interpretation on an ever-developing com-1on law of arbitration. A cursory examination of typical agreements will isclose an indefinite number of them.

NOTHER GRIEVANCE DISPUTE

`urning now to the second kind of grievance dispute under discussion, amely, where a collective agreement is totally silent on the issue to be arbi-ated, we must come to grips at the outset with a persistent and cherished •lklore surrounding the reserved-rights theory—a theory ironically that is 1ore often endangered by its friends than by its foes. Those who resolutely eclare as an article of faith that when the contract is silent on an issue, the union should forfeit on the very face of it the right to invoke arbitration fail to consider the size and strength of the contemporary American labor movement. Their realism, or lack of it, is on a par with those passionate opponents of compulsory arbitration who join the popular outcry against Big Labor's right to call strikes in important industries. They are apparently unaware of the actual alternatives posed by the problem—not whether Big Labor should or should not be allowed to strike, but whether it should be allowed to strike or be compelled to arbitrate.

The foregoing analogy is highly relevant to the question of whether union should be held to have yielded its right to arbitrate any and all matters on which the contract is silent—a view, it may be added, not shared by the U.S. Supreme Court. In adopting the contrary viewpoint, the Court reviewed the legislative intent of the Taft-Hartley Act and made an observation basic to the application of the reserved-rights theory of management

> Plainly the agreement to arbitrate grievance disputes is the *quid pro quo* for an agreement not to strike. . . .
> . . . the entire tenor of the [legislative] history indicates that the agreement to arbitrate grievance disputes was considered as *quid pro quo* of a no-strike agreement.[5]

In a later case the Court made the following additional pertinent observation:

> In the commercial case, arbitration is the substitute for litigation. Here arbitration is the substitute for industrial strife.[6]

Max S. Wortman, Jr., and Frank L. McCormick have highlighted the Court's reasoning as follows:

> Managerial freedom is based upon legal rights when property is concerned. However, when jobs and the wages, hours and working conditions of those jobs are considered, managerial freedom is not based upon legal rights, but upon the economic strength of the employer and of the employees.[7]

Stanley Young has elaborated on this point as follows:

> Management has confused its legal rights and economic power. Under individual bargaining, the buyer's economic power was of such a nature that it often enabled him to propose terms on a "take-it-or-leave-it" basis The individual employee, as a seller, had insufficient bargaining power

[5] *Textile Workers Union v. Lincoln Mills,* 353 U.S. 448, 455 (1957).
[6] *United Steelworkers v. Warrior & Gulf Navigation Co.,* 363 U.S. 574, 578 (1960).
[7] Max S. Wortman, Jr., and Frank L. McCormick, "Management Rights and the Collective Bargaining Agreement," *Labor Law Journal,* vol. 16, no. 4, April, 1965, p. 196. The passages quoted were condensed from a fuller treatment of this topic by Morris Stone in *Managerial Freedom and Job Security,* Harper & Row, Publishers, Incorporated, New York, 1964, p. 1.

to reject a proposal effectively or to submit counterproposals. Thus, out of a fear of unemployment, the seller often was willing to accept a wide range of employment terms unilaterally imposed by the buyer. The employer used economic coercion in the threat of discharge rather than legal control to achieve employee compliance.

Because the employer had the economic ability to purchase such subservience over relatively long periods of time, the buyer of labor came to assume that he was entitled to such a relationship as a matter of legal right, instead of recognizing the economic fact that such a condition reflected a labor market condition. *When employees subsequently organized into unions and changed the relative bargaining power between buyer and seller, employers erroneously interpreted the change as a modification of managerial prerogatives, rather than a reduction in their economic power.* [Italics supplied.][8]

The employer cannot, solely because of his legal ownership of physical assets, compel workers to obey or carry out his decisions. He tries to persuade them to do so by offering various kinds of inducements. Perhaps Neil Chamberlain put it more realistically when he observed:

The inducement generally takes the form of money—a wage or salary paid to the employee in return for his compliance with management's decisions. But there is no reason why those people whose cooperation is needed if the physical assets are to be put to use may not demand something more than money as a condition of their supplying their services. What conditions may they impose? They may impose any conditions except those which are specifically banned by law. There is nothing which can prevent them from demanding, as the price of their cooperation, that management must give them a voice in matters of production, or sales, or location, or even the selection of supervisory personnel. Whether they can win such demands depends, of course, upon the degree of their bargaining power—but it is equally true that whether management can avoid such demands, if made, depends not on its legal status as owner or agent of private property but on *its* bargaining power.[9]

It would be difficult to overstate the importance of the corollary conclusions which flow from these observations. The principle affirmed in the Lincoln Mills case of 1957 and reaffirmed in the trilogy of 1960 enunciates the fundamental bargain struck by the parties. To put this in simple language by repeating a statement in the opening chapter, the union signs away its right to strike (its members withholding their services) for a fixed period of time in exchange for a contract guaranteeing acceptable minimum rates of pay and working conditions.

[8] Stanley Young, "The Question of Managerial Prerogatives," *Industrial and Labor Relations Review,* January, 1963, p. 244.
[9] Neil W. Chamberlain, *The Labor Sector,* McGraw-Hill Book Company, New York, 1965, p. 344.

The grounding of employee rights in this bargain is the key to the wor *ability of the reserved-rights theory.* When the bargain concept of employe rights is coupled with the reserved-rights theory of management, a pragmat frame of reference is fashioned for contract interpretation which enables th parties to bypass their ideological conflicts over the genesis of managemer rights as contrasted to employee rights. When arbitrators have strayed fro: this balanced concept of the reserved-rights theory, courts of last resort ha redirected their steps appropriately. With a reference frame *groundir employee rights in the bargain which produced the binding collective agre ment,* we are now able to fix logically the status of those benefits or workir conditions which were in effect prior to negotiations and are not mentione in the agreement.

THE TORRINGTON CASE—JUDICIAL REVIEW OF ARBITRATION AWARD[10]

Arbitrators are divided in upholding management's rights to abolish modify such benefits or working conditions by a declaration during contra negotiations. The decision of a U.S. District Court in Connecticut reversi an arbitrator who required a stronger affirmative action by an employer highly instructive in this regard.

At issue was a benefit of twenty years standing not mentioned in the co tract permitting employees one hour off with pay to vote on Election Da During negotiations, in a context of major issues which later precipitated strike, the employer announced orally the withdrawal of the election benef The union, of course, objected, but the issue was minor compared to othe under consideration. A new agreement was not reached until the culmir tion of a seventeen-week strike. The new contract was silent on the electi benefit, but then all previous contracts had been silent on it. Sub quently, the union took the issue to arbitration, arguing that an unint rupted past practice of twenty years constituted an implied obligation on t employer's part to continue the benefit into the new contract. The arbit tor concurred with the union, ruling that to discontinue a benefit of su long standing required more than a simple announcement by the emplo during negotiations and that until there was language in the contra expressly discontinuing the benefit, it was still an implied part of t agreement.

[10] *Torrington Co. v. Metal Prods. Workers, Local 1645,* U.S. District Court, Connectic 237 F. Supp. 139 (1965). For an elaboration of the principle behind the court's reas ing, compare the example at the beginning of Chap. 1. For further discussion of t case, see Chap. 14, pp. 274–280.

The District Court vacated the arbitrator's award with an incisive opinion stating in part:

> Labor contracts generally affirmatively state the terms which the contracting parties agree to; not what practices they agree to discontinue. This agreement made no provision for "paid voting time" and the arbitrator exceeded and abused his authority when he attempted to read into the agreement this implied contractual relationship.[11]

There is little doubt that if the employer had waited until the agreement had been consummated and had afterward announced the withdrawal of the election benefit, the court would have found against him. Most arbitrators hold that when a contract is silent on an established benefit it cannot be withdrawn until the contract is open for changes and the employer announces a withdrawal of the benefit at some time during negotiations. Failure to do so may result in the benefit being continued into the new contract.

Although this criterion has occasionally been enunciated as a flat rule, it is not without some deviation when drastic changes in company operations have eliminated all justification for the benefit. Consider, for example, an employer who had for many years allowed his machine operators to use the last ten minutes of their shift as a washup time. The contract was silent on the practice. Then, while the contract still had two years to run, he automated the machine shop by introducing numerically controlled machine tools. Numerically controlled cutting tools receive their instructions in the form of coded numerical instructions (on punched paper tape), which direct the equipment to position the part to be machined, control the flow of coolant, select the proper machining speeds and feeds to be used, and control all the machinery operations such as drilling, milling, boring, and turning.

The plant manager explained to the arbitrator: "From machine operators the men have really become machine monitors—attendants, that's all. They have about as much occasion to soil their hands as a typist or a bookkeeper has. We revoked the washup time because there was no longer any reason for it."

The arbitrator in that particular case ruled for the employer, and perhaps a majority of arbitrators would have done the same. But it is a safe conjecture that a good many arbitrators would have held that the company had an implied obligation to continue the washup time until the expiration date of the contract.

[11] See Appendix B for full text of Torrington arbitration opinion and award, as well as text of subsequent federal court decisions. See also Appendix C for two law-review articles, by Benjamin Aaron and Edgar A. Jones, Jr., respectively, commenting on the Torrington case.

As a matter of fact, arbitrators have also applied the doctrine of implied obligations to government agencies in collective-bargaining disputes with unions and their employees. The account of one such dispute as reported in the *New York Times* is a case in point. Arbitrator Arthur Stark ruled that the Lindsay administration must honor a nine-year-old tradition permitting city employees to leave work an hour early from mid-June to mid September. The mayor's office did not contest the short workweek for July and August, begun about forty years ago before city offices had air conditioning. But his administration contended it was not required to permit city employees to leave their offices at 4 P.M. instead of 5 from mid-June until mid-September. The arbitrator ruled that the city could restore the regular work hours only by negotiating with the eight unions involved in the dispute. The city agreed to honor the ruling but promised to raise the question again in negotiations the following year.

As reported by the *New York Times:*

> Mr. Stark's ruling consisted of two decisions involving about 100,000 employes. One decision settled the dispute between seven unions representing Career and Salary Plan employes who do not have a formal labor contract with the city. The second decision dealt with the dispute between the Social Service Employes Union and the city in which the union has a contract regulating wages, hours and working conditions
>
> In his ruling on the dispute between the seven unions and the city, Mr. Stark said that the short work-week in June and September had been renewed each year by directive and that he found no indication that the city government had reserved the right to rescind the practice.
>
> Mr. Stark held that the practice established a consistent hour pattern and if this was changed it could be done only through negotiations, even though a formal labor contract does not bind the city and the seven unions.[12]

The Lindsay administration had argued it was not bound by the annual directives. After Stark's ruling, Deputy Mayor Costello announced that Mayor Lindsay had been pressing for economies as well as better service and that the question of a full thirty-five-hour workweek would be raised in the next negotiations with the unions. In explaining his decision on the dispute with the Social Service Employes Union, Stark said he had been requested to interpret the clause in the labor contract governing work hours in which "the parties have agreed not to change the length of the existing work-week."

The arbitrator went on to say:

> Had it been the city's intent to reserve the right to withhold part of the summer schedule, that intent could have been made clear at the ba

[12] The *New York Times,* June 20, 1966.

gaining table. *In the absence of any such caveats, however, the union had a reasonable right to rely on the consistent practice extending back to 1957.* [Italics supplied.][13]

Mr. Stark added that the "summer schedule cannot be considered a gift or gratuity, in my judgment; rather it has become an integral part of the hours of work of affected city employees." He noted that:

> A change in city administration, under these circumstances, cannot affect this conclusion. There are undoubtedly many areas where a new administration can revise, alter, amend, and change policies, practices and procedures.
> But in labor relations it is essential that understandings and firmly established practices be maintained until modified through negotiations.[14]

DOCTRINE OF IMPLIED OBLIGATIONS

The "doctrine of implied obligations" is an important corollary to the reserved-rights theory of management. The implied-obligations doctrine acknowledges the employer's right to alter or abolish employee benefits when the contract is open for negotiations, but once a new contract has been signed, he is no longer free to withdraw existing benefits. He has an implied obligation to maintain them, including those benefits which were not revoked by him during negotiations and to which the contract makes no reference.

To elaborate on the underlying premise of the U.S. Supreme Court, management is precluded from taking away an established benefit during the term of an agreement because the union is precluded from strike action to preserve that benefit. Stated even more pointedly, the employer may not induce the union to sign away its right to strike and then proceed unilaterally to abolish an established benefit, but must wait until the union has got back the consideration it gave up when the bargain was made.

The problem now presents itself: What if the employer exercises his reserved right (assuming the contract is silent on the question) to rationalize his operations by introducing new methods, new jobs, combining old jobs, and so increasing his efficiency as to justify a drastic reduction in his work force? Does not a laid-off employee have a valid claim that the employer has unilaterally deprived him of an established vital benefit (the job itself) during the term of a binding contract? Arbitrators for the most part have denied such claims, ruling that, absent an express provision guaranteeing the continuation of a job, a contract does not ordinarily bar the employer

13 *Ibid.*
14 *Ibid.*

from laying off employees for various reasons, including increased efficiency attained by new equipment or new methods of utilizing old equipment. Employees may, however, enter a claim for a higher rate of pay for the new jobs or the combination of old jobs on the ground that the proper rate for such jobs was not on the agenda when the current contract was negotiated. It may be added that arbitrators, when reviewing the rates for these jobs, give greater weight to such factors as increased effort and skills than to increased production.

Subcontracting is another vital area where a reserved management right is seen to overlap an employee benefit. If the collective agreement is silent on the question, a majority of arbitrators will rule that management has the right to contract out work provided such action does not result in layoffs or a reduction in wages or other benefits. If layoffs or impairment of benefits should occur, it is held that subcontracting violates the recognition provision of the agreement. A minority of arbitrators, however, place greater stress on management's reserved rights and hold that the only restriction they will impose on subcontracting is that management must act reasonably and in good faith.[15]

On few questions do arbitrators display as much unanimity in upholding management's right to manage as they do in the area of work assignments. An employee must obey orders, carry out assignments, and grieve afterward. He must not take matters into his own hands, resort to "self-help" by bypassing the grievance procedure. Even if the employee is subsequently found to be right and his grievance ruled meritorious, arbitrators will uphold harsh penalties by management for his failure to obey orders and grieve later. There are few exceptions to this stricture against self-help, the most important being an employee's refusal to carry out an assignment which he honestly believes will menace his safety or health, or might involve an immoral or criminal act.[16]

SUMMARY

The reserved right of management to manage, to run the business, is not a right that needs to be rooted in some historic genesis. It is a right inherent in management's responsibility for a capital investment of thousands, millions, and even billions of dollars, not to speak of the jobs dependent on the successful operation of the organization. To safeguard this right, it is

[15] For further discussion on subcontracting see pp. 46–48.
[16] For discussion of an additional exception see pp. 221–224.

unnecessary for management to rule out all employee claims which are not spelled out in the collective agreement. Not all problems can be solved by an oversimplified reference to fundamental principles. When fundamentalists reject a pragmatic solution by going outside the fixed-term contract, when they turn to history for guidelines, by probing into the genesis of the relationship between managers and employees, then they invite ideological conflict. They open up a Pandora's box of irreconcilable social and economic philosophies ranging from the unregulated laissez faire right of individuals to bargain in the marketplace to total government ownership and control of the means of production and exchange, from pushcart vending to steel mills and hydroelectric plants.

Management has no need for recourse to ideological sanctions for its right and responsibility to manage. A relative conflict of interest between those who manage and those who are managed cuts across ideological lines. Basic responsibilities and basic principles of enlightened management in an advanced industrial society are just as applicable to a tractor factory in Moscow as to a tractor plant in Fort Wayne, Indiana. The extent to which the managerial function is no respecter of ideologies is perhaps best exemplified by the reaction of union officials when their own office staffs become unionized. The behavior of union officials as employers engaging in collective bargaining with representatives of their own office and clerical work force does not differ in any significant respect from the behavior of the average employer in industry negotiating with a union. Some union officials as employers have even been known to tell representatives of the Office and Professional Employees Union, "If they're not happy working for us, why don't they look for a job somewhere else?"[17]

To conclude, labor arbitration in this country has gained wide acceptance as a pragmatic process, utilizing the reserved-rights theory of management as a basic frame of reference and incorporating into the reserved rights the fact of implied obligations to employees—obligations grounded in the collective agreement as part of the bargain struck by the parties.

[17] The *Los Angeles Times* of Oct. 15, 1966, reported that two office employees were picketing a militant AFL-CIO union local in a dispute with the union over a wage claim. The union officials endured the picketing for a week and then sought a superior court order (presumably from an "injunction judge," using hallowed labor terminology) to ban the picketing. The union also filed suit against the two pickets for $100,000 damages. Ironically, it may be added, the judge hearing the case was, before his appointment to the bench, a prominent attorney representing several large unions.

As another case in point, no paternalistic employer of the old school could have greeted more explosively the unionization of his work force than did that revered patriarch David Dubinsky, retired president of the International Ladies' Garment Workers' Union, when his organizing staff formed a union and asked to negotiate a collective agreement governing their salaries and other conditions of employment.

Chapter 4

Semantics of contract language: principles

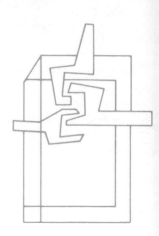

■ With the development in the late 1930s of the written agreement as the core of the collective-bargaining relationship came the standardization of basic provisions in the agreement. An experienced labor relations representative could now run a practiced eye through a contract he had never seen before and, as he flipped over its pages, discourse inaudibly to himself:

> Well now, the recognition provision covers all production and maintenance but excludes office, sales, and engineering. That's standard. Union security—a union shop modified by a grandfather's clause— employees now in the union must stay in and new employees must join, but old-times don't have to. Hmmmm. Union must've had a rough go organizing this plant. Probably still plenty of friction on the foreman– shop steward level. Grievance and arbitration procedure—standard. Management-prerogatives provisions take up half a page—but on a close reading it's standard. Management must've wanted all that language for psychology, to slow down rambunctious union militants. Seniority— a "relatively equal" provision for promotions and a "sufficient ability" provision in layoffs and recall. Vacations—now, here's an odd eligibility clause. . . .

Inevitably such standardization of key provisions accelerated a trend toward more uniform principles of contract interpretation. Many of these principles, with necessary modifications, have been imported from commercial-contract law. So basic are these criteria that those involved in contract administration, particularly the adjustment of employee grievances, are advised to consider them carefully in the sequence in which they are discussed. A note of caution, however: These standards should serve as guides and not become rigid, undeviating blueprints to be followed as methodically as though labor relations were an exact science. They should never supplant human relations, human judgment, on the job level.

SPECIFIC LANGUAGE IS CONTROLLING OVER GENERAL LANGUAGE

The first of these principles may be phrased in this question: *Is there SPECIFIC LANGUAGE in the contract covering the issue in dispute?* The word "specific" must be underscored. It should not be taken in this instance to mean "clear, exact, unambiguous," although dictionary definitions and common usage of the word stress concepts of clarity and precision. "Specific" has another meaning far more pertinent in contract interpretation, a meaning which is the ranking definition in Merriam-Webster's Abridged Dictionary, Seventh Edition: "constituting or falling into a named category."

Specific Language Can Be Ambiguous

Now it should be apparent that a contract provision can constitute or fall into a named category and yet be loosely written, vague, and ambiguous in its treatment of that category. For example, a standard contract provision reads:

> Supervisors may perform work in the bargaining unit in emergencies only, or for the purposes of instruction.

Unquestionably, this provision deals specifically with a named category— supervisors performing work in the bargaining unit—yet the language can hardly be considered precise, exact, or unambiguous. There is much room for argument as to what constitutes a true emergency[1] or what are the limits, if any, to bona fide instruction. Nevertheless, such specific language will

---

[1] Prof. Thomas Kennedy has illustrated this point as follows, referring to the quoted provision regarding supervisors' work in their bargaining unit: "I recently had an

take precedence over general language, the latter being language that deals with the issue, not as a named category, but by inference only.

An Example of General Language

> Section 1. Short vacancies of less than 30 days duration may be filled without posting at the option of the Department Head.

At issue was an employee's birthday, a category listed in another provision of the contract as one of eight paid holidays in the calendar year. The aggrieved employee had asked to work his birthday holiday, which would have entitled him to earnings at 2½ times his straight-time hourly rate. The department head asserted an option under section 1 to deny the employee's request and to assign another employee (for whom it would not be a holiday) to work the job at the straight-time rate.

Does section 1 cover the issue specifically? The answer, of course, is no. Nowhere in the provision is "holiday" mentioned as a named category. The named category treated by section 1 is "short vacancies" defined as "vacancies of less than 30 days duration." A holiday might logically be considered a short vacancy of one day duration, but such a conclusion would have to be inferred from the general language of section 1 defining a short vacancy. Such an inference, it must be stressed, would be superseded by any specific language on holidays covering the issue.[1]

An Example of Specific Language

So controlling is specific language in contract interpretation that when the contract is entirely silent on a particular matter, the moving party is often better advised to let well enough alone than to negotiate language which does not clearly spell out its expectations. Consider the following language proposed by a union and accepted by management:

> It is agreed that all work shall be performed as much as practicable by union labor in the employer's own shop. In the event that all work cannot be rendered in the shop of the employer, the employer may

---

arbitration case under an almost identical clause where a supervisor repaired a truck in a garage early in the morning rather than call in a mechanic because to have waited for the mechanic would have delayed the departure of the truck. Query: Was this an 'emergency'? Don't we have, therefore, in the contract clause on supervisors' work an example of 'general language' just as we have 'general language' in the contract clause on short vacancies? In the one case, 'emergency' was not specifically defined to include a situation where a truck would be held up for twenty minutes and in the other, 'short vacancies' was not specifically defined to include a one-day birthday holiday."

contract his work to union shops only; provided that if union shops will not accept such work or are unobtainable for such work, then the employer may contract such work elsewhere.

From a surface reading of the provision, it would appear that the union had made an impressive gain. Impressive to the uninformed: actually, the union's position would have been stronger if it had allowed the contract to remain silent on the issue. When the collective agreement is silent on sub-contracting, a large majority of arbitrators will not sustain management if the subcontracting results in layoffs or impairment of established employee benefits. Two important exceptions to this rule are:

1 Where subcontracting has been a customary mode of procedure for the company, as in such industries as apparel, construction, and the manufacture of transportation equipment.
2 Where there has been a drastic change in underlying conditions of the jobs in question.

An example of the latter is afforded by the case of a furniture manufacturer who was sustained by an arbitrator when he laid off employees in his wood-shop during a period when the only wood available to him for one of his staple items had to be purchased precut.

Absent these exceptions, many arbitrators will hold that subcontracting violates the general language of the union-recognition provision. They will rely on Samuel Williston's principle that every contract contains:

. . . an implied covenant that neither party shall do anything which will have the effect of destroying or injuring the right of the other party to receive the fruits of the contract; in other words, in every contract there exists an implied covenant of good faith and fair dealing.[2]

JUDICIAL AND ARBITRAL INTERPRETATION OF LANGUAGE

Williston's principle has been given arbitral elaboration in the following extract from an article by Ralph Seward:

A great deal is made of the differences between the approach of arbitrators and the approach of the courts toward the interpretation of a labor agreement. There *are* differences. They are parallel to the differences between the courts and administrative agencies or the differences between the opinions of any specialized group of men and any non-

2 Walter H. E. Jaeger, *A Treatise on the Law of Contracts*, 3d ed. replacing Revised Edition by Samuel Williston, Baker, Voorhis & Co., New York, 1957, vol. 5, sec. 670, p. 159.

specialized group of men. But there is little difference in the basic process of adjudication by rational implication from written language. There is little difference between that process as carried on by arbitrators and that process as it has been carried on by the courts as long as there has been law in this world. Arbitrators are certainly not the first to read into written agreements an implied obligation of good faith and fair dealing. Unless arbitrators are to divorce themselves from the entire course of legal history, it must be recognized that there is a pressure in human beings toward the expression of basic unwritten concepts of justice and fair dealing which will not stay out of judicial procedures, which will find expression and which must and should find expression.[3]

From Williston and Seward they will conclude with Cox that:

In the absence of other evidence . . . the provisions of a collective bargaining agreement establishing wages and labor standards impliedly impose upon the employer an obligation not to seek a substitute labor supply at lower wages or inferior standards. The implied promise would, for example, prohibit subcontracting for this purpose.[4]

But when specific language on subcontracting is written into the agreement, it is not within the province of the arbitrator to go outside that language (except to fill gaps of ambiguity) to determine the intent of the parties. It is his duty to find out what was meant by the language that the parties themselves used. Standard arbitration criteria, which would have prevailed when the agreement was silent, are now superseded by the specific language. In the negotiated language quoted (p. 46), the phrase "as much as practicable" could conceivably be interpreted to permit subcontracting for reasons of economy and efficiency even if the bargaining unit were decimated. Many arbitrators might satisfy themselves that subcontracting was done in good faith to effect legitimate economies and would then uphold management's action, regardless of its effect on established employee benefits not spelled out in the agreement or incursions into the bargaining unit.

CLEAR AND UNAMBIGUOUS LANGUAGE IS GENERALLY CONTROLLING OVER PAST PRACTICE

Returning now to the question which asks whether there is specific language covering the issue, let us assume that such specific language is found. A careful reading of the disputed provision should then answer this second

---

[3] Ralph T. Seward, "Arbitration and the Functions of Management," *Industrial and Labor Relations Review,* January, 1963, p. 239.

[4] Archibald Cox, *Law and the National Labor Policy,* University of California, Institute of Industrial Relations, Monograph Series, no. 5, Los Angeles, 1960, pp. 75–76.

question: *Is the language clear and unambiguous with respect to the issue?* If the words of a provision are clear and free of doubt as to their meaning, then the arbitrator must stop right there. He may not go behind the language to probe for an intent other than the one disclosed by a simple reading of the provision. The language, it is said, speaks for itself. In contract law an agreement is not ambiguous if the arbitrator can determine its meaning with no other guide than knowledge of the simple facts on which, from the nature of language in general, its meaning depends. For the arbitrator to infer a different meaning by resorting to other criteria such as past practice would ordinarily constitute an abuse of his authority, one of the major grounds on which the courts will vacate an arbitration award.[5] He would be adding to, or subtracting from, the contract—powers he may not arrogate to himself without an express grant from the parties.

The Case of the Stationary Engineers' Lunch

We proceed now to the presentation of an extreme example of enforcement of the clear-language principle. The case involved a large rubber company in South Los Angeles. For some thirty years its stationary engineers had occupied themselves in the boiler room with no designated lunch period during their entire shift. Although their main responsibilities (to keep the boilers from blowing up) were great, their tasks were not onerous. Most of the time the men sat around keeping a watchful eye on the pressure gauges and making notes in the log. Occasionally one of them would get up and turn a knob to regulate the pressure or touch a rag to the remnants of oil seepage, while another might be leisurely munching a sandwich. Major adjustments and repair work were occasional, and, for the most part, the men were able to relieve one another with minimal inconvenience.

The contract, however, included a provision that "all employees in the bargaining unit shall have a thirty-minute lunch period, except for the following ...," and the stationary engineers were not listed as one of the exempt classifications; nor could any other provision of the contract be construed to exempt them. Since the union in thirty years had never made an issue of a designated lunch period for the engineers, the company regarded the matter as settled and did not try to amend the language to

---

[5] We hasten now to acknowledge that there are arbitrators of considerable stature who would take issue with such an unqualified statement of the primacy of clear language over a long-established practice. For the most influential exposition of this contrary viewpoint, see Benjamin Aaron, "The Uses of the Past in Arbitration," *Arbitration Today*, Jean T. McKelvey (ed.), *Proceedings of the Eighth Annual Meeting, National Academy of Arbitrators*, BNA, Inc., 1955.

bring it into conformity with its practice. Then an entirely new slate of union officers took over following a bitter election campaign featured by charges that the old officers were "pie-cards," lazy and indolent. The new officers, avid for victories to demonstrate their effectiveness, filed a grievance on behalf of the engineers and pushed it all the way to arbitration.

In vain did the company point to an unchallenged past practice of thirty years. The arbitrator sustained the union, holding that the omission of the stationary engineers from the exempt classifications inescapably and unambiguously placed them in the category of employees entitled to a thirty-minute paid lunch period. The failure of a party, the arbitrator wrote, to enforce the clear language of an agreement does not constitute a waiver of its right to expect future enforcement of the language.[6] But, added the arbitrator, enunciating another established principle of contract administration, by its failure to enforce clear language, the union did forfeit any and all claims of the stationary engineers for damages in the past.

UNAMBIGUITY IS NEVER ABSOLUTE

Two points must now be stressed about unambiguous language in a written instrument. First, like beauty, it is often in the eye of the beholder. Not infrequently, both parties will argue that the contract language unambiguously supports their respective claims, and the arbitrator will not only disagree with them both but will even declare a third meaning to be unambiguously expressed by the language! Needless to say, the arbitrator's declaration, like that of the baseball umpire, is the one that stands.

Second, language is never unambiguous in an absolute sense. It is unambiguous in respect to a given issue. The same language in respect to any number of other issues will be hopelessly vague and uncertain in meaning.

So primary a criterion is clarity of language in contract administration that arbitrators admit of many shadings and graduations in their characterizations of disputed provisions. Language is said to be clear, implying

---

[6] "... a party's failure to file grievances or to protest past violations of a clear contract rule does not bar that party, after notice to the violator, from insisting upon compliance with the clear contract requirement in future cases." Frank Elkouri and Edna A. Elkouri, *How Arbitration Works*, revised ed., BNA, Inc., 1960, p. 281. For similar views, see *Nat'l Fireworks Ordnance Corp. v. Int'l Ass'n of Machinists, Local 502*, Sept. 29, 1954, 23 LA 289, Arbitrator Livingston Smith; *Minneapolis-Moline Co. v. United Elec. Workers, Local 1146*, Nov. 14, 1951, 17 LA 497, Arbitrator William B. Lockhart; *Bethlehem Steel Co. v. Indus. Union of Marine & Shipbuilding Workers, Local 13*, Mar. 24, 1950, 15 LA 688, Arbitrator I. Robert Feinberg; *Serrick Corp. v. United Auto. Workers, Local 459*, Jan. 12, 1951, 15 LA 918, Arbitrator Bert L. Luskin; all BNA, Inc.

that it is not pellucidly clear; its transparency is obscured by shadings; it is something less than unambiguous. An unambiguous provision, in lawyers' language, is one that "can be nailed down on all four corners." The degree of clarity in language can range from the exactitude of the proverbial four corners to the relative imprecision of merely pointing in a direction, so that arbitrators enunciate as a criterion, "If the language points in one direction and the practice points in another, go with the language." There may be exceptions to this rule, but in the vast majority of cases it is applicable.

The principle of clear contract language prevailing over past practice has been expressed repeatedly in numerous arbitration awards, of which the following formulation is typical:

> Paragraph 5 is clear on its face. There is no ambiguity in this clause. An omission of words in a clause does not create an ambiguity. Plain and unambiguous words are undisputed facts. The conduct of Parties may be used to fix a meaning to words and phrases of uncertain meaning. Prior acts cannot be used to change the explicit terms of a contract. An arbitrator's function is not to rewrite the Parties' contract. His function is limited to finding out what the Parties intended under a particular clause. The intent of the Parties is to be found in the words which they, themselves, employed to express their intent. When the language used is clear and explicit, the arbitrator is constrained to give effect to the thought expressed by the words used.[7]

Arbitrator Harry Platt has stressed that where the contract language is clear and unambiguous, evidence of past practice is "wholly inadmissible."[8]

Referring to the matter under discussion, the second question posed may now be reformulated: *Is the contract sufficiently clear in respect to the issue that the mutual intent of the parties can be discerned with no other guide than a simple reading of the pertinent language?* As elaborated previously, if the answer is yes, then the issue is disposed of by the language alone. But what if the answer is no, if the language is not clear? Then, by application of Aristotelian logic, it must be ambiguous.

---

[7] *Phelps Dodge Copper Prods. Corp. v. Int'l Union of Elec., Radio & Mach. Workers, Local 441*, Feb. 28, 1951, 16 LA 229, 233, Arbitrator Jules J. Justin, BNA, Inc. For similar views, see *Sun Rubber Co. v. United Rubber Workers, Local 58*, Mar. 11, 1957, 28 LA 362, Arbitrator Harry J. Dworkin; *Texas-U.S. Chem. Co. v. Brotherhood of Painters, Decorators & Paperhangers, Local 328*, Dec. 17, 1956, 27 LA 793, Arbitrator Charles A. Reynard (Chairman); *Wallace Barnes Co. v. United Auto. Workers, Local 712*, Nov. 30, 1956, 27 LA 662, Arbitrator Robert L. Stutz (Chairman); *Am. Window Glass Co. v. Window Glass Cutters League*, Jan. 11, 1956, 26 LA 105, Arbitrator Clair V. Duff; *J. A. Bergren Dairy Farms v. Int'l Brotherhood of Teamsters, Local 536*, Nov. 16, 1955, 25 LA 472, Arbitrator Joseph F. Donnelly (Chairman); all BNA, Inc.
[8] *Penberthy Injector Co. v. United Steelworkers, Local 2395*, Nov. 30, 1950, 15 LA 713, 715, Arbitrator Harry H. Platt, BNA, Inc.

Ambiguous and Unambiguous Language
Are Reciprocal Opposites

Although ambiguous and unambiguous language are opposites, they are in a reciprocal relation to each other—that is, they are defined one through the other. To illustrate, there was the frustrated negotiator who jabbed a finger at a disputed contract provision and insisted, "This language is plainly ambiguous." Then when his hearer did a double take, he stumbled on: "I mean it's clearly ambiguous—crystal clear."

Language is said to be "unambiguous" when on a simple reading it clearly and plainly suggests but a single meaning. It follows that language must be declared "ambiguous" when on a simple reading it is susceptible to more than one interpretation by persons of competent skill.

For many years philosophers, sociologists, and semanticists have proclaimed, and experimental psychologists have demonstrated, that the perceptions people have of the objective world are to a great extent shaped by their needs and desires—above all, those needs and desires which stem from self-interest. Not surprisingly, in a large number of disputes over ambiguous contract language, neither contending party is able to perceive the ambiguity. Both become obdurately convinced as they read aloud to each other, with appropriate speech tones and voice-intonation patterns,[9] that the language yields one meaning and one meaning only, which unambiguously supports their respective claims. Only when the fact of disagreement is pointed out to them, that persons of competent skill have found the words susceptible to conflicting interpretations, do they relent and acquiesce to a ruling that the language is ambiguous.

THE NATURE OF LANGUAGE: SOME BASIC CONCEPTS

S. I. Hayakawa highlights one of the most common misconceptions of the nature of language in the following:

> The intellectually naive often objectify language as if it were something "out there," to be examined independently of speakers or hearers. But language, to be language, must have meaning and meanings are not "out there." Meanings are semantic reactions that take place *in people*. A language is therefore not just the sounds and the spellings, but more

[9] Linguists tell us that voice intonation is made up of three elements: stress, pitch, and juncture. "Stress" is the degree of loudness or softness with which we utter syllables; "pitch" is the range of voice tone from high to low; "juncture" is a way of breaking or stopping the speech flow—the imperceptible pause in an utterance which makes the difference between "I scream" and "ice cream" or "two lips" and "tulips."

importantly the whole repertory of semantic reactions which the sounds and spellings produce in those who speak and understand the language.[10]

The following short passage reveals the incredible gap between the meaning intended by a noted author and the confused meaning of the few words he put down on paper.

The mother was a small farmer's daughter.[11]

Only the writer can reveal who or what was small—the mother, the farmer, or his farm.

Historically, Speech Preceded Writing

Labor negotiations involve both oral and written discourse, two fundamentally different forms of communication whose differences must be recognized and respected:

Men talked before they wrote; and ideally, if we want to understand the tools of communication and expression which our writing system gives us, we should first understand the resources of our speech, from which our writing is derived. Otherwise we are likely to forget that the marks which we make on paper when we write do not completely and accurately represent the sounds which we make when we talk.[12]

For example, the following short simple contract provision, when written on the blackboard, has seldom failed to divide a class as to its meaning:

An employee who does not work the day before the holiday or the day after the holiday will not be paid for the holiday.

Some students, depending on their voice-intonation patterns when they read the provision aloud or to themselves, insist that the employee need only work one day, either the day before or the day after the holiday, to qualify for the holiday pay. Others will argue with equal vehemence that both days, the one before and also the one after the holiday, must be worked for the employee to qualify.

In all likelihood the negotiators who originally drew up the provision were unaware of the ambiguity in the language. It is not hard to reconstruct what probably happened. The spokesman for one of the negotiating

---

[10] S. I. Hayakawa (ed.), *The Use and Misuse of Language,* Fawcett Publications, Inc., Greenwich, Conn., 1962, pp. viii–ix.

[11] Joyce Carey, *The Captive and the Free,* Harper & Row, Publishers, Incorporated, New York, 1959, p. 117.

[12] James Sledd, *A Short Introduction to English Grammar,* Scott, Foresman and Company, Chicago, 1959, p. 20.

teams must have drafted a tentative understanding in longhand and read it aloud to his counterpart on the other side of the table. The adversary negotiators listening intently to the voice-intonation patterns of the reader undoubtedly parroted them as the discussion continued. To those in the conference room, only one meaning of the language seemed possible, the meaning suggested by the voice-intonation patterns they used in common. With the passing of months and then of years, old negotiators departed from the scene one by one to be replaced by new negotiators. Many of the new people read the language differently, using another set of voice-intonation patterns producing a meaning entirely different from the one contemplated by the framers of the provision.

Coordinate Structure and Markers of Parallelism

All too often such controversies over contract language become embittered by charges of duplicity simply because the parties are unaware of the fundamental differences between written and spoken discourse. The ambiguity in the provision could have been flagged if just one of the negotiators had remembered his high school grammar and had recognized the coordinate structure of the sentence they had adopted. All coordinate constructions are parallel, and the language provides special markers of parallelism to preserve clarity. Ambiguities can be prevented by the use of conjunctive forms like "both . . . and," "either . . . or," and "neither . . . nor." The provision should have read:

> An employee who does not work *either* the day before the holiday *or* the day after the holiday. . . .

or:

> An employee who does not work *both* the day before the holiday *and* the day after the holiday. . . .

Daily newspapers, which unavoidably are written on the run, are a ready source of linguistic mishaps. The head on a Sunday feature article reads, "The Arab World—Why Ties That Bind Easily Come Apart." When we extract the sentence, "Ties that bind easily come apart," it becomes apparent that if the word order remains unchanged, the meaning intended by the writer can be imparted with certainty only through oral communication. Without voice intonation we do not know whether the subject of the sentence is "Ties that bind easily" and the predicate "come apart" or whether the subject is "Ties that bind" and the predicate "easily come apart." Did the writer mean, "Ties that bind *easily* come apart *easily*," or did he mean, "Ties that bind come apart *easily*"?

Ambiguities, Patent and Latent

The foregoing sentence "Ties that bind . . . ," and the holiday eligibility provision "An employee who does not work the day before the holiday or the day after . . . ," are examples of language which is said to be "patently ambiguous" in meaning. A patent ambiguity is one which appears on the very face of the instrument; it is an ambiguity which arises because the language used is defective, obscure, or insensible.

Not all ambiguities arise from defects in the language of a contested provision. Take, for example, the disputed language previously referred to involving short vacancies defined as vacancies "of less than 30 days duration," which, according to section 1, could be filled "without posting at the option of the Department Head." Since an observed holiday is unarguably a short vacancy of one day duration, it would seem on a simple reading of the section that the right of the department head to fill the vacancy at his own option was unambiguously spelled out. And so it would be if consideration of the issue were confined solely to the language of this section. But there happened to be another provision in the agreement, listed as section 5, which read:

> If it is necessary to work a regularly assigned position on a holiday, the regular incumbent of said position shall be used; except that if the incumbent requests and is given permission to lay off on such holiday it shall be filled by the senior qualified employee in the department who accepts such work when offered. . . .

Returning now to the problem involving the right of an incumbent to work his regular job on his birthday holiday: Sections 1 and 5 are in direct conflict with each other. Section 1, taken separately, declares unambiguously that the incumbent can work his birthday holiday only at the option of the department head. Section 5, taken by itself, asserts with equal clarity that irrespective of the wishes of the department head, the incumbent has a right to work on his birthday. Both sections are flawed by a "latent ambiguity." Language is said to possess a latent ambiguity when it is clear and intelligible and suggests but a single meaning, but some extrinsic fact or extraneous evidence makes the language susceptible to more than one interpretation by persons of competent skill. Sections 1 and 5 are extrinsic to each other and contradict each other; therefore, each creates a latent ambiguity in the other.

It goes without saying that section 5, to the extent that it deals with the birthday holiday specifically, is controlling over section 1, which deals with the holiday in general terms only.

A common type of latent ambiguity manifests itself when an annual-wage-review provision pegs the hourly rate for the classification of, say,

Machinist at the rate set by selected companies in the industry locally. The latent ambiguity becomes known when the parties discover that the job title Machinist in the selected companies covers a wide variety of duties and skills. A Machinist in one company need only perform repetitive tasks operating a turret lathe. In another company the same job title requires that the man read blueprints, do his own layout and set-up, and operate every machine in the department from engine lathe to milling machine to boring mill to precision grinder. Reliable accurate information on job content acceptable to both parties is virtually unobtainable, and the wage-review provision becomes unenforceable.

SELECTIVE EXPOSURE AS A CAUSE OF AMBIGUITY—
OTHER SOURCES OF AMBIGUITY

The discussion so far has been confined to ambiguities which creep unnoticed into contract language to bedevil the negotiating parties later. People unfamiliar with collective bargaining, especially those with a casual knowledge of behavioral psychology, assume that ambiguities in contract language are largely the unintended result of sloppy writing stemming in great part from what psychologists call "selective exposure." Selective exposure is the propensity we all have for exposing our senses primarily to information that reinforces our needs, beliefs, and ideas. Most of us have by instinct developed techniques, of which we are but dimly aware, for rejecting or reshaping unwelcome facts that conflict with our fundamental needs and outlook. Critics of collective bargaining who hold that selective exposure is the chief source of human conflict are forever castigating the parties in dispute over contract language for not getting the language "right" in the first place. They reason thus: ambiguities in language cause disputes; ergo, eliminate ambiguities when the language is written and you eliminate disputes in embryo. Such folk remedies for eliminating conflict are, as any semanticist knows, deceptively simple—or, to turn the phrase around, simply deceptive. Quoting Irving J. Lee:

> In spite of the ease of demonstrating that a relatively few words are used to represent a vastly greater number of life facts, there persists, rather widely spread among those eager to philosophize, the curious notion that it is possible to discover the one "real and proper" meaning of any word.[13]

[13] Irving J. Lee, *Language Habits in Human Affairs*, Harper & Brothers, New York, 1941, p. 35.

In more sweeping terms, our working language, which totals less than 500,000 words,[14] must, through an infinite variety of forms and functions, represent the life facts of a world infinite in space and time. As stated by Edgar A. Jones:

> It would be nice were collective bargainers to be moved to write unambiguous and comprehensive agreements, each vacuum filled with its respective intent, each provision in logical tie to each other relevant provisions, so that arbitrators would not longer be pilloried for amending, altering, and modifying the collective unagreement.[15]

Another function of language pertinent to this discussion is the artful use of ambiguity to inhibit and prevent conflict. A comment extracted from an editorial in a morning newspaper provides the following illustration:

> For DeGaulle is a man of purposeful ambiguities, which permit retreat or compromise without necessarily appearing to do so.

The phrase "purposeful ambiguities" is an apt one. As a matter of widely known fact, most contracts abound with purposeful ambiguities, which denote statements over issues neither side will concede or go all out to win. The failure of the parties to reform the language and eliminate such ambiguities when the contract is open for negotiations amounts to a tacit understanding that the ambiguities may be negotiated at a later time during the contract term, when the ultimate disposition of unsettled issues becomes binding arbitration.

Those whose sense of symmetry and order in language is offended by the presence of ambiguities should be careful not to tamper with the wrong ones. The blemish in the language may be akin to the birthmark in the classic tale of that title by Nathaniel Hawthorne. The narrator tells of a scientist with a wife whose perfect beauty was marred for him by a birthmark on her cheek. He successfully concocted an elixir which when swallowed by her caused the blemish to fade away. But the birthmark was a blemish in outward appearance only. It was so rooted in her inner life-force that as it disappeared her life-force ebbed out with it until she had expired. So too, there are ambiguities in collective agreements which cannot be prematurely removed without upsetting a delicate and vital balance in the rela-

---

14 *Webster's Third New International Dictionary, Unabridged,* 1961, notes in its preface on p. 7a: "This dictionary has a vocabulary of over 450,000 words." This number, of course, can be reduced to far fewer root words.

15 Edgar A. Jones, "Problems of Proof in the Arbitration Process: Report of West Coast Tripartite Committee," *Problems of Proof in Arbitration: Proceedings of the Nineteenth Annual Meeting, National Academy of Arbitrators,* BNA, Inc., 1966, p. 169.

tionship between the parties of which the ambiguity is but a surface manifestation.

It should be stressed at this point that although purposeful ambiguities are quite common, they account for only a small proportion of the ambiguities which abound in the written instrument. An even larger proportion of contract ambiguities are the result of misunderstandings or of careless or clumsy writing. But by far the largest proportion are rooted in the limitations of language itself, both written and oral. On these limitations Harry Shulman observed:

> No matter how much time is allowed for the negotiation, there is never time enough to think every issue through in all its possible applications, and never ingenuity enough to anticipate all that does later show up. Since the parties earnestly strive to complete an agreement, there is almost irresistible pressure to find a verbal formula which is acceptable, even though its meaning to the two sides may in fact differ.[16]

It is a greater feat than is often realized when opposing negotiators are able to write language which covers clearly areas that they agree upon without inadvertently encroaching upon areas outside the scope of their agreement. For one to be able to put down on paper clearly and fully the mutual intent of the parties on a particular item and yet manage to keep the writing from going beyond their intent requires an appreciation of the subtle shades of meaning possible in language and a talent for expressing meanings in precise terms.

But, to repeat, the most frequent problems which arise during the life of a contract are those which were not anticipated by the parties when the language was drawn up, except in a general sense. Yet astute, highly sophisticated labor relations people are known to strain at defective and obscure contract provisions until they have convinced themselves that the language unambiguously supports their interpretations. So hemmed in do they become by their selective perception of key words, phrases, and sentences that they often neglect the search for pertinent facts outside the language to support their respective positions. One might hope that when opposing representatives with years of experience are able to read contrary meanings into disputed language, they would back up and less confidently proclaim that the language is so clear that it is susceptible to one interpretation only, their own.

The chapter following will explore in detail a number of major problems arising from semantic misconceptions and some basic standards developed in contract administration for resolving these problems.

---

[16] Harry Shulman, "Reason, Contract, and Law in Labor Relations," *Harvard Law Review*, vol. 68, no. 6, April, 1955, p. 1002.

SUMMARY

An examination of many reported arbitration decisions suggests there is widespread, although not unanimous, agreement among arbitrators as to some basic standards for interpreting contract language. Foremost among these criteria are:

1 Specific language is controlling over general language.
2 Clear and unambiguous language generally prevails over past practice.

Specific language refers to a constituted or named category; *general language* deals with the issue by inference. Within the specific-general structure, an arbitrator may use other guidelines to determine the relative priorities of the meaning. Specific language takes precedence over general language, especially if the language is clear and unambiguous. Ambiguity and unambiguity are polar opposites, each of which is defined through the other.

An important theme relates to determining the meaning of contract language by noting the presence of patent or latent ambiguities. A *patent ambiguity* appears on the face of the instrument and arises because the language itself is unclear or defective. A *latent ambiguity* is due to extrinsic factors which make possible more than one reasonable interpretation of the language.

The nature of language has been considered with respect to its impact on contract negotiations and administration. As Shulman observed, ambiguous language is often used to disguise disagreement. He was referring to the calculated or intentional ambiguity employed by the parties in negotiation "when they know they cannot agree on more precise statement and prefer to take a chance on future application rather than break up in total disagreement."[17]

---

[17] Harry Shulman, "The Role of Arbitration in the Collective Bargaining Process," in *Collective Bargaining and Arbitration,* University of California, Institute of Industrial Relations, Los Angeles and Berkeley, Calif., 1949, pp. 21–22.

Chapter 5

Semantics of contract language: case studies

■ The five cases in this chapter are intended to illustrate some important problems in contract administration where the language of the agreement is in dispute. These cases are presented in a sequence which, it is hoped, will allow the reader to move logically from one principle of contract interpretation to another. The first case (Leadman promotion) illustrates the principle that clear language generally supersedes past practice. The second case (discharge for dishonesty) demonstrates how the meaning of a term can be standardized by reference to the dictionary definition. The third case (vacation eligibility) delineates how the standardization of contract terms has extended the principle of assigning dictionary definitions to words of doubtful meaning. The last two interrelated cases (Saturday overtime) provide an interesting example of how the meaning of language can change by the introduction of new evidence.

[1] The authors wish to acknowledge their debt to Thomas Kennedy of Harvard University, who made a number of helpful suggestions regarding the organization and presentation of the case material in this and other chapters.

CASE NO. 1. LEADMAN PROMOTION—STANDARDIZATION OF SENIORITY PROVISIONS

The following example of the assignment of a standardized meaning to a basic contract item, adding another area of certainty to a major collective-bargaining topic, deserves an extended presentation. This case also includes a valuable discussion on seniority. At issue was the interpretation of the following contract provision:

SECTION XXI—LEADMEN

D. In the selection of Leadman the most senior employee in the Section where the opening occurs, and then in the Department, shall be given first consideration for the appointment to Leadman provided he possesses the qualifications, ability and physical fitness to perform the job and his conduct and attendance records are satisfactory.[2]

The grievant, Lloyd Payne, was the senior employee in the section (fourteen years) who had bid on a Leadman vacancy and had been passed over for another employee with ten years seniority. At the heart of the controversy was application of the phrase "first consideration." Both parties agreed that for the senior employee to be given first consideration, he must be the first prospective appointee to be reviewed as to his qualifications, ability, and other factors listed in XXI(D).

Union Position: Senior Employee Met Job Requirements

A sharp difference arose between the parties when the union argued that if the senior employee met the requirements of the provision, the employer should then proceed no further, but was obligated to appoint him Leadman. The company insisted that XXI(D) did not preclude management from considering other prospective appointees in the order of their seniority, subjecting them to the same tests as those put to the most senior employee. The procedure adhered to by management was for each prospective appointee to be considered one after another in a descending order of their respective seniorities. Then management would select the employee with the highest seniority who was deemed the most capable. In short, for the senior employee to be entitled to the Leadman job, he must be as well qualified at least as any and all of the junior employees under consideration.

[2] *Hughes Aircraft Co., Aerospace Group v. Electronic & Space Technicians, Local 1553,* Jan. 25, 1965, 43 LA 1248, 1249, Arbitrator Howard S. Block, BNA, Inc.

Company Position: Past Practice Requires Senior Employee to Be the Most Qualified

At the arbitration hearing the company supported its interpretation of XXI(D) with conclusive proof of a six-year past practice of adhering to the appointment procedure now in dispute. Of sixteen appointments made in that period, only three times was the most senior employee selected to fill the Leadman vacancy, and thirteen times a junior man was selected. Only two of these latter thirteen appointments were challenged by the union.

The strong showing of past practice made by the company was unavailing. Applying an arbitral standard of even greater weight, the arbitrator sustained the union's position in an opinion which aroused widespread interest.

Arbitrator's Opinion

The arbitrator stated that the resolution of the dispute must be found in the interpretation of section XXI(D), which dealt specifically with the selection of leadman from eligible employees in the section where the opening occurred. He ruled that since this provision dealt expressly with the grievance, it must take precedence over any general language elsewhere in the contract which might conflict with it. In other words, section XXI(D) was controlling.[3]

Did Grievant Get First Consideration?

According to the arbitrator, the language of the provision stated clearly that the most senior employee in the section where the opening occurred should be given first consideration for the appointment. There was no disagreement on this matter between the parties. The problem arose in the application of other standards or tests set forth in section XXI(D); the senior employee must possess the qualifications, ability, and physical fitness to perform the job, and his conduct and attendance records must be satisfactory.

The union contended that if the senior man met those standards, he should receive the appointment. The company, however, interpreted the language of section XXI(D) as giving it the right to subject the senior employee to a further test of comparison with other eligible employees. According to the company, section XXI(D) reserved to it the right to promote a junior employee whom it considered more capable and better qualified to fill the vacancy than the senior man. In short, the company claimed that the senior man should be given the position only if he was also the most capable man. The union disputed this interpretation and argued

[3] *Ibid.,* 1251–1252.

that the senior man must be measured against the requirements of the job without regard to other eligible employees, and if he met the requirements, the appointment should be his.

Strict Seniority versus Modified Seniority

To place the problem in perspective, the arbitrator presented as follows some background discussion of seniority practices prevalent in industry today:

> During the past three decades of collective bargaining in the major industrial centers of the country, seniority provisions have become well-nigh standardized. According to Elkouri and Elkouri, *How Arbitration Works*, pp. 383–386 inclusive, seniority falls into two basic types:
> 1 Strict seniority without qualifications, and
> 2 Modified seniority.

Three Types of Modified Seniority

There are three basic categories of modified seniority described and generally defined as:

> a. *Relative Ability Clauses*—Which generally provide that as between employees relatively equal in ability and other qualifications, the senior employee gets the job; under such a provision comparisons between qualifications of employees are necessary and proper.
> b. *Sufficient Ability Clauses*—If the senior employee has the ability and meets the other qualifications of the job he is selected. Comparisons between eligible employees are unnecessary and improper; the job must be given to the senior employee if he meets the requirements, no matter how much more competent some other employee may be.
> c. *Hybrid Clauses*—When seniority and relative ability are taken together and weighed against each other by comparing the relative difference in seniority and ability of competing employees. Thus, an employee high in seniority but low in ability could be passed over for an employee low in seniority but substantially higher in ability; whereas, if the junior employee were only moderately higher in ability than the senior employee, he probably would not get the job.[4]

Ruling: Section XXI(D) is a "Sufficient Ability" Seniority Provision

After analyzing the language of section XXI(D), the arbitrator came to the inescapable conclusion that section XXI(D) fell into the "sufficient ability" category of modified seniority provisions. If the senior employee met the requirements of section XXI(D), the language of the provision unambiguously entitled him to the appointment without the necessity of comparison with junior employees.

[4] *Ibid.*, 1251.

Ruling: Grievant Was Not Given First Consideration

The arbitrator said he was unable to read into the provision the express or implied right of management to go beyond measuring the senior employee to the requirements of the job. According to the language of section XXI(D) all employees in the section where the opening occurred were eligible for consideration, but the senior employee was to be "given first consideration for the appointment," provided he possessed the qualifications set forth therein.

In his opinion, the arbitrator observed:

> To say that the most senior employee receives "first consideration" in a comparison between other employees is to say nothing, because his lot becomes no different than any other eligible employee and renders this provision of the Agreement virtually meaningless. If meaning is to be given to the express language, then the senior man who satisfies the criteria set forth in Section XXI-D should be awarded the job. For the Arbitrator to rule that Management can subject the senior employee who meets the enumerated requirements to an additional test of comparison with other eligible employees is to add language to Section XXI-D which is simply not there; if the Arbitrator were to read such language into the Agreement by implication, he would be exceeding the scope of his authority.[5]

Ruling: Clear Language Supersedes Past Practice

The arbitrator then considered the testimony in the record of a past practice where on thirteen occasions in the previous six years section XXI(D) was applied to give the appointment to a junior man. However, he felt it was unnecessary to deal with this testimony or with the union's rebuttal argument since there was no evidence to prove that on any or all of the thirteen occasions the senior man met the requirements of the job. In any case, past practice was considered irrelevant to interpretation of section XXI(D). The arbitrator stated the principle as follows:

> It is axiomatic in the interpretation of Collective Bargaining Agreements that when the clear language of a Contract points in one direction and the practice points in another, the Arbitrator must base his decision upon the language of the Agreement.[6]

CASE NO. 2. DISCHARGE FOR DISHONESTY—MEANING STANDARDIZED BY ASSIGNING DICTIONARY DEFINITIONS

A major aspect of the use of linguistic and semantic principles to resolve contract ambiguities deserves an extended discussion. We begin with the assignment of meaning to single words and terms when the meaning

5 *Ibid.,* 1251–1252.
6 *Ibid.,* 1252.

ntended by the parties is unknown or is in doubt. In such instances, a eputable dictionary definition may be controlling. The case of Roger C., a district route manager of a large metropolitan daily newspaper, focused on he application of this criterion. Roger C. was discharged for

> . . . knowingly, fraudulently and dishonestly obtaining two General Electric clock radio prizes (total worth $25.00) from the company under the false representation that he had procured eleven subscriptions for which he was entitled to prize credit. They were phoned-in orders which belonged to the company, and he knew that he was wrong in claiming credit for them and receiving the prizes. The company rules and regulations are crystal clear that all orders coming in over the company's telephones to the branch offices are the sole property of the company, with no credit going to any other party.

Mindful that the arbitrator would subject to a severe scrutiny the discharge of an employee with twenty years service, the company in its brief graphically depicted its stake in the subscription program:

> The Company distributed more than $209,000.00 in merchandise, prizes and trips in 1963 alone to its carriers, as well as cash prizes to its dealers exceeding $134,000.00 in the same year—an aggregate of more than $343,000.00. The potential loss to the Company from misappropriation, theft and other dishonesty under such a program is staggering and the best protection is honest employees.[7]

Although the union contested the discharge as such, it was not the basic ssue before the arbitrator. The weight of evidence was so overwhelming hat Roger C. had knowingly and willfully claimed credit and received prizes for subscriptions which belonged to the company that the arbitrator had no hesitation in ruling that there was "good and sufficient cause" for his discharge. But the question posed to him in the submission agreement was:

> Was Roger C. discharged for good and sufficient cause amounting to dishonesty?

At issue was an accumulation of $5,300 in severance pay. The contract specified three counts on which an employee's severance pay would be forfeited: (1) if he quit; (2) if he provoked his discharge for the purpose of collecting severance pay; and (3) if he were discharged for dishonesty. The arbitrator, moved by the plight of Roger C., who he felt would be punished enough by denying him reinstatement to his job, turned to the dictionary, hoping that he could save the grievant's severance pay. A perusal of a number of dictionaries forced him to the "melancholy conclusion" that it was necessary at the outset to determine the meaning of the word "dis-

---

[7] This case is taken from an unpublished arbitration award of one of the authors; it is not identified further because of the nature of the charges involved.

honesty." Since the contract did not provide a definition, the arbitrator followed an established principle of contract interpretation:

> . . . that in the absence of a showing of mutual understanding of the parties to the contrary, the usual and ordinary definition of terms as defined by a reliable dictionary should govern.[8]

Both parties had quoted definitions of dishonesty taken from standard dictionaries. The arbitrator himself consulted a number of standard dictionaries including Webster's Third New International Dictionry, Unabridged. None of these definitions differed in any significant degree. Because of its clarity and succinctness, the arbitrator selected the definition cited in the union's brief taken from Black's Law Dictionary, where dishonesty was defined as "disposition to lie, cheat, or defraud; untrustworthiness; lack of integrity."

The arbitrator was very careful to state that he did not consider Roger C. guilty of theft. The charge was an infraction of company regulations on the order of punching another employee's time card or falsifying production records—infractions which could warrant dismissal on the first offense, but which managerial consensus did not regard as theft in the strict sense of the word.

The arbitrator stated that if he were asked to decide whether or not the discharge was for theft, he would need go no further to absolve the grievant. But the discharge was for alleged dishonesty—a much broader term suggesting a moral or ethical breach of conduct on the grievant's part. The matter of intent was at the heart of the question. In taking credit for the phone orders, was the grievant forgetful, did he make a careless mistake, or was he fully aware of the company regulations he was breaking? The evidence in the record pointed inescapably to the latter conclusion. The arbitrator then reviewed painstakingly the virtually airtight case against the grievant and denied his claim for severance pay.

CASE NO. 3. VACATION ELIGIBILITY—STANDARDIZED MEANINGS CAN BE ASSIGNED TO SOME BASIC CONTRACT ITEMS

The standardization of basic contract items has produced a logical and inevitable extension of the principle of assigning the dictionary definition to words and terms of doubtful meaning. As basic contract items become standardized, a lexicon of standardized meanings for these items is developing to be assigned like dictionary definitions when the parties do not make

---

[8] Frank Elkouri and Edna A. Elkouri, *How Arbitration Works,* revised ed., BNA, Inc. 1960, p. 207.

the language of the items clear. A controversy over vacation eligibility between a nationally known cosmetics firm and the union of its employees will illustrate the application of one such standardized criterion.

Late in 1964, after several months of negotiations, the parties finally reached agreement on a new contract. The old contract had provided for a three-week vacation after ten years seniority. The new contract granted annual wage increases and shortened the eligibility for the third week of vacation from ten years to five years seniority. The pertinent language of section 14A(4) of the new contract boiled down to the following simple statement:

> Effective October 1, 1965, employees who have completed five years of seniority . . . shall receive three weeks vacation. . . .[9]

The dispute flared up in the spring of 1965 when the company posted the following rules on vacation eligibility:

> 1 Any employee with five years or more of service whose vacation eligibility date *falls* on October 1, 1965, or after, shall be granted three weeks of vacation.
> 2 Any employee with five years or more of service but less than ten years whose vacation eligibility date occurs *prior* to October 1, 1965, will not be eligible for three weeks of vacation until his vacation eligibility date.
> 3 All employees with ten or more years of service will receive three weeks of vacation.[10]

Position of the Parties Summarized

The following condenses an exchange between the parties over this issue, and is *not* a verbatim transcription.

The company industrial relations director explained to an outraged union committee: "The language of 14A(4) is unmistakably clear. An employee whose vacation eligibility date [the anniversary date of his hire] falls before October 1, 1965, must have ten or more years seniority to get three weeks vacation. An employee whose eligibility date falls after October 1, 1965, can get three weeks if he has five or more years seniority."

"Are you trying to tell us," the chief steward demanded, "that if a guy's eligibility date accidentally falls before October 1, 1965—even if he has nine and a half years seniority—that he'll have to wait till his eligibility date in 1966 to get three weeks?"

"You can read 14A(4), can't you? It says so as plain as day."

"But that means people with eight and nine years seniority will get only

---

[9] *Max Factor & Co. v. Warehouse, Processing & Distribution Workers' Union, Local 26*, Dec. 10, 1965, CCH 66-1 Arb., § 8207, Arbitrator Paul Prasow.
[10] *Ibid.*

two weeks vacation this year, while people with five or six years seniority lucky enough to have their vacation eligibility date fall after October first get three weeks this year."

"Not many," the industrial relations director tried to assure him. "We have the figures from Accounting. Most of the people won't be eligible for the third week vacation until 1966. That was the intent of 14A(4)."

"Who says so?" the chief steward flared. "It was certainly not *our* intent, let me tell you."

"May I remind you," the industrial relations director said, tight-lipped, "that we granted very generous annual increases in the new contract, aside from the third week vacation—15 cents this year, 13 cents in 1966, and another 15 cents in 1967. Why 2 cents less in 1966? Because that's the year we calculated to pick up the heavy cost of the third week vacation—the equivalent of about 2 cents per hour per employee—and with the 13-cent wage increase it brings the economic package in '66 to 15 cents. Three 15-cent years across the board. And now you fellows want to eat your cake and have it by trying to move up the third week vacation in 1965."

The arbitrator who decided the issue candidly agreed with the union that the employer's interpretation of vacation eligibility for the third week would lead to "harsh, inequitable and illogical results." Nonetheless, he affirmed a weightier consideration than the obvious merits of the union's position. The long-range desires of the parties to diminish or eliminate areas of arbitral discretion by confirming established guidelines which transform these areas to areas of certainty impelled the arbitrator to sustain the employer's interpretation of the contract.

The arbitrator noted that the issue of employee eligibility for vacation benefits has historically been a frequent source of controversy in labor-management relations. In part the problem arises because there are three different types of years (annual time spans) upon which vacation eligibility may be based. Many disputes over this issue arise because when drafting the language of a vacation provision, one party may have in mind one type of year, while the other party may be thinking in terms of another type of year. These differences may not become apparent until individual employee vacations are scheduled, some time after the contract goes into effect.

Three Annual Time Spans

In most collective-bargaining agreements, vacation eligibility is based upon one of the following three different types of years:

    1 *The calendar year,* beginning January 1 and ending December 31.
    2 *The employee's seniority year,* based upon the individual employee's anni-

versary date of employment and continuing each succeeding year thereafter.

3 *The contract year,* based on the anniversary date of the contract. (In the case under discussion it would begin October 1, 1964, and fall on October 1 of successive years until its termination at midnight of September 30, 1968).

n the instant case, the union argued that an employee's vacation eligibility in section 14A(4) was based upon the *calendar* year. In other words, any employee who had completed five to nine years of seniority (and was otherwise qualified) at any time during the 1965 calendar year, from January 1 to December 31, was entitled to three weeks vacation under the contract.

The employer argued that it had been the intent of the parties to base the three-week-vacation eligibility in section 14A(4) on the second *contract year,* beginning October 1, 1965. Therefore, only those employees who met the seniority and other qualifications after October 1, 1965, could qualify or the third week of vacation.

The issue of vacation eligibility has been adjudicated so often over the years that its interpretation and application have become fairly well standardized. The major problem was to establish which of the three main time-span categories constituted the basis for granting vacation benefits. Once this could be ascertained, then vacation eligibility was automatically determined.

Ruling: Vacation Eligibility Is Based on Contract Year

After reviewing the record, the arbitrator noted that there was nothing ambiguous about the fact that eligibility in the disputed section was based upon the contract year and not the calendar year or the employee's seniority year. The language of 14A(4) clearly provided that vacation eligibility was determined by reference to the contract year whose anniversary date fell on October 1, 1965.

The real controversy was whether specifying the contract year in 14A(4) as the time span for the three-weeks-vacation eligibility precluded consideration of employee eligibility for this benefit *prior* to the October 1 anniversary date. For example, could an employee who completed the five-to-nine-years seniority requirement prior to October 1, 1965, claim a third week of vacation after that date? The answer to this question would be yes, if vacation eligibility were based on the *calendar year.* If vacation eligibility were based on the *contract year,* then the answer must be in the negative. Otherwise, the distinction and the very purpose of separating the calendar year from the contract year would be completely obliterated.

The arbitrator ruled that, when the agreement established vacation eligibility on the contract year, then an employee could not retroactively claim a benefit to which he would be entitled only if the time span were based on the calendar year. Numerous arbitrators have so ruled in prior cases, and these interpretations have become so well standardized that the arbitrator in the case under discussion said he was not inclined to disregard such established uniformity of vacation eligibility.

Maintaining Appropriate Time Spans Supersedes Harsh Results

In his opinion, the arbitrator stated that:

> No satisfactory resolution of this kind of issue can be arrived at by wandering in a semantic underbrush where the concepts become ever more illusive. If the Union's position were upheld, the ruling would in effect obliterate any purposeful distinction between a vacation eligibility based on a calendar year time span as contrasted to a contract year time span. The Union argues with considerable merit that to construe the contract as urged by the employer would lead to harsh, inequitable and illogical results. The Union graphically illustrates this contention by pointing out the manifest unfairness of granting a third week of vacation to a 5-year employee who by accident has the good fortune of a hiring-in date subsequent to October 1; while at the same time denying a third weeks vacation to another employee, with perhaps 9 years seniority, whose hiring-in date happened to fall prior to October 1.[11]

Acknowledging the union's contention that such a harsh result could not be taken lightly, the arbitrator said it must be balanced against the greater mischief which would be created by obliterating the distinction between the calendar year and the contract year. He noted that the words "Effective October 1, 1965," appeared only in section 14A(4); they did not appear in any of the other provisions of section 14 setting forth eligibility for one or two weeks vacation. He concluded that to rule as the union requested would require the arbitrator to in effect rewrite the language of 14A(4).

CASES NO. 4 AND 5. SATURDAY OVERTIME— "READ THE LANGUAGE. THAT'S ALL YOU NEED."

We conclude with an extended presentation of two interrelated cases which will demonstrate, we trust, a fundamental tenet of semantics—that there is strictly speaking, no such thing as an innate meaning of words, but only the

[11] *Ibid.*, p. 3726.

sense or context in which they are used. The employers in both cases belonged to, and were represented by, a huge association of retail grocery stores.[12]

The first case to come before an arbitrator involved a chain of supermarkets called Brothers Stores. At issue was a claim by a clerk-checker, Gloria D., that she had worked four hours on a Saturday and was paid at straight time when she should have been paid at time and a half. Her regularly scheduled workweek was five consecutive eight-hour days beginning on Monday and ending on Friday. On the Tuesday before the Saturday in question, she had worked only the first four hours and had then taken the afternoon off, with the permission of her supervisor, in order to take her son to a doctor.

The union and the association representatives scrutinized the three provisions of the master contract pertinent to the issue and unhesitatingly came to opposite conclusions. There was no undertone of doubt in their assertions. Each side read a meaning into the language so transparently clear as to cast doubts on the literacy of anyone able to read a different meaning. "We'll stipulate the simple facts of the case, all of them," both parties told Arbitrator Henry Blake. "You read the contract language. That's all you need. Just read the language and tell us if Gloria D. has or has not a valid claim."

The parties were sparing in their presentations. For the most part they aired their opinions of the contested language with little reference to facts extrinsic to the contract. In less than two hours they adjourned, leaving a somewhat bewildered arbitrator staring at the following language:

ARTICLE XIII—WORK PERIODS

(A) Forty hours shall constitute a normal week's work to be worked in five consecutive days within any seven day period, but no employee shall work more than five days during any such period without being compensated at the rate of time and one-half the regular rate of pay for all work performed on the sixth and/or seventh days.

(C) Eight hours shall constitute a day's work to be worked continuously except for a lunch period which shall not exceed one hour. In no event shall an employee be required to work more than five continuous hours without a lunch period.

ARTICLE XIV—OVERTIME AND PREMIUM RATES

(A) Overtime shall be paid all employees who work in excess of eight hours in any one day, or in excess of forty hours in any one week, at the rate of time and one-half the regular rate of pay.

---

[12] The parties in these two cases preferred to remain unidentified.

In denying Gloria D. overtime pay for Saturday, the company had pointed to article XIV(A). She had worked thirty-six hours from Monday to Friday and four hours Saturday for a grand total of forty hours. Article XIV(A) was crystal clear, said the company: time and one-half after eight hours in a day, or after forty hours in a week.

The union, of course, based its claim on article XIII(A), underscoring the part which read, ". . . no employee shall work more than five days during any such period without being compensated at the rate of time and one-half the regular rate of pay for all work performed on the sixth and/or seventh days."

The company rebutted by citing the opening words of article XIII(C), "Eight hours shall constitute a day's work to be worked continuously," contending that the passage gave meaning to the word "day" in XIII(A). Therefore, said the company, when Gloria D. took four hours off on a Tuesday, which was part of her normal workweek, she had not worked a day within the meaning of XIII(A).

On a simple reading of the provisions with no extrinsic facts outside the language to guide him, the arbitrator concluded that article XIII(C) was a connecting link, not only with XIII(A) but with XIV(A), giving a consistent harmonious meaning to all three provisions.

He wrote:

> It is important to note that while Article XIII (A) defines a normal work week as five consecutive days of work within any seven day period nowhere in Paragraph (A) is the term work day defined.
> The issue put succinctly is as follows: If an employee works part of a day, has she fulfilled the contractual requirement of a work day? Article XIII (C) is explicit in the following statement: *"Eight hours shall constitute a day's work. . . ."* [Italics supplied.] Nowhere else in the Agreement is a workday, as such, defined. In the opinion of the Arbitrator, the express language of Article XIII (C) is controlling and the question at issue between the parties is answered by the clear language of the above quote from Article XIII (C). Under the facts of this case The Grievant would have had to work five eight hour days, or otherwise have worked forty hours during her regular work week, in order to be entitled to overtime for the 4 hours which she worked on Saturday.

When Arbitrator Blake released his award, sustaining the position of Brothers Stores, he assumed that the issue was settled—for good or for ill, but nonetheless settled. However, the provisions he had ruled on were part of a master contract covering the industry in a large urban area, and the union had second thoughts about accepting an interpretation for one employer arrived at by analyzing the language of a master contract without reference to extrinsic facts in the industry. The union did not have to wait long for the identical issue to arise again.

ARBITRATING THE ISSUE A SECOND TIME

This time the employer was the Sunrise Supermarkets and the clerk-checker was Claire M., who had been paid four hours straight time for a Saturday morning instead of time and a half because she had been off the previous Monday afternoon on an excused absence. The new case went before Arbitrator Arthur Knowles. The hearings took two full days, and there was no argument this time—from the union at least—that the language proclaimed its meaning solely by word position and sentence structure. Arbitrator Blake's award was a prominent exhibit submitted into the record by the employer.

Blake sighed when he later learned of the new arbitration. He confided to an intimate: "If I had realized that this issue could be arbitrated over and over again down to the last member of the employers' association, I wouldn't have been quite so sweeping in my opinion. Not that I would've ruled differently. I'll still stand by my decision, but the flat statement I made, that article XIII(C) was so clear, so controlling"—he shook his head ruefully—"it was just too sweeping. I should've qualified the statement, acknowledged some ambiguity there. It was a slip of the pen."

Nonetheless, the employer's position in the second arbitration very much depended on the weight given to the Blake arbitration opinion and award—particularly Blake's unqualified statement that the "express" language of article XIII(C) was "clear" and therefore "controlling." Unquestionably, the Blake opinion alone would have easily tipped the scales in favor of the employer had the union not counterbalanced it with two other facts not introduced in the Blake arbitration.

First, the union was able to establish that the instant company's past practice had been to pay employees time and a half for working their sixth or seventh days as such even when they had taken off all or part of a day earlier in the workweek. To this the company replied that it had yielded in the past under pressure from the union, but was not now required to continue a practice which was contrary to the clear language (as verified by Arbitrator Blake) of the contract.

Second, the union subpoenaed as a witness Merle Dykstra, who had represented the local union many years before when the disputed contract language had been negotiated. His testimony carried more than ordinary

weight because of his status as area industrial relations director of a nation
wide food processing firm. Dykstra answered questions diffidently, no doub
because of the delicacy of his position as a management man giving testi
mony adverse to another management. He acknowledged that some fifteen
years before he had been the union's chief spokesman when the language in
dispute had been written. He then affirmed without qualification that th
meaning intended by the parties at that time coincided with the union'
current interpretation.

Dykstra's testimony and the evidence of past company practice were
extremely persuasive to Arbitrator Knowles. An arbitrator will not lightl
issue an opinion which contradicts a respected colleague on an identica
issue, and Knowles did not relish the role thrust upon him to function a
quasi-appellate arbitrator in a quasi-judicial proceeding. His ruling sus
taining the union is yet another cogent demonstration of how much the
meaning of language is derived from a variety of factors extrinsic to the
words and sentences in dispute. His opinion and reasoning are discussed
below.

The Second Arbitration Had a Different Record

Arbitrator Knowles began by stating the issue in his case as: whethe
work performed on sixth or seventh day of regular workweek, regardles
of how many days or hours worked during the workweek, was compensable
at the overtime rate of time and one-half. He noted that this issue had been
examined by Arbitrator Blake in a prior case involving the same union and
a different member of the employer group and that the company's interpre
tation of the contract language was found to be controlling. Knowle
observed that if the same record were before him, he would have had no
hesitancy in coming to the same conclusion as Blake. "What makes the cur
rent dispute so sticky," said Knowles, "is that testimony on the original
intent of the parties, plus testimony on past practice, has been added to the
equation. This complicates the factors which have to be weighed in relation
to each other."

Arbitrator Blake Had Said Language Was Clear

In summarizing the company's position, Knowles said the employer con
sidered the contract as clear and unambiguous, arriving at this conclusion by
juxtaposing XIII(C) and XIII(A). Article XIII(C) stated, "Eight hours
shall constitute a day's work . . . ," and nowhere else in the agreement was a
work day defined. Hence the company argued that when article XIII(A

referred to five days, it was referring to five 8-hour days by incorporating XIII(C) into its language. The company argued further that because the language of article XIII was unambiguous, the arbitrator was precluded from going any further and from considering matters such as past practice, which was outside the clear language and hence was inadmissible. The company also contended that the issue before Knowles was the same issue previously decided by Blake, where the latter had ruled that the language of article XIII(C) was controlling.

In summarizing the union's position, Knowles pointed to article XIII(A) on overtime and premium rates, which provided for payment of overtime at the rate of time and one-half for work in excess of eight hours in any one day or in excess of forty hours in any one week. The union argued that if article XIII(A) did not intend to call for overtime on the sixth or seventh day as such, then the language was superfluous. If the language was ruled to be ambiguous, asserted the union, its interpretation should prevail because the intent of the parties and their past practice were consistent with its reading of article XIII(A).

Arbitrator Knowles Said Language Was Ambiguous

Knowles reaffirmed the principle that an arbitrator's primary function is to interpret the intent of the parties. Arbitrator Blake in the prior case determined the intent of the parties by examining the language. However, nowhere did Blake say that the language in question was utterly devoid of ambiguity. Analyzing the language of the relevant sections, Blake noted that article XIII(A) did not define a work day and that only in article XIII(C) was a work day, as such, defined. Based upon the record in his case, Blake relied upon the language of article XIII(C) as controlling, leaving the implication that article XIII(A) was ambiguous standing by itself. Knowles agreed that Blake was correct in going outside article XIII(A) in trying to ascertain the intent of the parties. As such, XIII(C) became one measurement of the intent of the language in article XIII(A). Arbitrator Knowles suggested that Blake would agree that other measurements of intent could also be relevant, such as testimony of persons who first negotiated the language.

The thrust of Dykstra's testimony to Knowles was that the unequivocal intent of the language in the agreement meant that time and one-half should be paid for all work performed on the sixth and seventh days as such. When cross-examined on the omission of "as such" from the contract, Dykstra explained that those words were not included because fifteen years ago negotiators were not as expert in formulating contract language as they are today, and the phrase "as such" was not in common usage. Dykstra's testimony went unrebutted, since no witnesses were produced by the company to give any other version of what the parties intended.

Arbitrator Blake Actually Meant That Language Was Specific, Not Unambiguous

Arbitrator Knowles suggested that the parties had been misled by Arbitrator Blake's statement that "the express language of Article XIII(C) is controlling . . . ." Taken in the context of Blake's full decision and his recognition that the term "work day" is not defined in article XIII(A), Blake's statement should more properly have been understood as "the *specific* language of Article XIII(C) is controlling. . . ." The use of the word "express" implied that the language was unambiguous; all that Blake actually said was that the *specific* language was controlling, which, of course, is a different matter. Article XIII(A) did not define a work day, and, standing by itself, it could only be characterized as ambiguous, since one had to look outside the framework of (A) to ascertain whether the sixth and/or seventh day were intended to be premium days *as such*. Since article XIII(C) defined a work day, Blake elected to ascertain the intent of the parties by emphasizing article XIII(C). Knowles concluded that Blake had based his findings on XIII(C) alone because no other factors extrinsic to the contract language had been produced by the parties to guide him. For example, in the record before Blake, neither party had cited a past practice; therefore, past practice at Brothers Stores for this group had played no part in his decision.

Meaning of Language Changed by New Evidence

Arbitrator Blake had had little else but the actual language of the disputed provisions to guide him. The record before him had been bare of evidence of past practice or precontract discussions during negotiations. But the record before Arbitrator Knowles dictated a broader construction of the language in dispute. Knowles had no need to wander in a semantic underbrush straining with ambiguous language formulations to elicit the intent of the parties. A clear-cut past practice had disclosed how the parties themselves had resolved those ambiguities. Knowles said it was uncontradicted that up to six months previously, the company had in fact paid overtime for work on the sixth or seventh day as such. Moreover, from the time the company's practice started, no problem even arose on payment for the sixth or seventh day as such until the current dispute. Knowles observed that the parties were experienced in labor relations and recognized the implication and effect of the way they have lived together for a period of almost fifteen years. Finally, he concluded that "no past practice of any member of the Employer's Council was produced to show a practice contrary to this company and so neutralize the Union's showing. Therefore, even though the arbitrator is mindful of the value of prior awards, such prior awards are forceful when not only the issues and the parties, but the *record* is also the same." [Italics supplied.]

SUMMARY

To recapitulate, if Cases 4 and 5 illustrate nothing more, they demonstrate vividly that language consists of a limited number of semantic symbols (words) to convey ideas, facts, feelings—*meanings*. The meanings are not entirely in the words themselves, but depend upon a variety of factors extrinsic to the words and sentences used.

The point has been stressed repeatedly in this and the previous chapter that when a dispute arises over a contract provision, the intent of the parties is seldom manifested unambiguously by a simple reading of the language. Frequently one must look to factors extrinsic to the language in order to discern what the parties meant. Our next chapter will discuss the single most important criterion used to give meaning to the entire collective-bargaining agreement—the practice of the parties.

Chapter 6

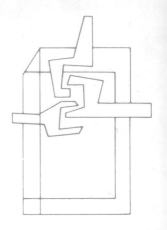

Past practice where there is contract language

■ The operation of an organization is the sum total of its practices—practices broadly described as methods for the production of goods and rendering of services. The point was stressed in Chapter 3 that the ultimate responsibility for the operation of the enterprise rests of necessity with management. In the popular vein: Somebody has to be the boss. People cannot aimlessly decide what they will do and how and when and where they will do it.

FUNCTIONS WHICH ARE EXCLUSIVELY MANAGEMENT'S

The operation of an organization—its practices—has been roughly divided into two main areas of responsibility. One area consists of those functions which are wholly the responsibility of management. Years ago, when representing the Steelworkers Union, Arthur Goldberg acknowledged that management's authority for the following basic functions was unarguably supreme and exclusive:

> Management determines the product, the machine to be used, the manufacturing method, the price, the plant layout, the plant organiza-

tion, and innumerable other questions. These are reserved rights, inherent rights, exclusive rights which are not diminished or modified by collective bargaining as it exists in industries such as steel. It is of great importance that this be generally understood and accepted by all parties. Mature, cooperative bargaining relationships require reliance on acceptance of the rights of each party by the other. A company has the right to know it can develop a product and get it turned out; develop a machine and have it manned and operated; devise a way to improve a product and have that improvement made effective; establish prices, build plants, create supervisory forces and not thereby become embroiled in a labor dispute. . . .

. . . In addition to these exclusive rights to do things without any union say, the exclusive rights to manage and direct should be very clearly understood by all parties. The union cannot direct its members to work stations or work assignments. The union does not tell people to go home because there is no work. The union does not notify people who are discharged to stay put. The union does not tell employees to report for work after a layoff (except perhaps as an agent for transmitting information in behalf of management). The union does not start or stop operations unless perhaps some urgent safety matter is involved and there is some contractual or other basis for such action.[1]

MANAGEMENT FUNCTIONS WHICH ARE SHARED

The other main area of responsibility may be summarized broadly as covering the terms and conditions of employment, including direction of the work force. Authority in this vital area is not exclusive to management, but may be subject to collective bargaining. The sharing of this authority is in some basic respects regulated by law, but even more fundamentally, the degree and extent of the sharing is determined by a balancing of strengths of the parties. The making of a first contract and its subsequent alterations is a legislative process—a process wherein the terms of the written instrument register concretely the ability of the union to modify and even veto management initiatives which had once gone unchallenged.

Can There Be a Pure Exclusive Management Function?

There are authorities who view with pronounced skepticism the demarcation of a sharp line between functions which are wholly management's and functions which involve employee benefits and hence are to be shared with unions as a subject of collective bargaining. Neil Chamberlain distrusts any

---

[1] Arthur J. Goldberg, "Management's Reserved Rights: A Labor View," *Management Rights and the Arbitration Process: Proceedings of the Ninth Annual Meeting, National Academy of Arbitrators*, BNA, Inc., 1956, pp. 123–124.

hard and fast line of demarcation, pointing out that any management function, however far removed it may appear at first glance to be from an employee working condition, is ultimately bound to influence working conditions and employee benefits dependent upon it.

Chamberlain adopted the Cartesian method, attempting to isolate a "pure" management function by eliminating from consideration one by one any operating function whose purity might be in doubt. By this process, he was able to extract *one* function which could be declared pure and unadulterated management. Attempting to isolate this pure management function, he reasoned that in order to enlist support for the operation of the enterprise, management must bargain not only with unions but also with other interest groups such as suppliers of materials, customers, stockholders, and performers of divergent functions (as say line and staff) in the managerial hierarchy.

> Each is seeking to fulfill the aspirations of its members through the medium of the corporation, thus preferring that the corporation take certain actions or make certain decisions rather than others, thus seeking to influence corporate conduct to the extent of its bargaining power.
> Because of the number of individuals and groups involved, because of the number of issues concerning which each has his preferences, because of the requirement that with respect to any issue only one resolution can be made, applying to all affected, and because of the further requirement that the decision on any issue must be consistent and compatible with the decisions on all other issues—because of all these conditions it is necessary that there be a *coordinator* of the bargaining.
> This task—*the coordination of the bargains of all those who compose the business—is the unique function of management.*[2] [emphasis supplied]

THE MAJOR–MINOR TEST OF MANAGEMENT FUNCTION

Other authorities, such as Cox, Dunlop, and the Elkouris, also recognize that there are no pure management functions which can be utterly divorced from collective bargaining in any and all circumstances. They advance a pragmatic solution often called the "major-minor test." When the employee benefit is minor and the contract is ambiguous or silent, the practice is considered a basic management function which can be altered or abolished at management's discretion. When the benefit is major, doubts are generally resolved in favor of the employees and the practice is considered a

[2] Neil W. Chamberlain, *The Labor Sector*, McGraw-Hill Book Company, New York, 1965, p. 349.

basic employee benefit which cannot be withdrawn until the contract is
open.[3]

Arbitrators of such stature as Saul Wallen and Richard Mittenthal
believe that the major-minor criterion leaves too much to the discretion of
the arbitrator. Says Mittenthal:

> To begin with, it [the test] is vague and inexact. What is major to one
> group of employees may be minor to all the others; what is major from
> the standpoint of morale may be minor from the standpoint of earnings
> and job security. There is no logical basis for distinguishing between
> major and minor conditions, unless the arbitrator is to concern himself
> with serious violations of the agreement.
>
> More important, this kind of test encourages arbitrators "to com-
> mence their thinking with what they consider a desirable decision and
> then work backward to appropriate premises, devising syllogisms to
> justify that decision. . . ." That is, if an arbitrator decides to enforce
> the practice he calls it a major condition, and if he decides otherwise
> he calls it a minor condition. To this extent, the test provides us with a
> rationalization rather than a reason for our ruling.[4]

The Major-Minor Test Is Workable

There is a persuasive logic to Mittenthal's objection, but it is flawed by
the singular omission of an alternative test. Decision makers are put in the
uncomfortable position of the motorist who was seeking a village somewhere
in the general vicinity and asked an old farmer for directions. After artic-
ulating several false starts, the old farmer concluded, "You just can't get
there from here nohow." In the workaday world, the parties must "get
there" somehow even if agreement is not formalized, even if it is only the
result of a default by one of the contending parties and is at best a temporary solution. When they do ask an arbitrator to draw the line for them,
he resorts willy-nilly to the major-minor test for want of a more acceptable
alternative. The deliberate weighting of the scales as to what is major and
what is minor to reach a desirable decision is an inescapable element of the
judicial process. There are limits, commensurate with his survival as an
arbitrator, to which he can allow a free play to his judgment. Such arbitral
free play tends to be exercised in borderline major-minor situations where
the merits of the case are glaringly in favor of the party which gets the
award.

---

[3] Frank Elkouri and Edna A. Elkouri, *How Arbitration Works,* revised ed., BNA, Inc.,
1960, pp. 274–275.
[4] Richard Mittenthal, "Past Practice and the Administration of Collective Bargaining
Agreements," *Arbitration and Public Policy: Proceedings of the Fourteenth Annual
Meeting, National Academy of Arbitrators,* BNA, Inc., 1961, p. 53.

CASE NO. 1. PAPER HANDLER'S GRIEVANCE—PAST PRACTICE GIVES MEANING TO CONTRACT LANGUAGE

A grievance over the assignment of a paper handler in a commercial printing firm illustrates the complexities of weighting criteria in just this kind of case. The grievance arose soon after the company had added an offset press to the five letter presses in its shop. The union charged that on certain runs of this new press on the night shift, the company had violated the contract as well as an established practice by failing to assign a paper handler to perform certain specified tasks alleged to be within the jurisdiction of the paper handlers' bargaining unit. These tasks were of two kinds: one was the moving of rolls of paper into position behind the press to enable the pressman to lock the rolls into the press; the other was the cleaning up of waste and the cutting of the waste when there was a break in the run.

Offset-press runs presented no problems on the day shift because there were always paper handlers servicing the letter presses who were available to do the necessary work on the offset press. But on certain nights, when none of the letter presses were in operation, the company had a regular run of the offset press to print a shoppers' newspaper involving a single sheet from one roll. No paper handler was assigned to these offset runs. Had a paper handler been assigned, he would have been entitled, according to the contract, to a full shift pay regardless of how much or how little work there was for him.

The company argued before the arbitrator that the paper-handler tasks for the press runs in dispute had been virtually eliminated. The day-shift paper handlers before going home would move the rolls behind and next to the offset press in preparation for the night run. As for waste around the offset press, the amount was negligible, as compared to the normal accumulation around the letter presses, and the company's instructions to the pressmen were to leave such waste for the day-shift paper handlers to clean up in the morning.

Did Practice on Letter Presses Apply to the Offset Presses?

The union pointed to a consistent past practice (of whose existence the memory of man knew not to the contrary) of assigning at least one paper handler to a shift when this same newspaper had been printed at night on a letter press and no other presses had been in operation. The reason for the practice was that every run entailed some work that was the exclusive jurisdiction of the paper handlers in accordance with section 4(b) of the collective agreement. Section 4(b) included as part of the paper handlers' jurisdiction "the stripping and make-ready of rolls for the presses" and "the weighing, checking and handling of waste paper."[5]

The company questioned the relevance of a practice applied to letter-press runs when the issue was the manning for an offset press. The union retorted, in Gertrude Stein idiom, that offset or letter press, a press was a press was a press and the past practice was applicable to all presses.

That some paper handlers' work, a minimal amount, was being performed on the disputed night runs was undeniable. At least two of the six rolls brought to the offset press by day-shift paper handlers, the two rolls placed on the side of the press (there was room behind the press for the other four rolls), would have to be moved again during the night run. As for the handling and disposal of waste paper, the area around the offset press was clean the morning after each run; therefore someone, perhaps a pressman, was doing this work. Privately the arbitrator estimated the amount of paper-handler work in question would add up to ten or fifteen minutes for one man; but in order not to quibble with the union in his written opinion, since he was going to rule for the company anyhow, he estimated the total at twenty to thirty minutes. The merits of the case, he felt, were conspicuously on the side of the company. Yet it is interesting to note how he weighted the criterion of past practice in reaching his decision.

The arbitrator was asked to decide the question of whether the company was required to assign at least one paper handler on the night shift when only the offset press was in operation. The offset-press operation presented no manning problem on the day shift because on that shift there were always paper handlers on duty to perform the tasks which were in dispute on the night shift. The night-shift tasks which the union claimed to have been deprived of in violation of section 4(b) consisted of handling and disposal of waste paper and, more important, the right to "make ready" the paper rolls for the press.

As to the first charge, the company denied that the relative cleanliness around the offset press after a night run was a result of assigning the handling and disposal of waste paper to the pressmen instead of bringing in a paper handler. The offset press, according to the company, was so fundamentally different from the letter press in its construction and operation that the amount of accumulated waste paper was minimal and easily disposed of by the pressmen without violation of the paper handlers' jurisdiction. The union flatly rejected the company's explanation but was unable to produce any evidence in support of its skepticism. The arbitrator felt

---

[5] *Rodgers & McDonald Publishers, Inc. v. Los Angeles Paper Handlers' Union 3,* June 13, 1966, unpublished arbitration award, pp. 2–3, Arbitrator Howard S. Block.

constrained, therefore, to resolve the doubt on this point in favor of the company and ruled that in the matter of handling and disposal of waste paper, there was no violation of the agreement.

Arbitrator Rules Practice on Letter Presses Does Not Apply to Offset Runs

Essentially, the case turned on conflicting interpretations by the parties of the all-important phrase "make-ready" as used in section 4(b). The arbitrator noted that when such a phrase is susceptible to more than one interpretation, a valid past practice is a basic criterion for discerning the mutual intent of the parties. The offset press had been introduced a year earlier, and since then the company had operated the night run without assignment of a paper handler. The arbitrator stressed that the mere existence of the past practice did not in itself bind the union because the union not only had withheld its acquiescence to the practice but had strongly protested its continuation.

The union pointed to the manning policy on the letter presses as the valid past practice which gave meaning to the phrase "make-ready." The company had always assigned at least one paper handler whenever a letter press, not to speak of the wood press, was operating day or night. The union urged application of the past practice of letter-press operation on a broad basis to encompass the offset-press runs for both shifts.

The arbitrator stated that in his opinion it was not enough to say that printing presses are printing presses, be they offset or letter, and that the practice of one automatically encompasses the other. "The true test," he said, "may be posed by the question: Do the *common features* of the two types of presses outweigh their differences?" The arbitrator illustrated the principle by intentionally using extreme examples: the practice of a propeller-driven airplane and that of a jet plane would not generally encompass each other; nor would the practice of a five-hatch freight ship be generally applicable to a huge transoceanic passenger liner.

The arbitrator acknowledged that past practice as a criterion should be broad enough to encompass minor or moderate distinctions between printing presses. However, when the differences were as substantial as those between the letter presses and the offset press, the arbitrator refused to rule that any and all past practices of the letter presses were indiscriminately and automatically binding on the offset press.

In his opinion, the arbitrator commented that:

> According to the testimony of Mr. J., it would take a maximum of five minutes for the Paper Handler to move two rolls of paper up to the

> press; his testimony is uncontroverted by the Union on this point. Based upon this testimony and a careful review of the record as to the nature and extent of the disputed duties, it appears to the Arbitrator that all of this work could be performed in twenty to thirty minutes per shift at most.[6]

Accordingly, he concluded that:

> In the absence of clear language in the Agreement as to the meaning of the phrase "make-ready of rolls for the presses" and, without the guidance of a valid practice to fill this gap of ambiguity, the Arbitrator does not feel justified in requiring the Company to assign a Paper Handler to the offset press on the night shift in order to perform twenty to thirty minutes of work. The Arbitrator rules, therefore, that the current practice of the Company first established when the offset press was introduced last year is not in violation of the Agreement and should remain undisturbed. It may be noted that while this practice does not require the assignment of a Paper Handler to the night shift when only the offset press is operating, it does include all the tasks on the offset press which the Paper Handlers have been performing when one or more of them are on duty.[7]

Why the *De Minimis* Rule Was Not Applied

A colleague of the arbitrator read the opinion critically and shook his head. It seemed to him that an unnecessarily lengthy and circuitous route had been taken to reach an obvious conclusion.

"You could've saved yourself all that writing," he told the arbitrator. "If ever I saw a clear-cut justification for the *de minimis* rule, this was it. Twenty minutes work, and the union was trying to get a full shift pay." He was referring to the rule of contract interpretation, *De minimis non curat lex,* meaning that the law does not concern itself with trifles.[8]

"*De minimis!*" the arbitrator frowned. "I'm supposed to resolve problems, not create them. Not even management tried to invoke the *de minimis* rule—and I'm sure they thought of it. Do you know how many different work-assignment practices there are in the industry that could be called *de minimis?*"

"I haven't the faintest idea."

"Well, neither have I," the arbitrator grinned, "and I wouldn't want to find out by standing up in a crowded theater, so to speak, and yelling '*de minimis!*' "

---

[6] *Ibid.,* p. 12.
[7] *Ibid.*
[8] Arbitrators, however, have accepted grievances over trifling amounts when it was clear that a major principle was at stake.

He paused and reflected briefly. "Perhaps I overstated the consequences. I'd rather put it in terms of that old proverb, 'In the house of the hangman, one does not talk of a rope.' "

The hinge of the paper handlers' claim, the arbitrator said, turned on the meaning of the phrase "make-ready" as used in section 4(b). A lengthy consistent past practice on letter presses had given meaning to that phrase for letter-press runs. The question was, did this past practice apply also to the offset press, to give the phrase "make-ready" an identical meaning for both types of presses? The arbitrator, by drawing a qualitative distinction between the practice of a letter press and that of an offset press, answered the question in the negative.

CASE NO. 2. SUPERVISOR PERFORMING BARGAINING–UNIT WORK—APPLICATION OF THE *DE MINIMIS* RULE INSTEAD OF PAST PRACTICE

Although the arbitrator displayed an understandable caution about invoking the *de minimis* rule in the printing industry, the rule is not infrequently invoked elsewhere. Consider the following case, where the issue was whether the work of a supervisor in operating a lift truck on February 23, 1959, constituted a violation of the agreement for which the grievant is entitled to pay:

Contract Clauses Involved

ARTICLE IX—MANAGEMENT

9.2 It is the policy of the Company that supervisors and other salaried employees of the Company at the plant shall not spend their time performing manual labor which is normally performed exclusively by members of the bargaining unit, except in cases of imminent safety hazards to persons or property, momentary assistance, instruction or experimentation. Clerical or laboratory work, other than the work presently performed by the Testers and the Small Batch S Utility men, shall not be construed as included within the scope of this paragraph.

ARTICLE II—HOURS AND WAGES

2.6 Employees scheduled to work on Saturdays, Sundays, or Holidays shall be guaranteed a minimum of four (4) hours of work within their department. Employees called in on special call (except during the day shift on a Saturday) shall not be required to continue working after completing the work for which they were called in, in order to receive the minimum pay.[9]

Background of the Case

February 23, 1959, was a plant holiday, since Washington's Birthday, which fell on Sunday, was observed on Monday. On that day, an outside contractor came to the plant with a crew of men to clean out a pit. It was a job which the outside contractor did for the company from time to time. The contractor, according to company procedure, should have advised the company in advance of his coming that he would be arriving on that date. The company then, according to its usual procedure, would have arranged with the guard on duty for the admittance of the contractor and would have prepared the area where the work was to be done. The contractor, however, did not advise the company that he was coming on this date. When he arrived, the guard, who recognized him from his previous visits to the plant, admitted him. The contractor went to the area where he was to work but found that the opening to the pit was obstructed by several pallets on which paint was loaded. He advised the guard of this fact, and the guard in turn advised Mr. F. of the situation. Mr. F. was a salaried supervisor who happened to be in the plant that day to catch up with some back work. Making use of the lift truck which was under one of the pallets, Mr. F. moved the pallets of paint a few feet.

Summary of the Union's Position

The union argued that this action on the part of Mr. F. constituted a violation of section 9.2, presented above. The union claimed that Mr. F. had improperly deprived a lift-truck operator of work and that he should have called in the appropriate employee to do the work. The union argued that since Mr. F.'s action was improper, the lift-truck operator should, under section 2.6, receive four hours straight-time pay. The union asserted that section 9.2 clearly governed the case. According to the union, none of the exceptions applied, since this was not a case of "imminent safety hazards to persons or property, momentary assistance, instruction or experimentation."

The union cited an instance which it maintained was substantially parallel, where a welder was called in on the night shift to do a very short job. It contended that the company should have followed the same procedure.

[9] *Sherwin-Williams Co. v. Paint, Varnish & Allied Prods., Local 1310,* Apr. 30, 1959, unpublished award and opinion, Arbitrator Morrison Handsaker (Impartial Member).

Summary of the Company's Position

The company maintained that the amount of work involved was so small as to be negligible. Mr. F. testified that it took him approximately ten minutes to move the pallets and that an experienced employee would have taken not more than five minutes to do the job. The company said that since there were no bargaining-unit members in the plant that day, Mr. F.'s action was the only practical solution to the problem. It would have taken a considerable length of time to have called another employee and to have gotten him into the plant. The company asserted that the contractor was concerned about the delay and did not want to have himself and his crew held up in performing the work. The company pointed out that since it had no notice of the prospective arrival of the contractor on the day in question, it could not have anticipated his coming and have had the area cleared of pallets. The company cited the *de minimis* rule, arguing that this was the sort of case in which the rule should govern. It maintained that the violation, if there was one, was so minor in nature that it should be disregarded as *de minimis*.

Opinion of the Impartial Member of the Arbitration Board

The impartial member of the arbitration board upheld the company with the following:

> It is clear that a very small amount of work was involved, and it is also clear that the Company could not have foreseen the need to have the area cleared since it did not know that the contractor would arrive on this particular day. Had a more substantial amount of working time been involved or if the Company could reasonably have foreseen the need for the work, the ruling would have been different. Since, however, such a small amount of work was involved, the need for which could not have been foreseen, the impartial member of the arbitration board rules that the "de minimis" doctrine applies and that the Company therefore has not violated the agreement.[10]

Importance of Past Practice in Interpreting Ambiguous Language

In general, the standard of past practice is used more extensively than any other for giving meaning to ambiguous contract language. Meaning can be established by the conduct of the parties, whether that conduct is b

[10] *Ibid.*, p. 3.

vords or by action without words. The rule was stated in an earlier case as ollows:

> It is a well settled principle of industrial arbitration that where past practice has established a meaning for language that is subsequently used in new agreements the language will be presumed to have meaning given it by past practice.[11]

Although there is ordinarily a meeting of minds when an agreement is reached, it is not enough that this be a subjective understanding. It is the expression of their mutual assent that obligates the parties in the contract-making process. It is not the subjective assumption of a meeting of minds, but their objective manifestation of mutual assent which binds the parties.[12]

CASE NO. 3. THE SCHEDULED WORK DAY AND HOLIDAY PAY—PAST PRACTICE GIVES MEANING TO AMBIGUOUS LANGUAGE

We present now an arbitration opinion on a controversy over the meaning of the phrase "scheduled work day" which includes an excellent dissertation on how mutual intent is ascertained by the conduct of the parties rather than by testimony as to their internal thought processes when the language was negotiated. The pertinent contract provision was:

> Section X (e): Employees working the scheduled work day before and the scheduled work day after a holiday, shall receive pay for the holiday. . . .[13]

The employer was a meat-packer in California's San Joaquin Valley, and the eight employees who initiated the grievance were represented by the Butchers' Union. In their grievance, the eight employees claimed pay for the 1963 Christmas holiday. They were laid off on Friday, December 20, 1963, and were returned to work on Monday, December 30. They performed no work during that intervening period. Between December 20 and December 30, the day on which the laid-off employees were recalled, the entire plant except for the killing department, the department to which these laid-off employees were assigned, was in operation. The employees

---

[11] *A. O. Smith Corp. v. United Elec., Radio & Mach. Workers, Local 1004,* May 23, 1954, 23 LA 27, 33, Arbitrator Paul Prasow, BNA, Inc.
[12] *Field-Martin Co. v. Fruen Milling Co.,* Minnesota Supreme Court, 210 Minn. 388 (1941).
[13] *Nobles Independent Meat Co. v. Butchers' Union, Local 126,* Sept. 8, 1964, unpublished arbitration award, p. 3, Arbitrator Adolph M. Koven.

worked the scheduled work day following their layoff, but not "the scheduled work day after a holiday" of the plant, since the rest of the plant was operating between December 20 and December 30.

Exactly the same situation occurred in 1959, 1960, and 1962. Employees were laid off from the "killing" section, but the rest of the plant was in operation. The laid-off employees were not paid for the holiday, but the union made no formal protest on those prior occasions. Section X had remained essentially unchanged for more than five years prior to the Christmas holiday, 1963.

The union argued that "the scheduled work day after a holiday" referred to the first day the grievants returned to employment from layoff. The company disagreed, contending that "the scheduled work day after a holiday" referred, not to the day on which the grievants returned from layoff, but to the scheduled work day for the entire plant, a day on which the grievants were still on layoff.

In his opinion, the arbitrator concluded that the disputed phrase was ambiguous:

> We come to the principal point in issue, namely, the meaning of subsection (e) and the requirement that the employee work "the scheduled work day before and the scheduled work day after a holiday" in order to qualify for holiday pay. In the Arbitrator's opinion that language is definitely ambiguous for he does not know from the words themselves whether "the scheduled work day after a holiday" refers to the employee's particular scheduled work day after a holiday or whether that language refers to the plant's scheduled work day after a holiday.
>
> Arbitrators differ on the meaning of this language. In *Ottumwa Foundry*, 30 LA 1081, the term "scheduled work day" was interpreted to mean "the employees scheduled day to work rather than the day the plant is scheduled to be in operation."
>
> That approach to "the scheduled work day" is rejected in *Hemp and Company*, 37 LA 1009; *Young Spring and Wire Corp.*, 41 LA 991; *Ultra Metal Manufacturing Co.*, 42 LA 111; *Lamson and Sessions Co.*, 37 LA 273; *Charm Tred Mills*, 12 ALAA 72, 159.
>
> *Hemp* reasons as follows: Where the Contract between the parties expressly provides that the employee to qualify for holiday pay must work on the last preceding scheduled working day before the holiday and on the first scheduled working day subsequent to the holiday, obviously he cannot work those days while he is on lay-off and to grant holiday pay in the presence of such provisions to men on lay-off would be to introduce new and different meaning into the provisions of the agreement.
>
> In *Young Spring and Wire Corp.*, when a lay-off was made in good faith and for recognized economic reasons, holiday pay was denied under circumstances similar to the case herein.[14]

[14] *Ibid.*, p. 10.

Practice Determines Meaning of "Scheduled Work Day"

The arbitrator took particular note of Lamson and Sessions, because in that case the presence of a clear past practice one way or another could determine the meaning of "scheduled work day."

> This is particularly true when established past practice places the meaning "scheduled *plant* work day" onto the words, and where lay-offs are not prompted by any desire to deprive the employee of holiday pay, but are caused purely by economic reasons.[15]

The decisive factor in interpreting "scheduled work day," therefore, appeared to be the existence of a strong and unbroken past practice, in which case the arbitrator would read the words either way, depending on that past practice.

In the case under consideration, a strong past practice had been established which indicated that the language meant "scheduled plant work day." There was no showing of bad faith in laying off the employees in the "killing" operation, nor was there any evidence that the layoff was for other than economic reasons. Under these circumstances, the arbitrator concluded that were he to sustain the union in its interpretation, he would be modifying the agreement so as to make it inconsistent with the parties' own past and controlling experience. Accordingly, he ruled that the company did not violate section X of the agreement in denying Christmas holiday pay in 1963 to the grievants.

CASE NO. 4. CARPENTERS' JURISDICTION—PAST PRACTICES CANNOT BE NULLIFIED BY SWEEPING GENERAL PROVISIONS

So authoritative is past practice as a standard for interpreting ambiguous contract language that arbitrators will not permit such practices to be nullified by general contract provisions which declare that the written instrument terminates all past understandings and is the complete agreement of the parties. Consider the following provision dated August 4, 1959:

> ARTICLE XXVIII—OTHER AGREEMENTS
>
> Section 2. The parties do hereby terminate all prior agreements heretofore entered into between representatives of the Company and the Unions (including any and all past understandings, practices, and arbitration rulings) pertaining to rates of pay, hours of work, and conditions

---

[15] *Lamson & Sessions Co. v. United Steelworkers, Local 3574,* Aug. 30, 1961, 37 LA 273, 275, Arbitrator Ralph R. Williams, BNA, Inc.

> of employment other than those stipulated in this Agreement between the parties.[16]

At issue was a jurisdictional claim of a Carpenters Union local protesting the assignment of boilermakers to such work as the installation of pre-fabricated bar-type aluminum gratings on a deepwater oil rig and the installation of aluminum rings in pressure tanks on a barge. The master contract covering all the crafts was ambiguous on the matter, but it had been a clear and consistent past practice of the company to recognize the carpenters' jurisdiction over all aluminum work. The arbitrator posed the key question and then answered it as follows:

> Does the reference concerning the elimination of past understandings in Article XXVIII eliminate those understandings which serve to clarify ambiguous contract language, which continues to exist in that and subsequent agreements? Obviously not, because to eliminate understandings which clarify an unclear contractual condition, would revert the parties to their original point of uncertainty which necessitated the understandings in the first place. Further, understandings and practices, which arise by virtue of ambiguous contract language, remain in force and effect until such time as contract language which necessitated the understanding is changed. Otherwise, uncertainty would result from a constant attempt to reach understandings over the same unclear contract provision which results in insecurity regarding the sanctity of a promise. Therefore, it must be held that the terms of Article XXVIII of the 1959 Agreement do not terminate the prior understandings of the parties relative to the jurisdiction of the Carpenters.[17]

CASE NO. 5. PREMIUM PAY DURING JURY SERVICE—PAST PRACTICE CONTROLLING OVER GENERAL PROVISION

The principle that a general provision canceling all prior understandings does not preclude the use of past practice to clarify ambiguous language is an important one and is worth elaboration in the following discussion of a published arbitration award. The case involved an interpretation of this contract provision:

> Employees who have completed sixty (60) days of continuous employment with the company who are called and report for service as a Juror, will be paid the difference between their base rate at straight time, and the fee paid for such Jury Service.[18]

---

[16] *Higgins, Inc. v. Carpenters Dist. Council of New Orleans, Local 584, United Brotherhood of Carpenters & Joiners,* July 5, 1961, 37 LA 297, 298, Arbitrator R. H. Morvant, BNA, Inc.

[17] *Ibid.,* 301–302.

[18] *Kelsey-Hayes Co., Heintz Div. v. United Auto. Workers,* Jan. 13, 1961, 37 LA 375, Arbitrator Lewis M. Gill, BNA, Inc.

The issue was whether the grievant, a night-shift worker, should have had a 10 percent night-shift differential included in his base rate for purposes of calculating the pay due him for jury service under the above provision. The union argued that the contract language was unclear or silent on the point and that a conceded past practice of including such a differential in jury-pay calculations established an interpretation of the language which could not be changed by unilateral decision of the company.

Past Practice versus Contract Provision Canceling All Prior Understandings

In arguing the negative, the company placed major emphasis on the following passage from section 8, article XV, of the collective agreement:

> All prior Agreements either oral or written are hereby cancelled and this Agreement and Supplements attached hereto shall constitute the entire Agreement between the parties.[19]

The company asserted that a major item in dispute during negotiations leading up to the then current agreement was management insistence on elimination of various past practices and understandings. The union did not deny this assertion, but it challenged the company's contention that it *achieved* the objective of a sweeping elimination of all past practices.

Past Practice Can Interpret Ambiguous Language

Specifically, the union argued that the provision cited by the company, whatever else it meant, certainly did not wipe out the effect of past practices which *interpreted* the contract language. The arbitrator concurred with the union, stating:

> I think the Union is undoubtedly right on this last point. The above language appears clearly designed to cover side agreements or understandings on subjects not covered by the contract, and may also apply to understandings or practices which are *contrary* to the plain meaning of the contract, but it certainly cannot be said to rule out consideration of how the parties have applied ambiguous contract language in practice.
>
> The contract, in other words, is the governing document, but the *meaning* of the contract is obviously a proper subject of inquiry, and evidence bearing on that question is surely not ruled out by the above provision.
>
> That brings us to the second contention of the Company, which is in my view the crux of the case.[20]

[19] *Ibid.*
[20] *Ibid.*, 375–376.

The arbitrator then addressed himself to the substance of the issue, and after an extensive analysis, he sustained the grievance. He concluded by heavily underscoring the restrictive nature of his decision:

> A word should be said in closing as to a general argument advanced by Company counsel at the hearing. He argued ably and at some length that the company was concerned here, not with the small amount of pay difference involved in his grievance, but with the broad principle of whether the Company should be saddled with a lot of past practices and side understandings which it had fought through a lengthy strike to eliminate before signing this current agreement.
>
> If it is not already clear from what has been said, it should be emphasized that the ruling here is strictly limited to the narrow issue posed in the present case.
>
> The ruling simply means that a consistent past practice of applying a contract provision in a particular way is given decisive weight as to the proper interpretation of that provision, where there is room for doubt as to what it means.
>
> I understand the Company's concern over the broader questions adverted to by counsel, but the issue here is a narrow one, and the particular facts before me require in my opinion the conclusion which has been reached.[21]

The relationship of practice to contract language goes much deeper than the clarification of ambiguities unforeseen by the parties. A great deal of language is written into the contract which is intentionally general because the parties could never agree on details for the application of the policies expressed by the language.[22]

SUMMARY

There are several approaches to the task of delineating the essential nature of the management function. For example, certain functions in operating an organization may be viewed as belonging exclusively to management, whereas others are considered as shared functions, i.e., subject to collective bargaining.

Some authorities maintain it is unrealistic to attempt to draw a sharp line between those management functions which are inviolate and those which are not. Neil Chamberlain, as a chief exponent of this view, also holds that, reduced to its ultimate, there is one "pure" function of management, which arises from the need to coordinate the bargain of all the different interest

[21] *Ibid.*, 377.
[22] Chap. 3, pp. 32–35.

groups which compose the organization. In his view, such coordination "is the unique function of management."

In tackling the same question, other authorities have devised what has come to be known as the major-minor test of management function. If the question involves a relatively minor employee benefit and the collective agreement is vague or silent, then management has the final say and can dispose of the matter at its sole discretion. On the other hand, if a relatively major benefit is involved, then disposition of the matter does not rest exclusively with management, but is subject to negotiations. Even though some believe that the major-minor determination of a line of demarcation leaves too much to the arbitrator's discretion, it has been generally accepted as a pragmatic solution to a most perplexing problem.

The criterion of past practice serves as an indispensable counterweight, balancing two opposing organizational requirements: stability and flexibility in operations. Past practice should provide the necessary stability to ensure continuity in key areas of the employment relationship, but it should not be pushed beyond the point where it impairs the exercise of legitimate managerial freedom of action. The line between stability on the one hand and flexibility on the other, that is, between practices which are binding and those which are not, must be drawn by the arbitrator on the basis of his evaluation of the record.

Chapter 7

Past practice when the contract is silent

■ Those practices of management which are not covered by any language in the contract and which intentionally or fortuitously confer benefits on employees go to the heart of the management-reserved-rights doctrine. They are in a sense the reverse side of the coin of that doctrine. In most instances they originate as reserved rights, as exercises of administrative initiative that may or may not become binding. The following observations by Ralph T. Seward on this topic cast a searching light on the interconnection between reserved rights and implied obligations:

> As this issue is faced in arbitration, it comes down primarily to a question of implied obligations. There is no inherent conflict between such obligations and the so-called doctrine of reserved rights. Of course, on the surface, it looks as though there is such a conflict. But what is the doctrine of management's reserved rights? The doctrine merely holds that management has retained those rights which it has not given up by agreement. The doctrine does not, however, answer the question of *what rights should management be held to have given up in the agreement.* That is the question with which arbitrators are faced. . . .
>
> And I detect, myself, no difference (I detect vast differences of *degree* but no difference in *kind*) between that kind of implication and the kind

of implications which management representatives themselves are con-
tinually asking us to find in the contract. For it is by no means the
unions alone that are asking us to imply things in agreements. There is,
I believe, quite as much argument from management for the reasonable
necessity of reading implications into the agreement as from unions.
Indeed, managements often argue that the existence of a management
right to continue some function or to start a new function should be
assumed, in *spite* of express language in the agreement.[1]

It is necessary at this point to differentiate between those employee benefits initiated unilaterally by management (sometimes by employees) which
become binding conditions of work and other such benefits which, regardless of how much employees have come to rely upon them, may be withdrawn at management's discretion. Benefits of this latter type may be
subdivided into (1) gratuities and (2) unintended benefits, which are incidental by-products of the organization of production and services.

Year-end Bonuses as the Most Common Type of Gratuity

Bonuses, especially Christmas bonuses, are a common source of controversy when they are discontinued by the employer as a gratuity. The following arbitration case dealt with just such an issue presented in clear-cut
form. The parties had agreed there was nothing in the contract providing
for the distribution of Christmas checks or the payment of a Christmas
bonus. The union's chief contention was that the company had each year
made a distribution of checks at Christmas and that therefore the matter
had become such an ingrained past practice that the company would be in
violation of the contract by failing to continue the practice. If the evidence
had been to the effect that a Christmas payment had been made each year
and that without any notice or action on the company's part the employees
had come to consider this as part of their perquisites, there would be a
problem as to its continuance. According to the arbitrator, however, the
evidence was undisputed that each year the company had made an
announcement that it would pay a Christmas bonus or make a distribution
of checks at Christmastime in some certain amount as a result of action by
the board of directors at that time.

> In the light of these factors, the arbitrator observed that: The rule has
> been pretty well ingrained that where the contract does not provide for a
> particular course of conduct, then the Company is not required to follow
> a line of conduct not required unless there could be established a long
> course of conduct on the part of the Company which created a condition

---

[1] Ralph T. Seward, "Arbitration and the Functions of Management," *Industrial and
Labor Relations Review,* Cornell University, January, 1963, p. 236.

of employment recognized by both parties. Unfortunately, in this case, the evidence refutes the establishment of such condition of employment, because each year the Company took special action and gave special notice to the employees of that action so that the arbitrator cannot hold that there was an established past practice since the announcing of the doing of an act prior to its performance would negative any indication that the conduct was something that had to be performed regularly. Under these circumstances, and while the arbitrator may have personal feelings in regard to Christmas distributions, in this particular instance, the evidence indicates that the Company had treated the giving of Christmas checks as its own voluntary act and had actually notified the Union each year to that effect. That being so, and the contract being completely silent on such distribution or the continuance of any past practices, the Arbitrator must hold that the Company was within its rights in withholding the distribution of Christmas checks in 1961.[2]

Catch-all Provisions Do Not Usually Convert Gratuities into Binding Practices

When arguing against the withdrawal of a bonus, unions will unfailingly cite any existing general provisions which require the maintenance of employee benefits in existence at the time the contract is signed. Arbitrators do not, as a rule, consider gratuities as benefits protected by such catch-all provisions, as is apparent from the following case.

In a dispute over withdrawal of a bonus, the union referred the arbitrator to article XXI of the agreement, which read:

> MAINTENANCE OF PRIVILEGES. The Company agrees that all existing privileges, advantages and favorable conditions which are presently enjoyed by the employees covered by the terms of this agreement will be continued by the company during the period of this agreement except that the vacation schedule shall be limited to the schedule provided for in Article XVI.[3]

The union argued that the article gave all employees the right to participate in bonuses and that the practice of granting them had now become an integral part of the wage structure so as to become a fringe benefit to be enjoyed at the end of the year. To show this intent, the union said that in order to obviate any conflict with a change in the vacation schedule, vacations were expressly excluded from the operation of article XXI. The union claimed that if it had been the intention to exclude the practice of granting bonuses, they too would have been specifically referred to in the article.

---

[2] *White Baking Co. v. Bakery & Confectionery Workers Int'l Union, Local 374,* Mar. 20, 1962, 38 LA 216, 217, Arbitrator Robert G. McIntosh, BNA, Inc.

[3] *Telemetal Prods., Inc. v. Int'l Union of Elec., Radio & Mach. Workers, Local 485,* Apr. 16, 1959, 33 LA 139, 140, Arbitrator Morton Singer, BNA, Inc.

The arbitrator ruled for the company with the following comments:

> After duly considering the facts, I am of the opinion that the Union has proceeded on specious grounds. I am convinced that if a bonus is purely a voluntary act, predicated solely on earnings, then no matter how long such bonuses were granted, if the bonus is a voluntary act, it can be stopped, dependent upon the Employer's balance sheet. This fact is supported by the Employer's statement that it had experienced a poor year and was in no position to grant a gift at year's end.
>
> There are certain practices which must be maintained after an agreement is entered into. But such practices are absolute, with no conditions attached. In the case at bar I am constrained to find that there is no practice which this Employer must maintain with regard to the payment of the Christmas bonus. A bonus of this nature does not fall within the purview of Article XXI. I shall deny the Union's request.[4]

Another union attempted to prevent the withdrawal of a regular Christmas bonus by citing from article X of the contract the following section designated as "Prior Agreements":

> Section 1. This Agreement terminates all existing collective bargaining agreements, as supplemented and amended between the parties, except where otherwise specifically provided herein; however, local working conditions, practices, or provisions of Agreements, written or oral, which already provide benefits that are in excess of or in addition to those provided for by this Agreement shall not be affected by this Agreement.[5]

The arbitrator ruled nevertheless that the bonus was a gratuity not covered by article X. He found there was no dispute between the parties that article X obligated the company to continue local working conditions and practices which provided benefits in excess of those specified in the express provisions of the agreement. There was also no dispute between the parties that neither the current agreement nor any previous agreement contained an express provision obligating the company to pay a year-end compensation (or Christmas bonus). It was therefore clear that the year-end-compensation payments made by the company to employees in the years prior to 1958 were benefits in excess of the express provisions of the contract. However, the arbitrator asserted that:

> The mere fact that the Company did make year-end compensation payments to the employees, . . . which were not provided for in the . . . Agreement, is not determinative of the issue. The real issue is, *"Did the payment of year-end compensation by the Company become a local working condition or practice, the discontinuance of which, in the year 1958, constituted a violation of Article X, or was such payment a gratuity?"* [Italics supplied.]

---

[4] *Ibid.*, 140.
[5] *Rockwell Spring & Axle Co., Newton Falls Plant v. United Steelworkers Local 4051,* May 28, 1959, 32 LA 664, 665, Arbitrator Joseph G. Stashower, BNA, Inc.

> The Arbitrator has come to the conclusion that the year-end compensation was not a local working condition, and that its discontinuance did not violate Article X. . . .

Recurrence of a Gratuity Does Not Constitute a Binding Practice

> . . . It is understandable that an employee who has received a Christmas bonus each year for several years, dependent upon his length of service with the Company, would be disappointed at the discontinuance of such payment by the Company at the end of any one year; it is further understandable that employees may arrive at a conclusion that such year-end compensation is part of the employees' earnings, the payment of which is deferred until the end of the year. But no matter how understandable this disappointment may be, and no matter how understandable the conclusion of the employees may be, it must be recognized that the Company can be required to continue such payment only where there is a firm contractual obligation so to do. Where the payment made each year was merely a gratuity dependent upon the discretion and determination of Management, there can be no contractual obligation to continue the payment during the life of any contract.
>
> The evidence indicates that each year a request for the year-end compensation payment was made by the Union Local President; it further indicates that it was made clear to the President of the Local that the decision as to whether a year-end compensation or Christmas bonus (and distribution of turkeys) would be made, rested with the higher echelon of Management. *A practice to be considered a practice binding upon a party, cannot require a separate decision each year. A practice, to be a practice, must in and of itself obligate the Company to follow a certain course of conduct; in this case, the payment of the year-end compensation.* [Italics supplied.]
>
> The conclusion that the year-end compensation was not a local working condition is further fortified by the fact that the Union itself urges that the payment of the bonus each year was a negotiated matter. If it was necessary to negotiate the payment of year-end compensation each year, then it cannot be considered as a local working condition or a practice; again it must be stated that a local working condition or practice is not one that has to be negotiated each year.[6]

Gratuities May Not Be Used for Bargaining

The foregoing cases enunciate basic criteria for defining a gratuity as such. An employer's failure to adhere to these criteria may result in transforming the gratuity into a binding practice. A gratuity is in the nature of a gift. It means paying more for a service than is required by agreement.

---

[6] *Ibid.,* 666–667.   .

The benefit must be a voluntary offering involving no mandatory exchange of consideration. It must be freely given, not demonstrably in response to pressure, and at no cost to the recipient. The donor of the type of gratuity under discussion is usually motivated by a desire to cultivate goodwill, build employee morale, and stimulate incentive.

The irony of many, if not most, controversies over such gratuities is that the employer has withdrawn the benefit precisely because the employees have come to rely upon it, have taken it for granted, thereby nullifying the original purpose of the benefit. In tight negotiations it is difficult for employers to resist using a bonus as an indirect bargaining chip, even at the risk of transforming it into a binding practice. Under the pressures of an impasse an employer will counter union dissatisfaction with his offer on wages and other cost items by pointing to the gratuity as proof of his generally beneficent attitude toward his employees. Even when he hastens to add that he does not know how much longer he can continue the bonus, he may not have escaped a psychological commitment to pay the bonus the next time it is due. The more he relies on the bonus to gain acceptance of his economic package, the more likely are the employees to regard the bonus as an integral part of the settlement. From a psychological commitment to a contractual commitment is a very short step indeed. The findings of Arbitrator Donald A. Crawford in a dispute over withdrawal of a Christmas bonus, described in detail below, show just how such a step is often taken.

THE CASE OF THE GRATUITY WHICH BECAME CONVERTED INTO A BARGAINING PRACTICE

The Christmas bonus is a part of the contractually established wages, and its continuance was part of the 1959 contract settlement.

The premise of the Company's case on the merits of the grievance is the same as in its argument on arbitrability; namely, that the Agreement contains no reference to the payment of a Christmas bonus. On this basis it concludes that the Company did not violate the contract when it did not pay the bargaining unit employees a bonus in 1959. Here again the Company disregards the substance of the matter at issue for the form.

As testified to by Knerr, the Company's chief negotiator, the 1959 contract renewal negotiations were settled after a work stoppage beginning September 1 and ending October 27, 1959. A sub-committee was set up to resolve the matter in dispute and on October 27 an agreement on a package deal was reached. The parties agreed on a wage settlement which provided increases of five cents to nine cents per hour in base rates in each year of the three-year contract. The Union estimates that the increase averages six and a half cents per hour per year.

It was at this sub-committee meeting on October 27 before the settle
ment was completed and the strike ended that Knerr replied, "No, I don't
assume so" to the Union's question whether the strike (or settlement
would have any effect on the payment of the Christmas bonus. The
Company contends that this answer was ambiguous and cannot be con
sidered as a definite understanding, agreement or commitment; that
inasmuch as the Christmas bonus could be continued or discontinued
solely at the Company's discretion, an ambiguous answer was the best
the Union could hope for under the circumstances; that further, knowing
that the bonus had always been considered a gift, the Union's repre
sentative recognized that there was no likelihood of success in attempt
ing to limit the Company's bonus.

But the Company overlooks important facts and considerations in
reaching this interpretation of the bargaining situation on the eve of the
settlement and the significance of Knerr's answer concerning the con
tinuance of the Christmas bonus. The employees had been receiving a
bonus in each of the 19 preceding years—admittedly in good times and
bad. For the past twelve years (since 1947) the amount of the bonus
had been the same, being paid in accordance with an employee's length
of service, so that the Union knew what the bargaining unit employees
could expect in additional year-end compensation. (Prior to 1947 the
employees were paid on the same basis, the compensation, however
being less: $50 for employees with two or more years of service; $20 for
employees with between one and two years of service; and $10 for
employees with less than one year of service). The employees were
never told by written notice, verbally or by a notation on their pay
envelope, that the bonus was a gift. And neither were the employee
nor the Union ever informed in the 19 years the bonus was paid that its
payment was subject to the approval of the Board of Directors of the
parent corporation (the Company is a division of the Chemetron Corpora
tion) in the light of financial conditions.

Furthermore, the Union knew from past experience that the Company
expected it to take into account the Christmas bonus in determining
whether a Company offer in settlement of a contract renewal was ade
quate. For what other meaning can be placed on the testimony of
Kerwin, President of the Company, that after negotiations had been
completed (but prior to submission of proposed settlements acceptable
to the Union negotiating Committee) he would sit around with some of
the men "for an hour or two talking about things in general, and trying
to inform them as well as I could about some of the problems that we
had, that were their problems also . . ."; that during such discussion he
would say, "You guys are lucky as hell; you are getting something [the
Christmas bonus] that you are not giving any consideration to"; "Boys
you don't know how darn lucky you are . . . getting things that maybe
other people weren't getting."

The Union counsel and participant in contract negotiations since
unionization, Louis H. Wilderman, testified that Company negotiators in
resisting demands for a pension plan until 1956, always pointed to the
Christmas bonus. Surely the Union was expected in contract renewal
to consider the Christmas bonus as a monetary benefit in evaluating

contract proposals. Kerwin's statement that he never asked that the Christmas bonus be given any consideration in connection with the negotiations or "official negotiations" does not alter this conclusion.

EFFECT OF STRIKE

Accordingly, when Knerr said, "No, I don't assume so" in reply to the Union's question as to whether the bonus would be discontinued, he was confirming what the Union had every reason to believe would be the answer. But either because it feared possible retaliation for the eight-week long work stoppage and/or perhaps a reaction to a wage settlement it thought the Company might have found less than satisfactory, it sought to anticipate an action that could very substantially reduce the 6½ cents per hour increase the parties had agreed upon as part of the package to settle the 1959 contract renewal. And the Union put the question of the continuation of the bonus directly to the Company. Against a background of a bonus nineteen times successively granted, in fixed amount regardless of economic conditions, which had never been referred to as a gift or described as subject to the discretion of the Board of Directors, and concerning which the members of the Union's negotiating committee had been reminded on more than one occasion that the bonus was a benefit they should take into consideration in evaluating a contract settlement—the significance of Knerr's answer was not in the term "assume" but in the words "No" and "don't." His answer was not ambiguous.

Nor was the point of the Union's question and his answer lost upon Knerr as is evidenced by his testimony under cross examination:

Q. Now, when you said, "No, I don't assume it will have any effect" you meant have any effect on the payment of the Christmas bonus, is that right?
A. That is right.
Q. And therefore, so far as you were concerned and as far as you knew there was nothing that indicated that the Company said or indicated, to the effect that the Christmas [bonus] would be discontinued or taken away. Is that right?
A. That is right, yes, sir.
Q. . . . When the people asked you the question, did you know they were interested in knowing whether they would get the Christmas bonus?
A. Certainly.
Q. And when you answered the question, did they accept your answer?
A. I don't know.
Q. Did they ask you any further questions?
A. No.
Q. So that disposed of the bonus question, is that right?
A. That is right.

Thus, regardless of whether the Union used the word "strike" or "settlement" in the question asked of Knerr, the impact of the inquiry was mutually clear to both the Union and Knerr: were the employees going to get the bonus? And when Knerr agrees that the matter of the bonus was disposed of in the 1959 contract negotiations with this question and answer, he recognized he had said or done nothing that would indica‹ that the Christmas bonus would be discontinued. As Knerr must hav‹ realized, had he answered "Yes, I assume the strike will have an effec on the payment of the bonus" or "I don't know," that obviously th‹ negotiation of the renewal of the 1959 contract would not have bee‹ disposed of at that point.

Accordingly, the Arbitrator finds under the circumstances in this cas‹ that Knerr's answer was a commitment that the Christmas bonus woul‹ continue to be paid so that the 6½ cents per hour increase in hour‹ base rates for each of the three-year contract period would not b‹ reduced. Therefore, as part of the wage settlement, the bonus wa‹ incorporated as consideration under the October 27, 1959 Agreement ‹ preserve the average increase of 6½ cents per hour per year.[7]

Other Types of Gratuities

So far our discussion of gratuities that originate as a generous employe‹ offering has been confined to Christmas bonuses. There are, of course, large variety of other gratuities in this general category. For example, company which had for years allowed union officials to use one of the tw‹ conference rooms in the plant for meetings abruptly discontinued the pra‹ tice. Management had become suspicious that many of the meetings wer‹ concerned with internal operations of the union rather than collectiv‹ bargaining matters to be taken up with the company. Arbitrator Sein‹ heimer ruled that permission to use the conference rooms was a gratuit‹ which could be unilaterally given and unilaterally revoked at any tim‹ He stated that in his opinion the company had a right to refuse use of th‹ conference room. He did not believe it made good sense from an industri‹ relations standpoint to refuse reasonable use of the room to the union fc purposes concerning wages and working conditions and other contractu‹ relations. On the other hand, there was no reason, especially where th‹ contract was silent, for the company to provide space for union represent‹ tives to meet on matters concerning the internal operation of the union.

Following this line of reasoning, the arbitrator observed:

> It is logical that the Company know for what purposes the Union inten‹ to use the conference room, and they are obviously within their rights ‹ refuse the use of the space if they feel the room is being used for pu‹ poses other than those concerning relationships between the Compa‹ and the Union. The preceding, of course, in no way limits the Compa‹ from providing the space to the Union for these other purposes, if‹ wishes to do so. To repeat, this Arbitrator is merely stating that th‹ Company does have the right to refuse the claim by the Union, and th‹

[7] *Pennsylvania Forge Co. v. Int'l Ass'n of Machinists, District Lodge 1*, June, 196‹ 34 LA 732, 739–740, Arbitrator Donald A. Crawford, BNA, Inc.

the Company by permitting it to use the room for these other purposes does not, in this Arbitrator's opinion, establish a past practice in the sense that past practice affects wages and working conditions, seniority, discipline, discharge for rules infractions, etc. The contract is silent on the use of this room, and the fact is that the Company has unilaterally granted use of the room, and since it has unilaterally granted use, it can likewise refuse such use.[8]

Free Coffee Becomes a Binding Practice

Another employee benefit, a long-standing practice of providing free coffee during rest periods and at lunchtime, originated as a gratuity but was unwittingly converted by the company into a binding practice during a difficult period of negotiations. Quoting from Arbitrator Handsaker's opinion:

> When we look at the issue on the merits, the arbitrator . . . finds the Union argument persuasive. Of particular importance is the fact that the Company cited the provision of free coffee as a fringe benefit in the 1960 negotiation to counter a demand by the Union for medical insurance for dependents. The evidence is clear to the arbitrator that the provision of free coffee was cited to the Union as a fringe benefit which the workers enjoyed. Thereupon, in view of the extensive list of fringe benefits which the Company had cited, the Union withdrew its demand for Company paid medical insurance for dependents. The Union, therefore, had reason to believe that this was a Company-paid fringe benefit which would continue.
>
> Both the citing of this benefit in the negotiation session and the fact that this benefit had been enjoyed by workers for such a long period of time establishes the granting of this benefit, in the view of the arbitrator, as a past practice which is an implied part of the agreement.[9]

Unintended, Incidental Benefits

We turn now to an examination of the second kind of benefit mentioned early in the chapter. It is a benefit which originates, not from the generosity of the employer, but as an incidental by-product, an unintended result of the operations of the enterprise. A clear-cut example of such a benefit was the use of an employee parking lot adjacent to the main production plant of a company. An ancient brick warehouse in a state of disrepair had sat on the lot until management decided to have it torn down and converted to a

---

[8] *Columbus Auto Parts Co. v. United Auto. Workers, Local 30,* Feb. 6, 1961, 36 LA 166, 170, Arbitrator Walter G. Seinsheimer, BNA, Inc.
[9] *Beech-Nut Life Savers, Inc. v. Beech-Nut Cooperative Council,* Dec. 3, 1962, 39 LA 1188, 1191, Arbitrator Morrison Handsaker, BNA, Inc.

parking lot. In the next decade the company experienced an unprecedented growth, necessitating an expansion of its production facilities. The lot was made the site of a new wing of the main plant. Employees now had to park some distance away from the plant and walk ten minutes on an average to their time clocks. At the end of their shifts they had to walk back to their cars. A test claim by an employee for restitution of twenty minutes pay daily was not allowed by an arbitrator. Parking adjacent to the plant had been permitted only because the land had been available. It was a fortuitous benefit, the unintended result of razing the warehouse. Parking privileges were therefore revocable at any time management decided to put the land to another use.

THE CASE OF THE BACK-TO-BACK SHIFT SCHEDULE

The incidental nature of a benefit is not always as clearly discernible as it was in the parking-lot case. A not unusual type of grievance has arisen when some companies operating at full capacity (around the clock) have rescheduled their shifts from three to two. Employees in manufacturing customarily work eight-hour shifts. But three consecutive eight-hour shifts ("back-to-back") leave no time off for lunch. Many companies, for good reasons, one of them to avoid stirring up acute employee discontent, will adhere to industry norms and maintain at least eight hours take-home pay per shift. One company in order to provide a thirty-minute lunch break for each shift, reduced the second shift to seven and a half hours, and the graveyard shift to seven hours—needless to say, at eight hours pay for each of the shifts. A number of years later the company was able to discontinue the graveyard shift, eliminating back-to-back shift scheduling. The second shift was then rescheduled from seven and a half hours to a full eight hours with no increase in take-home pay.

The union argued without success in arbitration that the original shift reduction to seven and a half hours at eight hours pay was an *additional* premium for working nights (additional because the contract also provided 10 cents per hour premium pay for the second shift). The company was able to establish that the shortening of both night shifts with full pay was not intended as an extra premium for night work—that its purpose was to provide each of the three shifts working back-to-back with a thirty-minute lunch period. The second and third shifts were shortened unilaterally on management's initiative and had never been part of any settlement package in negotiations. Therefore, the full eight-hour shift without increased pay could be unilaterally restored at any time management deemed it practical.

EIGHT CRITERIA FOR DETERMINING THE
BINDING NATURE OF A PRACTICE

We have, so far, discussed two types of employee benefits not mentioned in the contract, both of them gratuities. One type of gratuity is *intentional* and the other *incidental* to the operations of the enterprise. We proceed now to employee benefits not spelled out in the contract, not in the category of gratuities, and which depend for their enforcement on a binding custom or practice. An arbitration opinion involving severance pay sets forth with exceptional clarity and precision criteria for drawing the distinction between binding and nonbinding practices. The claim for severance pay was made by the union on behalf of a group of salesmen who had been given an indefinite layoff because of unfavorable business conditions. The union asserted the existence of a past practice whose binding character was upheld by a general contract provision—which we now quote, followed by relevant excerpts from the arbitrator's opinion sustaining the union:

> Article 12: It is mutually understood and agreed that none of the provisions of this agreement constitutes any lowering of the working conditions existing prior to the execution of this Agreement.
>
> This section, more commonly known as a prior better benefits clause, is generally sought by a Union to insure and protect any favorable condition of employment relating either to wages or hours or working conditions which is not directly spelled out in the labor contract for any of a multiplicity of reasons, but which the parties have nevertheless come to agree is an accepted condition of employment.[10]

The union maintained that the clear intent of this provision was to preclude interpreting the contract, by virtue of its inclusion or exclusion of any specific language, in such a way as to negate any more favorable benefit which employees enjoyed prior to its execution. The "past practice" the union relied upon was based on the numerous occasions in the past (in times of layoff and even discharge) when the company had, after discussion and at behest of the union, given severance pay to affected employees in varying amounts which could be described as fair and reasonable in each instance.

The union argued that the net effect of this consistent action of the company was to remove the matter of severance pay from the category of a gratuity that could be unilaterally granted or withheld by the company and to give it the status of a benefit which employees could properly expect and rely upon and which the parties understood and accepted as mutually binding and enforceable.

---

[10] *Jacob Ruppert v. Office Employes Int'l Union, Local 153,* Oct. 19, 1960, 35 LA 503, 504, Arbitrator Burton B. Turkus, BNA, Inc.

On its part, the company maintained that the contract was barren of any mention or grant of severance pay at time of layoff, that such an essential element of employment would most certainly have been reflected and included in the contract if actually agreed upon, and that under no circumstances should the company be penalized or entrapped into a binding commitment by its prior gracious and gratuitous acts.

The arbitrator then proceeded to enumerate criteria for determining whether the practice was binding:

> The problem here presented is one which has vexed arbitrators with considerable frequency in the past. Certain indicia are sought with such regularity in these cases as to be signposts for future travellers down this, at time, tortuous road. Some of these are:
>
> 1 Does the practice concern a major condition of employment?
> 2 Was it established unilaterally?
> 3 Was it administered unilaterally?
> 4 Did either of the parties seek to incorporate it into the body of the written agreement?
> 5. What is the frequency of repetition of the "practice"?
> 6 Is the "practice" a long standing one?
> 7 Is it specific and detailed?
> 8 Do the employees rely on it?
>
> Rarely do the facts of any of these reported cases produce replies to these questions, universally affirmative or negative. This case is no exception—but the recognized and requisite criteria here appear with sufficient cumulative force and frequency as to sustain the position of the union. Assuredly, severance pay is a major condition of employment —and no parallel of the "Christmas turkey" situation. The practice was initiated, perpetuated and administered on a bi-lateral rather than a unilateral basis. The repetitive frequency of the practice is such that with all lay-offs (some six instances in recent years) severance pay has been granted to the affected employees, without exception. The practice is of long-standing and maturity. Finally, employees have assuredly come to expect and rely on the practice. Indeed, they could not reasonably expect or contemplate that the Company which had repeatedly and invariably paid substantial sums to all employees laid off would allow the remaining employees (or any of them) with generally greater seniority to leave empty-handed upon lay-off.[11]

MUTUALITY IS THE KEY TO A BINDING PRACTICE

If one were to seek an underlying purpose common to all eight points listed by Arbitrator Turkus, it would be that of assessing the element of

[11] *Ibid.,* 504–505.

mutuality in a practice. If the employee benefit is minor, then the practice is a basic management function and the element of mutuality is irrelevant. If the practice was initiated or administered unilaterally, the burden is on the party asserting its validity to establish a sufficient element of mutuality to make the practice binding. Mutuality or its absence may be proved by conduct in negotiation. The incidence of the practice may be so rare, or its duration so short, or its form and content so fragmentary, that employees can hardly be said to have relied upon it, and therefore a claim of mutuality is specious. In summary:

Practice Must Be the Accepted Way of Doing Things

> The circumstances under which local conditions or practices arise and the periods of time which must elapse before they take clear and specific form must, of necessity, vary from one situation to another. But the essence of a past practice is that it constitutes the parties' uniform and constant response to a recurring set of circumstances. It must be and become *the* accepted "way of doing things." The past practice rule applies only to a party who was in a position where he could be deemed to have assented to the practice. The party asserting a past practice bears the burden of proving it by a preponderance of the clear and definite testimony.[12]

Basic Steel Provides the Most Authoritative Criteria

The published arbitrations interpreting "local working condition" in the basic steel industry enunciate the most authoritative criteria that have been formulated on practice when the contract is silent. A "local working condition" (meaning a binding employee benefit) may be established by oral agreement or by a course of conduct initiated unilaterally, even without words. Regardless of how it is initiated, the course of conduct must occur with sufficient regularity and continue long enough to be accepted by both parties as the normal way of operating presently and in the future.

---

[12] *Nickles Bakery, Inc. v. Int'l Brotherhood of Teamsters, Local 585,* Nov. 13, 1959, 33 LA 564, 566, Arbitrator Clair V. Duff, BNA, Inc. See also Richard Mittenthal, "Past Practice and the Administration of Collective Bargaining Agreements," *Arbitration and Public Policy: Proceedings of the Fourteenth Annual Meeting, National Academy of Arbitrators,* BNA, Inc., 1961, pp. 31–33; Richard P. McLaughlin, "Custom and Past Practice in Labor Arbitration," *The Arbitration Journal,* vol. 18, no. 4, 1963, pp. 206–209; Saul Wallen, "The Silent Contract vs. Express Provisions: The Arbitration of Local Working Conditions," *Collective Bargaining and the Arbitrator's Role,* Mark L. Kahn (ed.), *Proceedings of the Fifteenth Annual Meeting, National Academy of Arbitrators,* BNA, Inc., 1962, pp. 123–124.

THE CASE OF THE BINDING PRACTICE
INITIATED BY EMPLOYEES

To illustrate, a group of employees at a Bethlehem Steel plant initiated a twenty-minute lunch period on company time without the express consent of management. They were known as "straight-through" employees, meaning they were scheduled to work a continuous eight-hour day, squeezing in an undetermined lunch break during working hours. Supervisors began to view the twenty-minute lunch break with arched eyebrows when straight-through employees were found eating with other employees in the department who were scheduled for an eight-and-a-half-hour day, of which half an hour was an unpaid lunch period. Since the straight-through employees had started their lunch break simultaneously with employees entitled to thirty minutes, the straight-through employees should have returned to work earlier. But many of them did not: they were taking a full thirty minutes, thus creating a problem in supervision of enforcing their prompt return from lunch. The problem, once it had become a focus of concern, led to an announcement by supervision that straight-through employees would henceforth be limited to a ten-minute lunch break daily, from 11:50 A.M. to 12 noon. A brief summary of the positions of the parties is followed by Umpire Valtin's opinion and award:

The union claimed that supervision's order had the effect of cutting in half the lunch period previously taken by straight-through employees. The union contended further that a twenty-minute lunch period had long and consistently been taken by straight-through employees; therefore such a practice was a "local working condition," which was protected by article II, section 3.

The company's defense was not entirely clear or consistent. Throughout the lower steps of the grievance procedure and well into the hearing, the company appeared to be challenging as a regular practice the claimed twenty-minute break. Toward the end of the hearing, the company took the position that (1) supervision had never instituted a twenty-minute policy; (2) even if the men had customarily taken a twenty-minute lunch period, supervision had not sanctioned it; and (3) without such sanction, the claimed practice could not properly be found to be a "local working condition" within the meaning of article II, section 3.

In upholding the union's claim as to the binding nature of the practice, the umpire commented:

> As respects the existence of the claimed practice, the evidence leaves little doubt in the Umpire's mind that "straight-through" employees had

regularly taken a 20-minute lunch period. The Union put on the stand six employees, all of whom have been in the department for a number of years and all of whom have at one time or another worked on continuous operations. Their testimony is consistent and accompanied by persuasive details. Neither cross-examination nor Supervision's own statements served to destroy the convincing character of the men's testimony. The Umpire unquestionably must find, he believes, that there *was* a long and consistent practice under which "straight-through" employees took a 20-minute lunch break.

There remains the question of whether this practice should properly be held to be protected as a "local working condition" under Article II, Section 3. It is clear to the Umpire that the answer lies in the affirmative:

The Practice Was Binding Even Though It Did Not Originate from Supervision

1 The mere fact that Supervision did not *direct* that a 20-minute lunch period be taken—in the sense of making and announcing a policy decision—obviously does not mean that a "local working condition" could not have emerged. The Agreement's definition of a "local working condition" simply does not require such supervisory origination.

2 As to the "sanction" point, it is not clear whether the Company refers to "sanction" in the sense of "express agreement" or "sanction" in the sense of "tolerating" or "acquiescing." Either version, however, constitutes an untenable defense in this case. As to the first, the answer again is that a practice, to constitute a binding "local working condition," need not be accompanied by *express* consent or agreement on the part of Supervision. As to the second, the difficulty is that the evidence does not support a finding that Supervision did not tolerate, or acquiesce in, the 20-minute lunch break. On the contrary, the evidence indicates that at least some members of Supervision were aware of the fact that "straight-through" employees were taking 20 minutes for lunch. For example, in many instances it seems to have been the departure of the Assistant Foreman from the office, and his appearance in the shop, which "signalled" the end of the 20-minute period.

Umpire Finds Supervision's Acquiescence To the Practice Must Be Presumed

The Umpire believes, moreover, that in the case of a practice so long continued and so widespread, Supervision's awareness—even if not directly proved—must reasonably be presumed. This is *not* a case where but a handful of employees took a liberty and for a time "got away" with it. It is *not* a case which presents mere leniency in the face of departures from known and understood rules. It is a case, rather, of a long-standing practice which was consistently followed by the "straight-through" group as a whole—a group of employees which on some occasions consisted of as much as 70 per cent of the department's workforce. In these circumstances, the Umpire does not see how he can realistically give weight to the allegation that Supervision was unaware of the practice.

The Umpire thus rejects the Company's arguments, and concludes that the "20-minute" practice had assumed the status of a binding "local working condition."

In so holding, the Umpire is not addressing himself to the matter of the starting time of the lunch period for "straight-through" employees. In connection with the testimony bearing on the existence of the claimed practice, certain starting times were specified. The issue presented for decision, however, is not whether the lunch periods for "straight-through" employees should start at any particular hour, but whether such employees are entitled to a lunch period of 20-minute duration.[13]

The employees' grievance was granted, and the company was ordered to restore the "local working condition" in question.

Practice Almost Always Originates with Management, Not with Employees

It should not be assumed from the foregoing case that practices initiated by employees are other than exceptions to the general rule that the administrative initiative of running an enterprise is a basic function of management. Management practices are much more likely to partake of mutuality than employee practices. Employee benefits are generally instituted through management rather than through unilateral practices of employees.

THE CASE OF THE SELF-CONSTITUTED LEADMAN

The grievance of John Kramien, an employee of the Altec-Lansing Corporation, foundered on this principle. Kramien was classified as a Packer in the packing section of the shipping and stores department. He had originally been the only Packer in the deparment. Over a period of years, as the volume of work grew, the number of packers increased to five. Kramien contended that even before the Packer crew had reached this size, he had begun to assume the duties and functions of a Leadman, although still officially classified as a Packer. He now asked that he be given the title

---

[13] *Bethlehem Steel Co., Lebanon Plant v. United Steelworkers, Local 1374*, Oct. 15, 1959, 33 LA 374, 375–376, Umpire Rolf Valtin, BNA, Inc.

and pay for the job he was actually doing, Packer Leadman or Leader. At the arbitration hearing Kramien and other union witnesses made a strong and almost persuasive showing that he was in fact doing the work of a Packer Leader and was misclassified as a Packer. The qualification "almost persuasive" must be reiterated because Kramien's argument was fatally flawed by the very nature of the job title that he claimed.

Quoting from the arbitration board's opinion:

> It would seem to the Arbitration Board that in the absence of any clear-cut definition of a Leader's job (either in the Agreement or in plant practice), a determination of this matter must rest upon the degree of authority, if any, which Management has granted Kramien, either explicitly or implicitly, to direct the work of others in the Packing Section. It cannot be over-emphasized that even though a Leader's job is within the bargaining unit, it is still in essence a supervisory job. The distinguishing characteristic of any supervisory job, no matter how limited in scope, is the delegated authority and responsibility for directing and maintaining the work of other employees. From the record in this case it would appear that there was no explicit delegation of authority. At no time has Management officially authorized Kramien to act as a Leader.[14]

The union had argued there was an implicit delegation of authority in management's permitting Kramien to carry on duties beyond those of a Packer. In support of its claim, the union submitted a description of a series of incidents in Kramien's work which occurred on November 20, 1953, as examples of his Leader's duties. The arbitration board did not necessarily agree that the incidents required more of Kramien than would be expected of the most senior and experienced Packer in the section. Nevertheless, it accepted the union's contention that part of the work Kramien performed could be considered to fall within the scope of a Leader's duties. Training of new packers and expediting the work in the section were cases in point. However, the arbitration board pointed out it was not necessary to distinguish which of the duties performed were those of a Packer or those of a Leader. For Kramien acknowledged in his own testimony that he could not and did not exercise the one vital function which distinguished a supervisor (even on the lowest rung of the supervisorial ladder) from the most highly skilled nonsupervisory employee, namely, the power or authority effectively to enforce plant discipline and direct the activities of others. Such powers could not be assumed or undertaken voluntarily by the employee, but had to be delegated by management.

[14] *Altec Lansing Corp. v. Int'l Union of Elec., Radio & Mach. Workers, Local 1501,* Feb. 28, 1954, unpublished arbitration award, p. 6, Arbitrator Paul Prasow.

Grievant's Lack of Authority to Discipline Employees Was Decisive

In his testimony Kramien had admitted that although he had observed several instances of lack of discipline and loafing on the part of a few men from time to time, he had kept silent for good and sufficient reasons. His testimony on this point is noteworthy:

> **Q.** In other words, no one has ever told you that you have the authority to discipline, correct or even recommend that?
> **A.** No, no one ever told me that.
> **Q.** And you never have?
> **A.** I mentioned that at the meeting not long ago and got it clarified with Mr. Ward.
> **Q.** In other words, you have observed these things but you have not had the authority to do anything about it?
> **A.** I didn't feel it was my duty or authority to be a stool pigeon. If I was a Leadman it might be different.
> **Q.** If you had been a Leader it would have been different?
> **A.** Yes. I might have had some authority to report it directly to the supervisor and cooperate with him to pick up some of this lost motion and get production moving a little faster.[15]

A great deal more testimony along this same line was placed in the record to underscore that there was no implicit delegation of authority to Kramien by the company.

Under stringent cross-examination, Kramien was compelled to acknowledge a further untenability to his position:

> **Q.** Did you ever hear of an employee appointing himself as a Leader?
> **A.** I never heard of that but that is not what I am asking. I am asking them to consider the request.
> **Q.** Then it is a request, not a demand?
> **A.** It is a request. I can't appoint myself.
> **Q.** No, and you are not demanding that you be a Leader?
> **A.** I am requesting consideration of the appointment.[16]

In denying the grievant's claim, the Arbitrator was impelled to observe that there was no doubt that Kramien's initiative and industrious attitude deserved to be recognized and rewarded in some way. Nevertheless, this did not mean that management had to set up a Leader position which was not then in existence or apparently contemplated. Unless or until management conferred upon Kramien the authority to exercise some degree of disciplin-

---

15 *Ibid.*, pp. 7–8.
16 *Ibid.*, p. 8.

ary control and guidance upon the employees assigned to him, he could not validly claim to be performing a Leader's job in the full sense.

Practice Is Based on Underlying Conditions

In general, the practice of the parties, their observable activity, and the objective circumstances surrounding their course of conduct are what reveal their reasonable expectations in the present and for the immediate future. The binding character of a practice is linked directly to the underlying conditions of its origin and subsequent development. Sylvester Garrett, discussing a dispute over manning in the basic steel industry, had this to say on the relationship between the form of a practice and its substance:

> Thus the mere fact that a given number of men are scheduled for a given operation over the years does not *of itself* establish the existence of a local working condition governing crew size. It is the *relationship* between this course of conduct, and some *given set of underlying circumstances* which is important in determining whether there has been a recurring response which has evolved as the normal and accepted reaction in dealing with the problem. Such a relationship, in the minds of the parties, easily and reasonably may be determined or inferred where they have worked out a specific agreement, written or oral.
>
> But without actual agreement, the party relying upon a post-1947 local working condition based on custom must be prepared to show not only the custom, but to identify the underlying conditions to which it is addressed and which in effect have called it into being.[17]

When Underlying Conditions Change, Then Practice Can Change

When the underlying conditions of a binding practice not mentioned in the contract remain unchanged, the employer cannot unilaterally withdraw the practice until the contract is open for negotiations. When the underlying conditions do undergo a significant change, then the causal relationship between the new conditions and the old established practice is said to be broken. As pointed out in previous case studies,[18] most arbitrators hold that if the underlying basis for the practice changes, management may alter or discontinue the practice even while the contract is in effect. There is no fixed rule on how long *after* the underlying conditions have changed man-

---

[17] *United States Steel Corp., Fairless Works v. United Steelworkers, Local 4889,* Oct. 10, 1959, 33 LA 394, 404, Arbitrator Sylvester Garrett, BNA, Inc.
[18] See, for instance, Chap. 3, p. 39.

agement can wait before changing, eliminating, or modifying the practice. Some arbitrators have ruled, however, that an undue, unreasonable delay in making the change suggests that the new conditions have not significantly altered the underlying basis for the established practice and that therefore the practice must be continued for the contract term.

THE CASE OF THE TIME LAG
IN CHANGING THE PRACTICE

One company, for example, had unilaterally granted its employees a twenty-minute paid lunch period in the early 1940s when it had first scheduled its production on back-to-back shifts. When the graveyard shift was eliminated several years later, the company discontinued the paid lunch period for the day shift but continued it for the second shift. After several more years, the company discontinued the paid lunch period for the second shift, with the explanation that a policy of retrenchment was necessary and that the lunch period was being abused. The union maintained that granting the twenty-minute lunch period on the second shift had become an established past practice and therefore the company could not discontinue it unilaterally. To do so, according to the union, would have the effect of reducing the wages of second-shift employees.

The issue was whether the company had violated the agreement, or disregarded an established practice when it had unilaterally discontinued the paid lunch period. There was no express language in the agreement providing for a paid lunch period on the second or any other shift.

The arbitrator ruled that the second-shift paid lunch period had become an established practice because the company had waited too long after discontinuing back-to-back shifts to withdraw the benefit. In an opinion worth quoting, the arbitrator described how the lunch benefit had become transformed into a binding practice and therefore could not be unilaterally discontinued by the company.

> For a practice to ripen into an established past practice as it is known in the Arbitration process, it must be followed with such consistency and over such period of time that the employees may rely and reasonably expect such practice to be continued as a permanent working condition of the shift, even though the same is not specifically mentioned in the Agreement. The Company, even though it had no contractual obligation to inaugurate a paid lunch period or continue the same after it terminated such practice on the first shift, did continue to grant the same to the second shift continuously for a period of many years, even though the purpose or reason for which it had been originally established had

long expired. In so doing the employees assigned to the second shift reasonably came to rely and expect that such paid lunch period would be continued permanently and was a working condition of said shift. Such reliance and expectation was reasonable in view of the length of the time that it had been granted by the Company and the fact that the purpose for which it had been originally established had been terminated. These employees came to consider the paid lunch period as much a part of the shift differential as the rate they received.[19]

In reply to the company's claim that the lunch benefit could be withdrawn because it was being abused by employees, the arbitrator commented:

The argument by Management that the employees had abused the paid lunch period by eating before the lunch period had actually begun, playing cards, reading, sleeping and shutting down their machines during such period, is not persuasive. The Company's supervisory personnel admitted on cross examination by the Union, and upon questioning by this Arbitrator, that they had not taken any effective steps to stop such alleged abuses or to invoke disciplinary measures on the offending employees to correct the situation.

The Company has, and did have, adequate remedies to overcome the abuses complained of. It could have issued written warnings and disciplined those employees who failed to follow reasonable work instructions. It could have and may now establish reasonable rules for the conduct of the employees while in the Plant and enforce the same. Under Article VI, Section 6.1 B, the Company has the express right to require employees who are granted a paid lunch period to keep their machines running while eating lunch whenever practicable.[20]

A TYPICAL MANNING DISPUTE IN BASIC STEEL

The principle enunciated in the foregoing case—that a reasonable and proper causal relationship must be shown between changes in the underlying conditions of a practice and the elimination of the practice—is of sufficient importance to warrant another case examination, this one taken from basic steel. The controversy, a common one in the industry, was over the issue of manning—here, the ratio of helpers to journeymen boilermakers.

For many years the plant practice had been to assign one Helper to each boilermaker. However, early in 1948, certain changes began to take place in the underlying work conditions: welding operations increased, but riveting work declined; the company installed jib cranes, gantry cranes, and hoisters. The net effect of these changes was to decrease the helpers' work

---

[19] *Cooper-Bessemer Corp. v. Int'l Ass'n of Machinists, Lodge 90,* May 19, 1961, 36 LA 1464, 1467, Arbitrator Vernon L. Stouffer, BNA, Inc.
[20] *Ibid.*

load and to increase their idle time. Finally, around mid-1954, the company decided to lay off five helpers while adding two boilermakers. A month later the company laid off four more helpers, leaving thirteen boilermakers and two helpers. After that time the boilermaker force was enlarged considerably, while the number of helpers never went beyond eight. For the pay period ending May 20, 1958, there were twenty-eight boilermakers and eight helpers. In effect, the company had eliminated the practice of assigning one helper to each boilermaker, but it was not clear just when that decision had been made. On October 11, 1955, a grievance was filed by two union representatives, one of them a boilermaker, protesting the company's action in altering the practice.

Although the arbitrator had to treat various aspects of the grievance, such as its arbitrability, the main focus of his concern was the time lag from the changes in the nature of the work and of the equipment to the ultimate drastic alteration of the 1 to 1 ratio between helpers and boilermakers, which had constituted a "local working condition":

> The real issue is whether the underlying basis for the existence of this crew relationship was changed or eliminated by the Company; and, if so, whether the changed circumstances warranted the termination of this crew relationship. For clearly, in order to prevail in a case of this kind, Article One, Section 3 (d) obliges the Company to show a reasonable and proper causal relationship between the change in the established working condition and the change in the basis for the existence of such working condition.
>
> The Company eliminated the local working condition in question because of its belief that the workload of the Boiler Maker Helpers had declined to the point where they were no longer required to give a full day's work for a full day's pay. In other words, it concluded that if the one-to-one ratio were maintained between Boiler Makers and their Helpers, the latter would never have enough work to keep busy for an entire turn. The reasons for this alleged decrease in the Helpers' workload were the introduction of certain mechanical equipment in the Boiler Shop and the change in emphasis from riveting to welding.

The Company Waited Too Long to End the Practice

> The fact is, however, that any decrease in workload occurred long before June 1954, when the practice was evidently terminated. The new equipment was brought into the plant as early as 1946. Three or four hoisters were being used part time in the Boiler Shop by 1948 and the gantry crane was installed in 1950. This equipment served to mechanize and simplify the handling of materials, an important function of the Helpers. Yet, the Company continued to abide by the old crew relationship from 1950 to 1954 in spite of the supposedly lower workload for Helpers. Since riveting requires more men than welding, the continuing switch to

welding also resulted in less work for Helpers. But this was a very gradual process with the workload decreasing only slightly from year to year. In short, between 1946 and 1954 there may have been substantial changes in workload but those changes had already taken place by 1952 and 1953, without the Company altering the established practice. Notwithstanding these changed conditions, the Company continued to assign one Boiler Maker Helper to each Boiler Maker. And nothing happened in 1954 to change conditions from what they were in 1952–53. The workload which supported this practice in 1954 may have been far different from what it was in 1946 or 1948. But the Company's inaction during that period had in effect by 1954 founded the practice upon an entirely different workload. Accordingly, I am convinced that there is no reasonable and proper causal relationship between the change in the workload and the elimination of the local working condition. The Company had no right under Article One, Section 3 to cease assigning a Boiler Maker Helper to each Boiler Maker. This ruling does not mean that the Company must have a Helper for every Boiler Maker now working. All it means is that the Company must have at least one Helper for each Boiler Maker actually working.[21]

There Is No Fixed Time Period
For Establishing a Binding Practice

An element of past practice, often crucial, which deserves at least a brief discussion is the element of longevity, duration, repetition—or, to paraphrase a familiar saying, how many swallows make a summer? Quoting Richard McLaughlin:

> No precise formula or "time limitation" can reasonably be specified. While it does not shed a great deal of light on a possible solution to say that it must be a "significant" period of time, that the practice should be long established, that it should be readily ascertainable over a "reasonable period of time" or that the practice must have existed for a sufficient length of time to establish a "pattern," it is not at all feasible to devise a more concrete measuring stick.[22]

THE CASE OF A BINDING PRACTICE
FROM A SINGLE INSTANCE

A score (or even two score) of scattered exceptions to a daily practice of many years might not be enough to impair the validity of the predominant practice. A single instance, on the other hand, was declared by an arbi-

---

[21] *Republic Steel Corp., Gadsden Plant v. United Steelworkers, Local 2176,* Aug. 3, 1956, 27 LA 263, 264–265, Arbitrator Harry H. Platt, BNA, Inc.
[22] Richard P. McLaughlin, "Custom and Past Practice in Labor Arbitration," *The Arbitration Journal,* vol. 18, no. 4, 1963, p. 210.

trator to be sufficient to give meaning to the following contract provision, article 13(C):

> If an employee is required to perform work in a classification carrying a lower rate, no reduction in rate shall be made, except in case of demotion due to reduction in force.[23]

The grievance arose out of a strike in 1959. It arose because a group of men belonging to a union not on strike, as determined by the arbitrator, were assigned to a number of jobs paying a variety of rates. On the lower-rated jobs the men were paid the reduced rate instead of their regular rate.

The union pointed to a closely similar situation from years before when the company had been struck. As summarized in the arbitrator's opinion:

> The principal relevant past practice occurred in connection with the 1955 strike at Kennecott. At that time, as in 1959, the employees of the mine, milling, smelting and refinery operations went on strike. This substantially reduced the power needs of the Employer, as it did in 1959, leading to a management decision to fill its limited needs by buying power from the Utah Power and Light Company. This, however, then, as in 1959, required that a skeleton crew of employees be hired to do certain switching and related work. As a result the Employer retained some nine employees, chosen on the basis of seniority in the power station. In most of the cases, to judge by the testimony of the manager of the power house, . . . these employees did work in lower rated classifications. However, at that time they were paid rates in every instance, corresponding to the job classification in which they were normally employed rather than the lower job rates.[24]

On the basis of the foregoing course of conduct, the arbitrator held for the union. The gist of his reasoning is contained in the following extract from his opinion:

> Certainly, understandings reflected in past practice are of far greater significance in interpreting collective bargaining agreements than commercial agreements. This is because of the characteristic looseness with which such contracts are typically drawn; a looseness which not occasionally makes the task of construing their language almost an act of divination. Such considerations as this have led to the approach suggested by an arbitrator in a quotation advanced in the Employer's brief. In another contest: "By a time honored rule of construction *the meaning given to the words of the contract by the practice of the parties to the contract has controlling weight.*" [Hearst Consolidated Publications, 26 LA 723.] [Italics supplied.]
>
> I am inclined to follow that rule in this case. While the past practice here consists of only one instance, it is hardly, in the nature of things,

---

[23] *Kennecott Copper Corp., Utah Copper Div. v. Int'l Brotherhood of Elec. Workers, Local 1438*, Apr. 25, 1960, 34 LA 763, 769, Arbitrator Sanford H. Kadish, BNA, Inc.
[24] *Ibid.*, 770.

likely that there would be many, since the situation arises at the expiration of the union contracts every three years when a strike is called.
The 1955 strike was the last instance when this arose and the situation
is so fully parallel, in my opinion, as to warrant subordinating the strict
language of Article 13 (C) to the understanding reflected in that significant past practice.[25]

In general, a long and enduring past practice is not likely to be inval-
idated by a few exceptions. Not many practices could stand the test of
undeviating uniformity. Most arbitrators will usually hold that a practice is
binding if it shows a clear, predominant pattern. Infrequent exceptions will
not normally upset the practice unless they are discriminatory. In the latter
event, the arbitrator may either hold the company responsible for adverse
effects of the discriminatory treatment or invalidate the practice.[26]

SUMMARY

The exercise of administrative initiative when the contract is silent goes to
the heart of the management-reserved-rights doctrine. Most practices not
mentioned in the agreement begin as exercises of management reserved
rights. "Management reserved right" is but another term for a practice
outside the bargain between the parties. When such a reserved right
becomes part of their bargain, it is said to have ripened into a binding
practice. In short, a binding practice is a reserved right plus mutuality.
Mutuality, when the contract is silent on a practice, is the essential ingre-
dient which transforms the practice into an implied obligation. Mutuality
is the connecting link, the common denominator of management reserved
rights and management implied obligations. The implied-obligations doctrine conflicts with the reserved-rights doctrine only in the sense that it
sets boundaries to the reserved-rights doctrine. By setting these boundaries,
the implied-obligations doctrine completes the reserved-rights doctrine and
thus becomes an integral part of the latter.

[25] *Ibid.*, 771.
[26] *Todd Shipyards Corp. v. Indus. Union of Marine & Shipbuilding Workers, Local 9,*
Feb. 10, 1968, 50 LA 645, Arbitrator Paul Prasow, BNA, Inc.

Chapter 8

Contract administration: substantive determination versus modes of procedure

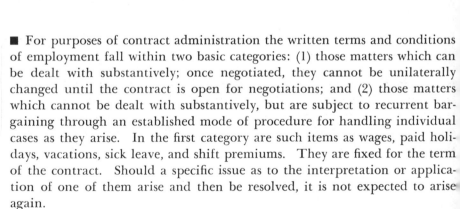

■ For purposes of contract administration the written terms and conditions of employment fall within two basic categories: (1) those matters which can be dealt with substantively; once negotiated, they cannot be unilaterally changed until the contract is open for negotiations; and (2) those matters which cannot be dealt with substantively, but are subject to recurrent bargaining through an established mode of procedure for handling individual cases as they arise. In the first category are such items as wages, paid holidays, vacations, sick leave, and shift premiums. They are fixed for the term of the contract. Should a specific issue as to the interpretation or application of one of them arise and then be resolved, it is not expected to arise again.

The second category includes such areas as modified seniority, discipline and discharge, and provisions generally whose application turns on such phrases as "insofar as practicable," "whenever possible," and "reasonable effort." Also in this category are strictures against management actions which are deemed arbitrary, capricious, discriminatory, or generally unreasonable. These broad terms have been given concrete meaning by a large, constantly developing common law of published arbitrations. It is a common law featured by guidelines for resolving individual grievances, a common law which assures relative stability to the modes of procedure for handling recurrent grievances of this type. Undoubtedly, more than half the grievances filed are in this second category, where the written instrument serves no more than as a means of invoking binding arbitration. It is not the broad general language which guides the arbitrator, but the accepted common-law criteria for the issue in dispute.

Example of a Substantive Ruling

One example of a contract item dealt with substantively is an *unmodified straight seniority clause*—based, say, on employee classifications—governing layoffs and recall. The sole factor in the application of such a seniority clause is the employee's length of service. The employee with the most seniority may be the least competent of those in his classification, yet he must be the last to be laid off and the first to be recalled. Presumably, if he does not meet minimum standards of job performance, he may be terminated for incompetence, but if he remains on the job, he holds his place at the top of the seniority list.

Examples of Modes of Procedures
For Deciding Recurrent Issues

By contrast, a *modified seniority provision* is not a contract item which can be dealt with substantively; rather, it must be considered a mode of procedure for resolving individual grievances of a recurrent type. Consider, for instance, a "relative ability" seniority provision applied to layoffs and recall. The senior employee must be relatively equal in fitness and ability to his junior competitors for his seniority to govern. Should management deviate from strict seniority by declaring a junior employee to be superior in fitness and ability, a grievance could be initiated by one or more senior employees. The "relative ability" provision would not be challenged substantively, but each specific deviation from straight seniority could be contested. The judgment of management in each instance would be subject to established tests and other objective criteria used in contract administration.

Not even a "sufficient ability" seniority clause for promotions is dealt with substantively. The senior employee may be disqualified on the ground that he does not possess sufficient ability (minimum requirements) for the job vacancy in question. Here, too, the judgment of management may be challenged for each specific departure from straight seniority and may be reviewed in the light of various tests and other criteria established in the common law of arbitration.

CASE NO. 1. THE DOWNWARD PROMOTIONS— A SUBSTANTIVE DETERMINATION AND MODE OF PROCEDURE

The distinction between contract language that deals with a matter substantively and language that establishes a mode of procedure for handling recurrent grievances on a matter is well demonstrated by a dispute over promotions in a good-sized manufacturing concern.

The pertinent contract language was the short, simple opening sentence of section 2(A), "Seniority shall govern in all cases of layoff, rehiring, transfer and promotion." On a close reading, the meaning of the sentence could hardly have been plainer—promotions: straight seniority without modification—or so it seemed. But the issue was not a promotion in the usual sense, an upward movement to a higher-paying job; the issue was the right of an employee to bid his seniority laterally or even downward to fill a vacancy in a lower-paying job.

For several years the company had interpreted the word "promotion" to mean only an upward movement to fill higher-paying jobs. Management had denied bids by employees who wanted to fill job vacancies on their own wage level, or would have even taken a wage cut to fill vacancies on lower-rated jobs. The union selected the grievances of three employees to test in arbitration the company's interpretation of section 2(A). All three grievants had bid their seniority unsuccessfully to fill vacancies on lower-rated jobs. The rationale behind the bidding of grievants Caro, Sebastian, and Ibarra is summarized below.

Mr. Caro was classified as a Plant Utility Operator with an hourly rate of $3.03. He bid for the job of Receiving Clerk which had an established rate of $2.985 per hour, or 4.5 cents below his rate. He was fifty-four years old and had been employed by the company for approximately twenty-three years. His job required heavy physical exertion and involved principally maintenance, repair, and some painting work. He gave the following reasons for desiring to change jobs: (1) he was at the end of the promotional line in his job, and in his opinion, the Receiving Clerk job would open many possible avenues for promotional opportunities; (2) because of his age, he wanted a job which would be less strenuous in order to prolong his work expectancy; (3) he had in the past worked as a Receiving Clerk for the company for some years and preferred that job to his current classification;

(4) certain aspects of his job were considered physically hazardous to him. He was allergic to certain paints and suffered skin reactions from chemicals that he had to handle occasionally. The boiler room, where he spent most of his time, was noisy, and this affected his nerves.

The second grievant, *Miss Sebastian,* at the time of her bid was employed as an Order Filler at an hourly rate of $2.355 per hour. She bid on the job of Clerk, carrying a rate of $2.33 per hour, or 2.5 cents below the Order Filler rate. She was twenty-five years old and had been employed by the company for more than six years. Her reasons for desiring to change jobs were the following: (1) the Clerk's job was office work, and thus she could avoid the continuous standing and physical exertion required in her job as Order Filler; (2) she could advance higher in the line of promotion as a Clerk than she could in her Order Filler's job; (3) the Clerk job seemed far more interesting, and in that position she would compete only with women, whereas in the Order Filler job she had also to compete with men.

At the time of his bid, the third grievant, *Mr. Ibarra,* was employed as a High-lift Operator, carrying an hourly rate of $2.58. He had held this job 2½ years. He bid for the job of Machine Attendant, carrying the rate of $2.42, 16 cents per hour below his job as High-lift Operator. The main reason he gave for wanting to move from his job as High-lift Operator was that it provided no clear line of progression. Although other warehouse jobs might be open to him if he could qualify, it seemed unlikely that the experience gained in his present job would qualify him for any of them. He bid for a job at the bottom of a line which eventually progressed into highly skilled and well-paid work. The Machine Attendant's spot was essentially a learner's job, from which he could move to Machine Setup Man, carrying a rate 30 cents an hour above that of the job held when he made the bid. From there he could advance to Machinist, carrying a rate 66 cents above the rate he received on the High-lift Operator's job. His relative seniority among those in the machine shop would seem to offer a prospect of advancement as rapidly as he could learn the work qualifications.

"Promotion" Is an Ambiguous Term

Central to the arguments of both the company and the union was their conflicting interpretation of "promotion." At first glance the word seemed utterly devoid of ambiguity, yet published arbitration opinions were as divided on its interpretation as were the parties themselves. To the company "promotion" meant a step-up in wages. Without increased wages, such intangibles as employee preference or potential advancement to higher skills were irrelevant; the true test of a promotion was increased wages. Wags have phrased this point of view thus: "If a thing is worth doing, it is worth doing for money."

The union argued for a broad interpretation of "promotion" in the following summary of its position:

Promotion: "Upward Only" versus Preferment

> The word "promotion," as used in this context, means far more than a higher-paying job. It embraces any job carrying a preferment to the bidder. The word "preferment," as used in the decided cases, has been held by Arbitrators to mean: a situation where the job bid upon opens opportunity for advancement, although the job itself carried a lower rate than the bidder's actual job; and jobs having safer, cleaner, or healthier working conditions and more advantageous work hours. The test applied in these cases is whether there is some objective, substantial advantage to the employee. The Union contends that measured by this standard, it is clear that in each of these three cases, a promotion was involved.[1]

On its part, the company pointed to arbitrators who had characterized a promotion as an upward movement to a higher-paying job or one involving greater responsibility. However, the company's strongest argument was the existence of a consistent past practice of several years, known to the union from its inception and unchallenged by the union in subsequent negotiations. Section 2(A) was never intended, the company asserted vehemently, to give senior employees an automatic right to fill vacancies according to their whims or moods. Such a license to play "musical chairs" would drastically undermine the stability of company operations.

The arbitrator's written opinion is of particular interest because of his three-pronged approach to the problem. First, he dealt with the pertinent sentence of section 2(A) *substantively:*

> The *apparent* Issue in this case, at first blush, is the contrary interpretations given by the Parties to the word "promotion" as used in Section 2 of the Agreement. The Arbitrator stresses the word *apparent* because a closer scrutiny of Section 2 suggests that the word *promotion* is not especially relevant to this Issue. If it were, the Arbitrator would find his road clear. He would not have to choose between those authorities who broadly define promotion as embracing virtually any job carrying a preferment to the bidder and those authorities who limit promotion to an upward movement to a higher paying job. He would find that a clear past practice of several years' duration, known to the Union, gives meaning to the word promotion, and that any ambiguities in the application are to be construed in accordance with that practice.

[1] *Max Factor & Co. v. Warehouse, Processing & Distribution Workers' Union, Local 26,* Dec. 14, 1965, CCH 66-1 Arb., § 8092, p. 3345, Arbitrator Howard S. Block.

The Union's defense that its failure to raise the Issue in subsequent negotiations is counter-balanced by the Employer's failure to raise the Issue, does not square with standard Arbitration criteria. *The Party whose interpretation of ambiguous language is contradicted by an established practice has the obligation in negotiations of clarifying the ambiguity in its favor if the practice is to be discontinued or changed.* [Italics supplied.]

Arbitrator Finds Issue Is Transfer, Not Promotion

We find, however, that the key word in Section 2 in respect to the Issue is not *promotion* but is the word *transfer.* Section 2(A) lists transfers as one of the circumstances under which seniority will govern. The Arbitrator cannot assume that the word *transfer* crept into the opening sentence of Section 2(A) by a semantic accident and is therefore superfluous. He must adhere to the principle that all words used in an Agreement should, if possible, be given effect. The fact that a past practice existed denying requested lateral and downward transfers does not give the Arbitrator the authority to "subtract" the word transfer which is expressly stated in the Agreement. He rules, therefore, that the Company cannot reject a bidder *solely* because the vacancy involved a lateral or downward transfer.[2]

By ruling that job bids could not be rejected solely because they were lateral or downward, the arbitrator disposed *substantively* of one part of the problem. By pointing out that the issue turned on the word "transfer," not "promotion," he clarified the ambiguity in that aspect of job bidding once and for all.

"Transfer" Is an Ambiguous Term

Second, the arbitrator addressed himself to the word "transfer" and found at once an ambiguity in its application:

It cannot be said, however, that the language "Seniority shall govern in all cases of . . . transfer . . ." is so unambiguous that it speaks for itself. Unlike promotions, lateral and downward transfers are not always or even usually left to the choice of the employees. Conspicuously absent, for instance, is language covering transfers requested by the employees as contrasted with transfers ordered by Management. It is difficult to believe that the intent of Section 2 is to compel a rigid adherence to seniority in any and all transfers, whether requested by employees or initiated by Management against the desire of affected employees. Such a sweeping interpretation of Section 2 would have to be spelled out in detail before this Arbitrator would believe that the Parties were so indifferent to the possibility of transfers becoming a

[2] *Ibid.,* pp. 3346–3347.

> game of musical chairs, which could be very disruptive to a Company's operations.

Arbitrator Establishes Three Tests for Transfer Bids

> The absence of specific language implementing the word *transfer* in Section 2(A) suggests that the job bids involving a lateral or downward transfer should be reviewed in the light of standard Arbitration tests as to whether the Employer was arbitrary, capricious or discriminatory.[3]

Here we see that because of his concern over the consequences, the arbitrator drew back from dealing substantively with the word "transfer." Instead, he established a *mode of procedure* for reviewing individual grievances based upon three tests posed in the question, was management arbitrary, capricious, or discriminatory? The three test words were not chosen for mere rhetoric. They have been implemented by many volumes of published arbitrations. They are basic criteria for reviewing management's actions in several areas upon which the contract is silent or which are covered by broad general language such as the "just cause" provision governing discipline and discharge.

The Three Tests Applied to Individual Grievances

Third, having established a mode of procedure for dealing with transfers as a recurrent type of issue, the arbitrator reviewed the grievances before him, applying the three tests of the procedure:

> Proceeding now with the application of these criteria, and since there were no allegations of discrimination by any of the Grievants, the Arbitrator will attempt to balance their right under Section 2(A) to bid for jobs involving lateral or downward transfers against the Employer's right to a reasonable stability in its work force.
>
> As to Caro and Ibarra, persuasive reasons were advanced for the transfer requested by each; Caro, a 23-year employee, seeks to maximize both his work longevity with the Company and future promotional opportunities by this transfer to Receiving Clerk, a job that he had previously performed with this Company. Ibarra's present job appears to offer very limited possibilities for advancement whereas the job for which he has bid would afford him the opportunity to learn highly skilled work paying substantial sums above his present potential.
>
> No reasons were advanced by the Company for denying these two transfers other than its position on the Issue of "Promotion" to lower-rated jobs which has already been considered. Under the Arbitrator's view of the facts as applied to the Agreement, the Company's action in denying the transfer requested by Caro and Ibarra is deemed arbitrary and therefore improper.[4]

[3] *Ibid.*, p. 3347.
[4] *Ibid.*

The arbitrator did not, however, sustain the grievance of Miss Sebastian. He was not convinced that her requested transfer reflected a genuine desire to increase her promotional opportunities. He noted that her request semed to arise "more as a matter of personal work preference than from factors which are capable of objective evaluation." He refused to require the company to grant transfers based primarily upon "the likes or dislikes of particular employees," because this would be a sharp departure from customary industrial practice. In his opinion, Miss Sebastian's case presented a situation where the employee's right to seek a lateral or downward transfer under section 2(A) was outweighed by the company's need for a stable work force. Accordingly, the arbitrator ruled that her bid was properly denied by the company.

Arbitrator's Findings and Arbitrator's Award

It is important to note that although the focus of the case argued by both parties was the grievances of three employees, the arbitrator's findings on their individual claims were not included in his award. The omission was dictated by the question stipulated in the submission agreement:

> Under Section 2 of the Collective Bargaining Agreement, can an employee under the job bidding procedure successfully bid on a same-rated or lower-rated job?[5]

Until the hearing, the parties had been unable to agree on a formulation of the issue to be arbitrated, and the submission had not mentioned the individual grievances. Accordingly, the arbitrator's award simply read in full text as follows:

> Upon a full consideration of all of the evidence and argument on the Issue involved, it is the decision of the Arbitrator that under Section 2 of the Collective Bargaining Agreement, an employee can bid on a same-rated or lower-rated job under the job bidding procedure.[6]

A Ruling on Promotion as a Preferment Is Usually Made through a Mode of Procedure

Also worth noting is the arbitrator's acknowledgment that the word "promotion," unilluminated by extrinsic factors such as past practice, is ambiguous on its face. Under the foregoing circumstances few arbitrators have interpreted "promotion" to grant senior employees an unrestricted

[5] *Ibid.*, p. 3344.
[6] *Ibid.*, p. 3347.

claim on job vacancies that involve lateral or downward transfers. Some have closed the door firmly to all such claims, with the substantive ruling that "promotion" means an upward movement to higher-paying jobs only. Others, perhaps a majority of arbitrators, have interpreted "promotion" to include preferment, ruling that senior employees may not be disqualified solely because they are bidding on lateral or lower-paying jobs. Such a ruling, however, has seldom been issued on a substantive basis to dispose of the issue once and for all. Usually the ruling has been enunciated on a mode-of-procedure basis using standard criteria for evaluating individual claims of preferment in job bidding laterally or downward.

CASE NO. 2. PROMOTION COULD INCLUDE MOVEMENT TO LOWER-RATED JOBS

The following analysis, taken from a published arbitration case, summarizes what appears to be the predominant arbitral opinion on the term "promotion," in the absence of extrinsic factors to give precise meaning to the word. In the case under discussion, the parties had cited a number of prior decisions supporting their conflicting interpretations of the term. The arbitrator looked up "promotion" in Webster's Third New International Dictionary and found that it included the word "preferment." After reviewing all the cited definitions, the arbitrator was persuaded that the term "promotion" could include, under appropriate circumstances, lateral transfers and even movement to lower-rated jobs.

Underlying the controversy was a conflict between two sets of rights. The company sought to minimize the inconvenience and economic loss resulting from the transfer of employees to less skilled or lower-rated jobs. The employees, on the other hand, wanted to maximize their opportunities for acquiring potentially higher skills and eventually qualifying for more desirable jobs. The basic problem was that of maintaining a proper balance between the employer's legitimate interest in efficient operations and the employee's natural goal to improve his situation by preferment, including transfer to a lower-rated job.

In the arbitrator's opinion, the touchstone which balanced these rights consisted of the objective standards which arbitrators Russell and Kates had applied, respectively, in Indiana Chair Company[7] and Mansfield Tire and Rubber Company.[8] These standards required the employee to show that the requested transfer to a lower-rated job was actually a preferment in

[7] 34 LA 856.
[8] 40 LA 1212.

eims of such factors as better working conditions, future promotional opportunities, more desirable shift hours, change in supervision, or improved social status.

In the case under consideration, the union had maintained there was no need to justify the requested transfers because the employees were entitled to this option under the labor agreement. Thus no evidence was submitted as to the grievants' reasons for wanting to bid downward. No showing was made that the working conditions, shift hours, long-run advancement possibilities, or other such factors in the jobs bid for were different from or better than the jobs already held.

The arbitrator acknowledged that an employee might have the right under the agreement to seek to change the existing situation in terms of job assignment and classification. However, he also held that "objective standards required the employee to make a showing that the transfer to a lower-rated job was neither whimsical nor capricious," because such change could result in significant loss of employer investment in the skills involved. Accordingly, the arbitrator ruled:

> It was incumbent on the employees to make a clear showing of actual preferment, and to dispel any impression that mere whim or caprice was involved. . . . Purely subjective and conjectural intentions on the employees' part are insufficient. The employer's needs and investment must also be given weight, based upon similar objective standards. Just as the Company may suffer some inconvenience when a bona fide "preferment" is established and exercised, so must the employee be prepared to undergo some inconvenience to remain on a job when there is no visible advancement in the short or the long run, or where the benefits to the employee are entirely in the realm of intangibles.[9]

Subsequent Reflections of the Arbitrator

In rereading the foregoing selection for this chapter, the arbitrator has had second thoughts on his phrasing of the statement "objective standards required the employee to make a showing that the transfer to a lower-rated job was neither whimsical nor capricious." Strictly speaking, management's action rather than the employee's is the proper subject of arbitral review. The sentence could more accurately have expressed the same thought by the following formulation: "Objective standards required the employee to make a showing that management was arbitrary, capricious, or discriminatory in denying the requested transfer to a lower-rated job."

---

[9] *Golden Bear Oil Co. v. Oil, Chem. & Atomic Workers Int'l Union, Local 1-19,* June 19, 1964, CCH 64-3 Arb., § 9181, p. 7088. Arbitrator Paul Prasow.

SUMMARY

Ambiguity in contract language can be dealt with substantively or by a mode of procedure. In disposing of the matter substantively the ambiguity is resolved once and for all during the life of the contract by a single determination.

However, there are some ambiguities that cannot be disposed of by one definitive adjudication, but must be considered on a case-by-case basis as they may arise during the term of the agreement. These matters are subject to recurrent bargaining through an established mode of procedure. A common mode of procedure for reviewing individual grievances consists of determining in each case whether management's action was arbitrary, capricious, or discriminatory. If the evidence does not establish the presence of any of these factors, then management's determination is upheld as representing a bona fide exercise of managerial discretion.

Chapter 9

Precontract negotiations

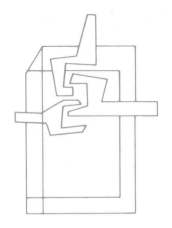

It is axiomatic in contract interpretation that the framing of the written provisions consists of acts of the negotiating parties, acts which represent their mutual intent. The genesis of intent is mental, a state of mind. But as a state of mind, the intent of a negotiator is rarely susceptible of direct proof. Intent must ordinarily be inferred from the facts, from behavior, whether it be by word or deed. The assertion by a negotiator of an intent which was not disclosed by him when contract language was written is irrelevant and immaterial. Intent must be communicated by some objective means. In the words of one arbitrator, "It's not your innermost thoughts, but what you said or did or didn't do that establishes your intent when the language is interpreted."

BARGAINING HISTORY DISCLOSES INTENT

It follows, then, that the formulation of words to convey meaning is as overt a course of conduct as the production of goods and the rendering of services. Therefore the bargaining history of a contract—the discussions of the negotiators as well as their other actions in the negotiating sessions—comprises a kind of practice that gives meaning to language in dispute.

One example of the decisive role of bargaining history in resolving a contract dispute is provided by the following controversy in a giant aerospace plant. The issue was phrased in a joint submission agreement as follows:

> Is the Company in violation of Article IV, Section 2, Paragraph (b), by requiring Stewards and Chief Stewards to obtain separate passes for each contact made for Union duties?[1]

Pertinent Contract Provision

ARTICLE IV, SECTION 2, PARAGRAPH (B)

> ... Each representative of the Union shall report to his regular place of work (1) at the commencement of his regular shift, (2) after any lunch period, and unless absent from his regular place of work in accordance with the provisions of this Article, shall remain there during working hours, unless permission of his supervisor not to so report has been given.[2]

Two unions are dominant in the aerospace industry. They are strongly grievance-minded, the processing of grievances being their life's blood. Chief stewards, and in some plants even stewards, customarily spend a large part of their working day away from their jobs investigating and processing employee grievances. The controversy in the instant case centered on the company's insistence on stricter control over the movements of union representatives. Where before they had been issued passes by supervision to make multiple contacts, a new policy limited the passes to single visits. After each separate visit the steward had to report back to his supervisor for another pass to make the next contact.

Company's Reasons for Change

The new system of granting passes to union representatives was established primarily to regulate a situation which was subject to abuse. The company did not intend to interfere with stewards carrying out legitimate activities. The company freely granted permission for a steward to leave his place of work, but it required a separate pass for each contact. According

---

[1] *Douglas Aircraft Co. v. United Auto. Workers, Local 148,* Dec. 12, 1962, 40 LA 201 Arbitrator Paul Prasow, BNA, Inc.
[2] *Ibid.,* 202.

to the company, this merely affected the manner or method of giving permission. The contract did not deprive the company of the right to require a separate pass for each visit. The new method of issuing passes was considered more efficient. It permitted a better check on the stewards' time, and it reduced waste and conflicting practices in various departments. The company claimed it was entitled to exercise such control over its personnel as long as such action was not in violation of the union's privileges or rights, as spelled out in the agreement. Union stewards were, of course, full-time employees and were expected to perform production work. The time they spent on in-plant union activities was paid for by the company, except that any time in excess of one hundred hours per month for 600 employees was shared with the union on a 50 percent basis.

From 1958 to 1962, Multiple Contacts On One Pass Were Permitted

The arbitrator reviewed the bargaining history of article IV, section 2(b), beginning with October, 1962, when the new policy was enunciated, and going back to the year 1956. For a number of years prior to 1962, the practice had been for supervision to release from their regular work assignment stewards or chief stewards who requested permission to contact other employees in connection with appropriate union activity. The supervisor would issue a form entitled "Employee Pass–Union Activity," which was used by the steward to make one or more contacts with other employees in the course of carrying out union activities. It was not unusual for the steward to make multiple employee contacts on one pass. During 1962, the practice was changed in a number of departments. The new practice required the stewards to report back to their regular place of work and obtain individual passes for each separate contact made for union duties. On August 2, 1962, the union filed a grievance alleging that the changed practice violated the agreement. On October 8, 1962, the company enunciated the changed practice as a uniform policy for all departments in the plant.

Prior to 1958, Contract Language (Requirement 3) Limited Each Pass to a Single Contact

Although article IV, section 2(b), was silent on the matter in dispute, the provision had not always been silent. Prior to negotiation of contract changes in 1958, article IV, section 2(b), had read as follows:

> Each representative of the Union shall report to his regular place of work
> (1) at the commencement of his regular shift,
> (2) after any lunch period, and
> (3) *immediately upon completion of any duties as a Union representative.* [Italics supplied.][3]

It is important to note that requirement 3 was removed from the contract effective May 19, 1958, expiration date of the agreement between the parties. From that time until approximately January, 1962, the record showed that multiple contacts by stewards were generally permitted, and that this policy prevailed in all departments until 1962. The changed practice (prohibition of multiple contacts) did not become a plant-wide policy until 2½ months after signing of the new agreement on July 23, 1962.

After Four Years, the Company Reinstituted Requirement 3 Unilaterally as a Management Reserved Right and Not by Negotiation

The company contended that reinstatement of requirement 3 was a legitimate exercise of managerial discretion, in accordance with company rights as expressed in article II, sections 2(a) and 2(b), the Management's Reserved Rights provision.

In his opinion the arbitrator replied that:

> Where the contract is silent on a particular point, the management's rights provision does not automatically take precedence over any other consideration. Other pertinent factors may be involved which have to be examined. The record in this case shows that prior to the 1958 negotiations, the contract between the parties expressly provided that the Union representative shall report to his regular place of work ". . . immediately upon completion of any duties as a Union representative." The Union argues *that this requirement was dropped during the 1958 negotiations in order to remove a restriction on shop steward mobility which management is now endeavoring to reinstitute unilaterally outside of negotiations.* [Italics supplied][4]

There was nothing in the record of the 1958 negotiations or subsequently which contradicted the union's interpretation. For four years, from 1958 until October 8, 1962, the practice of the parties, and the administrative policy of the company supported the union's contention. No explanation had been offered by the company for the removal of requirement 3 from the contract negotiated in 1958.

[3] *Ibid.*
[4] *Ibid.*, 204.

IT IS PRESUMED THAT WHEN THE PARTIES CHANGE THE LANGUAGE, THEY INTEND TO CHANGE THE MEANING

The arbitrator concluded that the parties must have had some motivation for taking the affirmative action in 1958 of deleting the third requirement from article IV, section 2(b). He commented:

> *It is an accepted principle in arbitration that when the parties change the language of their Agreement, there is a presumption that they intended a changed meaning.* [Italics supplied.][5]

The company argued that even if it had agreed to remove requirement 3 during the 1958 negotiations, this acquiescence in itself did not prevent it from reinstating the requirement at any future time as a company policy under the management-rights section. In other words, the company was not precluded for all time from reestablishing the requirement if such a step was deemed necessary for efficient operations and maintenance of adequate controls.

Arbitrator Rules: Requirement 3 Was Removed by Negotiations and Must Be Reinstituted by Negotiations

In principle, said the arbitrator, he would fully affirm the company's right to reinstate requirement 3 if the company deemed such a step necessary. However, the matter at issue was not the company's objective, but rather the method by which the objective had been attained. Under ordinary circumstances, appropriate plant rules could be promulgated by the company under the management-rights section provided such rules were not in conflict with the agreement. But, said the arbitrator, these were not ordinary circumstances:

> In the light of the 1958 change of contract language, and the subsequent practice of multiple contacts by Stewards until 1962, the Arbitrator is of the opinion that requirement No. 3 cannot be reinstated unilaterally. It seems to the Arbitrator that the appropriate method of reinstating requirement No. 3 would be through contract negotiations. Otherwise, it would be possible to reimpose unilaterally as plant rules specific conditions or requirements which had been deleted from the Contract through mutual agreement of the parties in negotiations.
>
> It is the Arbitrator's opinion that having once agreed in the give and take of contract negotiations to drop requirement No. 3, as was done in

[5] *Ibid.*

1958, the Company cannot now in 1962 unilaterally reimpose, outside of contract negotiations, that selfsame requirement.[6]

THE CONDUCT OF THE PARTIES DURING THE CONTRACT TERM CAN ALSO DISCLOSE THEIR INTENT

Not only can the conduct of the parties during contract negotiations illuminate their mutual intent; their conduct during the term of the contract can be equally crucial. Consider a practice initiated by management during a contract term, a practice covered by ambiguous language or mentioned not at all. A union charged with awareness of the new practice, if it keeps silent for an undue length of time, may be deemed by its inaction to have acquiesced in the practice. The binding nature of the practice becomes strongly reinforced if the union maintains its silence throughout a subsequent negotiation of the contract.

Another aspect of bargaining history which can be controlling is the settlement of grievances spawned by conflicting interpretation of contract language. An agreement on such grievances may become a binding precedent for future interpretations of the language in dispute.

A withdrawal of a grievance, however, will generally not constitute acquiescence to management's position if the union announces that its withdrawal is made "without prejudice" and with intent to press for a solution at a later time either by negotiations or by arbitration. A failure by the union to resolve the issue in a subsequent contract negotiation may fatally impair its attempt to keep management's action from becoming a binding practice.

THE INTENT OF THE PARTIES WHEN THE LANGUAGE WAS NEGOTIATED IS A PRIMARY CRITERION FOR ITS INTERPRETATION

In general, arbitrators will scrutinize closely utterances of the parties entered into the record as well as their other activities during the contract-making process. There is no higher standard for interpreting ambiguous language than conclusive proof of what the language meant to the parties when it was formulated. Such proof is often adduced by inference. Thus an attempt by a party in negotiations to reform ambiguous language to bring it into conformity with its interpretation can be a hazardous undertaking. If a pro-

---

[6] *Ibid.,* 205.

posal to clarify the language in question should fail, the party making the proposal will become highly vulnerable in a subsequent arbitration to a charge that it is trying to get from an arbitrator an interpretation it was unable to obtain in negotiations.

THE CASE OF THE STOLEN TOOLS

The resolution of a claim by a machinist that he be reimbursed for stolen tools highlights a typical application of the foregoing principle. The circumstances leading to the dispute may be summarized as follows: The grievant was one of approximately thirty machinists employed by the company. These machinists reported to work at a variety of locations throughout the plant. Some worked in the machine shop, and others were assigned from a central pool to specific areas in the plant for varying periods of time. For some time prior to the disputed incident, the grievant had been assigned to the compressor room. At the close of his shift on Friday, April 13, 1965, the grievant placed his personal toolbox, along with those of three other machinists, on a table in the compressor room and covered it with a canvas. His toolbox was locked. When he returned to work the following Monday, he found his toolbox has been pried open and approximately $75 worth of tools had been stolen. An investigation was conducted by the company, but the tools were never recovered.

The union charged that the company failed to provide adequate storage space for such tools and thereby violated section XXIX, paragraph (8), "General Conditions," of the then applicable agreement: "The Company agrees to furnish storage space for hand tools owned by employees." The union claimed the grievant was entitled to reimbursement for the stolen tools. The company denied any contract violation and disclaimed any liability.

As was to be expected, the union pegged its claim on the contractual requirement that the company "furnish storage space for hand tools owned by employees." The term "storage space," argued the union, implied a safe storage place. Quoting from the union's position as reported by the arbitrator:

> For example, the Grievant was required to leave his toolbox in the Compressor Room, covered only by a canvas, because there was no other place to put them. At this location, his toolbox was accessible to any number of employees who could walk in and out of the Compressor Room without being seen. The fact that he left them there, and that

> other employees have also done so for a considerable period of time, does not establish this to be an adequate provision for tool storage, as the Company has maintained. The Union asserts that, in the entire plant, there are virtually no sufficiently protected areas for tool storage.[7]

However persuasive may have been the merits of the grievant's claim, its entire foundation was undermined by a past history of unsuccessful attempts by the union to write language into the contract providing reimbursement for stolen tools. The impartial arbitrator as chairman of a tripartite arbitration board issued the following opinion:

> The Board, in carrying out its function of ascertaining the meaning of the disputed Contract provisions, must first look to the applicable language of the Agreement to see if the intention of the parties can be determined. When the language is clear, its provisions govern. It is only when the Agreement is not clear on the disputed points that Arbitrators resort to other criteria of interpretation such as past practice, negotiating history, etc., in an effort to determine and give effect to the mutual intention of the parties.
>
> In this case, the Contract is silent on the question of whether or not the Company is obligated to replace an employees' stolen tools and therefore, it is necessary to examine other indicia of intention. Where, as here, the subject has arisen during negotiations, the discussions on the point can be highly illuminating and in this case they are decisive.

A Party Cannot Get in Arbitration
What It Failed to Get in Negotiations

> It is clear from the record that during the negotiations in 1952 leading to the first Contract, when the theft problem was particularly acute, the Union proposed that "The Company replace tools . . . lost on the job." . . . During the 1956–57 negotiations, the Union proposed that the Company "Replace tools stolen." . . . These proposals were considered, discussed, and rejected. Against this background, the omission of a provision for the replacement by the Company of stolen tools is very meaningful. In the light of the bargaining history on this point, the conclusion is inescapable that the parties did not intend to make the Company responsible for the replacement of stolen tools. This Board would be exceeding its authority were it to add to the contract by interpretation what had been so clearly rejected during negotiations.[8]

It should be noted in the foregoing case that there was no record cited of the company ever having reimbursed an employee for stolen tools. And

---

[7] *Am. Potash & Chem. Corp. v. Int'l Ass'n of Machinists, Desert Lodge 886,* Oct. 17, 1966, 47 LA 574, 575–576, Arbitrator Howard S. Block (Chairman), BNA, Inc.
[8] *Ibid.,* 566.

now a hypothetical question suggests itself: What if the reverse had been true? What if the union could have cited a valid past practice of company reimbursement for stolen personal tools? In that hypothetical case, the past practice would have been controlling, and the arbitration board would have interpreted the company's obligation "to furnish storage space for hand tools" to mean "safe storage space," entitling the grievant in this instance at least to reimbursement for stolen tools.

A Failure to Bring Language into Conformity with the Past Practice Does Not Invalidate the Practice

"But," a dissenting reader might say, "what of the union's unsuccessful attempts to bring the language of section XXIX(8) into conformity with the past practice? Did not management's refusal to reform the language during negotiations render a prior practice null and void?" Such reasoning would be unassailable if the contract were silent on the benefit. But where there is language, ambiguous language to be sure, covering the benefit, then the past practice is inseparably joined to the language to give objective expression to the mutual intent of the parties. As pointed out in a subsequent chapter,[9] the mere repudiation of such a practice is not enough to change the meaning of the language. The responsibility devolves upon the party repudiating the practice to secure revisions bringing the language into conformity with its new interpretation.

THE CASE OF THE SEVEN–MEMBER GRIEVANCE COMMITTEE

We proceed now to another case where a company was charged with attempting to secure arbitral endorsement of a practice it was unable to write into the contract. At issue was the company's insistence that a union grievance committee be limited to a maximum of five members. The union complained that the company violated the agreement when it refused to meet with a union grievance committee of seven representatives. The matter was brought to a head on or about September 1, 1953, when, upon arriving at the scheduled meeting place, the company found that seven union representatives had assembled as a grievance committee. The superintendent informed the union that the company would listen to the union's

[9] See Chap. 14, pp. 274–280.

case as soon as the committee members were reduced to five or less as was the custom in the past. The union refused to reduce its committee from seven to five, and the meeting thereupon broke up. No agreement as to the size of the committee could be reached by the parties.

A Practice of Five Members Did Not Preclude a Committee of Seven

Although the contract placed no limits on the size of the union committee, the record was clear that with some few exceptions the committee had customarily been held to five members. However, more crucial to the arbitrator than the predominant practice was an unsuccessful attempt by the company to negotiate language restricting the size of the union committee. The following excerpt summarizes his principal reason for sustaining the union's position:

> The record in this case indicates that in prior negotiations attempts were made to include language in the Agreement limiting the number of Union Committeemen that might be present at grievance meetings. Apparently such attempts were unsuccessful, since the same language (establishing no such limitations) appeared in subsequent agreements. The Arbitrator is in no position to impose a limitation which was not arrived at in negotiations or by agreement of the parties. Although the Company's desire to limit the number of Union participants to a size suitable for efficient and rational consideration of the subject is certainly a legitimate and proper managerial aim, this matter must be resolved through mutual determination between the parties. What may appear to be reasonable for one situation, may be totally unreasonable in another case. Where there are no stated limitations in the contract, a reasonable number of grievance committee representatives will usually depend upon the facts and circumstances of the particular situation.[10]

It must be reiterated in the foregoing case that the contract was silent on the issue to be decided. The arbitrator had to consider whether the custom of negotiating with a five-member committee was an internal union matter, which could be unilaterally changed, or whether it was a binding practice. The failure of the company's efforts in negotiations to get language limiting the committee's size was decisive. The element of mutuality, an essential element of a binding practice, was demonstrably absent. The union's custom of negotiating with a five-member committee was held to be its own affair, subject to reasonable alterations.

---

[10] *Am. Smelting & Ref. Co. v. United Steelworkers, Local 4347*, Oct. 15, 1954, unpublished arbitration award, Arbitrator Paul Prasow.

Had There Been Language Limiting the Committee to Five, The Arbitrator Would Have Upheld the Company

Two questions now suggest themselves. First, had there been language regulating the size of the union committee, even highly ambiguous language, would the arbitrator have made the same decision? The answer would be an unqualified no. Assuming there had been ambiguous language covering the issue, all the essential elements would have then been present in the American Smelting case that had been present in the American Potash case of the stolen tools. The arbitrator would have held that a predominant practice of negotiating with a five-member committee had given meaning to an ambiguous provision regulating the size of the committee and that the practice was so inseparably joined to the language that the company's unsuccessful efforts to clarify the language would still leave the meaning of the provision unimpaired.

The Torrington Principle Does Not Apply Because of the Nature of the Issue

The second question that suggests itself relates to the principle expounded in the Torrington decision[11] of management's right, when the contract is open for negotiations, to withdraw a benefit not covered by any language. Suppose, with the contract silent, the company had not tried to write in language restricting the size of the union committee, but had made an oral declaration that henceforth it would deal with a union committee of not more than five. Would the onus have then been on the union, consonant with the Torrington principle, to get language into the contract removing the company's restriction on the committee size, or at least to get the company to withdraw orally its declaration?

The answer is that because of the nature of the issue the Torrington principle is not applicable to the American Smelting case. The size of a union committee, assuming it is not expanded out of all reasonable proportions, is an essential aspect of union recognition in collective bargaining. As between a five-member and a seven-member committee, it is difficult to regard the difference as an employee benefit—even an employee benefit of no monetary cost to the employer. The number of bargaining representatives to be designated should, within reason, be the exclusive prerogative of the respective parties. For the union's custom of negotiating with a five-

---

[11] *Torrington Co. v. Metal Prods. Workers, Local 1645,* 237 F. Supp. 139, (1965). For additional discussion of this case, see Chap. 3, pp. 38–39, and Chap. 14, pp. 276–279.

member committee to be converted by a unilateral declaration of management into a binding practice would constitute an unwarranted interference with the union's internal decision-making process.

The Size of the Committee Was a Purely Internal Union Matter

Such an interference with the internal operation of a union would be analogous to an employer strategem frowned upon by arbitrators and by the National Labor Relations Board. We refer to the refusal of some employers to make a significant offer in negotiations unless the union agrees to have the offer voted on by the membership in a secret-ballot election. At first blush, the employer's condition would appear to be quite reasonable and morally justified. From a more sophisticated point of view, the condition might seem to be designed to hamper the union's strategic flexibility. The timing and the method of presenting employer offers to a union membership may have a great deal to do with generating employee support for the union. In the American Smelting case Arbitrator Prasow decided for the union because of the company's unsuccessful attempts in negotiations to write language limiting the union committee; but even if the company had not impaired its position in negotiations, he would have still held that the size of the committee, within reasonable limits, was solely the internal affair of the union.

PROMISSORY ESTOPPEL DEFINED

Another course of conduct in negotiations subject to arbitral review involves the legal principle of "promissory estoppel." The estoppel principle has been lucidly enunciated in several law dictionaries. In Bouvier's Law Dictionary we find:

> He who by his language or conduct leads another to do what he would not otherwise have done shall not subject such person to loss or injury by disappointing the expectations upon which he acted.[12]

In Black's Law Dictionary we find:

> Estoppel in its broadest sense is penalty paid by one perpetrating wrong by known fraud or by affirmative act which, though without fraudulent intent, may result in legal fraud on another. . . .

[12] John Bouvier, *Bouvier's Law Dictionary and Concise Encyclopedia*, 8th ed. (3d revi sion by Francis Rawle), Vernon Law Book Company, West Publishing Company, St Paul, Minn., 1914, p. 1081.

> An estoppel arises when one by acts, representations, admissions or silence intentionally induces another to change his position for the worse.[13]

THE CASE OF THE DEFERRED INEQUITY INCREASE

A typical application of the estoppel principle to resolve a controversy was made at a major television studio. At issue was the compensation for script secretaries. During contract negotiations the union had argued that the script secretaries were entitled to an inequity increase over and above their classification rate because in the timing of television productions they had assumed responsibilities which had normally belonged to the associate directors. As reported by the impartial chairman of the arbitration board:

> At that time the Company proposed that the matter be deferred until the Union's claim could be looked into, and if it were found that the Script Secretaries were doing work beyond that called for in their job description, an upward salary adjustment would be made, or the additional duties would be taken away. The Union states that, relying on these assurances, it deferred its demand until after the Company's investigation had taken place. At some time after the signing of the 1955 contract, the Company announced the results of its investigation as indicating that the Script Secretaries were not being required to do work in any significant degree beyond their job description.[14]

The Company Is Estopped from Declaring the Issue Inarbitrable

The first matter before the arbitrator was a motion by the company to dismiss the union's complaint as not subject to arbitration. If the arbitrator were to find for the union, argued the company, the only remedies open to him would be either to create a new job classification or to increase the wages of the Script Secretary Classification, and both remedies would be in violation of the plain meaning of the following contract language:

> It is ... agreed that terms of a new agreement or changes in wages, hours or working conditions shall not be determined by arbitration.[15]

The arbitrator denied the company's motion by invoking the promissory-estoppel principle. Quoting again from his opinion:

---

[13] Henry Campbell Black, *Black's Law Dictionary*, 4th ed., West Publishing Company, St. Paul, Minn., 1951, p. 649.
[14] *Columbia Broadcasting Sys. v. Office Employes Int'l Union, Local 174,* May 9, 1956, unpublished arbitration award, p. 7, Arbitrator Paul Prasow (Chairman).
[15] Article 18, 1955 contract between the parties.

An examination of the entire record reveals that it was as a result of the Company's own suggestion that the Union was persuaded to defer the matter to a time subsequent to the signing of the contract. The Company's proposal to postpone the issue until the validity of the Union's claim could be determined, carried with it the assurance or commitment that the controversy would be treated as a classification matter subject to the contract grievance and arbitration procedures. This is amply supported by testimony of Company witnesses at the hearing. As a result, the Union ceased its efforts to attain a settlement of the issue through the traditional pressures of contract negotiations. In the opinion of the Arbitration Board, or a majority thereof, the Company is now estopped from claiming that the controversy is not arbitrable.

... To now sustain the Company's motion on dismissal would be to say in effect that there is no meaningful procedure or terminal point to resolve a disputed issue which, except for the Company's acknowledged commitment to treat the matter as a classification issue, subject to contract arbitration as a terminal point to grievance adjustment, might have been resolved through the normal processes of contract negotiations. Accordingly, the motion to dismiss is denied.[16]

THE CASE OF THE HOLIDAY-PAY ELIGIBILITY PROVISION

Another example of how decisive the estoppel principle can be is provided by an arbitral opinion resolving a controversy over employee eligibility for holiday pay. The pertinent contract language stated clearly that a regular employee with more than thirty days service "shall if he shall have worked the regular scheduled workday ... prior to the occurrence of such holiday and his scheduled workday subsequent to such holiday, receive eight hours pay at his regular hourly rate for each such holiday...." A separate contract section included a provision that "an additional day of pay or time off shall be allowed where a holiday occurs within a vacation schedule."

Did the Language Exclude from Eligibility Sickness, Excused Absence, and Death in the Family?

At issue was the departure by the company in the case of two aggrieved employees of a long-established practice of giving holiday pay to employees who did not work their regular scheduled work day before or after the holiday because of sickness, excused absence, or death in the family. The testimony of union witness Mr. E. was accepted at face value by the arbitrator because it went unrebutted by the company. Mr. E. confirmed that there was a past practice of granting holiday pay to those on excused absence or

---

[16] *Columbia Broadcasting Sys. v. Office Employees Int'l Union, Local 174*, pp. 8–9.

absent because of sickness or death in the family. Such testimony of a practice unsupported by the clear language of the contract would not of itself have been controlling. What did carry decisive weight was Mr. E.'s unrebutted version of what had transpired in the prior contract negotiations. The arbitrator ruled that statements of district manager L. in the negotiating sessions justified the invocation of the promissory-estoppel principle.

Crucial Testimony by Witness E. Was Accepted Because It Went Unrebutted

In upholding the union's position, the arbitrator said that since there was no contradiction of the important points made by Mr. E. on behalf of the union, he had to accept such evidence as entirely uncontroverted. The arbitrator noted that ordinarily the testimony of Mr. E. on behalf of the union would be regarded as self-serving statements as to past practice and the manner in which the previous district manager, Mr. L., interpreted the pertinent contract clauses. However, since the testimony was not in any way challenged or disproved, if it was erroneous, by company records, the arbitrator accepted it as fact and as an admission against interest by the company.

According to the arbitrator, Mr. E. had testified that from 1956 until 1959 the district manager on behalf of the company emphatically stated that holidays would be paid even if a person did not work the day before and/or the day after, provided such an employee was excused or was ill or had suffered a death in his immediate family. Mr. E. had further testified that the district manager expressed severe displeasure that the union even raised this point and did not trust management sufficiently to take into account the universally recognized exceptions under which an employee generally receives holiday pay although he may not work the day before and/or the day after such holiday. The arbitrator noted that on no less than four occasions during the hearing, Mr. E. stressed that Mr. L. on his own initiative had added, without any prompting from the union, an extra feature, namely, "the death of a member of an employee's immediate family," as warranting holiday pay in addition to absence due to illness or excuse.

THE DOCTRINE OF ESTOPPEL

Quoting from the arbitrator's opinion upholding the union:

> This case seems most unusual, interesting and important, in that it affords in our view a rather perfect situation in which the doctrine of

estoppel may justly be invoked and applied. True, the contract language is completely silent relative to excuses and does state that an individual must have worked the day before and the day after such holiday; it also provides that if a person is on vacation when such holiday occurs he will receive pay for that holiday. We cannot at all ignore the statements attributed to Mr. L. when such alleged statements evidently are completely supported by past practices. The Union did not press the point of spelling out the usual provisions which would have incorporated the three circumstances referred to by Mr. L., namely, sickness, excuse or death. The Union had every right to rely upon the unequivocal expression by Mr. L. of how he would interpret and apply the pertinent contract clauses. On the basis of all the foregoing, the fact that the Union had every right to rely upon the statement of the district manager, Mr. L., as well as the doctrine of estoppel, we have no choice in the subject case but to sustain in its entirety the position and the contention of the Union and to deny the Company position involving a narrower construction entirely at variance with the Company's past practice and own interpretation of the pertinent clauses in past years. If the application and interpretation of this clause which is identical with previous clauses is to be made sharply at variance with such past practice, then one of two things must be present: (1) The Company must not clearly inform and lead the Union to believe that the pertinent clauses would be interpreted as they have been in the past. (2) Or contract language in the next contract must plainly indicate, and under these circumstances, affirmatively so, that the past practice and application of these contract clauses will in the future be different and then spell that out accordingly and affirmatively. Jurisdiction is retained only for the purpose of clarification deemed necessary by the parties.[17]

Williston on the Implication of the Completeness of a Written Provision

Of particular interest in the foregoing case is that the arbitrator accepted testimony adding to the terms of a written provision even though an implication could have been fairly drawn that the written provision embodied the complete understanding of the parties. The word "implication" is used in the sense explicated by the following passage from Samuel Williston:

> A written promise to pay $50 is not in terms contradicted by an oral promise to pay $25 more, but the natural implication from the written promise is irresistible that $50 is the whole cash payment which the promisor is to make. This implication arises because as a matter of actual practice, one who was intending to promise $75 would put his promise in the form of a single promise to pay that sum, rather than in

[17] *Grief Bros. Cooperage Corp. v. Int'l Ass'n of Machinists, District 9,* Apr. 11, 1960 34 LA 283, 285, Arbitrator Joseph M. Klamon, BNA, Inc.

that of a written promise to pay $50 and a separate agreement to pay $25 in addition.[18]

PAROL EVIDENCE RULE DEFINED

The principle discussed by Williston is fundamental to the "parol evidence rule." This frequently invoked rule provides that where two parties have entered into a contract and have expressed it in writing which they intend as the final and complete statement of that contract, no evidence, oral or written, of *prior* understandings or negotiations is admissible to contradict or vary the written contract.[19]

The parol evidence rule, it should be reiterated, excludes evidence of *prior* understandings, but it does not relate to, or prevent proof of, oral understandings entered into *after* the written contract becomes effective, even when the written contract expressly provides that its provisions can only be changed or eliminated by a subsequent agreement in writing.

It would appear, therefore, that in the case previously cited, the parol evidence rule would not have been applicable to the contract interpretation in the first instance. The union's estoppel claim was based upon oral assurances given by the district manager which amounted to an oral commitment long *after* the holiday eligibility provisions had been drawn up. But even if the assurances of district manager L. had preceded the framing of the holiday eligibility provisions, the parol evidence rule could not have been successfully invoked because of exceptions to the rule. Parol evidence is admissible to show that the written contract when signed by the parties was voidable for fraud, mistake, duress, undue influence, incapacity, or illegality. A promissory estoppel is invoked as a protection against a promise which even though without fraudulent intent may result in fraud by legal definition. It follows then that whenever there is a clear, convincing, undeniable basis for a promissory estoppel, at least one exception to the parol evidence rule must be present—legal fraud. Another exception might well be undue influence. At the risk of being repetitive, it cannot be over-stressed with respect to oral understandings that the parol evidence rule applies only to those understandings reached *before* the written instrument becomes effective. Oral understandings made *after* the contract is executed by the parties do not come under the parol evidence rule.

---

[18] Walter H. E. Jaeger, *A Treatise on the Law of Contracts*, 3d ed. (replacing revised ed. by Samuel Williston), Baker, Voorhis & Co., Mount Kisco, N.Y., 1957, vol. 4, sec. 639, p. 1050.

[19] Laurence P. Simpson, *Simpson on Contracts*, Hornbook Series, West Publishing Company, St. Paul, Minn., 1954, p. 225.

The Stationary Engineers' Lunch Case Reexamined

To illustrate, let us reexamine a case reported earlier, the case involving the controversy at a large rubber company over a lunch break for stationary engineers.[20]   The contract language unambiguously provided a half-hour lunch period for all employees, excluding certain classifications.   Stationary engineers were not one of the classifications excluded, although, as a matter of fact, the stationary engineers had never had a formal lunch break, even before the company had been unionized.   When the first union contract was being negotiated the company had tried to list the stationary engineers among the exclusions, but union spokesmen had objected.

"No, no," they said, "we need every vote we can get to ratify this contract. Let's not stir anything up unnecessarily with language excluding the engineers.   We won't disturb the practice, we promise you, but don't write it in the contract."

ONLY UNDERSTANDINGS MADE PRIOR TO THE CONTRACT EXECUTION COME UNDER THE PAROL EVIDENCE RULE

The question now arises, would such an oral promise be admissible as evidence in a later arbitration?   On a strict application of contract law, it would not be admissible under the parol evidence rule, or if it were allowed into the record, it would normally be given no weight.   To strict constructionists the oral understanding would be inadmissible because it was made prior to execution of the contract.

What now, if, in a subsequent contract negotiation years later, the company again tried to list the stationary engineers among the lunch-break exclusions, and was put off by the same argument and the same promise from the union that the practice would remain undisturbed?   Would this new oral understanding be admissible as evidence?   Our answer is definitely yes.   From any point of view the parol evidence rule would not apply to the new oral understanding because it would have been reached in negotiations *after* the lunch-break provision had been *originally* negotiated by the parties.

Two Types of Prior Oral Understandings

To summarize, an important distinction must be made between two purposes for which prior oral understandings are advanced in arbitration:

[20] See Chap. 4, pp. 49–50.

1 A prior oral understanding may be offered in evidence to contradict the clear language of a written provision. The written provision taken as a complete and, above all, as an indivisible entity is characterized as a spurious agreement; the prior oral understanding, offered as a substitute, is purported to be the true agreement between the parties.

2 A prior oral understanding may be offered in evidence, not to contradict the language as such of a written provision, but to contradict an implication that the provision is the entire bargain made by the parties. The provision is not complete, it is argued, because it does not include additional benefits arrived at by prior oral understandings.

Arbitrators are much more prone to accept parol evidence in the latter instance then they are to admit parol evidence which directly contradicts clearly written provisions and which impugns the validity of these written provisions by attempting to reform the contract.

THE CASE OF MEMORIAL DAY PREMIUM PAY

A dispute over holiday pay at a unionized golf and country club was highlighted by the union's attempt to prove that a prior oral understanding had been reached which contradicted the plain meaning of the following written provision:

> Section 6. The following days shall be observed as holidays: New Year's Day, Washington's Birthday, Memorial Day, Independence Day, Labor Day, Thanksgiving Day, and Christmas Day.
>
> Employees working any of the above holidays shall be paid at the overtime rate of one and one-half times the straight time rate herein specified.[21]

At issue in arbitration was the union's claim that the compensation for work on Memorial Day, a contract holiday, should have been 2½ times the straight-time rate for hours worked. The employer pointed to the clear language of section 6 which specified that compensation for the holiday should be 1½ times the straight-time rate. The union argued that the facts leading to the controversy presented a classic case of promissory estoppel. The arbitrator reviewed the pro and con testimony at the hearing and found that at the initial negotiating meeting for the first contract, the union asked for 2½ times the straight-time hourly rate on specified holidays similar to that required in the contract with another golf course. The union claimed that at that first meeting the company agreed to pay the 2½-times rate if the union would accept contract language which specified the holiday rate as only 1½ times the straight-time rate.

21 *Del E. Webb Corp., Almaden Golf & Country Club v. Bldg. Serv. Employees Union, Local 77,* Jan. 17, 1967, 48 LA 164, Arbitrator Adolph M. Koven, BNA, Inc.

On its part, the company testified that at the negotiations it pointed out that the operation of a golf course required a seven-day-week, fifty-two-weeks-a-year schedule and that the premium rate demanded by the union was too expensive and unrealistic. The company also stated that it did not want Saturdays and Sundays to carry any premium rate.

According to the record, an informal meeting between a company and a union representative was held shortly after that first meeting. The union testified that the company again promised to pay the higher rate if its language was used in the contract and that because of this promise the union agreed to the "one-and-one-half" holiday-pay language in the contract. The company denied that any such promise was ever made.

A second negotiation meeting was held, at which time a company counter-proposal was allegedly made which included the 1½-times rate, the rate which appeared in the final contract. The union testified that after the contract was fully negotiated but before it was signed, the company again informally promised the union the higher rate. The contract in its final form, incorporating the 1½-times-rate language, was typed and prepared by the union.

The arbitrator, to understate the fact, was not persuaded by the union's argument; he disallowed the union's holiday-pay claim on seven separate grounds. We excerpt from the arbitration his dissertation on four of those grounds, pertinent to the subject of the chapter:

Was a Valid Estoppel Created?

The Union seeks to enforce what it says was an informal and oral promise to pay two and one-half times the straight time hourly rate for specified holidays in the face of a clear Contract provision calling only for time and one-half.

The Union's case falters for the following reasons: First, though it is true that arbitrators will sometimes decide issues specifically on the basis of estoppel (21 LA 199, 203; 20 LA 130, 136; 18 LA 306, 307; 17 LA 654, 661) to apply that doctrine, all the required elements of the doctrine must be present. In its usual application, estoppel is based upon a representation of fact which the party is not permitted to deny. The doctrine of promissory estoppel is distinct, and applies even though there is no misrepresentation: one who makes a promise upon which another justifiably relies may be bound to perform it, despite lack of consideration; i.e., the estoppel is a substitute for consideration. For instance, where it was undisputed that the employer gave an oral assurance on a matter during contract negotiations to induce the union to agree on a contract and end a strike, it was held that an estoppel had been created against the employer since the union had changed its position, suffering detriment, in reliance upon the assurance. Accordingly, the employer was held bound by the oral assurance, which limited the number of employees the employer could reclassify under a provision of the contract (*International Harvester Co.*, 17 LA 101, 103; to similar effect, 18 LA 306, 307).

Arbitrator Rules a Promissory Estoppel Was Not Proved

But a basic and essential precondition for invoking the doctrine of promissory estoppel is conclusive evidence that a promise was actually made. This basic precondition is lacking in the present dispute.   All that we have is an uncorroborated and unresolvable confrontation of conflicting testimony.   The result is that the Union failed to satisfy its burden of unequivocally and preconditionally providing that a promise had been made.   It therefore cannot begin to look to the doctrine of promissory estoppel for relief since the element of reliance, not to speak of justifiable reliance, cannot arise in the absence of convincing proof that a promise was actually made in the first instance.   But even if one concludes that a promise was actually made and that it was actually relied upon, a finding of justifiable reliance would be unwarranted.   The parties in this dispute were not novices at their trade of collective bargaining. They knew about such techniques as side letters and if the promise was reasonably intended to be taken as a binding and enforceable obligation, either the promise would have been reduced to writing or made in a context beyond an extremely informal get-together by only two men.   The net result is that under these circumstances no conclusion of justifiable reliance can follow.

Language Unequivocally Provided for Holiday Pay at Time and a Half

Second, where language of an agreement is clear and unequivocal, that language will generally not be given a meaning other than expressed. Parties to a contract are generally charged with full knowledge of its provisions and of the significance of its language (7 LA 708, 711; 3 LA 229, 232) and the clear meaning of the language is generally enforced even though the results are harsh or contrary to the original expectations of one of the parties (28 LA 557, 558; 20 LA 756, 758–759; 13 LA 110, 114).   In the case at bar, the language is obviously clear and unambiguous, and on its face, specifically provides for time and one-half for holiday pay.

Arbitrator Concludes Parol Evidence Rule Is Applicable

[Next,] . . . a written contract consummating previous oral and written negotiations is deemed under the parol evidence rule to embrace the entire agreement, and, if the writing is clear and unambiguous, parol evidence will not be allowed to vary the contract (See Wigmore, *Evidence*, paragraph 2400; *United Drill and Tool Co.*, 28 LA 677, 679–683).   This is said to be a rule of substantive law which when applicable defines the limits of a contract (2 Williston, *Contracts*, paragraph 631). Since the writing is clear and unambiguous and since none of the recognized exceptions to the parol evidence rule are present, the rule is obviously applicable in the present situation and operates to the disadvantage of the Union.

[Next,] where an agreement is not ambiguous, it is improper to modify its meaning by invoking the record of prior negotiations (18 LA 916, 918; 3 LA 753, 756). If a party attempts but fails in contract negotiations to include a specific provision in the agreement, an arbitrator will hesitate to read such provision into the agreement through the process of interpretation (27 LA 126, 128; 24 LA 224, 228; 21 LA 699, 702–703). Again, the unambiguous and clear character of the holiday premium pay provision precludes any modification, even if the Union's view of prior negotiations on this point is favored.[22]

Oral Understandings on Major Matters Should Be Avoided

The arbitrator's comment on the union's failure to secure a binding promise by the use of side letters was a point well taken. Oral, or gentlemen's, agreements on minor matters are unavoidable, but on major matters they should be discouraged as a source of disruption in the collective-bargaining relationship. Even when there are good reasons for not writing a major matter directly into the contract, it can be made binding for all practical purposes by the use of side letters. Side letters enable one or both of the parties to make binding (or at least not easily repudiated) concessions to each other without damaging their own or other people's interests at some other place. Thus a nationwide company can grant travel time, let us say, to a skilled group of employees in the sprawling Los Angeles area without publicly making it a precedent for its employees in other cities who do not need the travel allowance. Or a union can through side letters grant temporary relief on a costly fringe benefit to a newly unionized employer without incurring the wrath of a large group of unionized employers in the industry who are paying the fringe benefit.

Not All Promises Come under the Estoppel Principle

Another point made in the golf and country club arbitration deserving of elaboration is the element of consideration as it relates to the promissory-estoppel principle. The arbitrator noted that "one who makes a promise upon which another justifiably relies may be bound to perform it, despite lack of consideration. . . ." It should not be assumed from this statement

---

[22] *Ibid.*, 166–167.

that any and all promises made in collective bargaining justify invoking the estoppel principle.

THE CASE OF THE HOLIDAY SWAP

For example, there was the promise made by a local-union official to the industrial relations director of a manufacturing firm. For the first time in years the company was operating three shifts, filling a subcontract on a high-priority order for the Air Force. Late in October, the industrial relations director said to the union official: "We need your help. We don't want to shut down on Veterans Day, but we will if we have to. We don't want to pay the premium rate for working a contract holiday. We bid too close to the margin on this subcontract to pay premium rates. We'd appreciate it no end if you'd agree just this one time to make the holiday the Friday after Thanksgiving. Let us operate Veterans Day as a normal work day at straight time, and in exchange we'll shut down the day after Thanksgiving and make it a paid holiday. That gives everyone a four-day weekend. How about it?"

The union official pondered the proposal. "I don't think the membership will mind," he said. "If you're in that much of a bind, I'll okay the swap right now."

A week before Veterans Day, he reported his assent to the union executive board expecting a routine endorsement. Much to his discomfiture, he was reversed.

"Nothing doing," he was told by union militants. "Friday after Thanksgiving is not a contract holiday. We want 2½ times the straight-time rate for working Veterans Day. Any other arrangement is just chiseling us out of premium pay."

The industrial relations director, when told that the holiday swap had been vetoed by the union executive board, did not spare the union official. "You can't do this to me," he railed at him. "You're the top hand in the union, and you made a deal with me. I'm going to hold you to our agreement if I have to take it to arbitration."

Exchange of Consideration Was
Lacking in the Holiday Swap

Even if it were assumed (an assumption by no means warranted) that the union official had the authority to waive the contract provision making Veterans Day a paid holiday with a premium rate when worked, there was still lacking an essential element of a binding agreement, namely, an exchange of consideration. If the request to substitute the Friday after Thanksgiving for Veterans Day had been initiated by the union or had otherwise been acknowledged by it as a concession, then the arrangement would have been binding. In fact, however, the arrangement was a one-sided accommodation by the union to a request of management, with no apparent benefit acknowledged by the union, and hence the exchange of consideration necessary for a binding agreement was notably absent.

Estoppel Principle Requires That the Promise Must Be a Reasonable One

As to a promissory estoppel, the industrial relations director would have had to do more than prove that a promise had been made to him. He would have had to establish first that the promise was one which could be reasonably relied upon. To illustrate by exaggeration, a person would be singularly deficient in judgment were he to rely on a promise that he would be transported around Cape Horn in a 12-foot sailboat. The promise must be one on which the proverbial "reasonable and prudent" person of the law casebooks could justifiably rely.

By Relying on the Promise, the Promisee Must Have Suffered Damage

Assuming, as in this case, that the promise could have been justifiedly relied upon (both the industrial relations director and the promisor had shared this belief), a second element of promissory estoppel would have had to be present. The industrial relations director would have had to prove that he had been misled to his own detriment by the promise—that by relying on the promise he had in some way irreparably impaired his situation. It must be stressed that it is not enough for the one seeking to invoke the promissory-estoppel principle to prove that he has been damaged. He must show that the damage was suffered because he had acted or failed to act as a result of the promise—that the damage was not an inevitable consequence of his situation, but could have been avoided if he had not justifiably relied on the promise. The damage could be as simple as being deprived of the option of shutting down on Veterans Day to avoid paying the premium rate set by contract. The company might, for example, be compelled to operate on the holiday at premium pay because of irrevocable commitments made to suppliers or customers—commitments made because of a promise that it could operate the holiday at straight-time pay. The inability of management to prove that damage of this kind had been incurred prompted the company counsel to advise against arbitration, and the matter was dropped.

No Clear-Cut Trend in Arbitration
On Admissibility of Parol Evidence

In general it has not been possible, from an examination of published arbitrations, to discern a clear-cut trend on the admissibility of parol evidence to establish a promissory estoppel. Some arbitrators (a minority, to be sure) have been adamant in applying the parol evidence rule to exclude both oral and written, prior and collateral, understandings which contradicted the clear language of a contract or which amended a written provision that appeared on its face to be the complete agreement of the parties. Other arbitrators have rejected parol evidence which contradicted clear language but have admitted parol understandings which amended but did not contradict clear language. Still other arbitrators have gone all the way in admitting parol evidence to establish a claimed promissory estoppel. Edgar A. Jones, Jr., notes, moreover: "The modern judicial and legislative trend is definitely to dilute the parol evidence rule as an exclusionary device in litigation."[23]

AGENCY DISCUSSED: THE CASE OF
THE WAGE REOPENER

The matter of agency, specifically the authority of representatives of the negotiating parties to make binding agreements for their respective organizations, was mentioned only in passing in the case of the proposed swap of the Veterans Day holiday for the Friday after Thanksgiving. We turn now to a controversy over wages for a fuller treatment of the powers vested in an authorized agent to conduct precontract negotiations within the limitations imposed upon him when he acts on his own.

At issue was a contract wage-reopening provision, section (g) of article XIII, which read in part:

> The Union and the Company shall each have the right during the term of this agreement to reopen the general wage rates and vacation pay only for negotiation and to terminate this agreement by giving a sixty (60) days written notice of such intention to the other party.[24]

The dispute focused on conflicting interpretations of the phrase "general wage rates." The company argued before the arbitrator that the phrase

---

[23] Edgar A. Jones, Jr., "Problems of Proof in the Arbitration Process: Report of West Coast Tripartite Committee," *Problems of Proof in Arbitration: Proceedings of the Nineteenth Annual Meeting, National Academy of Arbitrators*, BNA, Inc., 1966, p. 174.
[24] *Metalcraft Prods. Co. v. United Furniture Workers, Local 1010*, Apr. 12, 1956, 26 LA 433, 434, Arbitrator Paul Prasow, BNA, Inc.

referred only to the guaranteed minimum rate for each classification as set forth in the contract—that incentive rates were excluded from consideration both by interpretation and by an oral understanding arrived at with an authorized union official when the wage reopener had been negotiated.

The Unratified Gentlemen's Agreement

As proof of the oral understanding, the company submitted in evidence a letter from Mr. G., a deposed business manager of the local union, acknowledging that a crucial consideration of the company's improved wage offer in previous contract bargaining had been his acquiescence to an oral understanding that incentive rates would not be part of the wage-reopening provision. The fervent indignation with which the union denounced Mr. G.'s letter was genuine. Ninety-five percent of the employees were on piecework, and had undoubtedly been unaware of any private understanding excluding incentive pay from the wage reopener. Even more to the point, the members of the union negotiating committee who had participated in the framing of the wage-reopening provision denied to a man any knowledge of the purported side deal between Mr. G. and the company. The following excerpts from the arbitrator's opinion sustaining the union show how he sought to resolve the issue while steering clear of the ticklish matter of agency posed by the problem:

Customary Usage of the Phrase "General Wage Rates" Includes Incentive Rates

Where incentive rates are part of a wage system, it is customary industry practice to include them as a subject of negotiations along with the minimum or base rates. A more restrictive interpretation which excludes incentive rates from negotiations, although sometimes provided for in a wage reopening clause, is not the common or prevailing practice. The word "general" in itself, either from the dictionary definition or customary usage, implies a broad or widespread coverage, rather than one specifically limited in application. Thus it would appear that the burden of establishing that the term "general wage rates" is intended to apply only to minimum rates, falls upon the party asserting this limitation. The reason is that such a narrow interpretation tends to be in conflict with the ordinary and popularly accepted meaning of the phrase. If it were the intent to exclude incentive rates from negotiations under the wage reopening clause in this agreement, appropriate language to this effect has not been inserted to make explicit such intent. . . .

. . . In determining the issue, consideration must be given to the circumstances leading up to the agreement as well as to the contract language itself. There is a sharp conflict in testimony as to the understanding reached during negotiations on the meaning and intent of the phrase "general wage rates." The chief negotiator for the Company has testified that there was an oral understanding just prior to signing the contract to the effect that general wage rates would not include incentive rates as an item for negotiation under the wage reopening clause. The Company supports this contention by submitting in evidence a letter from Mr. G., the Chief negotiator for the Union during the negotiations on this agreement, in which he states that "it was not intended to include incentives in the wage re-opener as shown in Section (g) of Art. XIII." On the other hand, two Union witnesses, who also participated in the same negotiations, as members of the Union's negotiating committee, testified that it was not their understanding that general wage rates would exclude incentive rates. Further that had it been made clear to them that such an exclusion was intended, they would not have signed a two-year contract.

Arbitrator Rules Mr. G.'s Letter Is Insufficient Proof
Of an Understanding to Exclude Incentive Rates

The Arbitrator has examined the record carefully with respect to the conflicting evidence and testimony on this point. Although it is quite possible that an oral understanding may have existed as claimed by the Company, it is not clear from the record whether such an oral agreement was understood and accepted by the Union negotiating committee as a whole, or by the membership when it ratified the agreement. Such evidence as does appear in the record would seem to indicate that the members of the Union negotiating committee accepted the written agreement at its face value without apparent awareness that incentive rates were to be specifically excluded from consideration during negotiations under the wage reopening clause. It seems to the Arbitrator that when an oral understanding appears to be a modification of the language of a written contract, and a counter claim is made that the alleged understanding was not held or accepted by the other party, there must be strong and compelling evidence to establish the existence of the oral understanding.

The Union has strongly objected to the introduction of Mr. G.'s letter in this proceeding on the grounds that he was expelled from membership in the Union and has now established himself as the head of an independent union which seeks to compete with Local 1010; and thus his letter would be a completely self-serving document. In the Arbitrator's opinion, Mr. G.'s letter in itself is insufficient to establish the existence of the alleged oral understanding, since he did not appear as a witness at the hearing and was not subject to cross-examination or interrogation by the Arbitrator. It is clear from the record that the oral understanding which may have been reached with Mr. G. was never reduced to writing, nor did it become a formal part of the agreement between the parties, and its existence cannot actually be verified. In the absence of more substantial evidence, the Arbitrator cannot consider the alleged oral understanding as modifying the language of the agreement.[25]

Colloquy between the Authors
On the Wage-Reopener Case

"Paul, you found for the union in the Metalcraft Products arbitration principally on the basis that the company had not presented convincing proof that it had come to an oral understanding with Mr. G. to exclude incentive pay from the wage reopener. Suppose the company had produced such proof, proof beyond question that an oral understanding had been reached. Would you have upheld the company?"

"No, not on a private understanding with Mr. G. At the very least, the understanding should have been ratified by the union negotiating committee, if not the general membership."

"Then why didn't you tackle the issue head on and rule that the oral understanding, even if proved, was not binding?"

"That was almost fifteen years ago. Arbitration criteria governing agency in collective bargaining weren't as well defined then as they are today. It was just too much for me to research and lay out broad guidelines for an oral understanding which had not been proved. I wasn't in an innovative mood at the time—not in that case."

"Generally speaking, Paul, what are the principal restrictions on the authority of union representatives to act on their own?"

"In the main, arbitrators would be dead set against understandings made by union representatives to waive or alter the express provisions of a contract—especially provisions involving employee benefits. They'd have to get ratification from the membership for such understandings to be valid. Arbitrators will not approve of wheeling and dealing with employee benefits provided for in the contract, unless these understandings are okayed by a vote of the bargaining unit. There are exceptions, of course."

"Such as?"

"Well, if the union representative has prior authority by virtue of the organization's constitution and bylaws. Officials of certain railroad unions for example, have the constitutional authority to negotiate contracts and sign them without ratification. Membership is scattered geographically over a wide area, and it's often hard to assemble a representative meeting. The union's theory of democracy is that if the membership doesn't like the contract negotiated for them, they can vote their officials out of office in the next election."

[25] *Ibid.,* 436–437.

"Can you suggest other important exceptions?"

"Not exceptions; I'd rather give the general rule. In collective bargaining, as in commercial law, people may be, in lawyer's language, 'clothed with ostensible or apparent authority' to act for their respective organizations. Shop stewards, grievance chairmen, personnel directors, plant managers have the authority to settle grievances on the spot—within limits, of course. A first-line foreman or a shop steward can't make or change major policies that are properly the responsibility of higher echelons in the grievance structure. But both parties are charged with knowledge of those decision-making areas of authority which are well-known facts of their collective-bargaining relationship. An employer is responsible for the coercive actions of a company representative who can hire, fire, and effectively direct the work force. A union is responsible for the actions of its major officers, especially paid officials. However, a union cannot ordinarily be held responsible for the conduct of its individual members, unless it is proved they were acting with the knowledge of and at the behest of the organization."

PRECONTRACT INTENT UNDISPUTED: THE CONTROVERSY OVER STEAMSHIP-BAGGAGE HANDLING

A study of precontract negotiations as a primary guide to contract interpretation must necessarily focus on basic criteria such as promissory estoppel, the parol evidence rule, and principles of agency. To conclude this discussion, a case is now presented involving a contract provision the intent of which was unquestioned in precontract negotiations. The employer was a steamship line operating a passenger vessel of Canadian registry which included in its regular itinerary various California and Mexican ports. In December, 1965, the company signed a contract with the Marine Cooks and Stewards Union (MCS) giving the union the right to handle all passenger-baggage handling—on embarkation, from the passenger on the dock to his stateroom; on debarkation, from the stateroom to a dock location designated by the passenger. The assignment of complete jurisdiction over passenger-baggage handling to MCS was unambiguously spelled out in section 2 of the contract.[26]

The company could not have been unaware of the likelihood that its assignment of total jurisdiction over passenger luggage to MCS would

26 "SCOPE OF CONTRACT WORK ASSIGNMENT: The Employees will assist or relieve Steward Department personnel in their normal duties; also the handling of passenger baggage being discharged from the Company's vessels to the dock and being taken abroad from the dock to said vessels."

bring about an encounter with the Pacific Coast Longshoremen's Union. Sharp jurisdictional conflict has characterized the relationship between the sailors and the longshoremen of the Pacific Coast for over three decades. It would not be easy to dissuade the longshoremen from asserting their traditional jurisdiction over passenger-baggage handling from the dock to the gangway on embarkation and from the gangway to the dock on debarkation. It is reasonable to assume, therefore, that the company relied not only on the support of MCS but also on a strong legal position based on clear contract language to deter the longshoremen from resorting to economic reprisals.

When the ship docked at Long Beach, California, not surprisingly to those aware of the longshoremen's penchant for direct action, all cargo handling was halted precipitously over the assignment of carrying passenger baggage. The company capitulated quickly and reassigned the baggage handling (except for shipside operations, which were not in dispute) to the longshoremen.

The arrangement was an unhappy one for the company. With MCS handling baggage on the ship and longshoremen handling baggage to and from the gangway and the dock, the double handling by rival unions required a duplication in costs. The company turned reproachfully to MCS, insisting it was the responsibility of the union to extricate it from an untenable jurisdictional tangle. The union invoked arbitration when the company talked of nullifying section 2 of the contract if the union did not take whatever steps were necessary to make possible its enforcement.

In analyzing the arguments of the parties, the arbitrator felt impelled to note at the outset that one area not in dispute was the meaning of the contract language covering the assignment of baggage handling. He noted that it would be difficult to conceive of how a disagreement on the meaning of section 2 could exist because the language of this section, as MCS correctly pointed out and the company conceded, clearly and unambiguously assigned the baggage handling in question to MCS. The arbitrator then went on to say:

> What then is the issue between the parties? Namely, that the Company has failed to carry out the express provisions of the Agreement. The Company argues that it has been frustrated in its desire to effectuate the mutual intent of the parties to this arbitration by a counter claim of jurisdiction made by the Longshoremen.
>
> At this point the Arbitrator must evaluate his own authority to rule in the instant case. The scope of an Arbitrator's authority is bounded by the written agreement of the parties. His function is restricted to the interpretation and application of the pertinent provisions to the dispute.

The Company's defense is based solely on the economic sanctions which might result from its enforcement of a written instrument, the meaning of which is not contested by the parties to this arbitration.

Arbitrator Refuses to Enforce the Agreement

The enforcement of a Collective Bargaining Agreement as distinguished from the interpretation and application of that Agreement is not a part of an Arbitrator's function. The question presented in this proceeding is not one of interpretation and application, but rather one of enforcement. The Arbitrator is restricted to the resolution of conflicts over the meaning of an agreement, and no dispute exists between the instant parties in that regard. The resolution of this dispute, the Arbitrator ventures to suggest, must be sought before an appropriate agency such as the NLRB or the Courts; it cannot be found in an arbitration proceeding.[27]

The arbitrator then concluded that the agreement was clear and unambiguous and no dispute existed between the parties as to its meaning; therefore there was no arbitrable issue in the case. Since the arbitrator ruled that no dispute existed, he simply referred the entire matter back to the parties.

SUMMARY

When called upon to interpret ambiguous language, the arbitrator's primary responsibility is to determine, if possible, the mutual intent of the parties. He may accomplish this objective by inquiring how the parties themselves have interpreted the language during the term of the agreement (*past practice*); or he may review the bargaining history of the agreement—what the parties said and did during making of the agreement (*precontract negotiations*).

The bargaining history—the discussions and actions of the parties as well as other significant circumstances which led to the making of the agreement —may provide valuable clues to the meaning of the language in dispute. The parties' conduct prior to signing the contract may reveal their mutual intent just as clearly as their activities during the contract term.

The arbitrator's study of precontract negotiations as a guide to interpretation of ambiguous language is often based upon the legal principles of promissory estoppel, the parol evidence rule, and the criteria of agency. In

[27] *Princess Cruises Co. v. Marine Cooks & Stewards Union*, Mar. 28, 1966, unpublished arbitration award, pp. 6–7, Arbitrator Howard S. Block.

essence, *promissory estoppel* prevents a person from repudiating his promises and inferential declarations made during negotiations which caused another person to change his position to his disadvantage because he was relying on the first person's conduct or statements. The *parol evidence rule* provides that where the parties have entered into a written agreement which they intend to be the final and complete statement of their contract, then no evidence, oral or written, of *prior* understandings or negotiations is admissible to contradict or change the terms of the written agreement. *Agency* refers primarily to the authority of representatives of the negotiating parties to make binding agreements for their respective principals.

Chapter 10
Evidence and proof

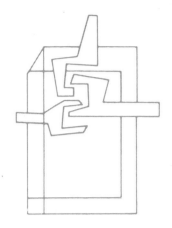

■ Arbitration, it has been emphasized, is a quasi-judicial process—judicial in that the arbitrator's award is binding and enforceable in the courts, quasi-judicial in that legal standards of contract interpretation and legal rules of evidence are not strictly adhered to by the arbitrator. A point made in the first chapter bears repeating: The quasi-judicial character of the process must be maintained if its usefulness is to be preserved. If arbitration were to lose its present flexibility by aping courtroom proceedings and obliterating the distinction between the two, then arbitration would lose its reason for existence.[1]

RULES OF EVIDENCE APPLIED FLEXIBLY

The fact is, however, that the approximately 350 persons who do most of the arbitrating rely just as heavily on legal rules of evidence for resolving questions of fact as they do on commercial-law criteria for interpreting labor

[1] See Chap. 1, p. 13.

agreements. Basic principles of proof are not arbitrarily concocted rules of the game. They have evolved out of the bitter travail of Western man; they are the end product of centuries of his social practice. Essential to an arbitrator's function, therefore, is a knowledge of the most important rules of evidence, and especially of the logic behind them, and an expertise in the application of those rules in a quasi-judicial proceeding. Questions of evidence and of proof focus on the quasi-judicial character of arbitration.

But first to draw the distinction between "evidence" and "proof," two terms used interchangeably in ordinary conversation: Evidence is the *medium* of proof; or, to reverse the definition, proof is the *effect* or *result* of evidence. Proof is the establishment of a judgmental fact by evidence. Without evidence there is no proof, but evidence by itself without inference leading to a judgment is not proof. Proof is a conclusion drawn from the evidence.

Fight Theory versus Truth Theory

When grappling with problems of proof, arbitrators generally find a middle ground between two pertinent methods of adjudication. One method is based upon the "adversary" principle, which draws a sharp line between the function of the judge and the function of the advocate. Under the adversary system the judge sits to decide the case based on a record produced by the contending parties, not by his independent investigatory zeal. As described by Judge Jerome Frank:

> Our mode of trials is commonly known as "contentious" or "adversary." It is based on what I would call the "fight" theory, a theory which derives from the origin of trials as substitutes for private out-of-court brawls.
>
> Many lawyers maintain that the "fight" theory and the "truth" theory coincide. They think that the best way for a court to discover the facts in a suit is to have each side strive as hard as it can, in a keenly partisan spirit, to bring to the court's attention the evidence favorable to that side. Macaulay said that we obtain the fairest decision "when two men argue, as unfairly as possible, on opposite sides," for then "it is certain that no important consideration will altogether escape notice."[2]

The contrasting method of adjudication, based on the "truth" theory referred to by Frank, permits the judicial inquirers a wide investigatory range to uncover the objective facts. Although the adversary procedure prevails in English-speaking lands, the "judicial inquiry" method is not uncommon in Continental Europe. Harvard law professor Lon L. Fuller

[2] Jerome Frank, *Courts on Trial: Myth and Reality in American Justice,* Princeton University Press, 1950, copyright 1949 by Jerome Frank, p. 80.

explains briefly the why and how of the "investigatory," or "truth," method
of adjudication:

Fuller on Truth Theory

> Why have courts and trials at all? Why bother with judges and juries,
> with pleas and counterpleas? When disputes arise or accusations are
> made, why should not the state simply appoint honest and intelligent
> men to make investigations? Why not let these men, after they have
> sifted the evidence and resolved apparent contradictions, make their
> findings without the aid of advocates and without the fanfare and
> publicity of a trial?
>
> Arrangements tending in this direction are not unknown historically.
> One of them has at various times and in various forms been familiar on
> the European continent. This is the institution of the investigating
> magistrate, *le juge d'instruction, der Untersuchungsrichter.* In important
> criminal cases this official makes his own investigations and reaches his
> own conclusions on the basis of the evidence. To be sure, he has never
> been given the power to make a final determination of guilt. Yet his
> findings tend to influence the trials that follow; the form he has given
> to his inquiry tends to shape the proceedings in court and often tips the
> balance in cases of doubt.
>
> No such office or institution exists in the countries of the common
> law, including the United States. Why do we reject an arrangement that
> seems so reasonable in its quiet efficiency? In answer I might simply
> draw on the European experience and quote a French observer who
> remarked that in cases where the *juge d'instruction* reaches the conclu-
> sion that no prosecution should be brought, it is usually with a tinge of
> regret that he signs the necessary documents.[3]

Fact-finding, or judicial-inquiry, methods of adjudication, as distinguished
from the adversary method, will continue to be an integral feature of labor
arbitration so long as the proceedings remain quasi-judicial. The trend of
labor arbitration, as a cursory reading of published cases will disclose, is
increasingly adversary in method, but the trend can be counted on to stop
short of obliterating the quasi-judicial character of arbitral adjudication.

It would be fitting, perhaps, for the great John Henry Wigmore to have
the last word on this topic, as expounded in his monumental work on
evidence:

Wigmore on the Adversary Principle

> Our system of Evidence is *sound on the whole.*
>
> In the first place, it was and is based on *experience of human nature,*
> —and that is saying a great deal for it. It was not created by legislative

---

[3] Lon L. Fuller, "The Adversary System," in Harold J. Berman (ed.), *Talks on American
Law,* Vintage Books, Random House, Inc., New York, 1961, pp. 35–36.

fiat,—like our Patent law. It was not devised by chambered jurists,—like the German Civil Code. It was not (for the most part) founded on anachronistic tradition,—like some of our Property law. It simply grew. And it grew during the last two centuries, so that its human nature basis is not, in time, far enough away to be possibly out of date.

That human nature is represented in the witnesses, the counsel, and the jurors. All three, in their weaknesses, have been kept in mind by the law of Evidence. The multifold untrustworthinesses of witnesses; the constant partisan zeal, the lurking chicanery, the needless unpreparedness, of counsel; the crude reasoning, the strong irrational emotions, the testimonial inexperience, of jurors,—all these elements have been considered. Tens of thousands of trials have forced them out into the open, where thousands of judges have observed them; and their observations have profited by them, in thinking out principles and formulating rules.

All this has not been created out of nothing; it rested on a solid basis of experience in human nature at trials. And that human nature has not essentially changed. The main basis is there yet. The changes have not been in the great factors.

The rules of Evidence, then, are to have at least that presumption in their favor which sensible critics always give to the conclusions of experience, even when all of the data of that experience are not specifically known to the critic.

In the next place, *that human nature*, in the same factors, *will always be with us.* Witnesses, counsel, jurors, will continue to exhibit similar weaknesses. The trial will always be struggle, revealing nakedly those weaknesses. And there will always have to be some apparatus for testing and checking those weaknesses. We can expect to improve the apparatus, but not to ignore the weaknesses. And just as long as man continues to be a reasoning animal, and to desire to profit in his narrow personal task by the combined experience of others, just so long will trial judges crave and devise generalized rules for making some headway through the welter of lies and errors and doubts and inferences that is heaped up before them at a trial.[4]

The quasi-judicial character of labor arbitration is in no aspect more noticeable than in the great flexibility of the hearing procedures, which are singularly free from technical rules of admissibility of evidence. All evidence pertinent and material to the issue must be accepted.

Why Arbitral Admissability Is Broad

At least two good reasons for a wide latitude in hearing procedures are advanced: First, the rules of evidence were developed historically as guideposts for juries made up of persons who lacked experience in analyzing

[4] John Henry Wigmore, *A Treatise on the Anglo-American Systems of Evidence in Trials at Common Law,* 3d ed., Little, Brown and Company, Boston, 1940, vol. 1, p. 262. Includes the statutes and judicial decisions of all jurisdictions of the United States and Canada.

evidence and who could easily be gulled into bringing in verdicts based on emotion rather than on reasoned, dispassionate consideration of evidence. Judges and arbitrators are by training and experience quicker to detect sophistry and are impervious to the chicanery of opposing counsel; hence they may and do dispense with many of the time-consuming safeguards retained in a trial by jury. Second, in civil litigation the contending parties are not compelled to live with each other, as they do in labor arbitration, after a verdict has been reached. The parties to a court suit meet as enemies and usually part as enemies regardless of who wins and who loses the verdict.[5]

Although in the end it is the arbitrator who determines what evidence is relevant and material, he is not likely to disregard the well-known admonition of the late Harry Shulman that "the more serious danger is not that the arbitrator will hear too much irrelevancy, but rather that he will not hear enough of the relevant."[6] Refusal to admit material or relevant evidence is one of the few grounds on which the courts will refuse to enforce an arbitral award. As many arbitrators freely say, why exclude doubtful evidence and run even a remote risk of having an award vacated by the courts when the purpose of exclusion is served by allowing in the evidence with a veiled suggestion that it will probably be given little or no weight?

There is, however, a major exception to the above practice. Generally not admissible or at least given little weight are offers of compromise made by either party in an effort to settle a grievance in the steps prior to arbitration. To admit such offers into the arbitration record not only may unfairly prejudice the position of the party who made the offer, but could seriously inhibit future attempts at grievance settlement through negotiations.

To illustrate this principle: it is not uncommon in a discharge grievance for the company or union to propose reinstatement of the dismissed employee, *but with no back pay.* In effect, this offer amounts to reducing the discharge penalty to a disciplinary suspension. Such offers are usually made primarily in the hope of resolving the grievance without going to arbitration. If the offer is rejected and the case submitted to arbitration, it would be unfair to the party who made the offer if the compromise proposal were admitted into the record as evidence. Once the parties proceed to arbitration, all prior offers to settle are usually withdrawn and the contest now becomes "double or nothing."

As a corollary to the principle of arbitration favoring the inclusion of

---

[5] If arbitration is also looked upon as an educational process for the parties and their constituencies who attend the hearing, then broad admissibility of evidence serves another important function.

[6] Harry Shulman, "Reason, Contract, and Law in Labor Relations," *Harvard Law Review*, vol. 68, no. 6, April, 1955, p. 1017.

evidence over exclusion, arbitrators place great weight on testimony which is subject to cross-examination as opposed to the admission of hearsay evidence which denies the opposing party any opportunity for cross-examination. Unsupported letters, affidavits, and other written documents are often admitted into the record "for what they are worth," meaning they will be given very little weight by the arbitrator because they are not subject to cross-examination. Here again Wigmore expresses a basic philosophy of jurisprudence adhered to by most arbitrators:

> The vital aspect is that we are not to credit *any man's assertion* until we *have tested it by bringing him into court* (if we can get him) and *cross-examining him.* Now the development of this art of cross-examination, during two centuries, is the great valuable contribution . . . and modern psychological science . . . has shown us something of the hundred lurking sources of error that inhere in all testimonial assertions; and we perceive that our traditional expedient of cross-examination was the main way to get at these sources of error, and that it owes its primacy to permanent traits of the human mind. To abandon our insistence on the necessity of this test [cross-examination] would be to surrender the best single expedient anywhere invented for getting at the truth of controversies.[7]

Courts Uphold Broad Arbitral Admissibility

A memorandum opinion of the U.S. District Court of the Central District of California vacating an arbitration award provides an especially lucid treatment of admissibility of evidence in an arbitration proceeding. The award reviewed by the court involved the discharge of an employee for alleged misconduct during a bitterly contested strike. The stoppage marked by intermittent massing of pickets with ensuing violent scuffles on the picket line, continued for more than four months until a strike settlement agreement was signed. The agreement provided for arbitrating the discharges of a number of strikers for alleged misconduct on the picket line.

After receiving an award reinstating Mary J., the company petitioned the District Court for review. The company asked to have the award vacated on grounds that the arbitrator had refused to permit Officer Gottesman, one of two police officers who witnessed the alleged rock-throwing incident, to complete his testimony at the arbitration hearing and refused to consider the testimony of this witness in arriving at his award. Officer Gottesman was called by the company after the union had rested its case on the alleged rock throwing by Mary J. during the strike at the plant on April 17, 1965.

[7] *Op. cit.*, p. 277.

The company had discharged Mary J. in accordance with its understanding of the provisions of the strike-settlement agreement. The only issue involved was whether Mary J. had engaged in strike misconduct. The company had argued before the arbitrator that Gottesman was properly called as a rebuttal witness. The union had objected that the evidence was cumulative and not proper rebuttal. Although Gottesman was allowed to testify in part on direct examination and was cross-examined by union counsel, the direct examination was not completed and no redirect was permitted.

The arbitrator stated in his award that he disregarded in its entirety the testimony of Officer Gottesman because, in his opinion, the witness should have appeared as part of the company's principal case and his appearance as a rebuttal witness was not timely.

"Ping-pong" Rebuttal Procedure Rejected by Arbitrator

In his written opinion the arbitrator observed:

> By way of explanation of this ruling, it is the view of the Arbitrator that orderly procedure in arbitration requires each party to present the whole of its case-in-chief before it rests. If part of the principal case of a party is reserved and put on ostensibly as rebuttal, then the other party may request to re-open its case in order to meet the additional testimony, and a kind of ping-pong procedure may ensue which is confusing. Assuming that a prime purpose of the arbitration is to convey to the arbitrator as clear an idea as possible of the facts and arguments in the case, the method of whole presentation will serve this end and the method of incomplete presentation to be completed as rebuttal will not.[8]

In its petition to the court, the company asserted that Officer Gottesman was an impeaching witness properly called on rebuttal and that by refusing to permit the witness to testify in full and consider his testimony as evidence in the matter, the arbitrator had refused to hear evidence pertinent and material to the dispute, in violation of the provisions of Section 1286.2, California Code of Civil Procedure, and Title 9, United States Code, Section 10(c), resulting in prejudice to the rights of the company and denying it a fair hearing.

After a hearing, the union's motion for summary judgment was denied on October 31, 1966. A hearing on the motion to vacate was held on November 29, 1966, at which time both oral and documentary evidence was received by the court.

---

[8] *Harvey Aluminum, Inc. v. United Steelworkers*, July 26, 1966, unpublished arbitration award, p. 2, Arbitrator Spencer Pollard.

The opinion of the court encompasses such a thoroughgoing discussion and analysis of the quasi-judicial nature of the arbitration process that particularly relevant sections are quoted at some length here. The text on pages 172–178 comprises direct quotations from the court itself:

Legal Rules of Evidence Are Not Required in Arbitration

It is well established that rules of evidence as applied in court proceedings do not prevail in arbitration hearings. The Supreme Court of California in *Sapp vs. Barenfeld*, 34 Cal. 2nd 515 (1949), denied a petition to vacate an arbitration award on the grounds that the complaining party had made no attempt at the hearing to produce the evidence which it later argued that the arbitrator had failed to consider. At page 520 the court stated:

"It has never been the law that arbitrations are subject to all rules of judicial procedure save those relating to the form of questions. 'The essence of arbitration is its freedom from the formality of ordinary judicial procedure.' (*Canuso v. Philadelphia*, 326 Pa. 302, 307 [192 A. 133].) All relevant evidence may be freely admitted and rules of judicial procedure need not be observed so long as the hearing is fairly conducted. The hearing may be in the nature of an informal conference rather than a judicial trial."

The rules of the American Arbitration Association are not binding upon arbitrators but do set guide lines as to hearing procedures. Rule 28 concerns "evidence" and states in part:

"28. Evidence—The parties may offer such evidence as they desire and shall produce such additional evidence as the Arbitrator may deem necessary to an understanding and determination of the dispute.... The Arbitrator shall be the judge of the relevancy and materiality of the evidence offered and *conformity to legal rules of evidence shall not be necessary.*" [Italics supplied by court.]

In Arbitration All Relevant Facts Are Admissible

Arbitrator Aaron of UCLA Law School observes in his article, "Some Procedural Problems in Arbitration," 10 Vand. L. Rev., 739, 743–744 (1957):

"The contrast between the objectives and procedures of an arbitration hearing and those of a law suit has been so generally noticed by arbitrators, lawyers, and laymen that one is puzzled by the ubiquity of certain procedural arguments in arbitration. Of these, surely the most senseless is the dispute over which side should proceed first. An insistence that the other side has the burden of going forward implies a plaintiff-defendant relationship in which the former must set up a prima facie case before the latter is obligated to respond. But this concept is plainly inapplicable to an arbitration proceeding. As an extension of the grievance procedure, an arbitration hearing serves many purposes, not the least of which is to give the grievant the satisfaction of knowing that the other party has been compelled to account for its conduct before an impartial third person. . . .

"Despite the generally accepted principle that arbitration procedures are necessarily more informal than those of a court of law, objections to evidence on such grounds as that it is hearsay, not the best evidence, or contrary to the parol evidence rule, are still frequently raised in ad hoc arbitration. To the extent that these and similar objections are intended to exclude the proffered evidence, they generally fail. *The arbitrator is interested in getting all the relevant facts that he can; his principal objective is to render a viable decision, and any information that adds to his knowledge of the total situation will almost always be admitted.*" [Italics supplied by court.]

Evidentiary Rules Must Be Announced
Prior to the Hearing

No evidentiary rules were announced prior to the hearing by the Arbitrator nor are there any provisions as to rules or law re evidence or procedure to be applied set forth in the agreement between the parties providing for grievance-arbitration proceedings.

Had the arbitration hearing here involved been a trial in a court of law, the court, on the question of propriety of admission of evidence on rebuttal having been raised and objection sustained, would have expected the party offering the evidence in question to have made an offer of proof as to the allegedly admissible evidence and if denied, to have made a request to re-open its case. However, we are constantly cautioned by the parties and the authorities that the rules of evidence do not apply to an arbitration hearing, at least unless there is some provision for evidentiary procedure to be followed in the written agreement or by the Arbitrator. Respondent argues that the fact the Arbitrator is not *bound* by rules of evidence does not mean that he *must not* follow such rules. The court does not conclude from the authorities that it would be fair to preclude material evidence based on some technical rule of evidence without some warning that the rules of evidence or some portion thereof would be followed in the arbitration hearing. . . .

. . . The court concludes, in reviewing the situation presented, that it is concerned with the rights of the respective parties who are presenting their sides of the case, not the niceties of the rule of evidence with respect to rebuttal which was so strenuously argued by counsel. This the court believes should be true particularly where there was no announcement that the rules of evidence or any portion thereof would apply.

Although, as noted above, the rules of the American Arbitration Association are not binding on the parties or the Arbitrator, they do set forth what the parties, when entering into an agreement providing for grievance-arbitration procedure, can expect in the way of their right to present all of their side of the case without regard to the rules of evidence governing court proceedings. The court concludes that both parties have the right to assume that any arbitration hearing in which they may become involved, pursuant to their agreement, will afford them the opportunity of presenting *all* of their material evidence and *that the Arbitrator, before closing the hearing, will inquire of all parties whether they have any further proofs to offer or witnesses to be heard.* Rule 31 of American Arbitration Association.

Procedural Rules Should Not Exclude
Material and Pertinent Evidence

Since rules of evidence are not to be applied, it does not follow that the court should conclude that the right of the petitioner herein to introduce the pertinent testimony of Officer Gottesman should turn on the issue of whether such testimony was proper rebuttal in the circumstances, and this is true although the arbitration proceeding does require a degree of formality, though not that required in courts of law. Shulman, *Reason, Contract, and Law in Labor Relations*, 68 Harv. L. Rev., 1016–1017 (1955). At page 1017 of his article, Dean Shulman states with regard to rules of procedure in arbitration hearings:

"Rules of procedure which assure adequate opportunity to each party to prepare for and meet the other's contentions, or rules designed to encourage full consideration and effort at adjustment in the prior stages of the grievance procedure may be quite desirable. But they should not be such as to prevent full presentation of the controversy to the arbitrator before he is required to make final decision. For that would not only limit his resources for sound judgment, but would tend also to create dissatisfaction with the system."

No one questions that the parties have the right to introduce material and pertinent evidence. The testimony of Officer Gottesman was such evidence. It was precluded as not proper rebuttal and because it was not offered as a part of the petitioner's case in chief. The court is now confronted with the question of whether, in the circumstances, the petitioner had a fair hearing.

Error of law on the part of the Arbitrator would not warrant vacation of the Award. It follows that although the testimony of Officer Gottesman be deemed proper rebuttal, that would not be grounds for the relief sought by petitioner.

Judicial Rules of Evidence Should Not
Be Applied without Prior Warning

Whether there was a fair hearing is another matter. The refusal by the Arbitrator to hear all of the testimony of Officer Gottesman or to consider his testimony in making his Award turned on a rule of evidence which the court concludes should not have been binding on petitioner in the absence of some warning by the Arbitrator as to the evidentiary rules to be followed. The failure to receive and consider the material and pertinent testimony in the circumstances appears to have denied to the petitioner a fair hearing. Although the refusal to hear or consider the testimony of Officer Gottesman be assumed correct as not being proper rebuttal under the rules of evidence, since such rules are not to apply, the refusal to hear and consider the pertinent and material evidence also reflects an unfair hearing in violation of Title 9, United States Code, S. 10(c).

Respondent says that in approximately 99% of all arbitration cases the parties are represented by non-attorneys. The fact that the parties in the instant matter are represented by lawyers should not alter their rights to offer all material evidence at the hearing unless the Arbitrator made known the fact he would follow certain evidentiary procedure, which was not complied with by a party.

The respondent urges that the Arbitrator did not refuse to hear evidence pertinent or material to the controversy but "rather *insisted upon compliance with the simple rules applied uniformly in court proceedings with respect to order of case procedure."* [Italics supplied by court.]

Had the Arbitrator announced at the commencement of the hearing that since both sides were represented by lawyers he would expect them to comply with the rules applied uniformly in court proceedings or stated other evidentiary rules he would apply, the petitioner would be in a different position.

Courts Do Not Review the Merits of Arbitral Awards

The courts, of course, have no business weighing the merits of the grievance or reviewing the merits of an arbitration Award. Findings of the Arbitrator as to the facts or his interpretation of the law are not to be questioned by the court and obvious error in either is not grounds for vacating the Award *if* there has not been refusal to hear pertinent and material evidence *and* the hearing has been fair. . . .

In *Central Packing Co. of Kansas, Inc. vs. United Packinghouse Workers of America*, 195 F. Supp. 188 (D.C. Kan., 1961), the court, at page 192 of its opinion, states:

"A reasonable construction of any collective bargaining agreement is that the parties intend the arbitrators of their grievances to adjudicate within some procedural rubric. Although it was agreed that the arbitration decisions were to be final and binding upon the parties, implicit in such an agreement was the concept of decisions reached by a fair means."

To repeat, the issue before the court in the instant case is, did the Arbitrator consider all the pertinent and relevant evidence offered in arriving at his Award and was the hearing from an over-all concept fair to both parties, not whether the testimony of Officer Gottesman was or was not proper rebuttal, or whether the respondent did or did not throw a stone. . . .

Court Quotes Arbitrator Block in a Similar Case

There are exhibits and testimony received at the hearing on the motion to vacate which establish that in three prior arbitration hearings involving the within petitioner and the same strike, testimony of witnesses of petitioner, called after the respondent had rested his or her case, was admitted without objection except in the Matter of Anaya where the same objection was overruled. As stated above, in those matters the respondent Union was represented by home office lawyers of the Union, of which Mr. Lipson was one, and the witnesses called, as noted above, testified to substantially similar facts as the petitioner's witnesses in its case in chief.

When Mr. Lipson raised the specific issue as to rebuttal testimony in a subsequent hearing in the matter of Bertha M. [a dismissed employee in another arbitration under the same strike-settlement agreement], had on November 15, 1966, in which Mr. Tallent appeared for the petitioner, the Arbitrator, Mr. Block, in that hearing observed:

"Mr. Block: Mr. Lipson, I think you are urging the procedure to be followed that is not customarily followed or adhered to by most arbitrators and certainly not by this arbitrator. It has always been my view, and I think a view shared by most arbitrators with whom I am familiar, that the basic purpose of an arbitration hearing is to make certain that both parties are permitted to set before the arbitrator all the facts that have a bearing on the issue, not being particularly concerned whether it is labeled as coming in under the case in chief or rebuttal. So that when that question has arisen in the past I have not been overly concerned with the particular sequence, except that I think in terms of following orderly procedure I would urge the Company to put on its complete case as it sees it in chief but I certainly would not consider either the Company or the Union estopped from adding later evidence or testimony or documents, as the case may be, if it felt that such material was important to the ultimate decision in the case." (Ex. 12, pg. 4, line 22 to line 13, pg. 5.)

Again at page 75, lines 1 to 11, of Exhibit 12, the Arbitrator stated:

"Mr. Block: All right. Let's have it out now. Let me tell you what my practice has been in conducting a fairly sizeable number of arbitrations. Generally after each side has rested and just before the hearing is closed, I normally turn to counsel on each side and ask them if there is anything further. If they feel that there is anything further that might have been overlooked or whatever, then I let it come in. I am not concerned with affixing a label as to whether or not it's rebuttal or case in chief. I don't see any real reason for departing from that procedure in this case."

This procedure conforms to Rule 31 of the rules of the American Arbitration Association.

Certainly no party to an agreement providing for grievance-arbitration proceedings would be of the opinion it had received a fair hearing in a proceeding in which one of its eye witnesses to the incident involved was not allowed to testify or wherein his testimony was disregarded. Arbitration is encouraged by both state and federal governments. If employers and unions concerned are to engage in agreements providing for arbitration, they must have complete confidence in the proceeding. The denial of admission of material evidence on the grounds it was not proper rebuttal would be of no solace to the losing party who had been given to understand that arbitration hearings were informal proceedings not governed by the rules of evidence applied in court trials.

Orderly Procedures, Not Legal Technicalities, Should Prevail

This does not mean that the Arbitrator may not insist on orderly proceedings but it does not appear that legalistic technicalities are to prevail or control particularly where no statement of ground rules for the hearing is made by the Arbitrator in the initial stages. Likewise, the fact one's lawyer did not offer the testimony of an important witness at the proper time is little consolation to the party who might suffer. He knows that the hearing must be fair and certainly the party should not be penalized.

The Code of Ethics for Arbitrators, adopted by the American Arbitration Association, provides:

"The Arbitrator should allow a fair hearing, with full opportunity to the parties to offer all evidence which they deem reasonably material. He may, however, exclude evidence which is clearly immaterial."

In determining the next step to be taken in this matter, it is important to consider the need to bring arbitration proceedings to a conclusion as soon as reasonably possible. Such must be accomplished if disenchantment with arbitration in general is to be avoided.

Case Remanded Back to Arbitrator by Court

Petitioner cites Sections 1286.2, 1287 and 1288 (before 1961 Amendment) of the California Code of Civil Procedure, as authority for the remanding of the case to a new Arbitrator for re-hearing. It appears to the court that Mr. Pollard, who has heard all of the evidence to date, is the logical one to hear further evidence in accordance with the within Opinion and Order. . . .

For the reasons set forth above, it is hereby ordered, adjudged and decreed that the petition to vacate the Award herein is granted. The matter is remanded to Arbitrator Pollard for the taking of the testimony of Officer Gottesman, which the court finds to be pertinent and material, and such other evidence, if any, as the Arbitrator may deem appropriate in the circumstances, and the making of such Award as he deems proper after consideration of all the pertinent and material evidence.

The above Memorandum Opinion shall be deemed compliance with any Findings of Fact and Conclusions of Law that may be required under the provisions of Rule 52, Federal Rules of Civil Procedure.[9]

Credibility Is Solely Up to the Arbitrator

We proceed now to a discussion of what is perhaps the single most important criterion for evaluating testimony in an arbitration proceeding—the criterion of credibility. A score of witnesses can testify "yea" contradicting a lone witness who testifies "nay" on the same point of issue. It is the arbitrator's prerogative, if he is so inclined, to say, "I believe the one witness who testified 'nay,' and I do not believe all the other witnesses who testified 'yea.'" An arbitrator can accept the testimony of a single witness to tip the scales against a mountain of evidence which contradicts the witness he believes.

To illustrate more concretely, we present, in abridged form, three arbitrations which were decided on sheer credibility. All three cases involved discharges of women pickets for alleged misconduct in the Harvey Aluminum strike just discussed, and were arbitrated in accordance with the pertinent provisions of the written strike-settlement agreement. Strike-misconduct criteria warranting discharge were spelled out in section IX, paragraphs 2(A) and 2(B), of the agreement. The arbitrator had no authority to reduce the discharge penalty by prescribing a lesser penalty such as suspension or a reprimand. He could either sustain the discharge under paragraphs 2(A) and 2(B) or, if the grievant were found innocent of strike misconduct, order reinstatement and decide the amount of lost wages owed by the company. The following selections from the written arbitration opinions in the cases are sufficient to give a clear, unadorned picture of how the credibility principle is invoked to reach a decision:

CASE NO. 1: THE DISCHARGE OF BELLE M.

Company witnesses were Brewster, a company security guard, and Mendoza, employed by Wackenhut Security. Quoting from the arbitrator's findings and conclusions:

> We come now to the incident of July 28, when the Grievant was allegedly observed throwing a golf ball which hit a police officer. It is undisputed that this constitutes strike misconduct as defined in Paragraph 2 (A), if proved. The charge is categorically denied by the Grievant.

[9] *Harvey Aluminum, Inc. v. United Steelworkers,* U.S. District Court, Central District of California, No. 66-1426-EC, Memorandum Opinion and Order Granting Motion to Vacate Arbitration Award and Remand to Arbitrator for Re-hearing, pp. 4–6, 8–16, Judge E. A. Crary, 263 F. Supp. 488 (1967).

The issue is entirely one of credibility. There is very little disagreement about the circumstances and events of this particular evening. Mr. Brewster was stationed at B Gate during the period in question. There were about 75 to 100 people standing in the vicinity of the Company flagpole, which is approximately 10 feet north of B Gate. The flagpole is embedded in a concrete block, approximately 4 feet square, which is slightly raised above the ground level. The Grievant was standing next to the flagpole on this concrete block. The area was well illuminated. Brewster testified that he saw the Grievant throwing a white object "about the size of a golf ball" and she was promptly arrested. Mr. Mendoza identified the object as a golf ball; he saw it strike a police officer; while he did not see who threw the golf ball, his testimony corroborates that of Brewster in all other respects.

The Arbitrator is persuaded that these two men described precisely what they saw without coloring their observations one way or the other. He finds their testimony, coupled with a consideration of the sequence of events which followed, convincing beyond doubt as to the accuracy of the incident which they described.[10]

Accordingly, the arbitrator ruled that the grievant, Belle M., did engage in strike misconduct as that term appeared in article IX, paragraph 2(A).

CASE NO. 2: THE DISCHARGE OF DORIS M.

In the second case Doris M. was charged with two separate and distinct acts of misconduct. Although both charges were the subject of a single arbitration proceeding, they were treated separately to avoid confusion. The arbitrator observed that if it were determined that both charges fell in the category of paragraph 2(A) and/or paragraph 2(B) of article IX of the strike-settlement agreement, then the grievant need only be found guilty of one charge for the dismissal to be upheld.

The focus of Doris M.'s alleged misconduct was upon her activities while picketing the plant between the hours of 5 and 8 A.M. on April 5, 1965, the first day of the strike. On one count, she was charged with punching an employee named Pitchford four times on his side as he tried to cross the picket line to enter the plant. Second, it was charged that during the same period of time she placed a cup of coffee in the jacket pocket of Mrs. Frie, another employee who was crossing the picket line to enter the plant.

In examining the record in the Pitchford incident, the arbitrator noted that the disposition of this incident turned upon two factors: (1) the credibility of opposing witnesses Pitchford and Doris M., and (2) whether offenses charged fell within the arbitrator's authority under paragraph 2(A)

---

[10] *Harvey Aluminum, Inc. v. United Steelworkers,* Dec. 22, 1966, CCH 66-3 Arb., § 9001, Arbitrator Howard S. Block.

and/or paragraph 2(B) or fell within paragraph 2(C), which was outside the arbitrator's authority.

Mr. Pitchford testified that as he proceeded to go through the picket line on the morning of April 5, he was jostled, pushed, struck on the jaw, and hit about four times on the side. He further testified that the pressure of the crowd in shoving and pushing made him fall to the ground, breaking his lunch box and thermos bottle, and caused his glasses to be knocked down. At the arbitration hearing, Mr. Pitchford made a positive identification of the grievant as the person who punched him four times on the side, but he absolved her of any involvement in the pushing and shoving which resulted in the tumble he took.

Doris M. denied any physical contact with Mr. Pitchford. She testified that there were several other women milling about in the same area and suggested that in the confusion a case of mistaken identity was easily possible. In direct testimony, she answered the questions of the union attorney as follows:

> **Q.** You remember Mr. Pitchford testifying at the last hearing?
> **A.** Very well. Very well.
> **Q.** Did you see Mr. Pitchford fall down or see him knocked down or anything like that?
> **A.** No, sir, I did not.
> **Q.** Do you recall being in contact with Mr. Pitchford or any other employee, that is, in terms of pushing him, jostling him, kneeing him, or anything like that?
> **A.** No, sir, I did not.[11]

Credibility Is More Intuition than Logic

In his findings, the arbitrator stated:

> Other than such testimony pro and con by partisan witnesses, there is little in the record which casts additional light upon what actually happened. The disposition of this charge boils down to a matter of sheer credibility, and in the Arbitrator's judgment, the credibility of the key witnesses Pitchford and the grievant. Here the Arbitrator must venture on a subjective terrain which is fraught with uncertainty. Allowing that his impressions are rooted more in intuition than in logic, there is little else in the record on which he can reply. Mr. Pichford's testimony appeared to be restrained and limited. He did not accuse Doris M., as he could easily have, of pushing him to the ground. His identification of her as the person who punched him on the side four times was forthright and unequivocal. His testimony had, as the saying goes, a ring of truth

[11] *Harvey Aluminum, Inc. v. United Steelworkers*, Jan. 27, 1967, CCH 67-1 Arb., § 8085, Arbitrator Paul Prasow.

to it. It tipped the scales of credibility in his favor. The Arbitrator finds, accordingly, that the grievant did punch him as alleged.

Proceeding now to the second factor in the Pitchford incident: whether the punches of a specific woman, Doris M., were of sufficient potency to fall within the category of Paragraphs 2 (A) and/or 2 (B). Doris M. is a woman of average size and hardly of a type considered masculine or even athletic. If Mr. Pitchford were a man of average size, or at least of a sinewy or wiry build, the Arbitrator would be constrained to rule that Miss M.'s offense belonged distinctly in the category of Paragraph 2 (C), which is outside his authority. But Mr. Pitchford weighs less than 110 pounds and is exceedingly frail in build. He would not appear to be immune from damage of a substantial or at least disturbing nature even from the punches of a woman of undoubted femininity as Doris M. is. Accordingly, the Arbitrator rules that the griev-ant's actions fall within the category defined in Paragraph 2 (A), not to speak of Paragraph 2 (B), a category which is considered moot for the disposition of this case.

The other charge of misconduct in the Frie incident also becomes moot, in the Arbitrator's opinion, since the culpability of the grievant in the Pitchford incident is sufficient to sustain the dismissal.[12]

CASE NO. 3: THE DISCHARGE OF MARY H.

The third case involved a charge that on April 19, while picketing, Mary H. sprayed paint on various employees from a spray paint can which she had concealed under her coat. In his findings, the arbitrator observed that:

> The incident of the paint can on April 19, where bodily contact was made by spraying paint, a skin irritant to many and damaging to garments, unquestionably falls within paragraph 2 (A) if proved, not to speak of paragraph 2 (B). No weight can be given the motion picture of the incident. The Arbitrator was unable to make a positive identification of the Grievant, and neither was the Company except by inference from the general contours of a culpable woman in the film—an inference which cannot be considered sufficient proof.
>
> At this point the charge boils down to the credibility of two key wit-nesses: Mr. Brewster [plant guard] who unequivocally identified Mary H. as the person he had seen use the spray can a number of times before reporting her to a police officer; and Mary H., the Grievant, who flatly denied possession or use of the spray can. If there had been some doubt in the Arbitrator's mind that Mr. Brewster's testimony was delib-erately slanted or that his vision had been obscured by the turbulent scene of the incident, he would be bound to resolve that doubt in favor of the Grievant. But Mr. Brewster's testimony had the ring of truth to it. It was convincing. Arbitrators do not, as a rule, like to decide cases on

[12] *Ibid.*, p. 3305.

> purely subjective standards of the credibility of witnesses. But, in the instant case, the Arbitrator is convinced beyond personal doubt that Mr. Brewster gave an accurate account of the incident.[13]

After evaluating the record, the arbitrator ruled that Mary H. engaged in strike misconduct as that term was defined in section IX, paragraph 2(A).

In all three preceding cases the sword of credibility was wielded summarily to cut the Gordian knot of directly conflicting testimony. The arbitrator said flatly that he believed one witness and did not believe another. Also worth noting in cases no. 2 and 3 are the unconcealed misgivings of the respective arbitrators at the uncertainty and the subjective unreliability of credibility as a decisive criterion for an arbitral award. As so aptly put by UCLA law professor Edgar A. Jones, Jr.:

> Anyone driven by the necessity of decision to fret about credibility, who has listened over a number of years to sworn testimony, knows that as much truth must have been uttered by shifty-eyed, perspiring, lip-licking, nail-biting, guilty-looking, ill at ease, fidgety witnesses as have lies issued from calm, collected, imperturbable, urbane, straight-in-the-eye perjurers.[14]

Credibility Checklist

In the same report Jones enumerates eleven factors listed in the California Evidence Code to be considered when listening to a witness testify:

1 "his demeanor while testifying and the manner in which he testifies"
2 "the character of his testimony"
3 "the extent of his capacity to perceive, to recollect, or to communicate any matter about which he testifies"
4 "the extent of his opportunity to perceive any matter about which he testifies"
5 "his character for honesty or veracity or their opposites"
6 "the existence or nonexistence of a bias, interest, or other motive"
7 "a statement previously made by him that is consistent with his statement at the hearing"
8 "a statement made by him that is inconsistent with any part of his testimony at the hearing"
9 "the existence or nonexistence of any fact testified to by him"
10 "his attitude toward the action in which he testifies or toward the giving of testimony"
11 "his admission of untruthfulness.[15]

[13] *Harvey Aluminum, Inc. v. United Steelworkers,* Aug. 2, 1966, 47 LA 196, 199, Arbitrator Howard S. Block, BNA, Inc.
[14] Edgar A. Jones, Jr., "Problems of Proof in the Arbitration Process: Report of West Coast Tripartite Committee," *Problems of Proof in Arbitration: Proceedings of the Nineteenth Annual Meeting, National Academy of Arbitrators,* BNA, Inc., 1966, p. 208.
[15] *Ibid.,* pp. 207–208.

Sheer Numbers of Witnesses Do Not Establish Credibility

Factor 6 on the checklist should be of particular interest to litigants who assume (hopefully) that a preponderance of evidence can be established by sheer numbers of witnesses. Arbitrators are not persuaded, for example, by the subjective judgment of a foreman which is corroborated by a succession of other supervisors whose testimony is also unsupported by objective facts. The fact that a half-dozen zealous unionists concur with one another's judgment in testimony devoid of objective evidence does not make their statements less self-serving than those of a single shop steward.

If the credibility criteria extracted from the California Evidence Code seem unreliable at best, this unreliability is not the only important reason for a noticeable tendency of arbitrators to be sparing in using the code for resolving conflicting testimony. Not mentioned in any evidence code is the key question of the arbitrator's future acceptability to the parties. When the arbitrator says, "I believe John Doe," he frequently implies, "I do not believe Richard Roe"—which comes very close to calling Richard Roe a liar—a juxtaposition of belief and disbelief hardly conducive to an arbitrator's continued survival. It is much more satisfactory all around when the arbitrator can say: "I really do not know whom to believe in this case, and I decline to decide by intuition. My intuition may be no more than my unconscious bias."

The Tool of Presumption Is Preferred To Credibility Criterion

Rather than make an uneasy, highly uncertain credibility choice between opposing witnesses, an arbitrator will utilize a traditional legal device for determining the facts from conflicting evidence in the record. He will introduce a presumption which places a burden of proof on one of the parties. Presumptions are analytic devices for determining what evidence will be accepted and given full weight and what evidence will be given little or no weight. A presumption puts the burden on one of the parties to produce evidence sufficient to avoid a ruling against that party on the issue. The party shouldering the burden of proof is said to have "the affirmative of the issue," meaning that it is the party that would be defeated if the bare question to be answered were put to the arbitrator and no evidence were given on either side. Arbitrators who are concerned about future acceptability, a problem not shared by the judiciary, derive an additional benefit from the use of presumptions. How much less strained are the arbitrator's relationships with the parties when he can put the affirmative of the issue on Richard Roe and rule that Roe has not sustained the burden of proo instead of making a flat declaration that he believes John Doe and does not believe Richard Roe.

Burden of Proof Must Not Be Imposed Arbitrarily

Burden of proof, it should be emphasized, cannot be placed on a party haphazardly to assure a predetermined verdict; the affirmative of the issue must flow from the inner nature of the issue being contested. Consider, for example, a warehouse employee who was called into the superintendent's office and accused of pilfering merchandise worth $75. The employee wrote out a letter of resignation and left it with the superintendent. Out on the sidewalk the employee met the chief steward returning from his coffee break and told him what had happened.

"You were stampeded," the steward said. "Let's go back and get that resignation."

"Too late," the superintendent told them. "I've already turned it in to the personnel department. It's out of my hands now."

Pilferage, a euphemism for theft, is an act of moral turpitude, and a criminal offense if the company wishes to prosecute. Arbitrators are expected to conduct hearings on the presumption that the employee does not have to prove his innocence. The company has to prove his guilt beyond a reasonable doubt. Throughout the proceedings the employer has what is called "the laboring oar," or more precisely "the ultimate burden of persuasion" that the grievant committed the offense charged.

AFFIRMATIVE OF ISSUE AND ULTIMATE BURDEN OF PERSUASION ARE NOT THE SAME

The term "ultimate" has not been tacked on to "burden of persuasion" as a rhetorical embellishment. There are intermediate points of difference in litigation on which the affirmative of the issue may not lie with the party having the ultimate burden of persuasion. For example, when the case just mentioned came to arbitration and the grievant's letter of resignation was entered as evidence, the first question to be ruled on was, "Did the grievant in fact resign?" An affirmative answer by the arbitrator would have meant that the grievant had forfeited his claim for reinstatement at the outset, rendering moot a disposition of the pilferage charge.

On the witness stand the grievant testified that when confronted unexpectedly with the charge against him, he had been too stunned to think clearly and had allowed himself to be maneuvered into writing a letter of resignation "to keep my record clean." He also insisted that the letter had been handed to the superintendent with the understanding that it was not to be turned in until he had had a chance to talk to the chief steward.

The union urged that no weight be given to the letter because it had been entrusted to the superintendent as a "conditional delivery," that it had been sent to the personnel office while the grievant was still talking to the chief steward, and that, therefore, the condition that could have permitted the letter to be withdrawn had not been met.

The superintendent unequivocally denied that any condition had been attached by the grievant to his letter of resignation. He testified further that the grievant had voluntarily offered the resignation when confronted with the evidence against him, because he knew that his discharge was imminent.

There was no witness to the discussion between the two men, and no plausible basis for assuming a misunderstanding which could reconcile their diametrically opposed versions of how the letter came to be written. Was there a conditional delivery attached to the letter, or did the grievant dream up the condition later to save his job?

Basic Principles for Imposing Affirmative of the Issue

There were too many doubts in the arbitrator's mind to resolve the conflict in testimony on credibility. He therefore found that the affirmative of the issue of whether there had been a conditional delivery lay with the grievant, who had made the assertion. He then ruled that the grievant had failed to sustain the burden of proving that a condition had been imposed on the delivery of the resignation. The ruling was not in itself fatal to the grievant's case. The arbitrator also found that the resignation was not a voluntary act, but had been induced by the threat of immediate discharge, with the implication that resignation would result in a clean record. A forced resignation, according to an established arbitration criterion, is construed as a discharge, and is arbitrated as such. In the ensuing arbitration the ultimate burden of persuasion, that the grievant had been guilty of pilferage, still lay with the employer. In placing the burden on the grievant to prove that there had been a conditional delivery attached to his letter of resignation, the arbitrator was invoking a frequently employed principle of proof: *"that the affirmative of the issue is imposed upon the party whose contentions depart further from normal likelihood."* [Italics supplied.][16]

Suppose, for example, an employee whose shift ends at 4 P.M. goes home at 3:30 P.M. "The foreman said I could" is his excuse. "Just the opposite,"

---

[16] John MacArthur Maguire, *Evidence: Common Sense and Common Law,* The Foundation Press, Inc., Mineola, N. Y., 1947, p. 179.

replies the foreman. "He's twisting our conversation completely around. I told him he couldn't go early." Assuming an arbitrator does not decide the case on straight credibility, he would have to impose the affirmative of the issue on the employee. His normal quitting time is 4 P.M., and it is he who departed from normal likelihood when he clocked out at 3:30 P.M. To rule otherwise would provide a wide-open loophole for employees to fabricate excuses out of whole cloth to escape the consequences of their misconduct by relying on the employer's ultimate burden of persuasion in most discharge cases.

The burden of proof does not always depend on presumptions imposed by arbitrators. A burden-of-proof situation can develop from the sheer weight of evidence produced by one of the parties during the hearings. The evidence becomes so decisively one-sided in favor of a party that the arbitrator could not reasonably find against that party—in which case the burden of producing evidence to avoid an adverse decision falls on the other party. It is not unusual in a strongly contested proceeding for the burden of producing evidence to shift from one side to another.

Charges of Moral Turpitude Must Be Proved beyond Reasonable Doubt

We proceed now to the matter of degree or quantum of proof required for a party to be sustained on an issue. The law distinguishes three basic degrees of proof in the following ascendancy: (1) preponderance of evidence; (2) clear and convincing proof; (3) proof beyond a reasonable doubt. Arbitrators are not quite so precise in their requirements for proof. Pragmatically they draw a line between proof beyond a reasonable doubt and lesser degrees of proof deemed appropriate to the issue but not exactly defined. Proof beyond a reasonable doubt is required as a matter of course in disciplinary cases where an employee is charged with acts of moral turpitude such as theft, subversive activities, or aberrant sexual practices. In this connection Benjamin Aaron, a noted authority on arbitration and labor law, writes:

> Since upholding the disciplinary penalty for these or similar acts permanently brands an employee just as surely as a criminal conviction would, the arbitrator will generally insist in such cases that the employer prove his charges beyond a reasonable doubt.[17]

An arbitral opinion of UCLA professor Harold Somers reviewing the dismissal of an employee for alleged theft states:

[17] Benjamin Aaron, "Some Procedural Problems in Arbitration," *Vanderbilt Law Review*, vol. 10, 1957, p. 742.

Discharge for stealing involves an unfavorable reflection on the *moral* character of the employee which is almost impossible to erase and which will seriously hamper if not altogether prevent his getting a job elsewhere . . . and will even hurt innocent members of his family. He and they are branded for life. The company therefore has a very heavy obligation in such a case. It carries the burden of proving beyond a reasonable doubt—in its own conscience as well as before the arbitrator —that the employee committed the offense of stealing.[18]

THE CASE OF THE IRASCIBLE EMPLOYEE

Virtually all arbitrators share the viewpoint of Aaron and Somers in requiring the most stringent kind of proof to sustain a disciplinary action based on a charge of moral turpitude. But unanimity is notably absent when the issue considered does not involve moral turpitude. On such an issue the degree of proof required will vary according to the importance attached to it by individual arbitrators.

For example, in the newspaper publishing industry, where the application of the seniority principle is not deemed practical in the editorial and circulation departments because of the nature of the work, extremely generous severance pay is provided by contract to discourage layoffs. In fifteen to twenty years of service a rather tempting sum often in excess of $5,000 severance pay will accrue. To inhibit long-service employees who might come to regard the severance money as more important than the job, the contract provides further that eligibility for severance pay shall be forfeited if the employee quits, is dismissed for dishonesty, or provokes his dismissal for the purpose of collecting severance pay.

We present now an abridgement of a case concerned with the dismissal of a newspaper district circulation manager. Pertinent to our discussion was the imposition by the arbitrator of a more stringent degree of proof on the issue involving severance or dismissal pay than on the issue of discharge from the job itself. Of four alternative questions posed to the arbitrator in the submission agreement, three asked for a ruling on the basis for the discharge:

1 Was the discharge of Sherman P. a self-provoked discharge for the purpose of collecting dismissal [severance] pay?
2 Was the discharge of Sherman P. for gross misconduct?
3 Was the discharge of Sherman P. for good and sufficient cause?[19]

---

[18] *Marlin Rockwell Corp. v. United Auto. Workers, Local 338,* June 6, 1955, 24 LA 728, 729–730, Arbitrator Harold M. Somers, BNA, Inc.
[19] *Los Angeles Herald-Examiner, Div. of Hearst Publishing Co. v. Los Angeles Newspaper Guild,* Sept. 2, 1964, CCH 64-3 Arb., § 9218, p. 7244, Arbitrator Paul Prasow.

An affirmative answer to question 1 would mean that the grievant would lose his job and well over $4,000 in dismissal pay. An affirmative answer to question 2 would mean the loss of his job and also $268.40 in notice pay. Question 3 permitted alternatives. An affirmative answer to question 3 coupled with negative answers to questions 1 and 2 would mean the loss of his job but the retention of his dismissal pay and notice pay. Finally, a negative answer to 1 and affirmative answers to 2 and 3 would mean that Sherman P. receives dismissal pay of $4,000, but no notice pay of $268.40.

Arbitral Opinion and Ruling on Question 1

In regard to the first issue, the Company bases its contention that Mr. P's discharge was self-induced on his conduct for the three years he worked at the Cain Branch [referred to as such because Mr. Cain was Sherman P.'s supervisor]. Summarizing its position in the Company brief:

"The Company submits, however, that a person's actions and statements over a period of three years are certainly indicative of his frame of mind . . . and that Sherman's frame of mind was typified by his obsession to be fired and to collect his dismissal pay."

The Union's position may be summarized from its brief as follows:

"Sherman P.'s conduct and language in the events surrounding his discharge were the same as they had been for almost fifteen years, and about which he had never heard any objection, protest, reprimand or warning from the Company.

"Sherman's personality, conduct and performance were known to the Company and it was not shown that there had been any changes after Sherman transferred to the Cain branch."

The Arbitrator has scrutinized the entire record and evaluated the testimony of witnesses carefully before coming to the following conclusion: During the years of his employment since 1949, Sherman P.'s conduct was that of a high-strung, somewhat emotionally unstable individual, whose difficulties were compounded by an impairment in his hearing. Over all, though, despite occasional brushes with management, his job performance seems to have been acceptable until his transfer to the Cain Branch.

The record indicates that at the Cain Branch, Sherman P.'s relationship with supervision deteriorated rapidly. He become increasingly deficient in the performance of his duties, and irascible in his conduct, to a point which suggests an indifference as to whether or not his employment with the Company continued. Clearly his deficient job performance and testiness made for an intolerable situation not only to his supervisors, but no doubt to Sherman P. himself. To acknowledge P.'s indifference to his continued employment with the Company is not the same as suggesting that he actively attempted to induce his dismissal. Admittedly, the line between unmotivated irascibility and disagreeable conduct calculated to provoke dismissal is a fine one, often difficult to prove, but it is a line which must be drawn.

The Arbitrator concedes it is entirely possible, in the light of the grievant's contentious statements and belligerent attitude, that his dismissal may have been self-induced. But considering the generally acknowledged emotional instability of the grievant, other plausible explanations for his deplorable relations with the Cain Branch supervision are possible. In short, there is a reasonable doubt in the mind of the Arbitrator that P.'s dismissal was self-induced. In accordance with established arbitration principles, the Arbitrator must resolve that doubt in favor of the grievant, and rule that the Company has failed to sustain its burden of proof that the dismissal was deliberately, calculatingly, and with malice aforethought provoked by the grievant. Therefore, the Arbitrator answers the first question in the negative, and rules that P.'s discharge was not self-provoked for the purposes of collecting dismissal pay.

Arbitral Opinion and Ruling on Question 2

Proceeding now to the second question, the Arbitrator concurs with the following statement in the Union's brief:

"To sustain the assertion that Sherman P. was discharged for 'gross misconduct' would necessitate proof that Sherman P.'s conduct under the circumstances of the discharge was such as to be highly outrageous and excessive."

Specifically, the review of Sherman P.'s conduct will focus on the events of December 2, 1963. Sherman P. testified that he phoned the office at 9:05 a.m. to report his illness. Cain appears to have returned the call at about 9:45 a.m. Both witnesses testified that an acrid exchange took place between them, which appears to have centered on Cain's dissatisfaction with Sherman P.'s failure to call him at an earlier hour before he (Cain) had left home, thus making it more difficult to locate a substitute. The conversation ended abruptly when Sherman P. hung up. According to Cain, Sherman P.'s parting words were: "I won't argue with you, you son-of-a-bitch."

Sherman P.'s version of the conversation, when he was questioned by the Company, may be found in the following excerpt from the transcript:

Q. Were you absent on December 2, 1963?
A. Yes, I was.
Q. Did you call Mr. Cain at his home that morning?
A. No.
Q. Did you have any discussion with Mr. Cain that morning?
A. Did I have any discussion with him?
Q. Yes.
A. I received a call.

Q. From Mr. Cain?

A. Right.

Q. What did Mr. Cain say?

A. He said, "Why didn't you call me at home?" He said, "I'm having trouble getting somebody over here."

I said, "I called your office at 9:00 o'clock and Neva called me back, trying to get somebody back."

And he started, he said "Why can't you come to work? Are you sick?"

I said, "Yes, I'm sick." And he kept badgering, and I said "Son-of-a-bitch, leave me alone." I said "I'm sick," and I hung up.

Sherman P. also testified he had been absent on some occasions, that the nature of his illness was nerves, causing headaches and a tendency to throw up.

Sherman P. testified further that he was aware of Cain's requirement to call him early at home, rather than later at the office, when it was necessary to be absent. Sherman P. acknowledged that on past occasions one of his reasons for not calling Cain at home was his reluctance to make a toll call, and that, on hearing a statement to this effect from him, Cain "got a little upset." Cain described the situation in the following words:

"It was to notify, to call me at my home or Mr. Wall, we have two men there, one of us, oh, say between 7:00 and 8:00 o'clock. I didn't set up a certain deadline time, it was before, early in the morning, any time. I have even had them call me at 6:00 o'clock in the morning. But it was primarily before 8:00 o'clock to let me know they were unable to work and then I would, naturally, take care of it.

"And I was unable to get Sherman P. to do this. He claimed it was a toll call. He informed me that he didn't go to work until 10:00 o'clock, and that as long as he notified me before he went to work at 10:00 that was all that was necessary. I could not get his cooperation."

Cain admitted he had never told Sherman P. he could call collect. But he testified that he had told Sherman P. he would reimburse him for a phone call if requested.

He also stated he had taken up the problem of calling in absences with the Shop Steward and Mr. P.'s Shop Steward, Max Berger, testified that he was unable to recall a specific discussion with Mr. Cain on this matter. Berger's description of the practice of communicating absences to Mr. Cain was given in the following testimony:

"Well, it's taken for granted that anybody that's going to be sick or that anticipates not showing up that they would get in touch with Mr. Cain as quickly as possible in order for him, to enable him to get a substitute to take his place. This is just a matter of fact. I never even gave it a second thought.

"But, as far as I know, I don't believe I have ever read, acting as a Shop Steward, any specific regulation that you had to do it. I just took it as a matter of course."

Can a Supervisor Enforce Rules of His Own Making?

In the Union's brief, Mr. P.'s failure to call Mr. Cain at home is defended in the following words:

"Cain testified that on six occasions Sherman P. failed to call him at home to report that he was ill and would not come to work, and that on three occasions it 'created a problem.' Cain's testimony is vague as to when or how he instructed Sherman P. in this respect. Sherman P. testified he knew of no such rule. The Company did not make it a written rule, did not effectively attempt to enforce it, did not take any disciplinary action against Sherman P., did not caution or warn him that any future violations would result in discharge. Cain testified 'I never told Sherman P. that he would be discharged.' The Company never filed a grievance with the Guild concerning this alleged failure of Sherman P. to comply with a Company rule. Sherman P. did not fail to notify the Company that he was sick and would not be able to come to work. P.'s starting time was 10:30 a.m. He testified that on December 2, 1963, he phoned the office at 9:05 a.m. to report his illness. We submit that the Company has failed to sustain this allegation, or to prove that P.'s conduct concerning this alleged 'rule' constitutes cause for discharge."

Arbitrator Says Reasonable Rules Must Be Obeyed

The Arbitrator cannot accept this view of the circumstances summarized in the preceding quote, nor share the Union's conclusion. Whether Mr. Cain's insistence that he be called at home was a Company regulation, a personal policy, or merely an accepted practice, it was a reasonable requirement for which he could rightfully expect no less than the full cooperation of the employees under his supervision.

For a supervisor to permit a legitimate exercise of his managerial discretion to be so flagrantly ignored, would constitute an abdication of his responsibility, a failure to maintain the elementary discipline necessary to operate a business. From testimony of witnesses, including Sherman P., the Arbitrator is convinced that the grievant was fully aware of Mr. Cain's requirement on this matter. Although the Company issued no written formal reprimands or warning to Sherman P. (discounting Cain's testimony of a meeting with Max Berger and the grievant on this matter, since Berger was unable to recall such a meeting), there were a number of acrimonious discussions in 1963 between Cain and Sherman P., where Mr. P. was made fully aware of Cain's extreme dissatisfaction over his refusal to comply with the requirement, a refusal which amounted to willful defiance.

Warnings and Reprimands Need Not Always Be Formal

The Union argues that even if Mr. P. failed to call Cain at home, his dismissal was arbitrary because no warnings or reprimands had previously been given to him. Evidently the Union means that no *formal* warnings or reprimands had preceded Mr. P.'s dismissal. It seems to the Arbitrator that this contention must be evaluated in the light of the basic purpose of warnings and reprimands. In the Arbitrator's opinion, they are not mere formalities, but are intended to put the employee on notice as to his alleged misconduct, and to give him a genuine opportunity to improve before the Company resorts to more serious disciplinary penalties.

Even though formal reprimands and warnings may not have been issued to Mr. P., the record indicates he was given adequate opportunity to rehabilitate himself. It is clear from the record that Mr. Cain had several discussions with Mr. P. in futile attempts (among other things) to enlist his cooperation in phoning Cain's home in the event of Sherman P.'s anticipated absence from work. The fact that these discussions descended into mere wrangling does not absolve Mr. P. from his failure to respond and correct the lack of cooperation in his conduct.

In the Arbitrator's opinion, Supervision met its obligation to try corrective measures and apply rehabilitative pressures on Mr. P. before terminating him. Although Mr. P. may have tried to improve, his negative pattern of behavior seemed to persist despite these efforts.

Insofar as the telephone conversation of December 2, 1963, between Sherman P. and Cain is concerned, it is only necessary to accept the grievant's version as accurate, excluding any reference to Mr. Cain's testimony on this matter. Even allowing for Mr. P.'s illness and irascibility, one cannot avoid the conclusion that the grievant exceeded the bounds of propriety in that situation.

In the Arbitrator's opinion, Sherman P.'s apparently inflexible, determined refusal to cooperate with Mr. Cain in what appears to be a reasonable requirement can only be described as gross misconduct.[20] Accordingly, the arbitrator ruled that:

1 The discharge of Sherman P. was not a self-provoked discharge for the purposes of collecting dismissal pay.
2 The discharge of Sherman P. was for gross misconduct.
3 The discharge of Sherman P. was for good and sufficient cause.
4 Under the Contract, Mr. P. was entitled to receive dismissal pay in accordance with Article V, Sections 1, 2 and 3.[21]

Criminal Court Proceedings Are Relevant But Not Binding

We have included in our discussion a number of arbitrations on charges which could have led to criminal prosecution, but did not. The question now suggests itself, what effect, if any, would the findings of a criminal court have on an arbitration proceeding? Jones suggests:

> The standards of proof, the relevant policies at issue, the cost of judgment of the triers of fact, and the environment in which the respective hearings take place are sufficiently different to warrant the conclusion

20 *Ibid.*, pp. 7245–7248.
21 *Ibid.*, p. 7248.

that a decision in one tribunal should not bind the other, although it should be admissible as relevant evidence.[22]

THE CASE OF THE EMPLOYEE ACQUITTED IN COURT

Consider the case of Jack T., who was arrested with another employee en route home from work and booked on suspicion of burglary involving the theft of nickel anodes owned by his employer. Both men were discharged by the company before their court trials. The other employee was subsequently convicted of two counts of grand theft. Jack T. was acquitted. He was immediately reinstated with full seniority by the company, but he promptly filed a grievance claiming four months back pay for time off the job. There follows now an abridgement of the arbitrator's findings and conclusions on the issue:

> It is clear from the record that the discharge of Jack T. took place against a background of repeated disappearances of valuable nickel anodes and several different attempts on the part of the Company to apprehend the individuals involved. There is no doubt that the Company acted in good faith when it terminated the grievant for the reason given. The Company has a legitimate interest in protecting its property from loss by theft, as well as the right to take disciplinary action against those found guilty of wrongdoing. And with these objectives the Union states it is in full agreement. However good faith is not sufficient to establish just cause for a discharge. In terminating the grievant at the time of his arrest, the Company acted on the assumption that he was guilty of theft, and that this could be proved. However, this assumption did not materialize. Despite the Company's firm conviction that the grievant was guilty, the charges of theft against him were not established beyond a reasonable doubt in a court of law.

Judicial Determination of Innocence Is Often Decisive

> While the burden of proof is higher in a criminal proceeding than in a civil proceeding, such as an arbitration case, the effect of a judicial determination of innocence would place a greater burden on the Company than is usual or customary in arbitration when attempting to establish just cause for discharge. The record in this case would indicate that the Company has failed to sustain this burden of proof. The Arbitrator has examined the record carefully, including the transcript of the proceedings of the Court trial, and is of the opinion that he cannot disregard the effect of the criminal proceedings which determined that the

---

[22] Edgar A. Jones, Jr., "Problems of Proof in the Arbitration Process: Report of West Coast Tripartite Committee," *Problems of Proof in Arbitration: Proceedings of the Nineteenth Annual Meeting, National Academy of Arbitrators,* BNA, Inc., 1966, p. 206.

grievant was innocent of the charges lodged against him. Temporary suspension would have preserved his status pending findings of the court.

The Company argues that it should not be required to retain employees on the payroll who are considered poor employment risks, as Management believed Jack T. to be at the time of his arrest. Unquestionably, the Company has the right to make the decision as to whether an employee should be terminated in such a situation. That is a fundamental management prerogative inherent in the responsibility to operate the plant facilities safely and efficiently. However, the Company must be at the same time aware of the risk that if its judgment proves to be in error, and just cause cannot be established through due process, it may be required to reinstate the terminated employee with all rights unimpaired, possibly including back pay. In this case, the Company has been unable to establish the charge of theft made against Jack T. And the Company has voluntarily reinstated Jack T. in his old job with full seniority rights following receipt of the Court's decision clearing him of the charges. Having not been proven guilty, he must be presumed innocent. And if innocent, he should not suffer any penalties for wrongdoing. By depriving the grievant of back pay, the Company is in effect imposing a financial penalty on him for a form of misconduct which it has been unable to establish by clear and convincing evidence. The specific charge made against Jack T. by the Company at the time of his discharge was violation of Rule No. 19 involving theft of Company property. The Company cannot escape the consequences of its failure to prove this charge.[23]

THE DISCHARGE OF BERTRAM X.

The grievant's discharge for strike misconduct on the picket line presented an especially interesting arbitral problem because of two exhibits entered into the record, either one of which would have been controlling had it not been counterbalanced by the other. One was a photograph, quite damaging to the grievant's case, of a violent encounter between a group of pickets and a carload of nonstrikers, showing the grievant, his body halfway into the car, with an arm encircling the driver's neck. The other exhibit was a transcript of criminal court proceedings which had acquitted Bertram X. of charges arising out of the picket-line incident. The arbitrator's findings and conclusions now follow:

> In this case . . . the testimony of witnesses is sharply conflicting. It is not unexpected that in a situation so highly tensed and charged with emotion, eye witness accounts of the incidents should diverge so widely.

[23] *Rheem Automotive Co. v. United Auto. Workers, Local 509,* Dec. 17, 1956, 27 LA 863, 866, Arbitrator Paul Prasow, BNA, Inc.

In such situations the Arbitrator can only make the best judgment possible.

In their presentations both parties attempted to reconstruct the incident on the basis of what they considered to be the most likely sequence of events. The Union states that on the basis of testimony and admitted conjecture of what must have happened, Mr. X stooped down below the top of the car while attempting to take a picture of the passengers; while he was in this position, the car door was suddenly opened, probably by someone on the inside. At this point, Bertram X was ". . . either pushed in or tripped . . . so that he fell forward and into the car door."

The Arbitrator has carefully examined the entire record in this case, and believes that such an occurrence is remotely possible, but highly unlikely. The photographs of the encounter, introduced as exhibits by the Company, are of particular interest in this regard. Photographic exhibit 7 g-2 shows the situation after the door on the driver's side had been opened. In this picture Bertram X is standing alongside the car bent over, and the upper part of his body is thrust far inside the car, and his left hand is around the driver's neck. Despite the divergence of testimony of various witnesses, the Arbitrator is persuaded that photographic exhibit 7 g-2 depicts a fairly accurate portrayal of the situation. It is difficult for the Arbitrator to believe, in light of this picture and others, that Bertram X was either pushed or tripped or fell into the car. Accordingly, the Arbitrator is of the opinion that Bertram X was the aggressor in this case.

Judicial Determination of Innocence Is Not Always Decisive

The Union states that Bertram X has already been tried in a criminal court, and acquitted of charges arising out of the same incident. In this connection, the Union has introduced into the record a transcript of the court proceedings in which Bertram X was found not guilty of violating Sections 242 and 594 of the Penal Code. The Union asserts that since he has been cleared of these charges by a court, he should not be found guilty of the same charges by an Arbitrator.

In this connection, the Arbitrator agrees fully with the statement made by Arbitrator Simkin in a series of discharge cases which he decided, involving alleged misconduct on the picket line:

"Similarly, a 'not guilty' or 'guilty' finding in a court proceeding is not necessarily a compelling reason for the Arbitrator to make the same finding in the instant cases. A court decision is a finding as to whether an individual is guilty or innocent of violation of some particular stature. That is not the issue in these proceedings. The question here is whether there is 'just cause' for discharge or suspension." [*Westinghouse Elec. Corp. v. Int'l Union of Elec., Radio & Mach. Workers*, July 27, 1956, 26 LA 836, 842, Arbitrator William E. Simkin, BNA, Inc.]

The issue in the Bertram X case is: Did his action while engaged as a picket constitute misconduct? In the Arbitrator's opinion, based upon the evidence in the record, the question must be answered in the affirmative, and, accordingly, his discharge is sustained.[24]

SUMMARY

Arbitration is a quasi-judicial process, meaning that legal criteria of contract interpretation and legal rules of evidence may be applied more flexibly in an arbitration proceeding than in a court of law. The quasi-judicial nature of arbitration can be delineated by focusing on questions of evidence and proof. *Evidence* is the medium of proof, something submitted that furnishes proof. *Proof* is the effect or the result of evidence, the establishment of a judgment by evidence.

There are two contrasting systems of adjudication, the *adversary* and the *judicial-inquiry* methods. In the first, the adjudicator decides the case based on the record made by the contending parties or advocates. Under the second system, an investigating magistrate first conducts his own independent subsidiary proceeding to determine the truth of the matter and make recommendations. Arbitrators in the United States have generally steered a middle ground between these two systems, although the trend is clearly in the direction of the adversary method.

The most important criterion for evaluating testimony of a witness in an arbitration proceeding is that of *credibility*—the witness's believability. The arbitrator may believe one witness and disbelieve a multitude of others who give conflicting testimony. It is entirely within the arbitrator's judgment which testimony he will accept and which he will reject.

In cases where it is difficult to determine the credibility of opposing witnesses, the arbitrator may utilize a useful legal device for determining the facts. He may introduce a *presumption* which places the burden of proof on one of the parties. A presumption is an analytic device for determining the weight to be given to evidence. A presumption puts the burden on one of the parties to produce evidence sufficient to avoid a ruling against that party on the issue. The burden of proof may not be imposed arbitrarily, but must flow from the inner nature of the issue under consideration.

Having the affirmative of the issue is not the same as having the ultimate burden of persuasion. *The affirmative of the issue* is imposed on the party whose contention on a particular fact situation departs further from normal likelihood—although an arbitral ruling on that fact situation may not in itself decide the case. *The ultimate burden of persuasion* rests with

---

[24] *Vickers Inc. v. Int'l Union of Elec., Radio & Mach. Workers*, Aug. 4, 1962, 39 LA 614, 616–617, Arbitrator Paul Prasow, BNA, Inc.

the party having the "laboring oar" in the case as a whole, in the fundamental issue to be decided—the party which has the duty of producing evidence to sustain its position on the basic issue of the case.

Depending on the case, there are three degrees of proof which may be imposed upon a party to be sustained on an issue: (1) preponderance of the evidence; (2) clear and convincing proof; (3) proof beyond a reasonable doubt. In general, proof beyond a reasonable doubt is required by most arbitrators in disciplinary cases where the employee is charged with acts of moral turpitude. In most other cases, a preponderance of the evidence or clear and convincing proof is sufficient for a party to be sustained on the issue. The degree of proof will vary according to the importance attached to the specific issue of the case by the arbitrator.

In cases involving charges of criminal conduct against an employee, there is an essential difference in function between a court of law and the arbitrator. The judge is concerned with enforcing statutory policy or legislative purpose, whereas the arbitrator is interpreting a private agreement to effectuate the mutual intent of the parties. Since different criteria are applicable, it is not inconsistent for a judge to acquit a man on a criminal charge and for the charge later to constitute the basis for a "just cause" dismissal in the employment relationship.

Chapter 11

Managerial discretion: criteria for arbitral review

When Contract Is Silent or General

■ We proceed now to a discussion of the most important single presumption invoked to review managerial action when either the contract is silent or its language is too general for interpretation—the presumption that managerial discretion must be exercised reasonably and with a degree of prudence befitting the circumstances. It is important to note that the arbitrator is not called upon to review the wisdom of management's action. He might say to the employer: "I think you have acted unwisely, and if I had been in your place I would have acted differently. But the fact is, I am not in your place. It is your responsibility, not mine, to manage the enterprise, and I will not substitute my judgment for your own as to the wisdom of what you did.[1] I will, however, subject it to the test of reasonableness—review your exercise of managerial discretion to determine whether it has been arbitrary, capricious, or discriminatory." The application of these latter three criteria

---

[1] For example, in upholding an employer's decision to hire from the outside to fill a vacancy rather than promote from within, one arbitrator said he thought this was an unwise personnel practice, but that it did not appear to be a violation of the agreement.

is specifie tests of reasonableness is nowhere more clearly demonstrated than n the area of employee discipline and discharge.

THE CASE OF THE MANNING OF SKIMMERS

But first, we shall consider a case which was highly confusing to Arbitrator Prasow until a careful analysis of the record balanced out the contentions of he parties, leaving him with nothing to review except the wisdom of management's action, which he declined to do. The dispute took place at a copper-smelter plant over the manning of reverberatory furnaces. The employee classification at issue was called "skimmer." The company had assigned one skimmer to service four furnaces on the day in question. The union contended the management was bound by an oral agreement (resulting from an earlier work stoppage) and by past practice to assign one skimmer to each furnace. The company insisted that the assignment of one skimmer to four furnaces was consistent with its past practice and denied the union's version of the oral agreement.

Colloquy between the Authors

"In reading your written opinion, Paul, I had no trouble with your logic, he principles of proof you invoked, but I must say that the arguments over manning you reported were mumbo jumbo—too technical for me. I never did understand the real nature of the job in question."

"You've got nothing on me, Pete. I blinked when I read from the union's statement of the grievance that 'several men were required to perform work in the reverberatory department on the first down day of a six-day operation. Four furnaces were on holding fires, two slag trains were operating, slag was being tapped from two of these reverbs, and supervision had only one skimmer assigned to do this work,' etc., etc., etc. Then he witnesses got into the fine points of the operation, and I got even more confused. When I asked questions, they really lost me. When I asked to see the job, neither party thought it was necessary, implying that the issue could be decided without seeing the job. I took the hint and dropped the suggestion."

"And yet without knowing the job you were able to decide the issue?"

"Yes, it was like solving an algebraic equation without knowing the actual value of the x's and y's."

In deciding the matter, the arbitrator sought to reach a conclusion by applying basic principles of proof until all the mutually conflicting evidence balanced out. In essence, the case raised three basic questions:

1 Was there an oral agreement between the parties which required the company to assign a skimmer to each furnace under the conditions existing on
December 17, 1962?
2 Was there an established past practice whereby a skimmer was always
assigned to each furnace on a standby, or holding-fire basis?
3 Did the company violate the terms of the collective-bargaining agreement
when it did not assign a skimmer to each of the four furnaces on December 17, 1962?

Regarding the alleged oral agreement, the evidence was both conflicting
and inconclusive. The union maintained that during a similar dispute a
meeting was held in September, 1962, between company and union representatives which resulted in an oral agreement. According to a union witness:

> My understanding was that whenever there was a furnace with a holding
> fire, if any adjustments were to be made on that fire, any of the work
> that the skimmer normally does, that is done on that furnace, then a
> skimmer would be placed; or if there were any men working on that
> furnace, then a skimmer would be placed on the furnace. That was our
> understanding of the Company's position.[2]

On its part, the company denied such an oral agreement was ever reached,
and insisted it was never the intention to always assign a skimmer to each
furnace on a holding-fire basis. The company acknowledged that it agreed
to assign a skimmer if actual skimmer work had to be performed or if craft
employees were doing repair work upon the furnace. However, neither of
these conditions was present on December 17, 1962, according to the company.

Neither Party Could Prove Its Version
Of Oral Understanding

The arbitrator reviewed the record thoroughly and was unable to resolve
to his satisfaction the conflict on this point. Neither party had been able to
sustain the burden of proof as to its particular version of the oral agreement.
There were numerous assertions by partisan witnesses as to their understanding of the oral agreement, but these statements were insufficient and inconclusive in establishing that a mutual meeting of minds took place on either
party's version of the nature and scope of the oral agreement.

The arbitrator did not know which witness to believe, and was therefore
unable to employ the criterion of credibility to resolve the conflict in testimony. He then sought a solution by invoking the burden-of-proof principle, namely, that the proponent of a proposition is shouldered with the

[2] *Kennecott Copper Corp., Utah Copper Div. v. United Steelworkers, Local 4347*
Nov. 28, 1963, unpublished arbitration award, p. 8, Arbitrator Paul Prasow.

responsibility of proving its assertion. Each of the parties had presented its own version of the oral agreement, both versions directly contradicting each other. Neither party could produce evidence of its version, other than a bold assertion. Both assertions, the arbitrator ruled, in the absence of supporting evidence, nullified each other and had to be disregarded.

Neither Party Could Prove Its Own Version of Past Practice

The arbitrator then turned to past practice as a criterion and ran into the same difficulty. The testimony was equally conflicting as to past practice. Quoting the arbitrator:

> The Union contends the practice has always been to assign a Skimmer to each furnace on a holding-fire basis. The Company denies this contention and claims that the situation which prevailed on December 17, 1962, was a relatively new one, and therefore no valid past practice exists.
>
> It is a well-established principle of arbitration that for past practice to be given significant weight, it must be of sufficient generality and duration to imply acceptance of it as an authentic construction of the contract.[3] A few incidents in the past do not establish a valid practice. Whatever evidence there is in the record on past practice establishes only what neither side is contending in this case. Such past practice provides no guide to the resolution of the issue in this case.
>
> With regard to the agreement itself, the Arbitrator can find no express language therein which relates to the fixed assignment of Skimmers in the reverberatory department of the smelter. The Arbitrator must conclude that the contract is silent on the specific matter in dispute, and is controlled by the general language of the agreement.

Arbitrator Refuses to Substitute His Judgment for That of Management

> Since the record does not establish conclusively either the existence of a *valid past practice*, or a mutual meeting of minds on an *oral agreement*, or *specific contract language* dealing with the issue, the Arbitrator has no alternative but to uphold the management's decisions on the matter. It is not the function of the Arbitrator to substitute his judgment for that of management, which has the ultimate responsibility for the safe and efficient operation of the smelter, so long as he is satisfied that the Company's decisions were made in good faith and were not *arbitrary, discriminatory,* or *capricious.* If the Arbitrator finds that the Company's

---

[3] *Sheller Mfg. Corp. v. United Auto. Workers, Local 857,* June 7, 1948, 10 LA 617, 620, Arbitrator Robert E. Mathews, BNA, Inc.

action was neither arbitrary, discriminatory, nor capricious, then, regardless of whether or not he agrees with the Company he will not substitute his judgment for that of the management.

In this case, the Company made certain decisions on December 17, 1962, with respect to the assignment of one Skimmer to four furnaces on a holding fire status. The Union protested this action through the grievance and arbitration procedure. The assignments made on December 17 may be set aside only upon satisfactory proof that the decisions were not bona fide exercises of managerial judgment and discretion. In the Arbitrator's opinion, the evidence in the record does not establish that the Company's action in this case was arbitrary, capricious, or discriminatory.[4]

After considering all the evidence and argument of the parties on the issue, the arbitrator decided that the company could, without violating the contract, assign Skimmers to reverberatory furnaces on a one-to-four basis, instead of a one-to-one basis as claimed by the union.

THE CASE OF THE IMPRUDENT EMPLOYER

The presumption that managerial discretion must be exercised with a prudence befitting the attendant circumstances is well illustrated by an arbitral opinion on a very close case. The employer was a fair-sized daily newspaper whose editorial and circulation departments had long been represented by the Newspaper Guild. The publisher had never been friendly to the union but had tolerated its existence because for years it had been relatively inactive, its organization a hollow shell. The situation changed abruptly when the publisher acquired another newspaper, a smaller one some 35 miles away, and merged the two newspapers into a single publishing entity. A number of transfers of key editorial people in the main newspaper to the newly acquired newspaper created considerable uneasiness among the employees.

Frank K., employed as a Telegraph Operator in the main newspaper, was elected chairman of the guild unit. He was an extremely energetic, militant leader, who almost single-handedly revived the union and made it a highly effective force. He was pressing on to recruit office employees into the organization when his transfer was ordered to the out-of-town newspaper at the lower classification of Reporter, but without reduction in his salary. Employee indignation was so intense at management's action that a walkout

---

[4] *Kennecott Copper Corp., Utah Copper Div. v. United Steelworkers, Local 4347,* p. 11.

was barely averted by an agreement to hold the transfer in abeyance while the issue could be arbitrated. The guild, of course, charged that Frank K. was being transferred out of the main newspaper because of his union activity. The publisher's rebuttal that certain key people had to be assigned to the newly acquired newspaper was certainly not an explanation to be lightly dismissed. Following is the arbitrator's opinion on the matter:

> Finally, we come to the Union's main allegation, that the proposed transfer was contrived and given a surface plausibility in order to punish Frank K. for his past activities on behalf of the Union, and to minimize his future effectiveness by shifting him to the out-of-town newspaper. The difficulties of proving such a charge, however well founded, can be attested to by any NLRB Trial Examiner. It is known that these Examiners are not content with a minute scrutiny of component events and details, but frequently reach a conclusion by a sweeping survey of the total picture.

Arbitrator Observes That the Arguments of Both Sides Are Equally Persuasive

> Such a sweeping survey of the picture in the instant case, does not, on balance, produce a clear-cut answer. The role played by the grievant in the organizing activities of the Union was not that of a run-of-the-mill working union leader. The record suggests that he displayed an exceptional effectiveness that could hardly have been lost on the Company. Yet, this consideration is balanced by the merging in recent years of the facilities of these two newspapers, not to speak of the reconstitution of the bargaining unit. Against this background, the reorganization scheduled for the date in question, which included the proposed transfer of Frank K., has an undeniable plausibility.
>
> The Arbitrator, however, cannot leave off with the scales so evenly balanced. He must tip them one way or another. He must choose. In deciding which side of the scales to apply the heavier weight, he cannot but dwell on Frank K.'s exceptional prominence and effectiveness on behalf of the Union. Assuming, arguendo, that the Company had no ulterior motive in shifting Frank K. to the out-of-town newspaper, it seems doubtful from the record that this move was of sufficient importance to be worth flying into the face of the obvious suspicions of the Union members and braving the storm of protest which was bound to follow.

Lack of Prudence Tips the Scales against Management

> The Arbitrator is not convinced that the Frank K. transfer was so indispensable that a prudent person would have ordered this transfer in these specific circumstances, which included in the total picture a demotion in job title, if not in salary. It is this lack of prudence which nurtures a persistent doubt in the Arbitrator's mind as to the Company's motive

and impels him to resolve the doubt in the Grievant's favor rather than the Company's. While the Arbitrator does not believe that the sole motive behind the proposed transfer of Frank K. was to discriminate against him, he does find that it was the predominant one.[5]

Is Discharge "Industrial Capital Punishment?"

The point has been made that arbitrators are far from unanimous in their attitude toward employee discipline on charges which do not involve moral turpitude. It is clear, however, from a casual survey of published arbitrations that when reviewing employee discharges of most kinds, a large majority of arbitrators will impose the ultimate burden of persuasion on the employer. Several of these arbitrators have referred to employee discharges as "industrial capital punishment" and hold that, as is the case with capital punishment in criminal law, the employee must be considered innocent until proved guilty—that all doubts must be resolved in his favor.

The analogy of discharge with capital punishment has been criticized by a number of arbitral authorities as a gross oversimplification of the arbitration process in a vital area of labor relations. Arbitrator Benjamin Aaron has observed that:

> Those who are prone indiscriminately to apply the criminal-law analogy in the arbitration of all discharge cases overlook the fact that employer and employee do *not* stand in the relationship of prosecutor and defendant. It cannot be emphasized too often that the basic dispute is between the two principals to the collective bargaining agreement, that is, the company and the union. At stake is not only the matter of justice to an individual employee, important as that principle is, but also the preservation and development of the collective bargaining relationship. . . .
> . . . The case of the employee sleeping on the job, or of the worker accused of punching another man's time card—these and many others are often incapable of proof beyond a reasonable doubt, and the most the arbitrator can say is that, more likely than not, the penalty was justified. How much weight he gives to the doubts that inevitably arise may frequently depend on a variety of considerations having absolutely nothing to do with the amount of proof adduced in the particular case the employee's past record, his length of service, or the possibility of severe economic forfeiture resulting from discharge, on the one hand, or the effect of his reinstatement on the morale of supervisors and fellow employees, or the restraining influence it would have on a joint company union program for stamping out certain undesirable conditions, on the other. The one thing we may be sure of is that, if the arbitrator is familiar with the facts of industrial life and understands that his function

[5] Although these findings were taken from an actual case, the decision was not approved for publication. Therefore no citation can be given. The names and places are fictitious, but the excerpts are essentially unaltered.

is creative as well as purely adjudicative, he will not evaluate the evidence solely on the basis of rigid standards of absolute proof or presumptions of innocence.[6]

The Criminal-Law Analogy Does Not Apply in Industrial Discipline

Concerning this conclusion, the following remarks of Arbitrator Arthur Ross extracted from a discussion on this topic merit careful consideration:

> The analogy between criminal law and industrial discipline breaks down in another important respect. Unlike a criminal trial, the typical discharge arbitration is not a means of determining the guilt or innocence of the accused. On the contrary, it is a review of the *reasonableness of management's action* in a state of facts which, after the jousting and sparring are over, can be seen to be essentially uncontroverted. Some cases, it is true, actually turn on contested issues of fact. Did the grievant steal the screwdriver? Did he strike the first blow? Did he take command of the illegal walkout? But these cases are distinctly in the minority. More often the basic circumstances are clear enough (although any skillful advocate is capable of miring the hearing in endless confusion over trivial or peripheral details). Our real task is to decide whether these circumstances constituted just and proper cause for terminating the employment relationship in the face of the grievant's seniority and associated job property rights. If they did not, we reinstate the grievant. His state of mind and degree of guilt then become secondary problems which can be resolved by cutting or withholding back pay and by sternly admonishing him in the opinion—which, in all likelihood, he will never read. . . . [Italics supplied.]

For Employee with Long Service Stronger Proof Is Needed

> . . . In deciding whether to sustain or to reverse a disciplinary discharge, we consider numerous circumstances which really have little or nothing to do with guilt, innocence, mitigation, extenuation, or other criteria of criminal law. One of these circumstances is seniority. *Long service creates a presumption that the employee is capable of satisfactory performance, so that stronger evidence is needed before the contrary is established.* Moreover, the senior employee has developed a greater equity in his job, which is thought of as a species of property right. He has more to lose when he is terminated and finds it more difficult to get readjusted. We therefore tend to feel that an employer must be willing to put up with more from a long-service employee. [Italics supplied.][7]

[6] Benjamin Aaron, "Some Procedural Problems in Arbitration," *Vanderbilt Law Review*, vol. 10, 1957, p. 741.

[7] Arthur Ross, "The Criminal Law and Industrial Systems," *Labor Arbitration— Perspectives and Problems: Proceedings of the Seventeenth Annual Meeting, National Academy of Arbitrators*, BNA, Inc., 1964, pp. 148–149.

The validity of the foregoing observations by Ross are very well illustrated in the case of a truck driver who was dismissed for failing to report a relatively minor accident. Of particular interest in the arbitral opinion is the crucial weight given to the grievant's seniority in consideration of his reinstatement.

The grievant was not discharged for having an accident, but for failing to report an accident. The company claimed that his discharge was justified under a plant rule requiring an employee to report any accident, no matter how small. The arbitrator acknowledged that a rule requiring the reporting of accidents was not unreasonable and that a company was "entitled to protect itself from liability when its agent has been involved in an accident, and in order to do so its employees have a clear duty to report any accident, no matter how small." Therefore, to impose the penalty of discharge for a "willful" disregard of this rule was not considered unfair or unreasonable.

Balanced against the testimony of a number of company witnesses who either saw the accident or heard the noise of the impact, and of those who repaired the truck, was the story of the grievant, consistently adhered to from the beginning, that he was not aware at the time he had caused an accident; that he had been previously warned of the consequences should he fail to report and that after receiving that warning he did in fact report his second accident; that none of his three accidents, including the most recent, was major; and that he was discharged not for having an accident, but for failing to report it.

In his opinion, the arbitrator observed:

> We know that the grievant would not have been discharged if he had chosen to report this accident. Inherent in the evaluation of the evidence, therefore, is the strategic question of why did the grievant fail to report since he had everything to lose and nothing to gain by taking this course.
>
> The Company proposes that the grievant was "not very smart" and thought he could get away without reporting. It says the only reasonable deduction one can make from its evidence is that the grievant knew he had an accident but chose not to say anything about it.

Arbitrator Holds That Thirteen Years Service Requires Greater Proof of Intent

> There are two fundamental questions in this very close case. The first question is the degree of proof necessary to sustain grievant's discharge. The Arbitrator has in mind that grievant has been employed for a period of 13 years. . . . A termination of his employment under such circumstances would be the ultimate and most severe penalty which could be imposed. The Arbitrator must therefore require a very high degree of persuasive proof in order to sustain the discharge. In giving consider-

ation both to the testimony of the grievant himself that he did not know he had an accident, and also to the underlying question of why grievant would not have reported so trivial a matter in view of the warnings which had been given him, the Arbitrator is unable to say he is sufficiently convinced of grievant's "willful" disregard of the Company rule.

We come to a second question and that is the reinstatement of the employee and the question of back pay. In this respect it is to be noted that during the period that the employee was off the payroll he suffered a period of illness and would not have been available for work in any event. He is therefore not entitled to back pay for that period.

Arbitrator Rules That Less Stringent Proof Is Required on Issue of Back Pay

The Union has argued that if the employee is entitled to reinstatement, then as a logical consequence he must be entitled to full back pay. The Arbitrator cannot agree with this assertion in its entirety. While the evidence was not strong enough to convince the Arbitrator that employee's discharge should be sustained, the question of employee's monetary responsibility for the damage involved does not require the same high degree of proof. The ordinary rule of preponderant evidence will suffice. The whole issue of back pay is before the Arbitrator, and because there is no question of grievant's responsibility for the accident, the Arbitrator therefore concludes that some penalty should be imposed. It is the Arbitrator's judgment that the reinstatement of the employee be conditioned upon a further deduction from back pay of such amount of money damages as were actually incurred by the Company by reason of the accident.

Thus, ... the Arbitrator reinstates the grievant with back pay less what the grievant would have earned during the period he was unable to work because of illness and less the amount of money damages as were actually incurred by the Company by reason of the accident.[8]

BURDEN OF PROOF APPLIED TO MODIFIED SENIORITY CLAUSES

Another vital area of labor relations in which burden of proof is often imposed for the solution of problems is the application of a modified seniority provision. In the first case discussed in Chapter 5,[9] it was shown that when there is a "sufficient ability" seniority provision and the senior employee is bypassed in favor of a junior employee, then the burden of proof is placed on management to show that the senior employee is not

---

[8] *Borden Co., Sacramento Branch v. Chauffeurs, Teamsters & Helpers, Local 150,* June 23, 1964, unpublished arbitration award, Arbitrator Adolph M. Koven.

[9] *Hughes Aircraft Company, Aerospace Group v. Electronic Space Technicians, Local 1553,* Jan. 25, 1965, 43 LA 1248, Arbitrator Howard S. Block, BNA, Inc.

competent to handle the job in question. The senior employee must be evaluated in relation to the requirements of the job, and not to another employee.

When there is a "relative ability" seniority provision and the senior employee is bypassed, the burden of proof for bypassing is still placed on the employer by most arbitrators, but the degree of proof required is not so stringent as it would be in the case of a "sufficient ability" provision. Much would depend on the fact situation, as the following case demonstrates.

The employer was a hospital in the San Francisco Bay Area. Mrs. W., the senior employee, had been bypassed for Mrs. Z., a junior employee, who had been promoted to the position of Senior Appointments and Communications Clerk. The agreement between the parties provided in article VI, section 1, that in "laying off, rehiring and promoting, the principle of seniority in each department and craft shall govern; provided that merit and ability are approximately equal." Section 2 specified that in "filling vacancies in any position under this agreement, preference shall be given to the employees who are qualified for such positions."

In his findings and conclusions, the arbitrator stated:

> It is true that the determination of "relative merit and ability" is management's prerogative. It is also true that management's decision can be overturned by a showing that its judgment was arbitrary, discriminatory, or capricious. . . . But it is incorrect to say that only if management's decision is shown to be arbitrary, capricious, or discriminatory can management's decision be overturned. To say that is to shift the burden to the Union rather than to place an affirmative and positive burden upon the Company to show that its determination conformed with the Contract's requirements. Consistent with Saul Wallen's well-known description to the effect that "wages may be the heart of the contract, but seniority is the soul," Article VI gives primary consideration to seniority which can be disregarded only in the event of a convincing showing that merit and ability are not approximately equal. The burden which therefore rests on the Company is to demonstrate the lack of approximate equality. Unless there is shown to be a wide disparity in merit and ability between the two employees, seniority must govern as specifically set forth in Article VI.
>
> There is no doubt that Z. was a person of outstanding qualities and that she handled the position to which she was promoted in a highly satisfactory manner. But since the grievant was not given any opportunity to perform in that job, we do not know whether the grievant would have performed satisfactorily. All that we have is the Company's judgment of the grievant's merit and ability. But the record on this score is confused since, on the one hand, the Company was critical of her performance, but on the other, the Company, both in its documentary and oral evidence, judged her to be a satisfactory employee. For example, in connection with the Company's approval of the grievant, [Supervisor] P.'s

memorandum states that "Mrs. W. is a good worker who knows her job . . ." and the grievant functioned on the job properly; that the grievant "was doing a good job as Appointment Clerk"; and that the Company "didn't seriously question the ability of the grievant to perform this job." Moreover, some of the criticisms leveled at the grievant by the Company when placed within a different judgmental framework can be argued as positive qualities rather than deficiencies. For example, the grievant's possessiveness in respect to the pediatric appointment book can be viewed in a positive light or as the Company itself testified "I'm sure [W.] had the patients' requests in uppermost concern."

Thus, we come first to the central question of the general meaning of "merit and ability" and second, its specific application in the W.-Z. matter. The Company says that Z. had the greater merit and ability and therefore seniority considerations did not apply in favor of W. There are three aspects to the Company's interpretation and application of "merit and ability." First the Company ignores the factor of experience as a component of "merit and ability"; second it says that the greater qualities of Z. made it unnecessary to consider the experience factor; and third, it contends that, whatever experience the grievant had, that experience did not operate to qualify her for the promotion.

Arbitrator Holds That Experience is Crucial
In Determining "Relative Equality"

The Company is incorrect in all three aspects. Whether "merit" and "ability" are considered to be separate items or whether "merit and ability" are put together as a single concept, the factor of experience is always a crucial component of the equation in determining "relative equality." Though Z. was a highly competent employee and though she performed the job satisfactorily, it is nonetheless true that she was given that job without any experience at all. (The fluoroscopy appointments that Z. performed cannot be made to serve as the kind of "experience" required for the promotional job.) On the other hand, W. not only had experience in the Department but also had experience involving some of the functions of the promoted job. Without experience in the Department, there is no way that Z. could properly be promoted over W. on the basis of "merit and ability" unless the Company had been able convincingly to show that W. was unable to perform the job satisfactorily.

The Principal Appointments and Communications Clerk position is not a complicated job and is relatively low in the job classifications system. Though only a short period of experience in the Department is sufficient to qualify for the duties of that promoted job, it is nonetheless true that the job is subject to seniority considerations in the Contract. If a more competent employee is always promoted over a senior employee who is also able to satisfactorily perform the job, obviously the seniority provisions would be rendered meaningless. . . .

It is perfectly obvious that W.'s personal relationships with other employees in the Appointment Department left something to be desired, but it is another matter to conclude, in the absence of a clear showing, that her problems in this connection meant that she could not satisfactorily perform the senior job. In this regard, the Company failed to make a persuasive showing. Moreover, it is significant that though the Company's criticisms of her in their totality amount to a seriously detrimental evaluation, at no time did the Company ever issue any written reprimand on the grievant. To the contrary, we know that some of the Company's testimony runs in her favor.

Finally, that the Company on a prior occasion promoted a PBX Operator to Principal Appointments and Communications Clerk without objection by the Union is not controlling in the present situation. Under the Contract the Company is not forever barred from promoting another employee from outside the particular department or from filling a promotional job by way of an outside hire so long as it satisfies the burden of proving, when challenged by the Union, the lack of qualifications on the part of the senior person. For these reasons, the determination of each case turns on its own particular facts. Thus, in W.'s case, the conclusion must follow that because the Company was both unable to show that Z. had the prior experience or that W. could not perform the job satisfactorily, it failed to show that merit and ability were not approximately equal.[10]

Definition of Arbitral Standards

Continuing our discussion of the three arbitral standards for reviewing the reasonableness of managerial discretion, we find that Webster's Dictionary[11] defines "arbitrary" as "not governed by principle; depending on volition; based on one's preference, notion, or whim." The term "capricious" is defined as "governed or characterized by caprice; apt to change suddenly or unpredictably." The same volume defines "discriminatory" as "the state of being discriminating, distinguishing, or setting apart; a showing of differentiation or favoritism in treatment." Black's Law Dictionary, Fourth Edition, 1951, defines "arbitrary" as "fixed or done capriciously or at pleasure; without adequate determining principle." The term "discriminatory" means "in general, a failure to treat all equally; favoritism."

In Chapter 2 an incident at Copleston Machine Works was described where several employees were dismissed for participating in a game of dice on company property. In that case, the union was persuaded to sign a submission agreement which unduly limited the arbitrator's authority.[12] For obvious reasons, permission to publish the case was neither sought nor granted, and therefore the name of the company is fictitious. However, in

---

[10] *Kaiser Foundation Hosps. v. Hosp. & Institutional Workers Union, Local 250,* Jan. 18, 1968, unpublished arbitration award, Arbitrator Adolph M. Koven.
[11] *Webster's New Twentieth Century Dictionary, Unabridged,* 2d ed., 1958.
[12] See Chap. 2, "The Submission Agreement and the Record," p. 21.

another case[13] where the fact situation closely resembled that in Copleston Machine Works, permission to publish was given.

Nature of Just Cause

In the Spring and Bumper case, the arbitrator's authority was not limited by the submission agreement to a finding of fact on gambling, but rather embraced the broad issue of determining "just cause" in imposing the discharge penalty. The essential qualities of just cause have been most ably described by Arbitrator Joseph D. McGoldrick:

> It is common to include the right to suspend and discharge for "just cause," "justifiable cause," "proper cause." There is no significant difference between these various phrases. These exclude discharge for mere whim or caprice. They are, obviously, intended to include those things for which employees have traditionally been fired. They include the traditional causes of discharge in the particular trade or industry, the practices which develop in the day-to-day relations of management and labor and most recently they include the decisions of courts and arbitrators. They represent a growing body of "common law" that may be regarded either as the latest development of the law of "master and servant" or, perhaps, more properly as part of a new body of common law of "Management and labor under collective bargaining agreements." They constitute the duties owed by employees to management and, in their correlative aspect, as part of the rights of management. They include such duties as honesty, punctuality, sobriety, or, conversely, the right to discharge for theft, repeated absence or lateness, destruction of company property, brawling and the like. Where they are not expressed in posted rules, they may very well be implied, provided they are applied in a uniform non-discriminatory manner.[14]

Application of Arbitral Standards
In Determining Just Cause

In the Spring and Bumper case, three employees were discharged for allegedly violating the no-gambling rule. Management maintained they had participated in a dice game in violation of rule 7, which stated that "dice, cards, lotteries, coin-matching, betting, jack-pots, book-making or gambling in any of its forms is not permitted on company property." During a rest period several employees were observed watching what seemed to be the shooting of dice on the warehouse floor. Three individuals were identified

---

[13] *United States Spring & Bumper Co. v. United Auto. Workers, Local 509*, Oct. 4, 1946, 5 LA 109, Arbitrator Paul Prasow, BNA, Inc.
[14] *Worthington Corp. v. United Elec., Radio & Mach. Workers, Local 259*, Feb. 4, 1955, 24 LA 1, 6–7, Arbitrator Joseph D. McGoldrick (Chairman), BNA, Inc.

by a passing supervisor, who reported the incident to Personnel for appropriate disciplinary action. The employees were subsequently discharged for violating the rule prohibiting gambling on company property.

After reviewing the record, the arbitrator found that the company had been arbitrary, capricious, and discriminatory in imposing the penalty. *Arbitrary,* he said, because other forms of gambling on company property had been permitted without restriction. During the course of raising funds for construction of a hospital near the plant, management had encouraged employees to participate in a lottery, not only on company property but on company time. During a recent World Series, foremen and their subordinates had widely and publicly participated in the popular baseball pools. Since lotteries and baseball pools are clearly forms of gambling, the company was held to be arbitrary in that it selected one form of gambling (shooting dice) for severe disciplinary action but condoned and even encouraged other forms of gambling. The discharges were arbitrary in that they were *not governed by principle,* but were based upon the subjective preference of management.

The company's action was also considered *capricious,* in that rule 7 had not previously been enforced. The rule had been posted on the bulletin board for some time prior to the gambling incident, and all employees may have been aware of it. However, management had been quite lax in enforcing the rule. For the company *suddenly and unpredictably* to crack down and enforce the rule constituted a capricious act.

The discharges were held to be *discriminatory* in that three out of a half-dozen or more employees at the scene had been singled out for punishment while the others went scot free. There was no evidence that two of the three dismissed employees were actually gambling. They denied the charge, and the record contained no evidence that they handled any dice or money. Discriminatory treatment occurred because there was a failure to *treat all persons equally.*

WILLFUL MISCONDUCT VERSUS INCOMPETENCE

A failure to distinguish between willful negligence and employee incompetence has on more than one occasion resulted in the setting aside of a disciplinary penalty. Arbitrators draw a sharp line between shortcomings or deficiencies of employee performance which arise from incompetence and those due to negligence amounting to disregarding reasonable company rules and policies.[15]

---

[15] For an excellent in-depth discussion of these concepts, see Lawrence Stessin, "Incompetency," *Employee Discipline,* BNA, Inc., 1960, pp. 163–199.

Orme W. Phelps's observations on this distinction are well worth quoting:

> There is an important difference between incompetence on the one hand and misconduct, either personal or collective, on the other. Incompetence is morally neutral; misconduct is morally objectionable.[16] The former is a limited fault and often easily curable, by training, transfer, or the like, whereas the latter points to failings much more deep-seated, the eradication of which is difficult and questionable. Incompetence is related to a particular job or class of jobs. A man may be pleasant, honest, sincere, loyal, hardworking, and reliable, and still be incompetent. The work is just beyond him. As a result, he may be transferred, demoted, or even discharged with less stigma than the rebel, the drunkard, or the chronic absentee. The area of fault is circumscribed, being limited to his inability to do certain specified tasks.
>
> This is not true of misconduct, where the great majority of lapses are regarded as evidence of want of character in major or minor degree. At a minimum, they are violations of plant rules such as no smoking or staying within prescribed work limits, and thus point to irresponsibility, whereas at the upper limit they are clear evidence of lack of principle. Unrelated to a particular job, they are by implication transferable and may show up again anywhere in the plant.[17]

THE CASE OF THE STUCK TRUCK—
WILLFUL MISCONDUCT VERSUS POOR JUDGMENT

In deciding a case of two employees suspended for improperly parking a truck, the arbitrator tried to clarify the confusion surrounding the concepts of incompetence resulting from poor judgment and misconduct due to willful disregard of safety rules.

The two men had parked the truck off the main road, where it became stuck in the sand. In trying to extricate themselves, they began to panic. The more desperately they struggled, the more difficult became their plight. As they frantically raced the motor and spun the steering wheel, the tires dug deeper into the sand until the car was hopelessly in the rut. Eventually they had to send for a tow truck to haul them out.

In his opinion the arbitrator said:

> The Company evidently concluded that the conduct of X. and Y. in parking the truck and attempting to extricate it, constituted negligence or

---

[16] In a footnote the author says: "Discharge for incompetence is frequently called 'nondisciplinary' discharge, to distinguish it from dismissal for misconduct. This is the explanation of the frequent use of the double term 'discipline and discharge,' rather than subsuming dismissal under the general term 'discipline.'"

[17] Orme W. Phelps, *Discipline and Discharge in the Unionized Firm*, University of California Press, Berkeley, Calif., 1959, p. 60.

carelessness in the operation of a Company-owned vehicle. The Company stresses the safety program, and points out that when employees are furnished Company equipment they are held responsible for its proper use, care, and maintenance.

The Arbitrator would agree that the violation of a safety rule must be considered willful, even if it is established that the employee was not aware of the existence of such rule, but would have been in conformity with it if he had exercised reasonable care and diligence. Disciplinary measures to correct such lapses in employee performance are clearly in order. However, ... the line must be drawn between employee inadequacies and other deficiencies which are basically the result of an employee's overall or momentary inability to comprehend or cope with the necessities of the situation. In short, there are errors which are the result of *willfulness*, and errors which are the result of *faulty judgment* exercised in good faith by the employee.

Corrective Measures Differ for Negligence and Incompetence

The Company may certainly take appropriate measures to protect itself from an employee who, with the best of intent, is unable to meet the requirements of a specific situation. In such cases, management often resorts to transfers, demotions, or even separation from the job if there is no work available for which the employee is qualified. However, ... it is improper to lump together the two kinds of lapses in performance (error in judgment and willful dereliction) and impose punitive measures in the first category as well as the second. In cases involving errors of judgment, where the good faith of the employee is not in question, correction, yes—but punishment no! The distinction is often a fine one, but it bears repeating.

A suspension is punitive in nature unlike a written warning, for example, which may have for its purpose notifying the employee of an inadequacy not necessarily due to willfulness. A warning, oral or written, serves this purpose but a suspension goes beyond this purpose. It serves notice punitively by depriving the employees of work days, which ... is inappropriate where there has been a good-faith lapse in performance.

Management is under no obligation to carry indefinitely an incompetent employee. If rehabilitative measures do not suceed, the Company may have no alternative but to terminate him. It would be improper, however, to treat his inadequacies as willful so long as he endeavors to improve, but is simply unable to meet the requirements of the job.

A review of the evidence persuades the Arbitrator that on April 30, 1964, X. and Y. displayed poor judgment rather than willful misconduct. If they had exercised better judgment, they probably would not have driven into the sand in the first place. But once having found themselves in this predicament, their efforts to extricate themselves were motivated less by willfulness than by panic at the realization they had miscalculated.

Having once blundered into the sand, ... they compounded their error by resorting to frantic measures to extricate themselves. It is just this kind of conduct which has probably brought into the vernacular the apt expression for extreme frustration and futility: "spinning your wheels."

A careful review of the record convinces the Arbitrator that the circumstances of April 30, 1964, were due primarily to bad judgment on the part of X. and Y. To the Arbitrator, their conduct has no apparent elements of carelessness, negligence, or other willful deficiencies in performance. Accordingly, it would appear that the suspension was more punitive than corrective in nature, due to an understandable exasperation on the part of Supervision. Accordingly, ... the appropriate response would have been to put the employees on notice by written warning to be more cognizant of safety and to improve their understanding of necessary safety precautions.

The Arbitrator concurs fully with the Company's real concern for safety, which involves not only protection of equipment, but protection of life and limb as well. For this reason, the Arbitrator believes that a clear warning notice requiring a stricter adherence to safety rules and regulations was certainly in order. Although the Arbitrator finds that the suspension penalty was inappropriate, he is convinced there was ample basis for a warning with respect to poor judgment in the operation of a Company vehicle.[18]

Facts Obtained after Discharge

Arbitral review of managerial discretion in discharge cases is based on the evidence (including the employee's record) relied upon when the termination occurred. Arbitrators generally do not accept reasons other than those given at the time of dismissal.

Most managements avoid this potential difficulty by suspending rather than discharging an employee pending investigation of the charges. It sometimes happens that after terminating an employee, management finds it is unable to sustain the original charge. However, in the course of the investigation other grounds may be uncovered which could justify a discharge for just cause, but these grounds differ from those on which the dismissal was based. The question arises, may the company introduce such new evidence at the arbitration hearing? When confronted with such a situation, Arbitrator James J. Healy replied unequivocally with an observation which reflects the thinking of most arbitrators:

If a Company discharges a man, the reasons known to the Company at the time of discharge must satisfy the "just cause" principle; it is

18 *Gen. Tel. Co. of California v. Communications Workers,* Mar. 10, 1965, 44 LA 669, 672, Arbitrator Paul Prasow, BNA, Inc.

improper to include reasons discovered by Management after the decision to discharge has been made.[19]

POSTDISCHARGE CONDUCT

It is a well-established principle in arbitration that acts engaged in by an employee subsequent to his discharge may not be relied upon to determine the propriety of the dismissal.[20]

In refusing to admit evidence as to a jail sentence received by an employee several months after his discharge for excessive absenteeism, Arbitrator Eli Rock observed:

> I am not . . . familiar with any arbitration case in which a totally separate basis for discharge, occurring a substantial period of time after the original termination . . . has been permitted to become part of the original termination proceeding—over the objection of one of the parties. . . .
>
> I am primarily influenced . . . by the fact that the later possible discharge represents, in a very real sense, a new and separate, potential discharge case which, I must find, has neither been properly processed through the grievance procedure of the contract up to now, nor has been properly submitted to arbitration. . . .
>
> I must at this time decline to admit or to rule on this aspect of the Company's argument in the present proceeding. The latter finding is, of course, without prejudice to whatever rights the Company might have under the contract, regarding further actions it may wish to initiate. . . .[21]

During the course of a strike an employee in another case received a letter notifying him he was terminated as of February 17, 1964. Subsequent to that date, he was accused of further misconduct while engaged in picketing. The case went to arbitration with the following two stipulated issues:

1 Was K. discharged for just cause?
2 If the answer is no, what is the remedy?

At the hearing the company requested that evidence regarding K.'s alleged misconduct after his discharge of February 17 be permitted into the record. The union objected, arguing that evidence regarding postdischarge conduct

---

[19] *Swift & Co. v. United Packinghouse Workers,* Dec. 6, 1948, 12 LA 108, 115, Arbitrator James J. Healy, BNA, Inc.

[20] Some arbitrators make exceptions to this principle in the case of continued misconduct of strikers who have already received discharge notice. See *Westinghouse Elec. Corp. v. Int'l Union of Elec., Radio & Mach. Workers,* July 27, 1956, 26 LA 837, Arbitrator William E. Simkin, BNA, Inc.

[21] *Westinghouse Elec. Corp. v. United Elec., Radio & Mach. Workers, Local 107,* Nov. 3, 1960, 36 LA 1185, 1187–1188, Arbitrator Eli Rock, BNA, Inc.

is not admissible and should not be considered. In deciding the issue the arbitrator stated:

> The over-riding consideration . . . is the scope of the Arbitrator's authority as defined by the parties themselves in the Submission Agreement. Does the Submission Agreement of August 25, 1964, authorize the Arbitrator to consider evidence regarding K.'s conduct after February 17, 1964? In the Arbitrator's opinion, the answer to this question must be in the negative. The Arbitrator believes that if he were to go beyond the date of February 17, on either issue, he would be exceeding his powers as set forth by the parties themselves.
>
> Since it was stipulated that K.'s discharge took place on February 17, issue No. 1 really asks: Was K. discharged for just cause on *February 17?* The Arbitrator's authority is restricted to this date. Accordingly, the second issue appears to be: If the Arbitrator finds that K.'s discharge was not for just cause on February 17, what is the remedy? . . .
>
> In the Arbitrator's opinion K.'s discharge must stand or fall on the reasons given and the facts known as of February 17, 1964. The basis for the Arbitrator's ruling is that under the Submission Agreement of August 25, 1964, he lacks authority to review charges of alleged misconduct on K.'s part after February 17, 1964.
>
> The Arbitrator is fully aware of the Company's position that K. is an undesirable person unfit for employment . . . because of his misconduct *both prior to* and *after* February 17, 1964.
>
> However, the Submission Agreement under which this arbitration is being held is restricted to events which occurred prior to February 17, 1964. It does not refer to incidents which took place after February 17, 1964. The Arbitrator has no power to expand his authority or to amend the Submission Agreement. This is the joint responsibility of the parties. In the absence of such an amendment, the Arbitrator is of the opinion that the Submission Agreement as presently written does not authorize him to consider events which occurred after February 17. Accordingly his findings are limited entirely to events which transpired on or before February 17, 1964.[22]

Does the foregoing opinion mean that management is forever precluded from taking action against an employee who has engaged in postdischarge misconduct? Not at all. Suppose an employee is discharged for insubordination after a vitriolic argument with his foreman. When the employee returns the next day to pick up his paycheck, he runs into his foreman on leaving the office and follows up a torrent of invective by punching his supervisor in the face. If an arbitrator absolves the employee from blame in the initial argument culminating in his dismissal, the company may, of

---

[22] *Gen. Tel. Co. of California v. Communications Workers,* Sept. 14, 1964, unpublished arbitration award, pp. 2–4, Arbitrator Paul Prasow.

course, institute new charges against the employee for assaulting his supervisor and then fire him on the new grounds.

POSTDISCHARGE CONDUCT— MODIFICATION OF PENALTY

So far we have discussed postdischarge conduct of an *aggravating* nature. Does the same principle apply to postdischarge conduct of a *mitigating* character? Generally, yes, unless there are unusually strong and compelling reasons to take such conduct into account. That is, an employee's conduct after discharge, either good or bad, usually has no bearing on the case. The arbitrator must judge the situation at the time it occurred. In rare cases postdischarge conduct may be given weight by the arbitrator in deciding whether to uphold or modify the discharge penalty.

Take the case of a long-service employee whose record was unblemished for twenty of twenty-two years seniority. He was an excellent worker and was considered a valuable, highly skilled employee. However, during the last two years of his employment with the company, he was found drinking during working hours and was warned or disciplined on several instances. On the final occasion, he was discovered completely intoxicated while on the job and was dismissed immediately.

Subsequent to his dismissal, he took some very decisive steps to rehabilitate himself. He placed himself under the care of a physician, a specialist in dealing with such problems. He began to follow a strict program aimed at maintaining sobriety by complete abstinence from alcoholic beverages. He started attending meetings of Alcoholics Anonymous; he kept regular hours; he began to take medication prescribed by the physician. In the months between his discharge and the arbitration hearing, he had maintained complete sobriety, and his physician testified that the employee was considered a good risk who would remain sober. In requesting modification of the discharge penalty, the union stressed the employee's successful rehabilitation and the physician's favorable prognosis. The company acknowledged these aspects but stated that they did not alter the original basis for termination. The company maintained that the case must be decided on the facts known on the date of discharge. In treating these contentions, the arbitrator observed:

> It is true that in most grievance arbitrations, the basic issue to be determined is whether management's action was proper based upon the facts known at the time the action was taken. Normally the clock stops at that moment, and anything that occurs subsequently is irrelevant. How-

ever, there are occasions, especially in discharge cases, where events occurring after the incident giving rise to the grievance are given some weight by arbitrators. For example, the conduct of an employee after he has been discharged may be considered significant either for its mitigating or aggravating influence in determining whether the penalty should be modified.

It is a well accepted principle in arbitration and industrial relations that the primary purpose of industrial discipline is not to inflict punishment for wrongdoing, but to correct individual faults and behavior and to prevent further infractions. Both the Company and the employee lose when the employee is terminated. It is for this reason that discharge is normally invoked only as a last resort, after it has become abundantly clear that corrective measures will not succeed.

X. has a social-problem disease called alcoholism, for which there are no dramatic and quick cures. Current therapy focuses on attempts to arrest the disease and restore the person to a useful and respected role in society. This is no easy task, and most of the effort must come from the affected person himself. He must become aware of the problems that induced the disease; he must believe strongly that he has the ability to remain sober; and he must practice rigorous self-discipline in his personal habits and relations with others. The chances of successful rehabilitation are increased if the person has the understanding and cooperation of family, friends, and society itself. Some risks are certainly involved, but the gains from success are of such inestimable value to the person, his family, to the Company, and to society as a whole that they seem worth the effort. It is for this reason that the Review Board, or a majority thereof, believes that a modification of the discharge penalty is warranted.

It is important to note that X. does have 22 years of seniority with the Company; his record and reputation at least during 20 years of his employment were good; the lapses during the last two years of employment were all related to alcoholism; and there is the considered judgment that his future prospects seem favorable.

The above does not mean that the Review Board condones X.'s misconduct or minimizes the seriousness of his offenses. He merits the severest disciplinary measures short of permanent dismissal. He should be reinstated, but without any back pay, and the period of eight months since his termination should be recorded as a disciplinary layoff.

It it hoped that with reinstatement, X will continue to maintain without interruption his program of rehabilitation. It should be crystal clear to all parties concerned that any future deviation from strict sobriety on the job will warrant immediate termination.[23]

---

[23] *Texaco, Inc. v. Oil, Chem. & Atomic Workers Int'l Union, Local 1-128,* Dec. 26, 1963, 42 LA 408, 411–412, Arbitrator Paul Prasow (Chairman), BNA, Inc. For a similar case involving reinstatement without back pay of an employee whose rehabilitation followed his discharge, see *Chrysler Corp. v. United Auto. Workers, Local 961,* Apr. 8, 1963, Arbitrator Gabriel N. Alexander, 40 LA 935, BNA, Inc.

Admittedly, this is a most unusual case. It must be stressed that in the overwhelming majority of discharge arbitrations, the conduct of the employee after termination has no bearing on the issue before the arbitrator.

Consistency versus Uniformity in Administering Discipline

In carrying out a disciplinary program, there are compelling reasons for avoiding rigid uniformity. Thus if two employees violate the same rule and one is nearing retirement after twenty years service and the other is a young man of one year seniority, discharge would impose a far harsher penalty upon the employee who may lose his pension than upon the worker who has only one year of service. Arbitrators generally uphold managerial discretion in distinguishing among different cases.

Aaron has cogently stated the principle as follows:

> In considering the effects of past practice, [arbitrators] must be careful to avoid confusing uniformity with consistency. A consistency of purpose and of method may well produce a diversity in results, stemming from differences between individual personalities and situations. To put the matter another way, *it is not the fact of seeming inconsistency in past practice, but the cause of it, that ought to engage the arbitrator's attention.* What appears at first blush to be an arbitrary and capricious administration of a rule may prove on closer inspection to be a flexible and humane application of a sound principle to essentially different situations. [Italics supplied.][24]

In a case involving the imposition of lighter penalties for some employees who had participated in a work stoppage, the late Harry Shulman had this to say:

> Normally, when other considerations are equal, employees guilty of the same offense should receive substantially the same treatment. But the object of industrial discipline is future improvement, not retribution. The Union does not generally contend that penalties should be imposed automatically without regard for circumstances peculiar to the individual employees. In prior determinations, I have urged upon the Company that, in imposing disciplinary penalties, it should exercise a humane and statesmanlike discretion in each case rather than strike out automatically; and that in this exercise of humane and wise discretion, the employee's past record, a reasonable judgment as to his future prospects, and a reasonable estimate of the effect of the possible disciplinary measures on the general situation are important factors. When such factors are taken into account—as they are also in our courts—different treatment

[24] Benjamin Aaron, "The Uses of the Past in Arbitration," *Arbitration Today: Proceedings of the Eighth Annual Meeting, National Academy of Arbitrators,* BNA, Inc., 1955, p. 11.

for the same offense may very well result. Such civilized differentiation is not unjust discrimination.[25]

It must be noted, however, that despite the above there are some infractions considered so serious as to warrant summary dismissal on the first offense regardless of mitigating factors. These are the Class A offenses such as theft; sabotage; unprovoked assault resulting in serious injury; smoking in a restricted area creating extreme hazards to life, limb, and property; major acts of moral turpitude; and punching another employee's time card.

The Problem of Self-Help

Where a contract provides for grievance processing through an orderly procedure terminating in arbitration, there would seem to be no reason for a complaining employee to resort to "self-help." Yet many of them do and learn to their regret that even though the complaint was justified, their grievance was denied in arbitration because they had bypassed the prescribed procedure.

The problem arises in part because some employees believe they do not have to obey orders which clearly violate their rights under the agreement. The assumption is that a supervisor does not have the unqualified right to demand compliance with his instruction regardless of its fairness, timeliness, or compliance with contract provisions.[26]

This precise contention was made by a union in a case involving the discharge of nine employees for refusing to obey an order to work overtime. The men were requested to return to work after they had completed their regular eight-hour shift, taken a shower, changed to street clothes, and were in the process of clocking out. In stressing the importance of using the grievance procedure, the arbitrator stated:

> It is a well-established principle in arbitration that where a collective bargaining agreement contains a grievance and arbitration procedure, such procedure must be followed rather than a unilateral determination by employees that their complaint is justified. Employees must not take matters into their own hands. They should obey and carry out their assignments even if these are believed to violate the Agreement. When a controversy arises between Supervision and subordinates, the latter must utilize the grievance procedure for determination of the merits and for relief. There are, of course, some notable exceptions to this rule, namely, where obedience would involve an unusual health or safety

[25] *Ford Motor Co. and United Auto. Workers,* Aug. 14, 1945, Opinion A-197, sec. V, Umpire Harry Shulman.
[26] It is generally accepted that orders giving rise to serious safety or health hazards do not have to be followed.

hazard; and where performance would result in some immoral or criminal act.

The classic expression of this principle of observing the grievance procedure was stated by the late Harry Shulman, former Dean of Yale University Law School and Umpire between Ford Motor Company and the United Auto Workers Union:

"Some men apparently think that, when a violation of contract seems clear, the employee may refuse to obey and thus resort to self-help rather than the grievance procedure. That is an erroneous point of view. In the first place, what appears to one party to be a clear violation may not seem so at all to the other party. Neither party can be the final judge as to whether the contract has been violated. The determination of that issue rests in collective negotiation through the grievance procedure. But, in the second place, and more important, the grievance procedure is prescribed in the contract precisely because the parties anticipated that there would be claims of violations which would require adjustment. That procedure is prescribed for all grievances, not merely for doubtful ones. Nothing in the contract even suggests the idea that only doubtful violations need be processed through the grievance procedure and that clear violations can be resisted through individual self-help. The only difference between a "clear" violation and a "doubtful" one is that the former makes a clear grievance and the latter a doubtful one. But both must be handled in the regular prescribed manner." [Ford Motor Company, 3 LA 779.]

The Arbitration Board (as provided in the contract) is the final judge of whether a direct order of Supervision meets the tests of reasonableness, timeliness, or compliance with the Agreement. If employees make such a determination unilaterally and act accordingly, then they are subject to discipline for not following the grievance procedure, even if it is ultimately decided that their complaint was justified and Supervision was arbitrary.[27]

The Problem of Remedies in Arbitration

Closely related to the issue of self-help is the problem of providing adequate relief for an employee who proves his case through the grievance and arbitration procedure. If the employees in the above situation had worked overtime as ordered and it had later been determined that such request violated their rights under the agreement, to what would they have been entitled as a remedy? It was this question that the union raised in justifying the bypassing of the grievance procedure. In treating this issue, the arbitrator stated:

[27] *Globe-Union Inc. v. United Auto. Workers, Local 509*, Dec. 11, 1963, 42 LA 713, 720, Arbitrator Paul Prasow (Chairman), BNA, Inc.

The Union agrees in principle with the general rule that employees should follow the grievance procedure rather than resort to self-help. However, according to the Union, the instant case provides an exception to the rule, because there is no adequate remedy in the grievance procedure for the justified complaint of the employees. As the Union argues in its post-hearing brief:

"The Company could openly, admittedly and wilfully violate this section and order employees to work overtime. The employees would be forced to work overtime or be penalized. If the overtime was worked and the employees filed grievances the Company could admit the contract violation without penalty. The Company could repeat this violation indefinitely. The employees' right to '48 hours notice whenever possible' would become a hollow right without meaning or means of enforcement."

The Union has raised a most important problem which has long intrigued arbitrators. The question may be posed: What protection does an employee have against continued managerial action detrimental to his contract rights where invoking the grievance procedure would fail to provide appropriate relief or any effective penalty to prevent future violations by the Company?

There is no simple answer to this perplexing question. However, several observations are warranted. In the first place, the immediate objective in all such cases is to remove the detriment to which the employee was improperly subjected by issuing a "cease and desist" order, to prevent recurrence in the future. The Arbitrator can direct that the improper conduct be stopped.

In the second place, where the remedy is at the heart of the dispute, the parties have a number of approaches they can follow. They could limit the authority of the Arbitrator to determining whether or not the Agreement was violated, reserving to themselves the fixing of the remedy. An extension of this method is to provide that if the Arbitrator should find that a violation occurred, a specific remedy could be stipulated in the submission agreement. There are some cases where the parties are much better equipped than the Arbitrator to fashion a remedy, assuming they are willing to take on this responsibility. The Arbitrator's primary function is to interpret the agreement. All his powers in respect to remedies derive from the agreement and the submission to arbitration. Where the parties reserve the right to negotiate their own remedy, they could also provide that, in the event of failure to agree, the matter may be referred back to the Arbitrator for resolution of this problem. The latter procedure could be very important in enhancing the usefulness of abitration. But it is up to the parties to make this decision, and not the Arbitrator. Arbitration is no substitute for good faith collective bargaining.

The submission agreement is especially well adapted to a definition of the Arbitrator's authority on remedies. Where the remedy is important and the contract seems to make no provision for it, the parties may very well include in the submission their views on the remedy. This should be done before the hearing, when the outcome on the substantive issue has not yet been determined.

A basically different element is injected into the picture when a Union charges a Company with deliberately and repeatedly ignoring certain obligations under the Agreement. Here the source of the difficulty is not just the inability of the grievance-arbitration procedure to provide a remedy or penalty to discourage future violations. The real problem is the break-down in the relationship between the parties. Arbitration is not designed to deal with such problems. If an Arbitration Board finds a deliberate violation of the Agreement, it should say so. However, it would seem inappropriate for the Board to fashion a remedy to deal with intentional violations on exactly the same basis as unintentional ones. If one party or the other appears determined to evade the provisions of the contract, the best approach is for the parties to face the issue frankly, rather than expect the arbitration process to deal with a situation which is beyond its purpose. There is no evidence that such a situation is present in this case.[28]

A final comment on the matter of those who resort to self-help because no remedy is possible for the employee to be made whole for damages suffered by a clear-cut management violation of the contract. In those exceptional cases, depending on the specific circumstances of each event, the authors would be inclined to utilize two basic criteria applied by courts when considering petitions for injunctive relief:

1 Will the damage suffered by the petitioner be irreparable if he is subsequently proved to be the victim of an illegal wrongful action?
2 Will the damage to the petitioner be substantial enough to warrant restraining the other party, who might subsequently be proved to be in the right, and in turn suffer needless harassment, perhaps irreparable damage, by the restraining order?

If the aggrieved employee could meet the foregoing two tests as a justification for self-help, it would seem inappropriate for an arbitrator to permit an inflexible prohibition against self-help to become a protective shield for management actions in violation of the contract.

SUMMARY

The most important single presumption for reviewing managerial action when the agreement is silent or the language too general is that managerial discretion must be exercised reasonably. The three most common specific tests of reasonableness are that the action is not *arbitrary, capricious,* or

[28] *Ibid.,* 720–721.

discriminatory. The burden of proof rests with the grievant or his representative to establish the presence of one or more of these factors in order to have the arbitrator set aside the employer's decision.

The common assumption that discharge of an employee is comparable to capital punishment in criminal law has been attacked by a number of prominent arbitrators. The point has been stressed that "unlike a criminal trial, the typical discharge arbitration is not a means of determining the guilt or innocence of the accused." Rather it is "a review of the reasonableness of management's action" to determine whether it was arbitrary, capricious, or discriminatory. "Arbitrary" means "not governed by principle" and refers to action based on personal preference or selection. "Capricious" refers to conduct which is unpredictable—subject to sudden, unexpected, or unannounced change. "Discriminatory" means "showing . . . differentiation or favoritism in treatment"; there is "a failure to treat all equally."

The primary function of an arbitrator in hearing a discipline or discharge case is to determine whether the penalty imposed by management was for "just cause." There is no adequate definition of this important but elusive concept. All one can do is describe its essential qualities, as was ably done by one arbitrator as follows:

> No standards exist to aid an Arbitrator in finding a conclusive answer to such a question [definition of just cause] and, therefore, perhaps the best he can do is to decide what [a] reasonable man, mindful of the habits and customs of industrial life and of the standards of justice and fair dealing prevalent in the community, ought to have done under similar circumstances and in that light to decide whether the conduct of the discharged employee was defensible and the disciplinary penalty just.[29]

In reviewing discipline and discharge cases, arbitrators generally differentiate between *willful misconduct* and *incompetence.* As Arbitrator Phelps has noted, "Incompetence is morally neutral; misconduct is morally objectionable." The first is more limited and can often be remedied by additional instruction, counseling, demotion, or transfer. The second is more serious and more difficult to eradicate, having to do with a person's character or personality and involving varying degrees of irresponsibility or lack of principle. Different corrective measures are applicable to these two situations.

Arbitral review of managerial discretion in discharge cases is generally based on the evidence relied upon when the termination occurred. Unless there are very compelling circumstances, arbitrators do not accept reasons

---

[29] *Riley Stoker Corp. v. United Steelworkers, Local 1907,* July 11, 1947, 7 LA 764, 767, Arbitrator Harry H. Platt, BNA, Inc.

for discharge other than those given at the time of dismissal. Generally the clock stops at the time of discharge, and an employee's conduct after termination has no bearing on the merits of the case. However, in some unusual situations, postdischarge conduct may have an *aggravating* or *mitigating* effect on the arbitrator's consideration of the issue.

Finally, there is the matter of *consistency* versus *uniformity* in carrying out a disciplinary program. Some persons assume that a strict uniformity in administering discipline is necessary to avoid charges of favoritism or discriminatory treatment. In fact, however, a "consistency of purpose and of method may well produce a diversity in results. . . ." Significant differences in circumstances and in personality may well justify a flexible application of disciplinary penalties.

Chapter 12

Collective bargaining in the public sector

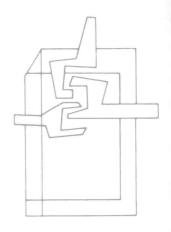

■ Both as to grievance adjustment and as to the negotiation of new terms of conditions of employment, collective bargaining in the public sector is undergoing a vast, far-reaching transition. Although strikes by public employees are prohibited by law in nearly every jurisdiction of the United States, such stoppages have occurred with increasing frequency in recent years. In the absence of satisfactory alternative procedures for dispute adjustments, public employee strikes have become commonplace in the urban centers of the nation. Most significantly involved in these walkouts, on a scale greater than those in the private sector, are professional groups such as teachers, social workers, nurses, and technicians. It seems advisable to us that a profitable discussion of collective bargaining in the public sector should not be confined to the simple adjustment of grievances, but should analyze public employment developments in some of their broadest aspects.[1]

[1] With an eye to this chapter, Edward Peters prepared a paper on some legal and philosophical concepts of governmental sovereignty and the settlement of public employee disputes in the light of emerging patterns in the public sector. This chapter is an edited version of his paper, which was read by Mr. Peters in 1968 to a conference on developments in public employee relations sponsored by the Public Personnel Association.

COMPARISONS BETWEEN CANADIAN AND
UNITED STATES LAW ON PUBLIC EMPLOYEES

Recently enacted federal legislation in Canada permits national government employees to choose between compulsory arbitration and the strike as the terminal point of dispute settlement. The choice, once made by the employee organization, is binding for a specified number of years. Interestingly enough, most of the employee organizations have opted for compulsory arbitration.[2]

Apparently the Canadian federal government has managed somehow to hurdle the legal and philosophical doctrine of sovereignty, the doctrine which holds that a public authority should be immune from collective-bargaining pressures in its decision making. How else can the willingness of Canadian public management to arbitrate new terms and conditions of employment be explained? Clearly the day is not far off when public management in the United States will have to make the same hard choice as did Canadian public management. A rigid, unbending advocacy of the sovereignty principle to ban strikes and rule out arbitration is as realistic as plugging up the spout of a teakettle on the assumption that the steam inside will dissipate, causing the fire underneath the kettle to burn out for lack of steam to sustain it. If public management in the United States reflects the same temperament as its counterparts in private industry, then it can be expected to follow a different course from Canadian public management. While management in both the private and public sectors of the United States will, in exceptional circumstances, arbitrate new terms and conditions of an agreement (i.e., interest issues), most employers will not accept compulsory arbitration of such issues as a fixed terminal point of dispute-adjustment procedures. Predominant thinking of public management in most states is to regard both alternatives, strikes and compulsory arbitration, as unacceptable for resolving disputes over interest issues. But assuming that public employee organizations reach a degree of strength and militancy to compel a choice, a fair prediction (allowing that forecasts in this area are more a matter of coin tossing than of logic) is that public management will prefer an economic contest to compulsory arbitration of new terms and conditions of employment.

---

[2] Municipal employees in Canada have had the legal right to strike for sometime, and even provincial employees (Saskatchewan and Quebec, to be specific) have been allowed to strike under certain conditions.

COMPULSORY ARBITRATION VERSUS STRIKES
IN PUBLIC EMPLOYMENT

For example, the Southern California Rapid Transit District (RTD), which provides such bus service as is available for an interurban area of 8 million inhabitants, bargains collectively with a number of old entrenched unions. It would not be difficult for the RTD to secure legislation banning strikes if it were willing to include compulsory arbitration of unresolved union contract demands. Of interest is the fact that one of the unions, which halted the buses for a week in 1960 in a wage dispute, has a constitutional provision that it must offer to arbitrate disputed issues before it can engage in a walkout. Yet the RTD management would much rather take its chances in an economic contest than allow an arbitrator to make binding decisions on its key labor costs. The agency's rejection of compulsory interests arbitration is not prompted as much by philosophical concepts of sovereignty as by the same hard-boiled considerations of operating a business as motivate management in the private sector of the economy.

Most states do not ban strikes in privately owned public utilities, even though these utilities usually have a monopoly of the most highly sensitive services. What could be more catastrophic (as any New Yorker can testify) than a sudden cessation of power and light in a densely populated area? Yet the only safeguard provided by federal law is the eighty-day-injunction procedures set forth in the Taft-Hartley Act, after which the union is potentially free, if it has the strength, to plunge a city into darkness. In general, government has been content to rely on the self-restraint of the parties. It has been left up to them not to create a situation where public clamor will reach such proportions that ad hoc legislation (as in case of the railway firemen) or more permanent dispute-adjustment machinery will be enacted to take the ultimate decision on disputed issues out of their hands. For decades in these vital industries no one has been able to come up with a more workable solution for disputes than voluntary mediation or fact-finding, which rely on the good sense of the parties not to make waves which will upset the boat. In short, there are no really satisfactory solutions in a free society, but only some solutions which are less objectionable than others.

NATURE OF COLLECTIVE BARGAINING
IN THE PRIVATE SECTOR

Those who would devise a practical third alternative to strikes or compulsory arbitration must grapple with a fundamental and inescapable fact of collective bargaining. The process is not entirely an exercise in logic and reason;

it is more than a joint search for immutable truths obscured by opposing points of view. A union in the private sector of the economy exists on the premise that it gets things for its members that the employer would not have given otherwise. The union must win victories to preserve itself, not in all contract negotiations, to be sure, but often enough to preserve the union's image of effectiveness.

Victory cannot be the private affair of a few professionals; it must be savored by the broad membership. The prelude to victory must be uncertainty, and in the private sector uncertainty is often staged when necessary. A so-called "sophisticated" employer is one who allows the union to win all or part of what he is prepared to give anyhow. The trick for him, of course, is not to be pushed beyond his bargaining expectations. All of which underscores the necessity for both parties to take bargaining positions which conceal their ultimate goals until the time is ripe for settlement. In summary, the negotiation of the collective agreement (as contrasted with grievance adjustment during the term of an agreement) is an adversary process.

NATURE OF COLLECTIVE BARGAINING IN THE PUBLIC SECTOR

This question now presents itself: considering the unique features of public employment, can the fundamental principles just discussed, the adversary nature of contract negotiations and all that it entails, apply to the public sector? Those who reply in the negative logically conclude that viable collective bargaining in the true sense cannot function in government employment. They point to the dispersion of authority both within the executive branch and between the executive and legislative branches. "Adversary to whom?" they ask. "The elected representatives of the people who vote on the budget? Adversary to the ill-defined management in the executive branch, so many of whom on the supervisory level are active in independent employee associations? When a representative of an independent employee association appears at a school superintendent's office to discuss a conflict between a teacher and a principal, in whose interest will the representative take an adversary position?"

The logic behind these objections would be unanswerable if it were not flawed in a basic sense. Logic must be rooted in the specific conditions of life, and when these conditions undergo a change, the logic loses its validity. The old logic is becoming detached from today's reality by a strong persistent trend toward collective bargaining by public employees. This central fact of employee relations in the public sector has galvanized both the AFL-CIO unions and the independent associations into a stepped-up competition with each other. It is a competition reminiscent in some important respects of the struggle in the 1930s when a demoralized AFL was stirred from its lethargy by a challenge from the newly emerged CIO and, as a result, labor relations in the private sector were completely transformed in a brief span of years. In the present period, with the notable exception of the American Federation of Teachers, the major gains of AFL-CIO affiliates have been among blue-collar employees and nonprofessional office personnel. The independent associations have managed to more than hold their own with the white-collar employees and to retain a near monopoly of professional groups.

To accomplish this purpose, these associations, some of whose most influential members are in management, have had to do a complete about-face. Painfully, public management is shedding the notion that it can make the most effective and knowledgeable presentation of the case for employee salary increases and other benefits. A strong persistent ground swell toward collective bargaining is forcing even those on the supervisory level into an adversary position where they can no longer sit on both sides of the bargaining table.

When employee organizations are weak and pliant, the dispersion of managerial authority is highly advantageous to those who control the public purse strings. But the absence of a definable management, whether by tradition or design, becomes a fatal weakness when dealing with a strong, militant employee organization. The organization can often seize the initiative and dominate the course of negotiations. Public management is finding out now what private industry learned decades ago: that a strategy of "divide and rule" works when competing employee organizations are weak, but when they are strong, the strategy backfires into "divide and be whipsawed." Not only does public management becomes whipsawed between strong employee organizations, but an ill-defined management negotiating team is easily undermined and undercut by political pressures exerted by employee organizations on the legislative branch.

Most people prefer order to chaos, and unions are no exception in this regard. They have always preferred to deal with strong (but not overly strong) management negotiating teams that can make commitments which stick rather than to deal with heterogeneous assortments of managerial interests that become paralyzed by internal disagreement over anything that makes meaningful negotiations possible. As one union representative who deals with an association of small retail bakeries put it, "A three-ring circus is all right once in a great while, but who wants it for a steady diet?" It can be said of this union official that the one thing he fears as much as a defeat by the employer association is a union victory which would atomize the association into an undisciplined assortment of warring individualists.

Role of the Independent Employee Association in the Public Sector

Probably the most unusual feature of the transition to collective bargaining in the public sector is the evolving new role of the independent employee associations. That they are or were company unions on the order of those once prevalent in the private sector is undeniable. But what should not be forgotten is that company unions in the private sector did not simply disappear because they were banned by the National Labor Relations Act of 1935. Those which were set up as paper organizations to function only when needed to beat off a bona fide union failed to gain the adherence of a significant number of employees and inevitably went out of business. But most of those endowed with an inner vitality that kept them active on behalf of their members ultimately "graduated" (to use a common expression of that day) into bona fide unions. Many of the new unions, typified by those in the steel and auto industries, were midwived by "graduated" company unions. The Academy of Motion Picture Arts and Sciences, known now largely for its annual Oscar awards, was originally formed by the producers in 1927 to forestall unionization of the talent categories. Its activities ultimately produced just the opposite result. The academy introduced the principle of collective bargaining, and the experience gained in academy relationships enabled the talent groups to form the strong guilds which bargain today.

AFL-CIO unions, most of which still regard the emphasis placed by independent associations on professional standards as an anemic substitute for collective bargaining, greatly misjudge the importance of this area of employee relations. It is true that many public agency policies which these associations try to influence, if grouped together as professional standards, would in private industry be treated as exclusive management prerogatives. It is also true that initially the concern of independent associations with professional standards reflected in no small degree the interests of supervisory public management which dominated these organizations. But the involvement of professional groups in the standards of their profession is an unshakable fact of life today, not to be reduced to a mere identification with supervisory interests and certainly undeserving of such quips as "Intellectuals of the world, unite! You have nothing to lose but your brains."

The Importance of Professional Standards as Bargaining Issues in the Public Sector

The involvement of teachers in educational policy, of social workers in welfare policies and programs, of other professional employees in the policies of their agencies is no longer a *substitute* for collective bargaining, but is a dimension *added* to the process. The inclusion of professional matters on the agenda for discussion was initially welcomed by public management before the independent associations began to "graduate."

The American Federation of Teachers (AFT) was progressing at a snail's pace as long as its main thrust was on teacher working conditions, with educational policy a subordinate consideration. The organization became a serious contender to affiliates of the National Education Association (NEA) when it boldly proclaimed that no one was more qualified to know what was best for the children than the teachers themselves. In recent years we have seen both organizations carry the banner of professionalism in a direct challenge to the sacrosanct public itself. Across the nation the school systems of one major city after another, and even of whole states, have been partially or totally shut down by teacher walkouts—walkouts highlighted as much by issues of educational policy as by salaries and other working conditions.

In Detroit, when told that the citizenry would not vote the appropriations necessary to meet teachers' demands, an AFT spokesman replied that people who would not appropriate money to maintain a quality school system needed the education more than the children. With that declaration the teachers walked out and stayed out until they got an acceptable settlement.

Some years ago the Florida NEA affiliate carried the challenge even further when it staged a mass resignation of teachers throughout the entire state. An AP dispatch quoted a spokesman for the Florida Education Association as follows: "We're not asking for anything right now except quality education. It is far better to abandon the children for a few days than to abandon them for the rest of their educational lives." To which the Governor replied at the time that the state would never, but never, turn education over to the unions by bargaining on curriculum changes, teacher assignments, class size, and related matters.

The attitudes of both teacher organizations appear to reflect the thinking of John Stuart Mill, who wrote that there are things of the mind which are felt least by those who need them most, and education is one area that cannot be left open to the free play of the market.

Mediation, Fact-finding, and Arbitration
In Public Sector Disputes

In many areas of the United States public management has been reluctant to utilize available professional mediators to resolve dangerous impasses with employee organizations. One reason for this extreme caution is a dearth of experience with the mediation process because of the erroneous assumption that the mediator is a kind of quasi fact-finder or quasi arbitrator who might under pressure make public statements and recommendations adverse to management's interest. Mediators in private industry carry on in no such manner, if for no other reason than that they would never get away with it.

A mediator is a go-between, a confidant of both parties, whose exploratory conversations on disputed issues are off the record. His public pronouncements are largely on procedural aspects of negotiations, such as expressions of foreboding that not enough progress is being made or optimistic observations that the parties are trying very hard, that some progress is being made, and that round-the-clock sessions are being scheduled.

A great deal of confusion is engendered by the failure to distinguish between three separate and entirely distinct functions: mediation, fact-finding (including advisory or nonbinding arbitration), and binding arbitration.

When so-called "mediators" or "mediation boards" have the reserved authority to make advisory or binding arbitration decisions, they are performing, not one function, but two of three separate functions. For a vocalist to accompany himself on the piano does not mean that vocalizing is piano playing or vice versa. Arbitration is a judicial process. When the arbitrator enters a situation, *negotiations stop* unless the parties want to continue talks outside the hearings in hope of avoiding a binding arbitration decision. When the mediator enters a situation, *negotiations are usually intensified,* because the parties still have to make their own decision, using the mediator as a new line of communication.

Which suggests the chief reason for a lack of enthusiasm for mediation among many experienced negotiators in public management—a belief that unless the persuasive powers of the mediator are reinforced by the threat of an economic contest, he is ineffective and can even become a new line of confusion rather than communication. The syllogism is as follows:

Major premise: Mediation is part of the collective-bargaining process.

Minor premise: Without the right to strike, effective collective bargaining is not possible.
Conclusion: Effective mediation is not possible.

When proponents of this syllogism apply it to disputes where the ultimate power of decision lies in compulsory arbitration, then a dissent must be noted. To those who insist that the threat of an adverse arbitration award does not generate enough pressure on the parties to make mediation effective one cannot resist saying, "If you haven't tried it, don't knock it." California mediators have had twenty years of experience mediating in such situations, and they form a significant part of the government agency's case load. The California experience is fairly typical of other parts of the United States and even more typical of Canada.

Most grievances dealt with in mediation sessions are resolved on their own merits through the application of human relations techniques. There is another technique for mediating grievances, but the proportion of professional mediators who have the requisite knowledge of arbitral standards to apply this technique is not large. There are aspects of the proceedings, some mediators feel, that make conferences of the following type more of a "bootleg" arbitration than a mediation discussion:

The parties first present their opening positions and arguments in a joint session with the mediator, maintaining throughout a keynote of informality. When the mediator has thoroughly familiarized himself with the disputed issue, he meets with the parties separately for deeper explorations. The separate discussions are intended to give the parties an off-the-record opportunity to check their positions against established arbitration criteria, in effect a common law of arbitration, and to get the mediator's objective assessment of their strength and weaknesses should they go on to a formal binding proceeding. A very high proportion of grievances undergoing this test (perhaps a higher proportion than grievances treated on a human relations basis) are resolved after the parties have each pondered the degree of risk in going forward. For those interested in a more elaborate description and analysis of the foregoing mediation technique, an article written years ago on preventive mediation is recommended.[3]

THE SOVEREIGNTY DOCTRINE IN PUBLIC EMPLOYMENT

It seems appropriate at this point to make some observations on the sovereignty doctrine as an impediment to collective bargaining. This analysis will focus on the contention that managerial sovereignty in the public sector

---

[3] Paul Prasow, "Preventive Mediation: A Technique to Improve Industrial Relations," *Labor Law Journal,* vol. 1, August, 1950.

precludes the kind of give-and-take characteristic of collective bargaining in the private sector. Reference is made not to naïve objections of people unfamiliar with collective bargaining, but to questions raised by highly sophisticated management representatives.

The unsophisticated declare flatly that the basic conditions of public employment are fixed by law, and are therefore not a proper subject for collective bargaining. Employee organizations, they say, must avail themselves of the same democratic processes for influencing government as are provided for other interested citizenry.

Experienced management negotiators know better. They are well aware that the collective-bargaining process has an inner dynamics of its own, that folk wisdom, character, honesty, integrity, straightforwardness, etc., cannot substitute for a knowledge of the rules of the game. The novice, who believes that collective bargaining is essentially an excursion in social uplift wants to cut through the ritual of negotiations on the assumption that the whole thing can be resolved "if we all sit down like intelligent persons, lay our cards on the table right now, and get this thing over with." Such an approach, as many well-intentioned public management negotiators are discovering to their chagrin, is fatal to successful bargaining.

"But," interposes the experienced management negotiator, "how the devil can we formulate a bargaining position and then time each move away from that position toward a realistic settlement without being undercut by public and private pronouncements from the legislative branch?"

The question goes to the heart of the problem of defining a management in the public sector. Until it is answered satisfactorily, employee-management relations will remain inherently unstable. In 1967, for example, a major California city had to weather a general strike precipitated by a press release issued by the city council announcing that there would be no salary increases, even as a management negotiating team was agreeing to salary increases that were less than those prevailing in the private sector.

The Problem of Informing the Public on Negotiations in the Public Sector

Not the least of the impediments to a definable management in the public sector is a narrow, overrigid interpretation in collective-bargaining matters of the public's "right to know." The basis of a democracy is an informed citizenry that must know what those who act on its behalf are doing and exert an ultimate control over their actions. But to argue from this principle that all public business, with no exceptions, must be conducted in a goldfish bowl is to make a travesty of the democratic process. Most of the unions which went in for goldfish-bowl negotiations had to eliminate the practice when a sizable number of their constituents in attendance got wise to the fact that the negotiators were just making speeches to the audience ("fertility rites" the proceedings were derisively called) and the real negotiations were taking place on the telephone or in secluded restaurants.

The point of these observations is not to question in principle the right of the public to attend the deliberative sessions of public councils, boards, and commissions. It is when this principle is carried to extremes, permitting no exceptions, such as collective-bargaining sessions, that the democratic process becomes subverted.

There was a time, in a bygone era, when newspaper people insisted that freedom of the press entitled them to print all the news of a labor dispute without consideration of its impact on the conflict. Today no newspaper of consequence would print, unless authorized by the parties, the terms of a tentative settlement before the union membership had a chance to vote on it. Despite bold union pronouncements that "we are standing firm on our demands," there is often a tacit understanding in the membership that these demands are inflated and will eventually have to be compromised. Considing the wide range of opinions in a membership as to what constitutes a suitable compromise, ratification meetings have to be handled with great delicacy and skill. If the press were to reveal prematurely the bare facts of a tentative understanding involving painful compromises, a raucous, disgruntled membership might drown out the attempts of union negotiators to explain the projected settlement in detail. The very strict Ralph Brown Act in California requires that public business be transacted in open public session. Yet an exception is made of the mediation agency in the Department of Industrial Relations. The California Labor Code expressly provides that the records of that agency are to be confidential except for arbitration awards.

The insistence that public management negotiate in a goldfish bowl sharply conflicts with the realities of collective bargaining. There is a Latin saying, *Abusus non tollit usum,* which translates loosely into "The abuse of a practice is not an argument against its proper use." It is granted that irregularities do crop up when there is unnecessary and excessive secrecy in government. However, if someone is playing stud poker with the taxpayers' chips, it would be foolish to handicap him by demanding in the name of democracy that he play with five cards face up against an opponent who keeps a hole card down. In this connection the following observation is most relevant:

> I must confess that I cannot conceive the bargaining process involving a three-way operation [between management, unions, and the public], and under our system of government we would be inclined to believe that the

> public is ultimately represented at the bargaining table through those
> who represent the state.[4]

This statement reflects a Canadian viewpoint, but a viewpoint just as applicable to our own system of government as it is to Canada. We must not underestimate the problem of reconciling a definable public management with our uniquely American political system of checks and balances, which tends to diffuse power and impede its concentration. But the United States is also the home of pragmatism, a philosophy which holds that the validity of a theory is based upon its utility for getting things done that have to be done.

Trilateral Negotiations in the Private Sector

It is doubtful if the decision-making authority of management is more widely dispersed in the public sector than it is in the privately owned San Pedro (California) fishing industry. Fishermen may not negotiate directly with canners because the antitrust division of the Justice Department, sustained by the High Court, has ruled that such negotiations would constitute a conspiracy to fix prices in restraint of trade. The fishermen's unions must negotiate with the boat owner's association, which in turn negotiates with the canners. The hitch, of course, is that the boat owners cannot give the fishermen anything which they do not first get from the canners. The boat owners, when they negotiate with the canners, have mixed emotions. The higher the price per ton they can get for fish, the larger their share of the proceeds. But if the canners balk and set a price for fish which does not satisfy the fishermen's unions (often in bitter rivalry with each other), then the fleet is tied up. This poses a catastrophic threat to the boat owners, who have enormous investments in their boats and equipment.

To complicate the struggle further, the California Fish and Game Commission, for conservation reasons, limits the sardine season to a fixed period of months, and the fish do not, in any event, linger in nearby coastal waters waiting for a dispute to end. The nuances and complexities of these trilateral negotiations would baffle a nuclear physicist. Yet no one familiar with the industry would deny that viable collective negotiations take place and that the underlying relationships between the parties are generally cordial.

A final observation on bilateralism in collective bargaining may be in order. One gets the impression sometimes, from the frequent emphasis

[4] Thomas J. Plunkett, "The Seminar in Retrospect," in Kenneth O. Warner (ed.), *Collective Bargaining in the Public Service: Theory and Practice,* Public Personnel Association, Chicago, Ill., 1967, p. 193.

placed on the coequal status of the parties at the bargaining table, that an important distinction between those who manage and those who are managed is being glossed over. Coequality in bargaining does not mean that management and employees have an equal say on how the agency is to be run. Whether it be in the public or private sector, management must retain the administrative initiative to operate the enterprise. The employee organization has the right, or should have the right, to protest those management actions it deems arbitrary, discriminatory, or generally unreasonable. But it must be understood that management still makes the initial decisions, with or without consultation of employee organizations, in the expectation that its decisions are to be complied with promptly. The employee organization on its part has the right to protest these administrative decisions and to seek redress through grievance-adjustment procedures. It is understood, of course, that if the employee organization's position is subsequently upheld (by arbitration, advisory or binding) then management will make appropriate adjustments retroactively.

In conclusion, the keystone of a definable management is its reserved right of administrative initiative to operate the enterprise. If, however, employee organizations are denied the right of redress by impartial intervention (mediation, fact-finding, or arbitration), then realistically they can be expected to assert a reserved right of their own to apply economic sanctions, whether these sanctions take the form of outright strikes in violation of the law and in defiance of public opinion or semilegal mass resignations and sickness epidemics.

Interest versus Rights Disputes in the Public Sector

The parallel drawn between the current upheavals in the public sector and the upheavals in the private sector during the turbulent 1930s was not a rhetorical indulgence. Common to both periods were the accelerated growth of employee organizations and their militant struggles for meaningful recognition. As Prof. Everett M. Kassalow of Wisconsin University has graphically observed:

> Strikes of public employees, once a novelty, are no longer unusual. During one three-month period, not so long ago, a casual check showed social workers' strikes in Chicago, Sacramento, and White Plains; slowdowns of firefighters in Buffalo and of policemen in Detroit; strikes among university maintenance employees at Ohio State, Indiana, and the University of Kansas Medical Center; a three-day "heal-in" by the interns and residents of the Boston City Hospital; "informational" picketing, with a strike threat, by the Philadelphia School Nurses' Association; teachers' strikes in a dozen communities, ranging from West Mifflin,

Pennsylvania, and Gibraltor, Ohio, to South Bend, Indiana, and Baltimore, Maryland. Such strikes and slowdowns among teachers, policemen, firemen, etc. have become daily occurrences.[5]

In coping with such impasse situations as described by Kassalow, public management has turned more and more to direct negotiations, fact-finding, and mediation. However, with regard to day-to-day grievances of public employees, it seems reasonably safe to predict that eventually they will be processed in much the same manner as in private industry today. With some modifications due to the nature of governmental employment, the arbitral procedures, practices, policies, and criteria for adjudicating grievances and disputes over contract interpretation will be borrowed largely from the private sector.

Tangible evidence of the trend in this direction is contained in recommendations of the President's Review Committee on Employee-Management Relations in the Federal Service. Two of the Committee's key recommendations on grievances, appeals, and interpretation of agreements provide that *"arbitration should be made available for the resolution of disputes over the interpretation and application of an agreement"* and *"exceptions to arbitrators' decisions should be sustained only on grounds similar to those applied by the courts in private sector labor-management relations. Procedures for considering exceptions to decisions should be established by the Panel."*[6]

In support of its recommendations, the Review Committee found that arbitration of grievances in the federal service had "worked well and has benefited both employees and agencies."[7] The Committee observed that:

> Many thousands of grievances have been settled without referral to arbitration. In those few instances in which the grievance was referred to arbitration, the arbitrators' decisions have been accepted most of the time. There have been some few instances in which agencies have rejected or modified the decision. Witnesses appearing before the Committee objected to an agency's unilateral right in this regard. The Review Committee feels that arbitrators' decisions should be accepted by the parties. Challenges to such awards will be sustained only on grounds similar to those applied by the courts in private sector labor-management relations, and procedures for the consideration of exceptions should be developed. . . .[8]

[5] Everett M. Kassalow, "Trade Unionism Goes Public," *The Public Interest*, no. 14, Winter, 1969, p. 118.

[6] *Report of the President's Review Committee on Employee-Management Relations in the Federal Service*, April, 1968, p. 12. The panel referred to was the Advisory Panel to the Review Committee consisting of such prominent arbitrators and scholars as Lloyd H. Bailer, Derek C. Bok, Leo C. Brown, S.J., Mrs. Jean T. McKelvey, and Lloyd Ulman.

[7] *Ibid.*, p. 14.

[8] *Ibid.*, pp. 14–15.

SUMMARY

Collective bargaining in the public sector, at all levels of government, has undergone a vast transformation since 1962, when President Kennedy first issued Executive Order 10988 on employee-management cooperation in the federal service.   Although applicable only to the federal government, this order had the same impact on public employment throughout the country as the National Labor Relations Act had on private industry.

While federal employees in Canada may choose between compulsory arbitration and the strike weapon in resolving impasses over interest disputes, such alternatives are not acceptable in the United States.   In this country public employees are legally prohibited from striking in all jurisdictions, although they can and do engage in strikes with alarming and increasing frequency.   Insofar as grievance and contract-interpretation disputes are concerned, the trend is in the direction of impartial arbitration, advisory or binding.

A basic question facing management and labor in the public sector is whether, considering the unique features of governmental employment, the fundamental principles involved in the adversary nature of contract negotiations can apply to the public sector.   Some reply in the negative, holding that the dispersion of authority, both within the executive branch and between the executive and legislative branches, makes it impossible to engage in the collective bargaining so characteristic of the private sector.

Others reply that the dispersion of managerial authority in the public sector has a varying impact upon negotiations depending upon the strength and militancy of the employee organization.   If the latter is weak and divided, dispersion of managerial authority is highly advantageous to those who control the public purse strings.   On the other hand, if the employee organization is strong and militant, it can often seize the initiative and dominate the negotiations, and dispersion of managerial authority becomes a fatal weakness.

There are usually two types of employee organizations in the public sector, the *independent association* and the *affiliated union*.   The latter has often looked upon the former as a company union dominated by public management.   However, a unique feature of the transition of collective bargaining in the public sector is the evolution of a new role for the independent employee association.   Just as many company unions of the 1930s graduated into bona fide unions, so have a number of employee associations in public employment graduated into independent and militant collective-bargaining representatives.   An important feature of this transition has been the emphasis of the independent association on *professional standards*. The involvement of public employee associations (representing such professional personnel as teachers, nurses, and social workers) in the policies of their agencies is no longer a substitute for collective bargaining, but is a dimension added to the process.

Public management is generally reluctant to call in the professional mediator to help resolve impasses with employee organizations over interest issues. This reluctance arises from inexperience with the use of mediators and confusion as to their role. In many jurisdictions no distinction is made between mediation, arbitration, and fact-finding—three entirely separate functions. A *mediator* is a go-between, a friend of both parties, who has no authority to make a decision and whose discussions with the parties are entirely off the record. In contrast, the *arbitrator* is a judicial agent who meets with the parties in a somewhat formal hearing and has authority to rule on the issues on an advisory or binding basis. When a mediator enters the situation, negotiations are usually intensified. When the arbitrator enters the dispute, negotiations stop. A *fact finder* investigates the dispute and issues a report on the issues, with or without recommendations for settlement.

Many persons knowledgeable in collective bargaining maintain that the sovereignty doctrine precludes the kind of negotiations characteristic of the private sector. The basic problem involves defining management in the public sector. Until this problem is solved, public labor relations will remain basically unstable. One impediment to a definable management in the public sector is a narrow interpretation in bargaining matters of the public's "right to know." The tradition in some governmental jurisdictions is that all public business, including collective bargaining, must be conducted in a goldfish bowl. The experience of private industry with goldfish bowl negotiations should prove a valuable lesson for those in the public sector. It eventually became apparent to all concerned that a goldfish-bowl session was simply a charade for the benefit of the audience and that the real negotiations were taking place privately and behind the scenes.

Direct negotiations, mediation, and fact-finding are being increasingly used in the public sector, especially in impasses over interest issues. Voluntary arbitration (advisory or binding) is rapidly becoming the standard method of resolving impasses over grievances and questions of contract interpretation.

Chapter 13

The legal basis of labor arbitration

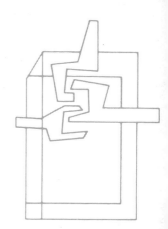

Introduction

■ In Chapter 1 the point was made that prior to 1940, arbitration was rarely used for resolving disputes over interpretation or application of a collective-bargaining agreement. Today, grievance arbitration not only is widely accepted by the parties but has become firmly embedded in our national labor policy as the preferred method for settling such labor-management differences.

Of the many forces responsible for this transformation in the past thirty years, two deserve special consideration:

1 The influence of the War Labor Board (WLB) in the period 1942–1945
2 The series of landmark decisions on grievance arbitration by the U.S. Supreme Court beginning in 1957

IMPACT OF WAR LABOR BOARD

The first of these forces has already been discussed, in the opening chapter. Suffice it to add that throughout its existence during World War II, the WLB consistently urged the parties to use voluntary arbitration procedures.

243

It wrote into literally thousands of collective-bargaining agreements those basic grievance-arbitration clauses which have now become standard in over 90 percent of all current agreements. By the end of 1945, when the WLB went out of existence, an unprecedented development had occurred:/For the first time in American industrial relations a viable, practical, *peaceful alternative to industrial warfare* had been widely adopted for settling disputes over the interpretation and application of existing collective agreements./

Grievance Arbitration: The Pioneering Stage

The significance of this development should not be minimized. It involved a historic exchange of rights: the union gave up its right to strike during the life of the agreement, and management gave up its right to make the ultimate decision on many aspects of day-to-day operations. In return management was assured of uninterrupted production during the contract term, and employees were assured of due process and just treatment. As Neil W. Chamberlain has so aptly noted, the grievance and arbitration procedure is:

> ... one of the truly great accomplishments of American industrial relations. For all its defects—the bypassing of some of the appeals stages, its use by the union as a political device to convince the employees that it is looking out for their interests, the slowness with which it sometimes operates—it constitutes a social invention of great importance. Although something similar is used in some other countries, it is perhaps safe to say that nowhere else has it reached the high stage of development that it has in the United States, in the sense that it is so widely employed and has achieved so much vitality at the local level.[1]

In the twelve years following the WLB's termination, the institution of arbitration began to evolve a discernible body of predictable criteria which provided the necessary uniformity for interpretation and application of collective agreements. It should be stressed that during this period the judiciary (particularly the federal courts) played a minimal role in shaping the arbitration process. The parties and the arbitrators shared primary responsibility (and credit) for adapting the emerging institution to the special needs and attributes of the industrial environment. Arbitration awards

---

[1] Neil W. Chamberlain, *The Labor Sector,* McGraw-Hill Book Company, New York, 1965, p. 240. In regard to Chamberlain's comment that the grievance and arbitration procedure is used "by the union as a political device to convince the employees that it is looking out for their interests,..." he is undoubtedly referring to activities of over-zealous union representatives who are known in legal circles as *"vexatious litigants"*— activities quite different from those of union officials who, on occasion, militantly pursue legitimate grievances, using a "bandwagon" approach to enhance their own image and that of the union in the eyes of the dues-paying voting membership.

were enforced largely by state courts relying on application of the common law or state statutes.

The Taft-Hartley Act and Section 301

Prior to 1947 Congress had consistently refrained from providing for federal enforcement of collective agreements. Nothing in the National Labor Relations Act (NLRA) of 1935, the Wagner Act, authorized the National Labor Relations Board to enforce such agreements, nor could the breach of a labor contract be treated as an unfair labor practice. Then Congress passed the Labor-Management Relations Act (LMRA) of 1947, the Taft-Hartley Act, and included Section 301, whose first two subsections were to have a most profound effect on the legal status of arbitration. The parties, the arbitrators, the federal and state courts, and legal scholars are still evaluating the momentous consequences of their impact.

In essence, Section 301(a) provides that suits for violation of contracts between an employer and a labor organization representing employees in an industry affecting interstate commerce or between any such labor organizations may be brought in any United States District Court having jurisdiction of the parties, without regard to the amount in controversy or the parties' citizenship.[2]

Section 301(b) states that any labor organization or employer in an industry affecting interstate commerce shall be bound by the acts of its agents, and any such labor organization may sue or be sued in the United States courts as an entity and on behalf of the employees whom it represents, and any money judgment against the labor organization in a United States District Court shall be enforceable only against the organization as an entity and against its assets, and not against any individual member or his assets.[3]

LINCOLN MILLS—EMERGING ROLE OF THE FEDERAL JUDICIARY IN LABOR ARBITRATION

Although a 1955 decision of the U.S. Supreme Court cast some doubt on the significance of Section 301,[4] it was the Lincoln Mills case of 1957[5] that provided the foundation for developing an elaborate system of federal substantive law on arbitration and the labor contract.

[2] Labor-Management Relations Act, Public Law 101, 80th Cong., 1st Sess., 29 U.S.C.A. § 185 (1947).
[3] *Ibid.*
[4] *Ass'n of Westinghouse Salaried Employees v. Westinghouse Elec. Corp.* 348 U.S. 437.
[5] *Textile Workers Union v. Lincoln Mills,* 353 U.S. 448 (1957). The full text of the Supreme Court opinion in this case, as well as the dissenting opinion of Justice Frankfurter, is contained in Appendix A, p. 294.

The essential facts in this case are as follows: The union had a collective bargaining agreement with the employer which provided that there would be no strikes or work stoppages and that grievances would be handled according to a specified procedure, including arbitration as the last step. The dispute involved several grievances over work loads and job assignments. Although the complaints were processed through the steps of the grievance procedure, no mutual settlement could be reached. The union then invoked the arbitration provisions of the contract, but the employer refused arbitration, declaring the issues nonarbitrable. The union sued in federal court under Section 301, seeking specific enforcement of the arbitration provisions. The District Court ordered the employer to comply with the arbitration section of the agreement. The employer petitioned the Court of Appeals, which reversed the lower court by a close vote. The union then petitioned the U.S. Supreme Court, which reversed the Appeals Court and ordered the company to comply with the arbitration provisions.

In upholding the applicability of Section 301 to collective agreements, the Court in Lincoln Mills affirmed four basic principles:

1 That either party could sue in the federal courts for enforcement of a collective agreement.
2 That federal rather than state law should be controlling in such suits.
3 That an agreement to arbitrate future disputes is enforceable in federal courts under federal law rather than in state courts under various state laws.
4 That the Norris-LaGuardia Act, which limits the issuance of injunctions by federal courts in labor disputes, does not apply to a union's suit seeking enforcement of an employer's promise to arbitrate.

Speaking for the majority, Justice Douglas summed up the Court's reasoning by stressing that an agreement to arbitrate grievance disputes is the *quid pro quo* for an agreement not to strike and that Section 301 expresses a policy that federal courts should enforce these agreements on behalf of or against labor organizations. He also noted that by implication Congress had rejected the common-law rule against enforcement of executory agreements to arbitrate.

In a conclusion with far-reaching implications, Justice Douglas stated that:

> The substantive law to apply in suits under § 301 (a) is federal law which the courts must fashion from the policy of our national labor laws. The Labor Management Relations Act expressly furnishes some substantive law. It points out what the parties may or may not do in certain situations. Other problems will lie in the penumbra of express statutory mandates. Some will lack express statutory sanctions but will be solved by looking at the policy of the legislation and fashioning a remedy that will effectuate that policy. The range of judicial inventiveness will be deter-

mined by the nature of the problem. . . . Federal interpretation of the federal law will govern, not state law. . . . But state law, if compatible with the purpose of § 301, may be resorted to in order to find the rule that will best effectuate the federal policy. . . . Any state law applied, however, will be absorbed as federal law and will not be an independent source of private rights.[6]

As the authors have stressed throughout this book, especially in Chapter 3, grievance arbitration (unlike commercial arbitration) is not a substitute for litigation, but rather a substitute for the strike. This concept is central to the Supreme Court's ruling in Lincoln Mills. For the first time the highest Court gave judicial recognition and sanction to this fundamental reality of collective bargaining.

A number of legal scholars and arbitrators expressed considerable concern over the Supreme Court's decision in Lincoln Mills, fearing it could lead to harmful judicial interference with the labor arbitration process. In a leading article on the subject, UCLA law professor Benjamin Aaron concluded that the Court's ruling was both a threat and a challenge:

The threat is clear: if the present trend toward seeking the enforcement or interpretation of collective agreements in the courts, rather than in arbitration, continues unchecked, the relations between employers and employees will eventually be governed, as Shulman warned, by "agencies of authoritative control from above removed from the unique atmosphere of the particular enterprise." Under such a system the arbitrator's function would cease to be the interpretation and application of the collective agreement under procedures devised by the parties, and would become more and more the interpretation and application of the federal law of arbitration. Moreover, under such a system the pressure on the losing party in an arbitration case to appeal the decision to the higher authority of the courts would be almost irresistible.

The challenge of Lincoln Mills, especially to members of our profession, is no less apparent; it is to demonstrate, by our actions and by our teaching, that the benefits of industrial self-government far outweigh its imperfections, and that arbitration, despite its weaknesses and abuses, offers far greater hope than litigation for the development of sound labor-management relations in a free enterprise system.[7]

Another distinguished professor of law also considered that Lincoln Mills posed serious problems for the arbitration process:

If the courts impose their approach to the construction of wills, trusts and tightly-drawn commercial contracts upon the interpretation of collec-

[6] *Ibid.*, 456–457.
[7] Benjamin Aaron, "On First Looking into the Lincoln Mills Decision," *Arbitration and the Law: Proceedings of the Twelfth Annual Meeting, National Academy of Arbitrators,* BNA, Inc., 1959, pp. 13–14.

tive bargaining agreements on the theory that those who seek judicial aid must accept existing judicial standards regardless of their workability in the new environment of labor relations, then section 301 and the *Lincoln Mills* case may severely damage labor arbitration and industrial relations. If professional arbitrators, the advocates who appear before them and the interested academicians go their separate way complaining of judicial ineptitude, there is little hope of achieving a workable accommodation. . . .

The ruling that the federal courts are to develop a substantive law of collective bargaining agreements also presents a challenge to labor specialists and the legal profession. The federal judges start with a clean slate. The Supreme Court has instructed them to fashion a law of collective bargaining agreements from the express provisions, the penumbra and the policy of our national labor laws. "The range of judicial inventiveness will be determined by the nature of the problem." [353 U.S. 457.] Outside of the area controlled by statute there is no more important treasury of experience than the record of grievance arbitrations. We may have been bemused by the precepts that justice requires deciding each case upon its merits and that no two contracts are quite the same, **but surely we have not labored at the administration of collective agreements for almost two decades without arriving at some generalizations upon which the unbiased can agree even though partisan interests preclude unanimity.** Perhaps only a few rules have developed, but I submit that there are attitudes, approaches, and even a number of flexible principles. More efforts may have to go into distilling generalizations from the amorphous mass of arbitration opinions before the courts can be expected to use them. Counsel will face the further problem of translating the ways of the industrial world into legal doctrines comprehensible to judges who lack industrial experience. However, if the professional arbitrators and labor lawyers who work with them can surmount these obstacles, the industrial jurisprudence which they have been developing might give wisdom and vitality to conventional law. [Italics supplied.][8]

In a separate concurring opinion on Lincoln Mills, Justice Burton, speaking for himself and joined by Justice Harlan, implied that he had some misgivings about the majority position. Declaring that he did not subscribe to the Court's conclusion that the substantive law to be applied in a suit under Section 301 is federal law, he nevertheless conceded that "some federal rights may necessarily be involved, . . . and hence . . . the constitutionality of Section 301 can be upheld. . . ."

In a strong dissenting opinion Justice Frankfurter reiterated his position set forth in Westinghouse[9] that 301 is a procedural section and cannot be "transmuted into a mandate to the federal courts to fashion a whole body of

[8] Archibald Cox, "Reflections upon Labor Arbitration in the Light of the Lincoln Mills Case," *Arbitration and the Law: Proceedings of the Twelfth Annual Meeting, National Academy of Arbitrators*, BNA, Inc., 1959, pp. 25–26, 29–30.

[9] *Ass'n of Westinghouse Salaried Employees v. Westinghouse Elec. Corp.*, 348 U.S. 437.

federal substantive law appropriate for the . . . problems raised by collective bargaining." In a caustic criticism of the majority's opinion, Justice Frankfurter complained that:

> The Court . . . sees no problem of "judicial power" in casting upon the federal courts, with no guides except "judicial inventiveness," the task of applying a whole industrial code that is as yet in the bosom of the judiciary. There are severe limits of "judicial inventiveness" even for the most imaginative judges. The law is not a "brooding omnipresence in the sky," . . . it cannot be drawn from there like nitrogen from the air. . . . But the Court makes § 301 a mountain instead of a molehill and, by giving an example of "judicial inventiveness," it thereby solves all the constitutional problems that would otherwise have to be faced.
>
> Even on the Court's attribution to § 301 of a direction to the federal courts to fashion, out of bits and pieces elsewhere to be gathered, a federal common law of labor contracts, it still does not follow that Congress has enacted that an agreement to arbitrate industrial differences be specifically enforceable in the federal courts. On the contrary, the body of relevant federal law precludes such enforcement of arbitration clauses in collective-bargaining agreements.[10]

THE STEELWORKERS TRILOGY[11]—FEDERAL COURT ENFORCEMENT OF ARBITRATION AGREEMENTS AND AWARDS

On June 20, 1960, the U.S. Supreme Court issued three landmark decisions which remain the most significant and sometimes controversial judicial rulings on the matter of labor arbitration. The cases provoked such widespread comment and critical evaluation that a voluminous literature concerning them soon emerged.[12]

---

[10] *Textile Workers Union v. Lincoln Mills,* 353 U.S. 448, 465–466.

[11] *United Steelworkers v. Am. Mfg. Co.,* 363 U.S. 564 (1960); *United Steelworkers v. Warrior & Gulf Navigation Co.,* 363 U.S. 574 (1960); *United Steelworkers v. Enterprise Wheel & Car Corp.,* 363 U.S. 593 (1960). For the full text of the Steelworkers Trilogy (majority, concurring, and dissenting opinions) see Appendix A, p. 294.

[12] See Benjamin Aaron, "Arbitration in the Federal Courts: Aftermath of the Trilogy," *UCLA Law Review,* vol. 9, 1962, p. 360; Gilbert A. Cornfield, "Developing Standards for Determining Arbitrability of Labor Disputes by Federal Courts," *Labor Law Journal,* vol. 14, 1963, p. 564; Harold W. Davey, "The Supreme Court and Arbitration: The Musings of an Arbitrator," *Notre Dame Lawyer,* vol. 36, 1961, pp. 138–145; Alex Elson, "The Supreme Court and the 'Private' World of Arbitration," *The Arbitration Journal,* vol. 18, no. 2, 1963, pp. 65–76; William B. Gould, "The Supreme Court and Labor Arbitration," *Labor Law Journal,* vol. 12, 1961, pp. 331–345; Charles O. Gregory, "Enforcement of Collective Agreements by Arbitration," *Virginia Law Review,* vol. 47, 1962, p. 883; Bernard D. Meltzer, "The Supreme Court, Arbitrability, and Collective Bargaining," *University of Chicago Law Review,* vol. 28, 1961, p. 464; Russell A. Smith, "Arbitrability: The Arbitrator, the Courts and the Parties," *The Arbitration Journal,* vol. 17,

In each of the three cases the Steelworkers Union was the moving party requesting the high Court either to order arbitration or to enforce an arbitration award. The following outline of the fact situations, the basic issues presented, the judicial decisions, and the reasoning is intended to serve as background for the ensuing discussion.

1 AMERICAN MANUFACTURING COMPANY

Fact Situation

The union sought to arbitrate the grievance of an employee who was denied reinstatement to his job after having settled a workmen's compensation claim against the company for an industrial injury. The union argued that the employee should get his job back because his physician had stated that he was able to perform his former duties and that his seniority rights under the agreement entitled him to reinstatement. The company rejected these contentions, maintaining that the employee was estopped from making his claim because he had only recently collected workmen's compensation for a permanent partial disability resulting from an occupational injury. The company also stated that the employee was physically unable to do the work and that a dispute over his reinstatement was not an arbitrable issue.

The collective agreement between the parties contained the standard grievance-arbitration procedure and a no-strike clause. When management refused to arbitrate, the union brought an action against the company under Section 301 of LMRA for specific performance of the arbitration clause. The District Court denied the petition and ruled that since the employee had accepted a settlement on the basis of permanent partial disability, he was estopped from claiming any seniority or employment rights. The Court of Appeals also denied the petition but gave different reasons, finding that the grievance was "a frivolous, patently baseless one, not subject to arbitration under the collective bargaining agreement." The matter was then appealed to the Supreme Court.

no. 1, 1962, pp. 3–22; Russell A. Smith and Dallas L. Jones, "Management and Labor Appraisals and Criticisms of the Arbitration Process: A Report with Comments," *Michigan Law Review*, vol. 62, 1964, p. 1115; Russell A. Smith and Dallas L. Jones, "Arbitration: The Emerging Federal Law," *Michigan Law Review*, vol. 63, 1965, p. 751; Franklin B. Snyder, "What Has the Supreme Court Done to Arbitration?" *Labor Law Journal*, vol. 12, 1961, pp. 93–98; "Symposium: Arbitration and the Courts," *Northwestern University Law Review*, vol. 58, 1963, pp. 466, 494–520, 632–644.

For the most comprehensive critical statement on the Steelworkers Trilogy and labor arbitration in general, see P. R. Hays, *Labor Arbitration: A Dissenting View*, Yale University Press, New Haven, Conn., 1966. For an excellent rebuttal to Judge Hays, see Saul Wallen, "Arbitrators and Judges: Dispelling the Hays Haze," *California Management Review*, Spring, 1967, pp. 17–24.

Basic Issue

What is the role of the federal courts when called upon to enforce a collective-bargaining contract containing an agreement to arbitrate future questions of contract interpretation?

Supreme Court Decision

They should enforce the agreement and order arbitration as long as the party seeking arbitration presents a claim which on its face is governed by the contract. The courts may not review the merits of the grievance under the guise of interpreting the agreement, which is the exclusive function of the arbitrator. The lower court's decision was reversed and arbitration of the grievance was ordered.

Court's Reasoning

> The function of the court is very limited when the parties have agreed to submit all questions of contract interpretation to the arbitrator. It is confined to ascertaining where the party seeking arbitration is making a claim which on its face is governed by the contract. Whether the moving party is right or wrong is a question of contract interpretation for the arbitrator. In these circumstances the moving party should not be deprived of the arbitrator's judgment, when it was his judgment and all that it connotes that was bargained for.[13]

The courts, therefore, are precluded from weighing the merits of the grievance or assessing the equity of a particular claim and from seaching for particular language in the written instrument which will support the claim. The agreement requires that all grievances involving contract interpretation be submitted to arbitration, not just those which a court deems meritorious. The Court observed that processing of even frivolous claims "may have therapeutic values of which those who are not a part of the plant environment may be quite unaware."

The Court has been severely criticized for adding "therapeutic values" as a "touchstone in judicial construction." Supporters of the Steelworkers Trilogy have interpreted the Court's reference to mean that since a union is a political institution, it must on occasion arbitrate a grievance because of membership pressure. Others have claimed that a full and frank airing of all aspects of the grievance at a hearing presided over by a neutral has a salutary psychological effect on the parties regardless of the ultimate decision by the arbitrator.

---

[13] *United Steelworkers v. Am. Mfg. Co.,* 363 U.S. 564, 567–568.

2 WARRIOR AND GULF NAVIGATION COMPANY

Fact Situation

The company had laid off about twenty maintenance employees in the bargaining unit after contracting out such work to other firms. A number of the laid-off employees filed a grievance protesting the company's action during the term of a binding contract and alleging a partial lockout in violation of the contract. The written instrument contained a no-strike, no-lockout clause and a grievance procedure culminating in arbitration. Included in the grievance procedure was a general provision that "matters which are strictly a function of management shall not be subject to arbitration under this section." The agreement was silent on the subject of subcontracting.

When management refused to arbitrate, the union sued the company under Section 301 of LMRA for specific performance of the arbitration clause. The District Court dismissed the union's petition finding that the grievance was not arbitrable because ". . . the contracting out of repair and maintenance work . . . is strictly a function of management not limited in any respect by the labor agreement involved here." A majority on the Appeals Court agreed with the lower court, holding that the collective agreement had withdrawn from the grievance procedure "matters which are strictly a function of management" and that contracting out fell within that exception. The union then appealed to the Supreme Court.

Basic Issue

What is the permissible scope of federal judicial inquiry into a labor agreement containing an arbitration clause when there is doubt as to the arbitration clause's coverage of the particular dispute?

Supreme Court Decision

In the absence of an express provision excluding a particular grievance from arbitration, the courts should not inquire into the merits of the dispute or seek to interpret the arbitration section. Doubts as to the scope of the arbitration clause in encompassing the particular dispute should be resolved in favor of coverage. The lower court's decision was reversed and the company was ordered to arbitrate the grievance.

Court's Reasoning

In an unusually detailed analysis of (a) the nature of the collective agreement, (b) the role of the arbitrator in interpreting the agreement, and (*c*) the limits of judicial review in arbitration cases, Justice Douglas expounded as follows:

A NATURE OF THE COLLECTIVE AGREEMENT

The collective bargaining agreement states the rights and duties of the parties. It is more than a contract; it is a generalized code to govern a myriad of cases which the draftsmen cannot wholly anticipate. . . . The collective agreement covers the whole employment relationship. It calls into being a new common law—the common law of a particular industry or of a particular plant.[14]

The Court then referred to the oft-quoted observation of Archibald Cox:

It is not unqualifiedly true that a collective-bargaining agreement is simply a document by which the union and employees have imposed upon management limited, express restrictions of its otherwise absolute right to manage the enterprise, so that an employee's claim must fail unless he can point to a specific contract provision upon which the claim is founded. There are too many people, too many problems, too many unforeseeable contingencies to make the words of the contract the exclusive source of rights and duties. One cannot reduce all the rules governing a community like an industrial plant to fifteen or even fifty pages. Within the sphere of collective bargaining, the institutional characteristics and the governmental nature of the collective-bargaining process demand a common law of the shop which implements and furnishes the context of the agreement. We must assume that intelligent negotiators acknowledged so plain a need unless they stated a contrary rule in plain words.[15]

A collective-bargaining agreement is an effort to erect a system of industrial self-government. When most parties enter into contractual relationship, they do so voluntarily, in the sense that in the absence of a monopoly situation they may seek to obtain the same benefits from alternative sources in the marketplace. This vital consideration is not applicable in the negotiation of a labor agreement. The choice is not between entering or refusing to enter into a relationship, for such choices are predicated on a preexisting open-shop situation. The parties must choose between a relationship governed by an agreed-upon procedure for the adjustment of day-to-day issues and a relationship where such matters are left to a temporary resolution dependent solely upon the relative strength, at any given moment, of the contending forces. Written labor agreements introduce orderly procedures to facilitate the complicated relationship, dealing with its most crucial and most minute aspects over a fixed period of time. The need to reach agreement, the scope of the issues considered, and the necessity for a concise read-

---

14 *United Steelworkers v. Warrior & Gulf Navigation Co.*, 363 U.S. 574, 578–579.
15 Archibald Cox, "Reflections upon Labor Arbitration," *Harvard Law Review*, vol. 72, 1959, pp. 1498–1499.

able document compel the parties to shape a written instrument which, as the late Harry Shulman so aptly put it, is ". . . a compilation of diverse provisions; some provide objective criteria almost automatically applicable; some provide more or less specific standards which require reason and judgment in their application; and some do little more than leave problems to future consideration with the expression of hope and good faith."

B ROLE OF LABOR ARBITRATOR VERSUS ROLE OF COURTS

The Court took judicial notice of the fact that the arbitrator performs functions which are not normal to a judge's activities, that the criteria considered by the arbitrator are often outside the judge's competence.

The labor arbitrator's source of law cannot be confined to the express provisions of the contract. Crucial to his consideration are the practices of the industry and the shop which become part of the collective-bargaining agreement under certain conditions. The arbitrator is usually chosen because of the parties' confidence in his knowledge of this "common law" of the shop and their trust in his ability to consider facets which are not expressed in the contract as criteria for judgment. The parties expect that their evaluation of a grievance will reflect not only what is clearly spelled out in the written contract but also, insofar as the instrument permits, the implicit realities of the relationships at the workplace bearing upon morale, tensions, and productivity. For the parties' primary objective in negotiating the grievance and arbitration provision is to further their common goal of uninterrupted production under the agreement, to make it serve their specialized needs. The ablest judge is at best an outsider who cannot be expected to bring the same experience and competence to bear upon the determination of a grievance, because he cannot be similarly informed.

C SCOPE OF JUDICIAL REVIEW

The Court noted, however, that Congress has, by Section 301 of Taft-Hartley, assigned to the federal judiciary the responsibility of determining whether the reluctant party has breached its commitment to arbitrate. For labor arbitration, however quasi-judicial a process, is a matter of contractual obligation, and a party cannot be expected to acquiesce to arbitration of a dispute which it was not required to arbitrate under the negotiated agreement. Yet to conform with congressional policy favoring settlement of disputes by the parties themselves through arbitration machinery, judicial inquiry under 301 must be confined strictly to the question of whether the reluctant party did agree to arbitrate the grievance or did agree to give the arbitrator power to make the award he made. "An order to arbitrate the particular grievance," cautioned the Court, "should not be denied unless it may be said with positive assurance that the arbitration clause is not susceptible of an interpretation that covers the asserted dispute. Doubts should be resolved in favor of coverage."

3 ENTERPRISE WHEEL AND CAR CORPORATION

Fact Situation

Unlike the first two cases, where the union sought enforcement of agreements to arbitrate, this dispute centered around enforcement of an actual arbitration award which the company refused to implement.

The union had requested reinstatement of several employees who were terminated because they left their jobs while protesting the discharge of another worker. A grievance was filed, and when the company refused to arbitrate, the union brought suit for specific performance of the arbitration agreement. The District Court ordered arbitration, and the matter was subsequently heard and decided by an arbitrator who reduced the discharge to a disciplinary suspension and ordered reinstatement with back pay for all time lost except for ten days suspension and minus earnings from other employment. The company refused to comply with the award, contending that the arbitrator's ruling was issued after expiration of the collective agreement and therefore he lacked authority to make the award. The union's motion for enforcement was granted by the District Court, but the Appeals Court reversed the lower court, holding that the employer's reasons for refusal to comply with the award were proper. The matter was then appealed to the Supreme Court.

Basic Issue

What is the role of the federal courts in enforcing an arbitration award?

Supreme Court's Decision

The courts should enforce the award so long as the arbitrator stays within the scope of the submission agreement and the award is based on his construction of the contract. The Appeals Court ruling was reversed, except for modification of the back-pay determination, and the matter was remanded to the District Court.

Court's Reasoning

> The refusal of courts to review the merits of an arbitration award is the proper approach to arbitration under collective bargaining agreements. The federal policy of settling labor disputes by arbitration would be undermined if courts had the final say on the merits of the awards. As

we stated in *United Steelworkers of America v. Warrior & Gulf Navigation Co.,* . . . the arbitrators under these collective agreements are indispensable agencies in a continuous collective bargaining process. They sit to settle disputes at the plant level—disputes that require for their solution knowledge of the custom and practices of a particular factory or of a particular industry as reflected in particular agreements.

When an arbitrator is commissioned to interpret and apply the collective bargaining agreement, he is to bring his informed judgment to bear in order to reach a fair solution of a problem. This is especially true when it comes to formulating remedies. There the need is for flexibility in meeting a wide variety of situations. The draftsmen may never have thought of what specific remedy should be awarded to meet a particular contingency. Nevertheless, an arbitrator is confined to interpretation and application of the collective bargaining agreement: [to reiterate an oft-quoted stricture,] he does not sit to dispense his own brand of industrial justice. He may of course look for guidance from many sources, yet his award is legitimate only so long as it draws its essence from the collective bargaining agreement. When the arbitrator's words manifest an infidelity to this obligation, courts have no choice but to refuse enforcement of the award.[16]

SUMMARY OF STEELWORKERS TRILOGY GUIDELINES

With these rulings, the Court elevated labor arbitration and the role of the arbitrator to an unprecedented status, not only in the eyes of the judiciary but also in the eyes of the parties, the arbitrators themselves, labor relations attorneys, and other labor specialists.

The decisions elaborated the following ground rules to guide the judiciary when called upon to enforce an arbitration agreement or an award:

1 In determining the arbitrability of a grievance, the court is limited to answering the following question: (*a*) Is there a collective agreement in existence? (*b*) Does the agreement provide for arbitration? (*c*) Is there a claim that the agreement has been violated? If the answer to all these questions is in the affirmative, then the court must order arbitration.

2 The court should not review the merits of a grievance or substitute its judgment for that of an arbitrator selected by the parties where the agreement provides for arbitration of disputes over its interpretation and application. It is the arbitrator's judgment and not the court's which the parties have bargained for. Arbitration should be ordered regardless of whether the court considers the grievance meritorious.

3 Although arbitrators are generally held to be better qualified than judges to rule on industrial grievances, they must confine themselves to interpretation and application of the collective agreement. An arbitrator's award is

---

[16] *United Steelworkers v. Enterprise Wheel & Car Corp.,* 363 U.S. 593, 596–597.

enforceable only so long as it draws its essence from the agreement; again, "... he does not sit to dispense his own brand of industrial justice."

4 Although doubts should be resolved in favor of coverage, the courts should refuse to order arbitration if it is clear on the face of the contract language that the claim has been excluded from arbitration.

The trilogy decisions seek to establish a realistic division of authority and expertise between the arbitrator and the courts. The rulings, and especially the opinions, vastly strengthen the United States system of private arbitration. The high Court concludes unequivocally that the public interest is best served by encouraging the use of voluntary arbitration to promote stability and harmony in labor-management relations. The conclusion is in sharp opposition to those who advocate the use of labor courts in the United States, indicating that the dominant trend in this country is not in the direction of a labor court. For the present, the issue of a centralized versus a decentralized system of industrial jurisprudence has been decided in favor of the latter.

Reaction to the Trilogy

The 1960 trilogy aroused deep concern in some managerial circles that the arbitrator's authority had been expanded to such an extent that a Pandora's box had been opened leading to virtually "open-end" arbitration. Interest was revived in limiting the arbitrator's powers by writing into collective agreements express restrictions on arbitration clauses. The intensity of this anxiety focused on management's rights. The trilogy was viewed as giving arbitrators such broad discretion on questions of arbitrability that they could engage in wholesale gap filling, amending the agreement freely and granting to the union concessions which were not obtained in negotiations. The misgivings of important management spokesmen were expressed typically as follows:

> Speaking for the majority of the court in all three cases, Justice Douglas' opinions shattered precedent. The opinions held that once an employer and a union agree to set up arbitration machinery it can be invoked in *any dispute not specifically excluded in the labor agreement.* Thus, any management practice that the union does not like under more than 90 per cent of the union contracts in American can be carried to arbitration, unless the particular practice has been specifically noted by management and negotiated as an exclusion from the collective bargaining agreement.
>
> This is the biggest challenge to management's rights, prerogatives, and responsibilities that a court has handed down in years. Justice Douglas' claim that it will promote industrial peace appears unrealistic since management must insist at the bargaining table that certain items

such as the right to subcontract be excluded from arbitration; not merely ignored by the contract but precluded in writing from future agreement. Instead of peace these Supreme Court decisions are capable of generating turmoil, for many management rights have now been held to be arbitrable subjects.[17]

The logic of the Court's position on this point is grounded on the principle that when the parties provided for arbitration of disputes over contract interpretation and application, they specifically bargained for an arbitrator's decision and not for a court's. This principle takes into account some fundamental differences between the arbitration and litigation of grievance disputes. When the parties agree to arbitrate such disputes, it is they—and they alone—who control virtually the entire process: they structure and formulate the grievance-arbitration section of their agreement; they select the arbitrator, define the issues, determine the scope of his authority, set forth the criteria he may consider, control the remedy, provide for the binding effect of the award, and even arrange for its enforcement.

In view of such private control over a widely used voluntary, industrial judicial system, it is not surprising that the Court upheld the principle that jurisdiction over a dispute involving contract application or interpretation rests with the arbitrator. In so ruling, the Court sought to effectuate the intent of the parties to ensure stability in their relationship through orderly change during the fixed term of their agreement.

Subsequent developments after ten years have not borne out the worst fears of critics of the trilogy that the high Court has given the arbitrator virtually unlimited authority to legislate in the most remote areas of industrial jurisprudence. /To question the propriety of affirming the arbitrator's jurisdiction over an issue on which the contract is silent, is to overlook the fact that the Court is not telling the arbitrator how to rule. The arbitrator may well decide, and in many cases has so decided, that the issue is not arbitrable.[18] / Judges are seldom specialists in labor arbitration, whereas by definition arbitrators are such specialists. When the contract is silent, the arbitrator is usually the most qualified neutral to determine the arbitrability of the question at issue.

Implicit in the reasoning of some of those who disagree with the trilogy is

---

[17] John R. Bangs and Frank A. Fraser, "The Impact of the Courts on Arbitration and the Right to Manage," *California Management Review*, Summer, 1963, pp. 55–56.

[18] In a survey of judicial and arbitration decisions, University of Michigan professors Russell Smith and Dallas Jones concluded that there is little validity to the premise that arbitrators are less inclined than courts to sustain claims of nonarbitrability. Russell A. Smith and Dallas L. Jones, "The Impact of the Emerging Federal Law of Grievance Arbitration on Judges, Arbitrators, and Parties," *Virginia Law Review*, vol. 52, 1966, p. 911.

that arbitrators are inclined to be impractical idealists whereas judges are practical, business-oriented conservatives. In this era of professionalism in labor relations, such assertions are the rhetoric of the past. It is well known that arbitrators who are "pro" either side do not survive as arbitrators. Most experienced neutrals follow well-established and predictable criteria in deciding a particular dispute, and their services are in constant demand. Individual arbitrators are selected or rejected by the parties, as contrasted to judges, who are imposed upon them without consultation.

Most critics of the trilogy subscribe to the reserved-rights theory of managerial authority, which was discussed in an earlier chapter.[19] Many experienced and widely acceptable arbitrators also hold to this theory. However, to these arbitrators the theory does not mean that any dispute on which the contract is silent must automatically and always be dismissed as nonarbitrable. An agreement's apparent silence on a matter does not preclude the possibility that the general provisions may be applicable. These provisions are not rendered meaningless merely because they do not deal specifically with the dispute. Both parties have preserved fundamental rights in the contract's general sections. To maintain that an issue is not arbitrable because specific language on the matter is absent is to take a position which may very well deprive either party of valuable rights under the general provisions.

EXTENSIONS OF THE TRILOGY—INJUNCTIVE RELIEF AND DAMAGE SUITS FOR VIOLATION OF NO-STRIKE PLEDGE

The 1960 Steelworkers Trilogy was followed in 1962 by another set of three major Supreme Court decisions on the arbitration process, but involving quite different issues. In *Sinclair Refining Company v. Atkinson,*[20] the employer claimed that the Oil, Chemical and Atomic Workers Union had violated a contractual no-strike pledge by engaging in a number of strikes over arbitrable issues. The company sued under Section 301 and asked the federal district court to issue an injunction against the union. The union countered by arguing that the employer's complaint must be dismissed because the court had no jurisdiction under the Norris-LaGuardia Act of 1932.

The basic issue presented to the court was whether Section 301 of Taft-Hartley had preempted Section 4 of Norris-LaGuardia, which, with some exceptions not pertinent here, prohibited federal courts from issuing injunc-

[19] Chap. 3, pp. 31–34.
[20] 370 U.S. 195 (1962).

tions "in any case involving or growing out of any labor dispute." The Supreme Court dismissed the employer's complaint, relying largely on Norris-LaGuardia restrictions which bar federal courts from issuing injunctions in such labor disputes. The majority concluded that since Section 301 of Taft-Hartley did not conflict with Section 4 of Norris-LaGuardia, there was no need to reconcile the intent of the one with the purpose of the other. However, in a strong dissenting opinion, the minority asserted that the two sections must be reconciled since they do coexist and apply to the case under consideration. The minority urged the Court to work out an accommodation of the two provisions "which will give the fullest possible effect to the central purpose of both."

After reviewing the sharply conflicting majority and minority positions of the Supreme Court in Sinclair, Aaron felt that on the basic issue the dissenters presented a stronger case. Having noted that Congress could not anticipate the conflict between Section 4 of Norris-LaGuardia and Section 301 of Taft-Hartley, he concluded:

> Consequently, one cannot see how Congress could have intended to preclude the possibility of injunctive relief against strikes for violation of such agreements. It would seem more reasonable to construe the ambiguous legislative history of section 301 as the dissenters did in the Sinclair case. The resulting accommodation of section 301 with section 4 of the Norris-LaGuardia Act seems no more tortuous and no less reasonable than the accommodation of Norris-LaGuardia with the RLA [Railway Labor Act] which the Supreme Court effected in the Chicago River case.[21]

Deep concern over the majority's apparent failure to recognize the realities of the strike situation is expressed in the following:

> According to the most recent interpretation of section 301 of the LMRA in the Sinclair case, unions may not be enjoined by federal courts from striking over grievances which they have agreed to arbitrate, even though they, as well as the employers with whom they deal, may be compelled to arbitrate those same grievances.) Although it may be true that complete mutuality of remedy is not always possible or even desirable, the refusal in this type of situation to secure for the employer the practical benefits of his promise to arbitrate offends one's sense of fairness and may be said to border on the preposterous. By agreeing to arbitrate unsettled grievances arising under the collective agreement, the employer trades a measure of his economic sovereignty for the union's promise to maintain uninterrupted production. When the union breaks that promise, the only effective remedy is an injunction against the strike; an order

[21] Benjamin Aaron, "The Labor Injunction Reappraised," *UCLA Law Review*, vol. 10, 1963, p. 342. See also his article "Strikes in Breach of Collective Agreements: Some Unanswered Questions," *Columbia Law Review*, vol. 63, 1963, pp. 1027–1052.

to the union to arbitrate, unaccompanied by an order to end the strike, is worthless.[22]

In addition to seeking injunctive relief, the company had also sued the union for damages under Section 301 for violating the no-strike clause. The question at issue was whether the employer's claim for damages could be litigated without submission to arbitration under the agreement. In *Atkinson v. Sinclair Refining Company*,[23] the Supreme Court ruled that the employer could sue the union for damages under Section 301 because the arbitration agreement itself made no provision for the processing of employer grievances against the union. In this case, the Court did examine the particular grievance and arbitration clause in the contract and concluded that since it did not provide for submission of employer grievances, the company could reject arbitration and pursue litigation instead. This ruling was considered consistent with the guidelines of Warrior and Gulf, where the Court had cautioned that:

> An order to arbitrate the particular grievance should not be denied unless it may be said with positive assurance that the arbitration clause is not susceptible of an interpretation that covers the asserted dispute.[24]

Implicit in the Court's ruling was that if the grievance and arbitration procedures were broad enough to cover employer grievances, then the company would be required to arbitrate rather than litigate the claim. This question was decided explicitly in the third decision of the 1962 series. In *Drake Bakeries, Inc. v. Local 50, American Bakery Workers*,[25] the company sued for damages under Section 301, alleging that the union had encouraged its members to strike, or not to report for work, in violation of a contractual no-strike pledge. The question before the Supreme Court was whether the lower court was correct in ordering the employer to arbitrate the issue of damages.

After examining the parties' collective agreement, the Court ruled that the company's damage suit was arbitrable because the contractual arbitration provision was broad enough to encompass such employer complaints. The Court concluded that if the company had intended to exclude such a fundamental issue from arbitration, there would be express language in the agreement to this effect. In the absence of such language, the Court decided, the employer was obligated to arbitrate the entire dispute, including any question of arbitrable authority .

[22] Aaron, "The Labor Injunction Reappraised," pp. 344–345.
[23] 370 U.S. 238 (1962).
[24] 363 U.S. 574 (1960).
[25] *Drake Bakeries, Inc. v. Am. Bakery & Confectionery Workers Int'l, Local 50*, 370 U.S. 254 (1962).

In a cogent comment on the three 1962 Supreme Court rulings, Russell Smith and Dallas Jones concluded that:

> *Sinclair I* [*Sinclair Ref. Co. v. Atkinson*] made no contribution to the federal substantive law concerning the arbitration process. But *Sinclair II* [*Atkinson v. Sinclair Ref. Co.*] and *Drake Bakeries* represented important developments of that law in three respects. First, they established the principle that, with respect to arbitrable issues, a party to the arbitration agreement has the right to insist upon arbiration in the first instance, rather than litigation. Second, they seemed to imply that there is no arbitral jurisdiction of an employer's contractual grievances unless the arbitration clause provides for the submission of employer grievances to arbitration, but that a court should order arbitration of such grievance, including a claim of breach of a no-strike agreement, if the arbitration process is available to the employer and there is a broad arbitration clause. In addition, *Drake Bakeries* rejected the employer's claim that it was excused from any duty to arbitrate because of the union's breach of its no-strike pledge.[26]

In regard to the last point noted above, the Supreme Court later reaffirmed the principle that the breach of a contractual no-strike pledge does not relieve the nonbreaching party from his obligation to arbitrate grievances covered by the arbitration section.[27] In fact, even a breach by both parties was not considered a valid defense for rejecting arbitration unless there had been a clear repudiation of the duty to arbitrate.[28]

INDIVIDUAL EMPLOYEE RIGHTS AND CONCURRENT JURISDICTION OF COURTS, NLRB, AND ARBITRATORS

Three other Supreme Court decisions of major significance to grievance arbitration warrant consideration. The central problem in each case was how to define the appropriate jurisdictional boundaries and roles of the three interrelated entities—the courts, the NLRB, and the arbitrators.

In *Smith v. Evening News Association*,[29] a building-maintenance employee and member of the Newspaper Guild brought suit in a Michigan court, as an individual and as an assignee of forty-nine other employees, against the association for breach of contract. He complained that during a strike of employees belonging to another union, the association had refused to permit him and the forty-nine others from reporting to their regular shifts although they were ready, able, and available for work. He also alleged that the

[26] *Op. cit.*, p. 836.
[27] *Packinghouse Workers v. Needham Packing Co.*, 376 U.S. 247 (1964).
[28] *Minnesota Joint Board, Amalgamated Clothing Workers v. United Garment Mfg. Co.*, U.S. Court of Appeals, Eighth Circuit (St. Louis), 57 L.R.R.M. 2521 (1964), BNA, Inc.
[29] 371 U.S. 195 (1962).

employer did permit certain nonunion personnel to report for work and paid them full wages even though there was no work available.

The trial court dismissed the suit on the ground that the action complained of could constitute an unfair labor practice and therefore the subject matter was within the exclusive jurisdiction of the NLRB. Although the Michigan Supreme Court upheld the lower body, the U.S. Supreme Court disagreed and reversed all prior rulings. The high Court held that state and federal courts are not deprived of jurisdiction in actions under Section 301 simply because the conduct involved was arguably an unfair labor practice.

In the Smith case, the Court established three basic principles to govern in situations where there appeared to be overlapping jurisdiction as between the NLRB, the courts, and the arbitrator:

1 The authority of the NLRB to deal with an unfair labor practice which also violates a collective agreement is not displaced by Section 301, but it is not exclusive and does not destroy the jurisdiction of the courts in suits under Section 301.
2 Suits to vindicate individual employee rights arising from a collective agreement are not excluded from coverage of Section 301. Rights of employees concerning rates of pay and conditions of employment are a major focus of the negotiation and administration of bargaining agreements and are at the heart of the grievance-arbitration machinery. To exclude these claims from the ambit of Section 301 would invalidate the congressional policy of having the administration of collective contracts accomplished under a uniform body of federal substantive law.
3 Section 301 does not exclude all suits brought by individual employees instead of unions. To do so would also frustrate rather than serve the congressional policy expressed in that section.

In a dissenting opinion, Justice Black noted, among other things, that the majority had failed to state under what circumstances and for what kinds of breach an individual employee could sue under Section 301, and "when he must step aside for the union to prosecute his claim."

In *Carey v. Westinghouse Electric Corporation*,[30] the International Union of Electrical Workers (IUE) was the certified bargaining representative of "all production annd maintenance employees" at a Westinghouse plant. Another union (federation) represented "all salaried, technical" employees. IUE filed a grievance claiming that certain federation-member employees in the engineering laboratory at the plant in question were performing production and maintenance work. Westinghouse refused to arbitrate the grievance, contending that the matter was a representation dispute within the exclusive jurisdiction of the NLRB. The New York State courts denied

[30] 375 U.S. 261 (1964).

IUE's petition for an order compelling arbitration. However, the U.S. Supreme Court reversed the state courts and ordered the controversy to be arbitrated.

In the majority opinion, Justice Douglas first distinguished between two different although related types of jurisdictional disputes: (1) whether certain work should be performed by employees in one bargaining unit or those in another, and (2) which union should represent the employees doing particular work. The majority then ruled that in either situation arbitration of the grievance under a collective agreement was not precluded and should be followed.

The logic of the Court's reasoning appears in the following excerpts from the majority opinion:

> Grievance arbitration is one method of settling disputes over work assignments . . . To be sure, only one of the two unions involved in the controversy has moved the state courts to compel arbitration. So unless the other union intervenes, an adjudication of the arbiter might not put an end to the dispute. Yet the arbitration may as a practical matter end the controversy or put into movement forces that will resolve it. . . .
>
> Should the Board [NLRB] disagree with the arbiter, by ruling, for example, that the employees involved in the controversy are members of one bargaining unit or another, the Board's ruling would, of course, take precedence, and if the employer's action had been in accord with that ruling, it would not be liable for damage under § 301. But that is not peculiar to the present type of controversy. Arbitral awards construing a seniority provision . . . or awards concerning unfair labor practices, may later end up in conflict with Board rulings. . . . Yet, as we held in *Smith v. Evening News*, . . . the possibility of conflict is no barrier to resort to a tribunal other than the Board.
>
> However the dispute be considered—whether one involving work assignment or one concerning representation—we see no barrier to use of the arbitration procedure. If it is a work assignment dispute, arbitration conveniently fills a gap and avoids the necessity of a strike to bring the matter to the Board. If it is a representation matter, resort to arbitration may have a pervasive, curative effect even though one union is not a party.
>
> By allowing the dispute to go to arbitration its fragmentation is avoided to a substantial extent; and those conciliatory measures which Congress deemed vital to "industrial peace" . . . and which may be dispositive of the entire dispute, are encouraged. The superior authority of the Board may be invoked at any time. Meanwhile the therapy of arbitration is brought to bear in a complicated and troubled area.[31]

The main difficulty with the majority position is that it leaves unanswered some very practical questions regarding (1) the impact of the arbi-

[31] *Ibid.*, 265, 272.

tration award on the other union which is not a party to the arbitration, (2) the vulnerability of the employer to damage suits under Section 301 from the nonparticipating union, and (3) the inability of the arbitration process to achieve a final disposition of the controversy involving conflicting claims of union jurisdiction.

The Carey decision is noteworthy because the Court invited arbitrators to handle jurisdictional disputes even though one of the unions was not a party to the proceeding. The Court ordered bilateral arbitration between the Company and one union, although the existence of an indispensable third party (a second union) had created a situation necessitating trilateral arbitration where two separate written agreements between the Company and two unions could be interpreted. /Justice Douglas's opinion could imply that he placed more confidence in arbitrators than in the NLRB to handle jurisdictional disputes practically. One reason for this may be the basically different functions performed: the arbitrator seeks to determine the meaning and intent of a private collective agreement; the NLRB is chiefly concerned with effectuating the policies and purposes of a federal statute./ Edgar Jones has described the NLRB-arbitrator functional difference thus:

> The Board's statutory policy is both affirmative—to encourage certain kinds of conduct—and negative—to preclude other kinds. Its view of the private interests involved is not like that of an arbitrator. As to statutory policy, the arbitrator's concern, if he entertains it at all, is more apt to be for assurance that no statutory proscription is violated in the circumstances. But it must be observed that arbitrators are so desirous of effectuating the mutual intent of the parties that many of them at this point in the relationship between the Labor Board and arbitration will not take cognizance of statutory proscriptions if to do so would frustrate a clearly evidenced intention of the parties. Of course, the problem is entirely altered when an ambiguous situation comes under scrutiny. Statutory policies, affirmative as well as negative, provide a reasonable basis for finding an intent of the parties to abide by the policy rather than to violate it. But, once again, the arbitrator's search is for the mutual intent of the parties, not the propriety of their conduct as measured by statutory concepts.[32]

Justice Black (joined by Justice Clark) issued a strong dissenting opinion in Carey stressing the impracticalities of the majority ruling:

> The employer, caught in [a] jurisdictional dispute, is ordinarily in a help-less position. He is trapped in a cross-fire between two unions. All he

[32] Edgar A. Jones, Jr., "The Name of the Game Is Decision—Some Reflections on 'Arbitrability' and 'Authority' in Labor Arbitration," *Texas Law Review*, vol. 46, July, 1968, pp. 888–889. Because of its importance in the field of arbitration law, the full text of Mr. Jones's article is reproduced in Appendix C, pp. 367–395.

can do is guess as to which union's members he will be required by an arbitrator, the Labor Board, or a court to assign to the disputed jobs. If he happens to guess wrong, he is liable to be mulcted in damages. I assume it would be equally difficult for him to prophesy what award an arbitrator, the Labor Board, or a judge will make as to guess how big a verdict a court or a jury would give against him. It must be remembered that the employer cannot make a choice which will be binding on either an arbitrator, the Board or a court. The Court's holding, thus subjecting an employer to damages when he has done nothing wrong, seems to me contrary to the National Labor Relations Act as well as to the basic principles of common everyday justice.

The result of all this is that the National Labor Relations Board, the agency created by Congress finally to settle labor disputes in the interest of industrial peace, is to be supplanted in part by so-called arbitration which in its very nature cannot achieve a final adjustment of those disputes. One of the main evils it had been hoped the Labor Act would abate was jurisdictional disputes between unions over which union members would do certain work. The Board can make final settlements of such disputes. Arbitration between some but not all the parties cannot.[33]

There is always the possibility, of course, that in a Carey-type work-assignment dispute, the arbitrator would dismiss the grievance. If so, the difficulties which so distressed the minority would not arise since the arbitration would "as a practical matter end the controversy." In a penetrating analysis of the Carey decision, Edgar Jones in another law-review article made the following provocative comment:

Reflecting upon the collective bargaining realities implicit both in Justice Black's dissenting observations and in Justice Douglas' reference to putting "into movement forces that will resolve" the dispute, an arbitrator may well pause at the final sentence in the majority opinion. "Meanwhile the therapy of arbitration is brought to bear in a complicated and troubled area."

Although the parties typically do not license their arbitrator to engage in preventive medicine, it is accepted that his reasoning when given latitude for choice by the collective agreement, will and should seek to reinforce the long range good health of the continuing relationship of the parties. Arbitration is not designed as a band-aid type of justice reacting to temporary, expedient necessity. The trouble which Carey creates for arbitrators is that sparring unions in this type of dispute are likely now to try to play the ancient game of forum maneuvering. That would tend to endanger the acceptability of arbitration by stimulating the dissatisfaction implicit in producing unworkable solutions to bitter problems.[34]

[33] Carey v. Westinghouse Elec. Corp., 375 U.S. 261, 275–276.
[34] Edgar A. Jones, Jr., "An Arbitral Answer to a Judicial Dilemma: The Carey Decision and Trilateral Arbitration of Jurisdictional Disputes," UCLA Law Review, vol. 11, no. 3, March, 1964, pp. 332–333.

SURVIVING COLLECTIVE BARGAINING RIGHTS
OF EMPLOYEES AFTER CORPORATE MERGER

The last case to be considered in this series on the functional boundaries of the courts, the NLRB, and the arbitrator is *John Wiley & Sons, Inc. v. Livingston.*[35] A small publishing firm called Interscience Publishers, Inc., had entered into a collective agreement with a union representing about half of its eighty employees. The agreement, to expire on January 31, 1962, contained an arbitration clause but did not include an express provision making it binding on successors of Interscience.

On October 2, 1961, Interscience merged with Wiley and ceased doing business as a separate entity. At the time of the merger Interscience had only one plant and did an annual business af about 1 million dollars. Wiley, on the other hand, was nonunion, had a much larger operation, doing an annual business of more than 9 million dollars, and employed about three hundred persons.

After the merger, the union claimed that it continued to represent Interscience employees now employed by Wiley and that Wiley was obligated to recognize the rights of these employees under the bargaining agreement with Interscience. The union also claimed that Wiley had to make certain pension-fund payments provided for under the collective agreement.

Wiley refused to accede to the union demands, asserting that the merger terminated the collective-bargaining agreement and that the union no longer represented former Interscience employees now working for Wiley. About a week before expiration of the Interscience agreement, the union petitioned a federal court under Section 301 to compel Wiley to arbitrate certain employee rights which the union claimed had survived the merger.

Although Justice Goldberg took no part in the case, the Supreme Court was unanimous in affirming the lower court's order submitting the dispute to arbitration. In his opinion Justice Harlan answered a number of troublesome questions, several of which had divided the lower courts for many years. These significant points are summarized as follows:

Question: Should a court or an arbitrator decide whether the arbitration provisions of the collective agreement survive the merger?
Answer: The court decides. ". . . whether or not the company was bound to arbitrate as well as what issues it must arbitrate, is a matter to be determined by the Court on the basis of the contract entered into by the parties. . . . The duty to arbitrate being of contractual origin, a compulsory submission to arbitration cannot precede judicial determination that the collective bargaining agreement does in

[35] 376 U.S. 543 (1964), 55 L.R.R.M. 2769.

fact create such a duty. Thus, just as an employer has no obligation to arbitrate issues which it has not agreed to arbitrate, so *a fortiori*, it cannot be compelled to arbitrate if an arbitration clause does not bind it at all."[36]

Question: What is the obligation of the successor employer regarding employee claims arising under a preexisting agreement between the merged company and its union?

Answer: The successor employer may be required to arbitrate such claims where there is a substantial continuity of identity in the business enterprise before and after the merger and where the union has not abandoned its right to arbitration by failing to make its claims known. ". . . the disappearance by merger of a corporate employer which has entered into a collective bargaining agreement with a union does not automatically terminate all rights of the employees covered by the agreement, and that, in appropriate circumstances, present here, the successor employer may be required to arbitrate with the union under the agreement."[37]

Question: Why is the successor employer obligated to arbitrate under a collective agreement to which he was not a party?

Answer: Because the objectives of national labor policy "require that the rightful prerogative of owners independently to rearrange their businesses and even eliminate themselves as employers be balanced by some protection to the employees from a sudden change in the employment relationship. The transition from one corporate organization to another will in most cases be eased and industrial strife avoided if employees' claims continue to be resolved by arbitration rather than by the relative strength . . . of the contending forces."[38]

Question: What is the effect of the merger on the rights of covered employees?

Answer: The merger does not in itself remove employee claims otherwise plainly arbitrable from the scope of the arbitration clause. Grievances which would have been arbitrable under the agreement prior to the merger survive the merger and the successor employer is obligated to arbitrate them. Even expiration of the agreement does not make moot employee claims to rights that accrued during the term of the agreement and survive its expiration.

Question: Who decides the merits of such employee grievances?

Answer: "Whether or not the Union's demands have merit will be determined by the arbitrator in light of the fully developed facts. It is sufficient for present purposes that the demands are not so plainly unreasonable that the subject matter of the dispute must be regarded as nonarbitrable because it can be seen in advance that no award to the Union could receive judicial sanction."[39]

Question: Does the court or the arbitrator decide issues of procedural arbitrability?

Answer: "Once it is determined . . . that the parties are obligated to submit the subject matter of a dispute to arbitration, 'procedural' questions which grow out of the dispute and bear on its final disposition should be left to the arbitrator."[40] The Court noted that many labor disputes cannot easily be broken down into their

[36] *Ibid.*, 2771.
[37] *Ibid.*, 2772.
[38] *Ibid.*
[39] *Ibid.*, 2774–2775.
[40] *Ibid.*, 2775.

"substantive and procedural aspects"—that procedural issues are often so inextricably intertwined with the merits of a dispute that it is impossible to separate them. "Questions concerning the procedural prerequisites to arbitration do not arise in a vacuum; they develop in the context of an actual dispute about the rights of the parties to the contract or those covered by it."[41]

ARBITRATION UNDER STATE LAW

Although judicial enforcement of arbitration agreements and awards has been largely preempted by the U.S. Supreme Court under Section 301 of Taft-Hartley, the states still exercise some control over enforcement of such agreements and awards within their jurisdiction. Section 301 of Taft-Hartley applies, of course, only to collective agreements in industries affecting *interstate* commerce, thus reserving to the states enforcement of such agreements in industries affecting only *intrastate* commerce. Also, there are significant areas of arbitral conduct, both personal and legal, that still lie within state jurisdiction.

State arbitration statutes vary considerably. Some are designed to deal only with commercial disputes, others have been amended to include labor disputes, and still others specifically exclude collective-bargaining agreements from coverage of the arbitration statute. In those states that have no arbitration statute of any kind, the common law is controlling.

Under the common law, agreements to arbitrate future controversies are not enforceable in the courts. Either party may withdraw from an agreement to arbitrate at any time before the award is rendered. Under statute law, however, an agreement to arbitrate is enforceable in the courts, and an order of specific performance can be obtained. Marion Beatty has succinctly contrasted some essentials of the two systems:

> The main difference between common-law and statutory arbitration is that under a common-law arbitration the award is enforced by an independent action upon it or upon the bond of submission, while a statutory award may be made the rule of the court, or a judgment of the court, and an execution issued on the judgment, this being a more summary method of enforcement. The principal advantage of common-law arbitration is simplicity, whereas the principal advantages of statutory arbitration are irrevocability of the agreement to arbitrate and its summary enforcement. An award resulting from a common-law arbitration has the effect of a contract and is enforceable as such. An award resulting from a statutory arbitration has the effect of a judgment.[42]

[41] *Ibid.* For a comprehensive analysis of the legal and economic ramifications of Wiley, see Thomas M. Patrick, Jr., "Implications of the John Wiley Case for Business Transfers, Collective Agreements, and Arbitration," *South Carolina Law Review*, vol. 18, 1966, p. 413.

[42] Marion Beatty, *Labor-Management Arbitration Manual*, E. E. Eppler and Son, New York, 1960, p. 19.

California has one of the most comprehensive arbitration statutes of any state.[43] In 1961 this statute was extensively revised and specifically defined to apply to collective-bargaining agreements. The revised California arbitration statute incorporates a good deal of the common law as well as case law which had developed over the years. No attempt will be made to provide a comprehensive analysis of the California statute, but the essential features are outlined below:[44]

Definitions[45]

1 An "agreement" to arbitrate is defined to include agreements between employers and employees or between their respective representatives.
2 A "controversy" to be arbitrated may include questions of law or of fact or both.
3 A "party to the arbitration" is defined to include a party (a) who seeks to arbitrate a controversy pursuant to the agreement, (b) against whom such arbitration is sought pursuant to the agreement, or (c) who is made a party to such arbitration by order of the neutral arbitrator(s) upon such party's application, upon the application of any other party to the arbitration, or upon the neutral arbitrator's own determination.
4 A "written agreement" includes one which has been extended or renewed by an oral or implied agreement.

Under the section entitled "Enforcement of Arbitration Agreements," a written agreement to submit to arbitration an existing or future controversy is valid and either party may secure a court order of specific performance unless there has been a waiver, or grounds exist for revocation of the agreement.[46]

Powers and Duties of the Arbitrator[47]

1 He appoints the time and place for the hearing.
2 He is responsible for serving notice of the hearing on the parties and on any other arbitrators.
3 He presides at the hearing, ruling on admission and exclusion of evidence and on other questions of hearing procedure. However, he is not required to observe legal rules of evidence or rules of judicial procedure.
4 He adjourns the hearing when necessary.

[43] California Code of Civil Procedure, Arbitration Statute, title 9, chap. 1, 1961.
[44] An exhaustive analysis of the old and new California statutes has been made by Eddy S. Feldman, a member of the California bar, in two law-review articles: "Arbitration Law in California: Private Tribunals for Private Government," *Southern California Law Review,* vol. 30, July, 1957, pp. 378–500, and "Arbitration Modernized: The New California Arbitration Act," *Southern California Law Review,* vol. 34, Summer, 1961, pp. 413–444.
[45] California Code of Civil Procedure, title 9, chap. 1, § 1280.
[46] *Ibid.,* § 1281.
[47] *Ibid.,* § 1282.

5 He is required to base his award upon information obtained at the hearing. Otherwise, he must notify the parties and give them an opportunity to reply.

6 He may grant a reasonable continuance for the purpose of a party procuring an attorney.

7 He may subpoena witnesses and documents.

8 He may administer oaths to witnesses.

9 He may order depositions to be taken, upon application by a party to the arbitration.

10 He must make proper service of a signed copy of the award to each party to the arbitration.

11 He may correct an award upon written application of a party to the arbitration or serve notice of denial of application to correct an award.

Enforcement of the Award

A party to an arbitration in which an award has been made may petition a superior court in the county in which the arbitration arose to confirm, correct, or vacate the award. The court is required to *vacate* an award if it is determined that any of the following things happened:[48]

1 The award was procured by corruption, fraud or other undue means.

2 There was corruption in any of the arbitrators.

3 The rights of the petitioning party were substantially prejudiced by misconduct of a neutral arbitrator.

4 The arbitrator exceeded his powers and the award cannot be corrected without affecting the merits of the decision upon the controversy submitted.

5 The rights of the petitioning party were substantially prejudiced by the refusal of the arbitrator to postpone the hearing upon sufficient cause being shown therefor or by the refusal of the arbitrator to hear evidence material to the controversy or by other conduct of the arbitrator contrary to the provisions of this title.[49]

The court may *correct* the award and affirm it as corrected if it is determined that any of the following things are true:[50]

1 There was an evident miscalculation of figures or an evident mistake in the description of any person, thing, or property referred to in the award.

2 The arbitrators exceeded their powers but the award may be corrected without affecting the merits of the decision upon the controversy submitted.

3 The award is imperfect in a matter of form not affecting the merits of the controversy.

If the arbitrator has not exceeded his authority and is not guilty of fraud, corruption, or legal misconduct affecting an award, then the court must

[48] *Ibid.,* § 1285.

[49] It is this subsection in the statute which causes many arbitrators to err on the side of admitting too much evidence into the record rather than that of excluding evidence of doubtful relevance or materiality.

[50] California Code of Civil Procedure, title 9, chap. 1, § 1286.6.

confirm the award, which then becomes a judgment of the court having the same force and effect as a judgment in a civil action and may be enforced like any other judgment of the court in which it was entered.

SUMMARY

This chapter has surveyed ten significant U.S. Supreme Court decisions construing Section 301 of Taft-Hartley as authorizing the development of a body of federal substantive law on labor arbitration. In the years since Lincoln Mills (1957), the Court has, without the benefit of a federal statute, established a broad and comprehensive system of remedial powers for the federal judiciary in enforcing arbitration agreements and awards. The "range of judicial inventiveness" has been singularly devoted to maximizing the use of grievance arbitration as a primary means for achieving industrial peace. As Gilbert Cornfield has observed in commenting on the Steelworkers Trilogy, "The action of the Supreme Court was designed to effectively place the public interest behind the growth and reinforcement of arbitration as an accepted and integral part of industrial life."[51]

The cases in this chapter were selected primarily because they constitute the major components of a new federal common law of arbitration. Other Supreme Court decisions related to the same problem area have been omitted because they did not seem to have the impact or the pioneering qualities of the others—whose general import may be summarized as follows:

Lincoln Mills made Section 301 the structural base for erecting the body of federal law. Henceforth, arbitration provisions in collective agreements were to be enforced by federal courts under federal law.

The Steelworkers Trilogy placed the entire federal judicial system squarely behind the labor arbitration process as the preferable method for resolving disputes during the fixed term of collective agreements. Henceforth, federal and state courts were to be greatly limited in their review of arbitration awards and agreements.

Sinclair I established the proposition that the Norris-LaGuardia Act precluded issuance under Section 301 of a federal injunction against a union engaged in a strike over arbitrable issues in violation of a contractual no-strike pledge.

Sinclair II held that the employer could reject arbitration and sue the striking union for damages in a federal court under Section 301 where the

---

[51] Gilbert A. Cornfield, "Developing Standards for Determining Arbitrability of Labor Disputes by Federal Courts," *Labor Law Journal,* vol. 14, 1963, p. 564.

collective agreement did not require the union to arbitrate employer grievances.

Drake Bakeries obligated the employer to arbitrate a claim for damages against the union, which struck in violation of a contractual no-strike pledge, since the collective agreement required the union to arbitrate employer grievances.

Smith v. Evening News held that damage suits by an individual employee or by the union could be brought against the employer in either a state or a federal court under Section 301, even though the action complained of could come under the exclusive jurisdiction of the NLRB.

Carey opened the door for arbitrators to handle union jurisdictional disputes on a bilateral basis, even though the NLRB has superior authority in this area and the other union was not a party to the arbitration.

Wiley established a number of basic principles delineating the respective roles of courts and arbitrators on issues of arbitrability involving survival of employee rights in a collective agreement after a change in the firm's ownership.

These ten cases seem to reveal most clearly the structure and development of the Court's philosophy on the arbitral process and the function of arbitrators. They provide a frame of reference which not only imparts a logical flow to the high Court's rulings but also establishes a necessary base for critical analysis of judicial attempts to fashion a body of federal law on labor arbitration.

State and federal courts have concurrent jurisdiction over suits to enforce arbitration agreements and awards. Where interstate commerce is involved, the state courts are required to follow the federal law as fashioned by the U.S. Supreme Court under Section 301 of Taft-Hartley. Arbitration of labor disputes under exclusive state authority (intrastate commerce) is governed by the common law or by an appropriate arbitration statute. State law is particularly important in setting bounds to arbitral conduct.

Chapter 14

The Torrington case

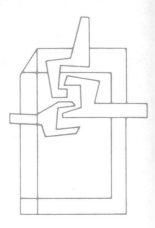

■ Because the issues and principles involved in Torrington[1] are basic to an understanding of labor arbitration and the dynamics of collective bargaining, the case warrants a chapter devoted largely to its consideration and implications.

As may be recalled from Chapter 3, the Torrington case centered on a long-established employee benefit (voting-time pay) not mentioned in the contract.[2] The company had abolished the benefit by an oral declaration during negotiations when the contract was open and the union was free to combat management's action in an economic contest. The arbitrator had ruled subsequently that the company had erred in eliminating the benefit without the union's consent, even though the union could have legally

---

[1] The Torrington case consists of three parts: (1) the opinion and decision of Arbitrator Thomas Kennedy; (2) the opinion and decision of the U.S. District Court; and (3) the opinion and decision of the U.S. Court of Appeals, Second Circuit (New York). All three parts are reproduced in full text in Appendix B. See also Appendix C for two law-review articles, by Benjamin Aaron and Edgar A. Jones, Jr., respectively, commenting on Torrington.

[2] For approximately twenty years, the employer had allowed up to one hour's pay for employees to vote on Election Day.

resisted by strike action. A United States District Court later vacated the award on the ground that the arbitrator had exceeded his authority. On appeal, the Second Circuit Court upheld the District Court.

DEFINITION OF THE ISSUE

At the outset, it is essential to define the issue with utmost precision. The Torrington case (and our discussion) involves (1) a long-established *past practice* on (2) a relatively *minor employee benefit* on which (3) the contract was *completely silent* and where (4) the employer announced *during negotiations* on a contract renewal his firm intention of discontinuing the practice in the future. It is important to note that all four elements must be present for a case to fall within the Torrington principle. The basic question was this: could a past practice on which the contract was silent become so firmly embedded in the agreement that during negotiations on new contract terms the practice could not be altered or eliminated without express mutual agreement?

Polarization of Opinion on the Issue

Commentators on Torrington are divided into two main points of view. Those who answer the question in the affirmative hold that the burden is on the employer to get language into the new agreement expressly discontinuing the long-established practice and that his failure to do so means that the practice is automatically continued as an integral part of the new agreement. This position is based in part upon the principle in commercial law that the conduct (practice) of the parties during the term of the written agreement can effectively amend that agreement.

The opposing point of view holds that once the employer has announced his clear intention during negotiations to discontinue the practice, the onus shifts to the union to secure language into the new agreement expressly continuing the employee benefit. Otherwise, the practice is automatically discontinued after execution of the new agreement. This position is based upon an interpretation of how collective bargaining fixes the institutional roles of the parties.

One of the most articulate spokesmen for the first group, who on this issue may be called "the broad legal constructionists," is Prof. Edgar A. Jones, Jr., of the UCLA Law School. In commenting on Torrington, Jones stated:

> The question was whether the benefit [voting-time pay] had already
> become part of the fabric of agreement, prior to its discussion in the

1963 negotiations. If so, the benefit surely could not be deleted solely by unilateral assertion. It would have to be cut out by agreement.

Perhaps the court's analytical difficulty may be traced to an unwillingness to accept past practice as amendatory of a written collective agreement. That view, however, has no legal basis. It is elemental contract law that the conduct of the contracting parties after execution of a written agreement can effectively amend that agreement. Whether the amendatory conduct has occurred becomes a matter of proof. If in fact it has occurred, it is inferable that the party economically disadvantaged by the amendment has in one way or another recouped that disadvantage by securing some other kind of concession or advantage in the course of collective bargaining. It may be that the benefit sought by Torrington in this case was the extra-contractual one of a community image as a civic-minded employer. Torrington's motivation is not relevant, however. Whatever it may have been, a bilateral commitment had resulted.[3]

The position of the second group, who may be called "the strict legal constructionists," was set forth succinctly by Judge Lumbard in his opinion reviewing the Torrington arbitration award:

Labor contracts generally state affirmatively what conditions the parties agree to, more specifically, what restaints the parties will place on management's freedom of action. While it may be appropriate to resolve a question never raised during negotiations on the basis of prior practice in the plant or industry, it is quite another thing to assume that the contract confers a specific benefit when that benefit was discussed during negotiations but omitted from the contract.[4]

A careful reading of Arbitrator Kennedy's opinion discloses that his award was anchored in part on a finding that the employer had not sustained the burden of proof that he had maintained the oral declaration during the give-and-take of bargaining sessions which had followed his announcement that he was withdrawing the election pay benefit. As Jones noted:

There had been a lot of milling around in the negotiations and enough track marks had been laid down by the backing and filling of the parties to obliterate any assured path to a conclusion one way or the other on the vote pay issue. The arbitrator made no egregiously erroneous award; arguably wrong, perhaps, but arguably correct, certainly.[5]

Although the authors are inclined toward Jones's version of the Torrington fact situation, the basic question still remains to be treated: can a prac-

---

[3] Edgar A. Jones, Jr., "The Name of the Game Is Decision: Some Reflections on 'Arbitrability' and 'Authority' in Labor Arbitration," *Texas Law Review*, vol. 46, July, 1968, pp. 871–872. This is the Jones article included in Appendix C.

[4] *Torrington Co. v. Metal Prods. Workers, Local 1645*, U.S. Court of Appeals, Second Circuit (New York), 62 L.R.R.M. 2495, 2499 (1966), BNA, Inc.

[5] *Op. cit.*, pp. 870–871.

tice on which the contract is silent become so firmly embedded in the agreement that it cannot be removed in subsequent negotiations except by mutual consent? The discussion which follows is directed toward that question without regard to the intrinsic merits of Arbitrator Kennedy's award.

The Authors' Position

On the Torrington principle the authors hold to the viewpoint of the strict constructionists. The broad constructionists would, in effect, reverse the inherent traditional roles of the parties in collective bargaining, namely, that the employer acts and the union reacts. The employer, as we have repeatedly stressed, must retain the administrative initiative to operate the enterprise, and the union may challenge employer decisions, either by exerting its economic ability to strike if contract negotiations are deadlocked or by invoking arbitration if the contract is in effect.

Those who believe that in this matter the scales should be weighted in favor of the union, that in all fairness the onus should be shifted to the employer in contract negotiations to obtain express acquiescence of the union, may in fact be doing the union a disservice. The broad constructionists in many instances may be closing off an avenue of retreat for a union reluctant to strike over a subordinate issue but unable to let the matter go by default because the employer must secure an affirmative assent to withdraw a long-established benefit. Union officials are thus given an unpalatable choice, either to put their jobs on the line with their constituents by becoming active accomplices of the employer in depriving the membership of an established benefit or to play it safe for themselves by taking a never-say-die position, even if this means drifting into a strike with an employer who has the economic strength to clobber them.

Union officials need the flexibility to allow certain issues tacitly to go by default in negotiations. They may not want to join the issue and risk the danger of a minor issue becoming an insurmountable obstacle to the signing of what is basically a satisfactory settlement. They would rather sign the contract; then, should the matter arise during the contract term through an aggrieved employee, they can explain that "the past practice was unilaterally eliminated by the employer; we never agreed to its discontinuance." A grievance is filed and taken to arbitration. Whatever the outcome, the union representatives can't lose. If they are upheld, they regain through arbitration what they really yielded by default in negotiations. If the award is unfavorable, they can blame the "chiseling" employer or the expendable arbitrator. In any event, negotiating-committee members are off the hook, innocent of complicity with the employer in the eyes of their constituency. They have accomplished their main objective: to ensure that the signing of the entire contract was not jeopardized by an impasse over a relatively minor fringe benefit.

Two Categories of Issues in Negotiations

The subject matter of most negotiations includes not only major issues which neither side is inclined to concede but also minor items over which neither side is willing to undergo economic warfare. On major subjects, the question of who has the burden of getting language into the agreement is seldom crucial. The parties will settle major issues one way or another, not by sweeping them under a rug, but by a balancing of strengths. Relatively minor items taken singly are seldom worth a fight, but their ultimate disposition may be decisively influenced by which party has the burden of getting language into the new agreement.

In the opinion of the authors, it is a mistake to place the burden on management to secure language on a subordinate issue. If an issue involves a past practice of such importance to the parties that they are willing to engage in an economic contest, the ritual leading to the disposition of the issue is seldom decisive. The procedural steps lead either to combat or to settlement. If the item is vital, the parties will take whatever action is deemed necessary to preserve or abolish the practice, in accordance with their conflicting objectives. However, the vast majority of practices on which the instrument is silent deal with relatively minor benefits. The contract is seldom silent on such matters as wages, hours, union security, seniority, limitation on the strike, etc. Subordinate benefits, such as washup time, voting pay, and Saturday holiday pay, often originate at the workplace without being registered in the written agreement. Such relatively minor issues rather than the major items are likely to come within the scope of the Torrington principle.

Recapitulation

If for the purposes of discussion we assume that the District Court's statement of the fact situation in Torrington is correct, then it would follow that the arbitrator had reversed the institutional roles of the parties: that the employer establishes the status quo, and the union, as the moving party, attempts to alter the status quo.[6] The onus is on the union, when the con-

---

[6] Prof. Frederic Meyers, who reviewed the entire manuscript, asserts that "the truth of this statement depends on the definition of when the war starts," holding that at times it is the employer who seeks to alter the status quo. The validity of Meyers' observa-

tract is open for negotiation, to get the employer's consent to its proposed alteration of the status quo. Union tenacity can keep an issue alive only until the contract is signed; then union proposals not agreed to by the employer go by default. Militant never-say-die declamations by the union on such issues should not obscure the fact of the union's inability to secure employer consent. The signed contract is the objective manifestation of the parties' assent, a binding assent which includes the elimination of those union proposals which were rejected by the employer during the contract negotiations.

The arbitrator in Torrington had ruled in effect that the union need not resort to its traditional weapon (an actual or threatened strike) to prevent the employer from withdrawing a long-established benefit; it need only stand pat, withholding its consent and waiting for the employer's next move, if any. To eliminate the benefit, the employer would have to secure the union's consent by persuasion, by barter, or by economic pressure. The union could hardly be expected to give up the benefit by persuasion alone when it need only say no to retain it. For the employer to barter with the union over the benefit would be analogous to buying property where the railway is coming through; and to attempt economic sanction such as a lock-out to secure union consent would be a hazardous undertaking legally, not to speak of other undesirable effects of a self-imposed shutdown.

THE TORRINGTON DECISION APPLIES ONLY WHEN THE CONTRACT IS SILENT ON THE ISSUE

So much for Torrington—a controversy, it must be reiterated, over an employee benefit on which the contract was completely silent. However, what about an employee benefit of long standing which is covered by contract language, but the language is ambiguous? For example, a contract provision reads, "Insofar as practicable, overtime shall be distributed equally on a departmental basis." A practice of many years had been to exclude from the arrangement employees who had been transferred into the department in an emergency for temporary periods. Temporary employees were not assigned overtime as long as there was a sufficient number of regular employees in the department available to work overtime. During

---

tion is unquestioned. The term status quo is used somewhat broadly by the authors to denote the basic managerial prerogatives (administrative initiative), which of necessity must be exercised by those who direct the organization over those who are directed. In that sense, the operating conditions at the workplace may be deemed a status quo created by management.

negotiations, when the contract was open, the company announced that it would henceforth interpret the provision to include in the equal distribution of overtime those employees assigned to the department for temporary periods. Because of the employer's failure to reform the language, his oral repudiation of the past practice was futile, meaning that he had to follow the previously established past practice of excluding temporary employees from overtime assignments.[7]

Based upon the courts' rulings in Torrington, we know that when the written instrument is silent on an employee benefit, the employer need only make an explicit oral declaration during contract negotiations to withdraw the benefit, it being understood that the oral declaration must not become obscured by the give-and-take pressures of hard bargaining. Responsibility for securing language to maintain the benefit then devolves upon the union. But such is not the case when there is language, however ambiguous, covering the benefit. The past practice is then inseparably joined to the language.

Quoting Richard Mittenthal:

> Because the practice is essential to an understanding of the ambiguous provision, it becomes in effect a part of that provision. As such it will be binding for the life of the agreement. And the mere repudiation of the practice by one side during the negotiation of a new agreement, unless accompanied by a revision of the ambiguous language, would not be significant. For the repudiation alone would not change the meaning of the ambiguous provision and hence would not detract from the effectiveness of the practice.[8]

Clear Language vs. Established Practice

A closing word now on the matter of a past practice which is contrary to the clear and unambiguous language of a contract. In Chapter 4 a criterion was presented that clear and unambiguous language in respect to an issue generally takes precedence over all other criteria, including a long-established past practice.[9] It was also acknowledged that there are highly influential arbitrators resolutely opposed to the endowment of such sovereignty to the criterion of clear language. Foremost among them is Benjamin Aaron. His

[7] *Hughes Aircraft Co. v. Electronic & Space Technicians, Local 1553*, May 20, 1967, unpublished arbitration award, Arbitrator Carl Benecke, S.J.

Frank Elkouri and Edna Asper Elkouri, *How Arbitration Works*, BNA, Inc., 1960, p. 279. "Where past practice has established a meaning for language that is subsequently used by the parties in a new agreement, the language will be presumed to have the meaning given it by past practice."

[8] Richard Mittenthal, "Past Practice and the Administration of Collective Bargaining Agreements," *Arbitration and Public Policy*, Spencer D. Pollard (ed.), *Proceedings of the Fourteenth Annual Meeting, National Academy of Arbitrators*, BNA, Inc., 1961, p. 53.

[9] Chapter 4, pp. 48–51.

article on past practice is a formidable challenge to the absolutism of clear language when it is confronted by a contrary practice of long standing.[10] Aaron advances two basic reasons for a flexible approach to the problem:

> In the first place, a collective agreement is something quite different from a life insurance contract or an agreement for the purchase and sale of goods. It is but a means to an end and, as Harry Shulman has so aptly observed,

> "The object of collective bargaining is not the creation of a perfectly meaningful agreement—a thing of beauty to please the eye of the most exacting legal draftsman. Its object is to promote the parties' present and future collaboration in the enterprise upon which they are dependent."

> In the second place, even the construction of commercial contracts is not as inflexible as is commonly supposed. Referring to the familiar statement that "usage is admissible to explain what is doubtful but never to contradict what is plain," Williston makes the following comment:

> "If this statement means that usage is not admitted to contradict a meaning apparently plain if proof of the usage were excluded ... it is inconsistent with many decisions and wrong in principle."[11]

Clear Language Affirmed Over Practice

Aaron, Shulman, and even Williston (not to mention others such as Wallen and Mittenthal) are an impressive array of authority on a question of such magnitude. Yet the trend of published arbitrations continues to favor clear language over past practice or any other criterion.[12] The clear-language criterion retains its primacy because of the deepening trend toward judicial arbitration. The striving after the fruits of two antithetic arbitral

---

[10] Benjamin Aaron, "The Uses of the Past in Arbitration," *Arbitration Today*, Jean T. McKelvey (ed.), *Proceedings of the Eighth Annual Meeting, National Academy of Arbitrators*, BNA, Inc. 1955.

[11] *Ibid.*, p. 4.

[12] Following are some typical arbitral affirmations of this basic principle: (1) "[The] union's contention that past practice permits employees to refuse overtime without consequential penalty cannot prevail in face of clear, unambiguous contract language." *Int'l Minerals & Chem. Corp. v. United Stone & Allied Prods. Workers, Local 188,* July 17, 1967, 49 LA 159, Arbitrator Leonard Oppenheim, BNA, Inc. (2) "Section 3 ... is clear and unequivocal and the meaning and intention thereof is not wanting. There should have to exist some contractual language which would create an ambiguity as to intent, in order to qualify the use of evidence of past practice. Here there is no contractual language which creates an ambiguity." *AMF Western Tool, Inc. v. United Auto. Workers, Local 562,* June 9, 1967, 49 LA 718, 725, Arbitrator Lewis Solomon, BNA, Inc. (3) "Management argues that it has been the past practice to place men in this job. However, where the contract is rather clear as to the procedure to follow in cases of bumping, the Arbitrator must follow the written agreement rather than past practice." *Paterson Parchment Co. v. United Papermakers & Paperworkers,* Apr. 11,

systems (consensus and judicial) has become an increasingly sterile endeavor to the parties. Shopping around for the "right" (meaning liberal or conservative) arbitrator and score keeping are on the wane. Certainty, predictability of criteria, is much more the focus of concern than the award itself. The award is often anticlimatic, a mere peg upon which to hang an opinion. A criterion enunciated by an arbitrator might favor a party on one grievance and then work against that party the next three or four times the same type of grievance arose.

In contract law, conduct can be manifested by words or by actions without words. In that sense the written instrument is also the practice of the parties, and in this country they have chosen to make it the core of their collective-bargaining relationship. On that fact alone, it seems to us that whenever the language of the instrument is clear on a matter at issue, there should be no higher proof of the intent of the parties than the instrument itself.

SUMMARY

The Torrington arbitration has aroused considerable controversy not only as to the permissible limits of judicial review but also as to the merits of the particular dispute. This chapter has been devoted to a consideration of

---

1966, 47 LA 260, 262, Arbitrator W. Roy Buckwalter, BNA, Inc. (4) "A cardinal rule of contract interpretation is that where the language is clear and unambiguous in an agreement, that language must be applied in accordance with its ordinary meaning and intent.... It is equally well settled that a past practice cannot control the application of clear and unambiguous contract language. The prior acts of the parties cannot be used to change the explicit terms of an agreement. Many arbitration precedents could be marshalled to show that no matter how well established a practice may be, it is unavailing to modify the clear terms of an agreement. This has been held to be true where the arbitrator believed that, on the basis of equity, past practice should have governed." *Westinghouse Elec. Corp. v. Int'l Union of Elec., Radio & Mach. Workers, Local 601,* July 23, 1965, 45 LA 131, 139, Arbitrator Paul M. Hebert, BNA, Inc. See also *Marathon City Brewing Co. v. Int'l Union of United Brewery, Flour, Cereal, Soft Drink and Distillery Workers,* Sept. 21, 1965, 45 LA 453, Arbitrator Robert M. McCormick, BNA, Inc. (5) "The arbitrator would be going far beyond his authority were he to disregard the clear contract language and extend and enlarge its content through the recognition of alleged practice and procedure. The practice claimed by the company is too fundamental a departure from the contract, to warrant its recognition in the arbitrator's award, which must be primarily governed by the contract terms." *Ohio Steel Foundry Co. v. United Auto. Workers, Locals 926 & 975,* June 26, 1961, 36 LA 1088, 1091, Arbitrator Harry J. Dworkin, BNA, Inc. (6) "In this case, where the applicable provision of the Agreement clearly preserves for each employer a discretionary right in relation to the authorization of overtime, the Company can not be held to have lost that right merely because it did not exercise that right in a particular fashion for a particular employee group." *Nat'l Brewing Co. v. Int'l Union of United Brewery, Flour, Cereal, Soft Drink & Distillery Workers, Local 38,* Aug. 29, 1958, 31 LA 300, 306, Arbitrator Mark L. Kahn (Chairman), BNA, Inc.

arbitral criteria and leaves to legal scholars a critique of judicial intervention in labor arbitration.

The Torrington case involved a twenty-year practice, on which the contract was silent, of granting one hour's paid time off for voting. During the 1963 negotiations, the company announced its intention of discontinuing the practice. A new agreement, signed in Jauary, 1964, at the end of a 17-week strike, contained no language on paid time off for voting. On Election Day in November, 1964, the employees were not given time off with pay to vote. Thereupon, the union filed a grievance, and the matter went to arbitration.

The arbitrator ruled that the company could not discontinue the practice unilaterally, but had to secure the union's consent. He ruled that since there was no mutual agreement during negotiations to discontinue the practice, the company had violated the 1964 agreement by refusing "to pay this benefit to employees on Election Day in 1964." The District Court vacated the award on the ground that the arbitrator had exceeded his authority. The Court of Appeals later affirmed this ruling by a divided vote.

Two opposing viewpoints have emerged as to the basic question involved. One group holds that in the context of the Torrington situation, the burden was on the employer to secure the union's consent before discontinuing the practice. The other group holds that if the union wanted the practice continued it had the responsibility of getting appropriate language into the new contract, or, at the very least, prevailing upon the employer to withdraw his oral declaration abolishing the practice.

The authors believe that the nature of the issue, the silence of the contract on the benefit, the institutional roles of the parties in collective bargaining—all gravitate toward placing the onus on the union and not on the employer to get language into the new contract. A failure to do so must be construed as the union having yielded on the matter in negotiations.

The three basic criteria developed in this chapter may be stated as follows:

1 If the contract is *silent* on the issue, then *Torrington* applies and mutual agreement is not required for the employer to modify or discontinue the practice when the contract is open for negotiations.
2 If the contract contains *ambiguous language* on the subject, then past practice is decisive in determining meaning and mutual consent is required in negotiations for the practice to be altered or abolished.
3 If the contract contains *clear* and *unambiguous language* on the benefit, then the language takes precedence over past practice and mutual agreement is required to alter or eliminate the benefit.

Chapter 15

What makes a mainline arbitrator?

(Colloguy between the authors)

■ "Paul, you've been an active arbitrator for over twenty-five years. For several of those years arbitration was your principal means of livelihood. You're an old-timer. How did you get started?"

"Like many if not most of the old-timers, I started with the War Labor Board. I was a graduate of the Wharton School at the University of Pennsylvania and studied under Prof. George W. Taylor. When Dr. Taylor was appointed in 1942 to be Vice-Chairman of the War Labor Board, he recruited a number of his students to the WLB, including me."

"Did most of the WLB staff continue as arbitrators after the war?"

"No, only a small fraction survived the rough-and-tumble of voluntary arbitration in the postwar years. Throughout this book, Pete, we've frequently referred to the 350 members of the National Academy of Arbitrators who do most of the arbitrating. 'Mainline' arbitrators, they're often called, to distinguish them from 'fringe' arbitrators trying to get into the main current."

"At what point did you personally cease to be a fringe arbitrator and consider yourself a mainliner?"

"Not on any one single case, I can assure you. A fringe arbitrator can be broken by a bad opinion on just one arbitration, but becoming a mainliner is a process rather than the result of a single spectacular case."

"Is there any condition or status you can describe which clearly defines a mainline arbitrator?"

"When you put it that way, Pete, I can make the line of demarcation between a fringe arbitrator and a mainliner quite distinct. When I was a fringe arbitrator, the losing party would scrutinize my opinion to find out where *I* was wrong. I knew I had arrived at the mainline stage when in many cases the loser would study my opinion to find out where *he* was wrong."

"You spoke of the rough-and-tumble of voluntary arbitration as contrasted to WLB dispute procedures?"

"Yes, it's important to note that the settlement of disputes under WLB rules and procedures was fundamentally different from private arbitration as we know it. When all but a few unions gave up their right to strike during World War II, the parties turned to us for the resolution of impasses over new terms and conditions of employment. Most private arbitrations are over rights issues. We handled mostly interest disputes. Even so, for ten or fifteen years after the war, most of the mainline arbitrators were people who had got their training in the WLB."

"The WLB dispute procedures, Paul, were for all practical purposes based on compulsory arbitration. What experience did you derive from the WLB that was applicable to voluntary arbitration?"

"It's true that in the absence of practical alternative procedures the parties had no real choice but to come to the WLB. But they were able to exert great pressures on us, too, and under the stress of those pressures we, meaning the WLB, formulated many of the criteria used in private arbitration today. Those of us involved in the formulation and application of these criteria, even indirectly, gained a rich experience. Of equal if not greater importance to the fledgling arbitrator was the battle conditioning he received in the rough, tough arena of collective bargaining. He learned to think, to make difficult decisions under fire; he learned to preside and function in an adversary system, and eventually he became seasoned, a veteran in the full sense of the word. Granted, his bad decisions were not as costly to him as they would have been to a private arbitrator—he could not be removed as easily—but for an apprenticeship, the WLB experience should not be underestimated."

"That explains how most of the mainline arbitrators got on the ground floor of private arbitration after the war was over. But twenty-five years have passed, Paul. Arbitrators grow old, they get sick, some die, others retire. Still others shift their interests to new endeavors; they become teachers or writers or labor relations consultants. Meanwhile the need for experienced arbitrators continues to grow. Where do the new ones come from?"

"You put your finger on the problem, Pete, when you said that the need was for *experienced* arbitrators. Not well-meaning novices, just out of graduate school, not retired partisans of collective bargaining imbued with a strong paternalistic conviction that they can be 'fair,' but real arbitrators, battle-scarred and battlewise. The parties will generally accept nothing less than an experienced arbitrator, sprung full-blown, I suppose, like Athena from the brow of Zeus. As we put it in our opening chapter, a would-be arbitrator has the same problem of acquiring experience as a would-be surgeon. No one wants to be operated on by an apprentice."

"I didn't realize, Paul, how close that parallel between the arbitration profession and the medical profession was until I read an article in the *Wall Street Journal* discussing the problem of providing experience to interns and resident physicians in a rising economy. There has been a steep decline in the number of so-called 'charity' cases, largely because of the great increase in medical plans and health insurance, not to speak of Medicare. The free-ward patients have traditionally provided young, inexperienced doctors with a wide variety of ailments to develop their skills rapidly—patients who would otherwise have received little or no medical treatment at all. Millions of people who in the 1930s would have crowded into the free wards are now covered by health plans, and are competing with the more affluent sectors of society for the services of physicians and surgeons with long experience. How will a new generation of medical school graduates and specialists get the practical training so indispensable to preceding generations of doctors?"

"I don't know, Pete, but having once hurdled medical school, the graduate is not likely to be forced into another profession. One way or another he'll acquire the necessary experience to go into private practice. Not so with fringe arbitrators. The most promising of them enjoy brief periods of acceptance; then come a few major arbitral opinions which do not sit well, and they're through. Good people, too, who, if they'd had anything like the WLB training the old-timers had, would go on to become established mainliners."

"It occurs to me that wartime industry had an experience parallel to that of the WLB in training skilled personnel. Industry was hard hit by skill shortages. In the United States nearly half the highly skilled prewar journeymen had learned their trades in Europe before coming to these shores. In the airframe industry, for example, toolmakers and jig and fixture builders had to be trained at a frenzied pace. Tooling-department employees who learned to read blueprints by taking cram courses in defense schools had projects thrown at them by aircraft engineers which were often way over their heads. They developed into skilled toolmakers by making one snafu after another, but it was worth it to industry and the defense effort because journeymen were created in one-fourth the time of a planned apprenticeship in peacetime."

"True, but major industry continues to maintain and expand planned apprenticeships for skilled trades in peacetime, and there the parallel with arbitration ends. There is no equivalent of the WLB to train arbitrators today—no widely organized apprenticeship program."

"In industry, Paul, when there is no planned apprenticeship, a semi-skilled worker, usually a helper, gets to be a journeyman by 'stealing the trade.' "

"Meaning what?"

"He watches the journeyman, bluffs about his experience and capability with each new supervisor to get more skilled assignments. He cultivates the goodwill of journeymen who show him tricks of the trade, until, by some process of osmosis from job to job, over an extended period of time he acquires the skills and status of a journeyman."

" 'Stealing the trade' is an apt expression, Pete. From my observation of the tortuous course pursued by a number of arbitrators who have emerged as mainliners in recent years, I think you've described exactly what most of them have had to do—steal the trade."

"Let's put the spotlight on an arbitrator we both know intimately, Paul, a former student and protégé of yours who is very much of a mainliner. How did Harry Blank attain a status where the losing parties tend to read his opinions to find out where they, and not Harry, are wrong?"

"Well, the first thing to note, Pete, is that Harry Blank is an attorney. Which means he has been grounded in principles of contract law and of judicial proof—a grounding which can be of inestimable help to a would-be arbitrator—or a downright hindrance, depending on the person."

"Why a hindrance ever?"

"Because arbitration, as we keep stressing, is quasi-judicial, not strictly judicial. An arbitrator must not only know the rules, but he must know when and how to deviate from them. The worst of all offenses is to break rules you don't even know exist. Many attorneys act as though arbitration is or should be conducted in a courtroom. They forget that not all contract law or rules of evidence are applicable. Arbitral flexibility makes them uncomfortable, and to them there is a problem of consistency. As they see it, either apply contract criteria and rules of evidence with the stringency of a courtroom or function as a simon-pure consensus arbitrator, solving problems by divination, by intellectual folk wisdom, so to speak. They discuss arbitration solely in terms of the 'precedental' value of awards—always awards, rarely the opinions leading to the awards."

"They forget, Paul, what great legal philosophers have tirelessly reiterated: that there is more than a little folk wisdom in legal criteria. Emerson's stricture against foolish consistency applies to arbitrators as well as constitutional judges. Undeviating adherence to legal criteria is just as unacceptable to the parties as arbitral awards which result from human caprice. Slavish adherence to criteria becomes a futile attempt to overcome inconsistencies inherent in the nature of things by imposing a uniformity greater than life will bear. Harvard law professor Paul Freund put it best in his study of the United States Supreme Court when he said, 'If the first requisite of a constitutional judge is that he be a philosopher, the second requisite is that he be not too philosophical.' But you do make the point, Paul, that Harry Blank is an attorney, and the Academy reports that about half the arbitrators in the nation are attorneys, most of them too young to have had War Labor Board experience."

"Yes, Pete, in the absence of a planned apprenticeship, it must be expected that most of those who fill the depleted ranks of the arbitration profession will be attorneys. When Harry was first launched on his career as an arbitrator, he had already had enough courtroom experience to be at home in an adversary system, and he also knew instinctively when and how to draw the line between court proceedings and arbitral proceedings. But merely having these intuitive abilities is not enough. The parties must be made aware of such abilities, not simply by the endorsement of established arbitrators, although such endorsements are essential to a beginner, but the parties will decide his ultimate acceptability by his arbitral opinions—note I didn't say awards, I said his opinions."

"Like your recent arbitration on the meaning of an overtime-assignment provision?"

"A most appropriate example, Pete. The case came before me as an employee's claim for two hours of overtime pay—a trifling sum of $9.40, involving the time and attention of two attorneys, a plant manager, a union president, a varied assortment of department supervisors and shop stewards, and, of course, the arbitrator. Whether or not I awarded for the grievant on his claim was irrelevant. Everything hinged on the reasoning leading up to my award. I could award for the grievant and yet reject the union's interpretation of the overtime provision or, as it happened, award for the company on the individual claim and do it with an opinion which reversed the company's policy on assigning overtime within a classification."

"Perhaps you should discuss this case in a little more detail."

"Perhaps I should, because the last I heard, the union was talked out of my favorable interpretation of the contract language because I had ruled against the grievant in the case."

"How could a thing like that happen?"

"It was the first arbitration the parties had had in years, and the local-union leadership didn't pay much attention to arbitral opinions. They were naïve scorekeepers who eagerly turned to the last page of my written opinion and read the award which denied the grievant's claim. They were so disappointed that they flipped back the pages and skimmed the arbitral opinion with unseeing eyes. All that penetrated their understanding was that the grievant's claim has been rejected, that they had lost the decision. From what I was told secondhand, the union chief steward said: 'One thing that arbitrator succeeded in doing: for the first time in ages, the union and the management agreed on something—that arbitration is for the birds. We lost the case, and we're unhappy—and the management's unhappy even though they won the case.' "

"How could it happen, Paul, that you could write an opinion at cross-purposes with your award?"

"Not cross-purposes, Pete; the award was in a sense irrelevant to the opinion. The issue, you see, was a policy the company had initiated of disregarding seniority when assigning people to work overtime—I'm talking of people within the same general classification who performed a variety of jobs. Plant management took the position that it would not assign an employee to work overtime on a job he had never performed before, even though the job fell within his general classification. The contract provided for seniority by classification in layoffs, recall, and promotions. The union argued that even though the grievant had never done the job, it was work within his general classification, and therefore he should be given a break-in period to prove he could qualify. I agreed with the union. There is a presumption that when employees, even with a diversity of tasks, are grouped together in a general classification, there must be some underlying connection between them, some common level of skills; otherwise the concept of a classification becomes meaningless."

"And yet on the specific issue of the grievant's claim you awarded for the company."

"Well, the grievant had been tried out on that overtime job before, and the company convinced me that, in *his* case at least, he'd had his chance and had muffed it. But on another employee in that general classification I might easily have gone the other way. Any individual claim would be an entirely separate and distinct matter from my basic interpretation of the contract language."

"What if you'd refrained from interpreting the contract and had simply ruled on the grievant's claim?"

"That would have been ducking the real issue. You don't seriously believe the parties went to all that trouble and expense for a trivial sum of $9.40, do you? They wanted that contract provision interpreted. If I didn't interpret the contract, what would be the point of a written opinion at all? An arbitrator's lot would be an enviable one if he could get by simply by issuing an award without giving reasons to justify his choice."

"Yet, Paul, the penchant of many people to keep score on the arbitrator, to chalk up the number of times he awards for management or for labor, is still prevalent and is still a formidable obstacle to fringe arbitrators."

"True, but it's nothing like it used to be. There was a period after World War II, for a decade perhaps, when both parties through their various organizations maintained two unofficial lists, one of unacceptable arbitrators and another of approved ones. If losing parties and winning parties had succeeded in reducing arbitral acceptability to the level of bad guys and good guys, professionalism would have become impossible, and the arbitral process in private industry would no doubt have been supplanted by a system of labor courts."

"Yet, Paul, the good-guy, bad-guy lists were never very effective. Those who compiled them forgot that it takes two to tango. The dialogue between the parties over those lists could be satirized as follows: 'I can't get you to accept my brother-in-law as arbitrator and you can't get me to accept your uncle, so how about Joe Doakes? At one time or another he's ruled against each of us. Let's use him again.' I don't mean to oversimplify the matter. For an arbitrator to rule against each side at one time or another is not in itself a virtue. He must show in his opinion that he understood completely the basic arguments of the parties, especially those of the loser. There is nothing more galling, I can tell you from my own experience, than to have an arbitrator decide against you with an opinion which reveals that he never really understood your position or the underlying issue."

"The underlying issue, Pete, is the submerged part of the iceberg, the nine-tenths hidden from view. When a person attains a level of understanding necessary to grasp the underlying issue, he can be said to have finished his apprenticeship. He is not yet a mainliner, he doesn't have a—a—well, for lack of a better expression, a personal following. While mainliners accept many referrals, most of their cases come to them from the parties by direct contact. At the very beginning of his apprenticeship Harry Blank had to rely for his occasional cases on referrals from me. With cases I couldn't squeeze into my calendar I would urge the parties to try Harry."

"Recommending an arbitrator, Paul, has its precarious aspects. You have to recommend him to the loser as well as to the winner."

"Well, Harry's heavy reliance on my overflow ceased when some of his more insightful opinions were published and other people in labor relations began to recommend him. At that stage arbitration was still a part-time endeavor for him. His cases came largely from the standard arbitration appointing agencies, always on the alert for new blood to fill in the panels they provide to interested parties. It took several years before the bulk of his cases came directly from the parties. First, he had to pass the most crucial test of all, the test that eliminates all but a handful of aspiring fringe arbitrators."

"You mean the moment of truth."

"Yes, but unlike the matador, the arbitrator doesn't face that moment in the hot glare of a mid-day sun while thousands of *aficionados* watch in breathless anticipation. He faces it alone in his study, long after his family and his neighbors have retired for the night. Sleeplessly, he reviews the record of the case in the light of discussion with one or two close colleagues. He and he alone must now decide. He has advanced his career thus far by adhering to established criteria applied flexibly. This case could be his turning point for good or for ill. It is a major case, if for no other reason than that the parties are a large influential corporation and a powerful union. He has been selected because one or the other of them has rejected all the established mainliners in the area and insists on a relatively new face to decide this issue."

"No doubt, the party with the weaker case."

"Of course. It's usually the potential loser who fears established arbitrators, because he senses the inherent weakness of his case."

"There are also other reasons, Paul. Many of those who could put up a strong argument are unable to cope with arbitral criteria. They don't want to acknowledge the validity of such criteria. 'The hell with technicalities,' they say. 'Let's decide the issue on right and wrong.' "

"Far more deadly to the fringe arbitrator, Pete, is the party who knows something of the principles of contract interpretation but is also aware that unless the issue is really clear-cut, the arbitrator doesn't have to abide by such principles, and who sees no reason why the arbitrator shouldn't depart from them in his case."

"Is it outright cynicism, Paul?"

"Not always, not usually. In Harry's case, he had to reckon with a party who was deeply and obdurately convinced of the rightness and justice of his position. The conviction of rightness had no relation in the party's mind to the express terms of the contract; his mood was reinforced by the fact that he had been playing the numbers game, and had decided it was 'his turn' to get a favorable award; if he didn't, the arbitrator was a charlatan, a tool of his opponent. There are more than a few representatives of powerful unions and of employers who work themselves into that state of mind. They know they can't bend the established mainliners to their will, so they kick the doors open to a fringe arbitrator like Harry Blank and give him his big chance."

"Under those kinds of pressures, I wonder if it was all worth it."

"As a regular diet, it wouldn't be; but remember we're talking about a man at the crossroads. He's at the crossroads when anxious telephone calls are made to him, calls with increasingly ominous undertones to ostensible inquiries as to when his award will be ready. The arbitrator is in for it. Shall he adhere to criteria, knowing that the loser will launch an angry campaign to have him blacklisted as an enemy of labor or a saboteur of management prerogatives, a naïve, destructive longhair who never met a payroll or got a callus on his hand? The temptation to buckle under pressure is strong. Shall he yield to expediency and change his award, or shall he hold fast? It is an intensely personal experience. There are no eyewitnesses. He toys with the consequences of changing his award. At worst, he suggests to himself, the party adversely affected will charge it off to a mistake, a blind spot. Why not?"

"All of that riding on a single case; to be broken so easily?"

"The arbitrator may not know it at the time, Pete, but he is not weighing a single case; he is weighing a basic, long-term approach to arbitration. If he folds under pressure in this single instance, the damage will probably not be fatal, but he must meet the test again, and then again, and soon there will be no more agains. From a fringe arbitrator he will regress to a has-been. If, on the other hand, he meets the test, there will be reprisals from the loser, a vindictive campaign in the tribal centers of labor relations. There will be damage, unavoidable damage, but it will not be fatal, provided—a most important proviso—provided he is right!"

"That's quite a proviso. All the knowledge of arbitral criteria there is can't make a person right. Being right is in the department of intangibles."

"Exactly. There are no mechanical yardsticks for being right in the judicial process. The arbitrator cannot hide behind contract criteria to escape responsibility for the correctness of his decisions. He must be right, not in easy abstract terms of truth, justice, and integrity, to be bandied about as Platonic absolutes. He must be right within the context of the specific situation. He must deal with the submerged nine-tenths of the iceberg and be as right in essence as though he were dealing with an exact science. He cannot evade the intangibles of the issue, in whatever form he chooses to grapple with them. He must produce a decision which encompasses the underlying reality of the issue before him."

"In short, Paul, he must know contract criteria, be able to apply them under the pressures of an adversary system, and above all come up with the right answer."

"Yes, Pete, it is along this lonely, jagged, twisted road he must travel for an indefinite period of time, until one day he becomes aware that he has survived. He has been working too hard. The frequent phone calls and cascade of cases which he thought were temporary have not eased up. So he calls the regional office of the American Arbitration Association, writes to the Federal Mediation and Conciliation Service and his state mediation service: 'No more cases until next September.' He has arrived.

"He is now a mainline arbitrator!"

Appendix A

U.S. Supreme Court landmark decisions on labor arbitration

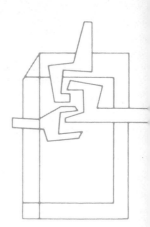

TEXTILE WORKERS UNION OF AMERICA V. LINCOLN MILLS OF ALABAMA

Supreme Court of the United States, 1957.
353 U.S. 448, 77 S. Ct. 923, 1 L. Ed. 2d 972.
(Footnotes Omitted)

MR. JUSTICE DOUGLAS delivered the opinion of the Court.

Petitioner-union entered into a collective bargaining agreement in 1953 with respondent-employer, the agreement to run one year and from year to year thereafter, unless terminated on specified notices. The agreement provided that there would be no strikes or work stoppages and that grievances would be handled pursuant to a specified procedure. The last step in the grievance procedure—a step that could be taken by either party—was arbitration.

This controversy involves several grievances that concern work loads and work assignments. The grievances were processed through the various steps in the grievance procedure and were finally denied by the employer. The union requested arbitration, and the employer refused. Thereupon the union brought this suit in the District Court to compel arbitration.

The District Court concluded that it had jurisdiction and ordered the employer to comply with the grievance arbitration provisions of the collective bargaining agreement. The Court of Appeals reversed by a divided vote. 230 F. 2d 81. It held that, although the District Court had jurisdiction to entertain the suit, the court had no authority founded either in federal or state law to grant the relief. The case is here on a petition for a writ of certiorari which we granted because of the importance of the problem and the contrariety of views in the courts. . . .

The starting point of our inquiry is § 301 of the Labor Management Relations Act of 1947, . . . which provides:

> (a) Suits for violation of contracts between an employer and a labor organization representing employees in an industry affecting commerce as defined in this chapter, or between any such labor organizations, may be brought in any district court of the United States having jurisdiction of the parties, without respect to the amount in controversy or without regard to the citizenship of the parties.
>
> (b) Any labor organization which represents employees in an industry affecting commerce as defined in this chapter and any employer whose activities affect commerce as defined in this chapter shall be bound by the acts of its agents. Any such labor organization may sue or be sued as an entity and in behalf of the employees whom it represents in the courts of the United States. Any money judgment against a labor organization in a district court of the United States shall be enforceable only against the organization as an entity and against its assets, and shall not be enforceable against any individual member or his assets.

There has been considerable litigation involving § 301 and courts have construed it differently. There is one view that § 301 (a) merely gives federal courts jurisdiction in controversies that involve labor organizations in industries affecting commerce, without regard to diversity of citizenship or the amount in controversy. Under that view § 301 (a) would not be the source of substantive law; it would neither supply federal law to resolve these controversies nor turn the federal judges to state law for answers to the questions. Other courts—the overwhelming number of them—hold that § 301 (a) is more than jurisdictional—that it authorizes federal courts to fashion a body of federal law for the enforcement of these collective bargaining agreements and includes within that federal law specific performance of promises to arbitrate grievances under collective bargaining agreements. Perhaps the leading decision representing that point of view is the one rendered by Judge Wyzanski in Textile Workers Union v. American Thread Co., 113 F. Supp. 137. That is our construction of § 301 (a), which means that the agreement to arbitrate grievance disputes, contained in this collective bargaining agreement, should be specifically enforced.

From the face of the Act it is apparent that § 301 (a) and § 301 (b) supplement one another. ⌈Section 301 (b) makes it possible for a labor organization, representing employees in an industry affecting commerce, to sue and be sued as an entity in the federal courts.⌉ Section 301 (b) in other words provides the procedural remedy lacking at common law. Section 301 (a) certainly does something more than that. Plainly, it supplies the basis upon which the federal district courts may take jurisdiction and apply the procedural rule of § 301 (b). The question is whether § 301 (a) is more than jurisdictional.

The legislative history of § 301 is somewhat cloudy and confusing. But there are a few shafts of light that illuminate our problem.

The bills, as they passed the House and the Senate, contained provisions which would have made the failure to abide by an agreement to arbitrate an unfair labor practice. S. Rep. No. 105, 80th Cong., 1st Sess., pp. 20–21, 23; H. R. Rep. No. 245, 80th Cong., 1st Sess., p. 21. This feature of the law was dropped in Conference. As the Conference Report stated, "Once parties have made a collective bargaining contract the enforcement of that contract should be left to the usual processes of the law and not to the National Labor Relations Board." H. R. Conf. Rep. No. 510, 80th Cong., 1st Sess., p. 42.

Both the Senate and the House took pains to provide for "the usual processes of the law" by provisions which were the substantial equivalent of § 301 (a) in its present form. Both the Senate Report and the House Report indicate a primary concern that unions as well as employees should be bound to collective bargaining contracts. But there was also a broader concern—a concern with a procedure for making such agreements enforceable in the courts by either party. At one point the Senate Report, supra, p. 15, states, "We feel that the aggrieved party should also have a right of action in the Federal courts. Such a policy is completely in accord with the purpose of the Wagner Act which the Supreme Court declared was 'to compel employers to bargain collectively with their employees to the end that an employment contract, binding on both parties, should be made. . . .' "

Congress was also interested in promoting collective bargaining that ended with agreements not to strike. The Senate Report, supra, p. 16, states:

> If unions can break agreements with relative impunity, then such agreements do not tend to stabilize industrial relations. The execution of an agreement does not by itself promote industrial peace. The chief advantage which an

employer can reasonably expect from a collective labor agreement is assurance of uninterrupted operation during the term of the agreement. Without some effective method of assuring freedom from economic warfare for the term of the agreement, there is little reason why an employer would desire to sign such a contract.

Consequently, to encourage the making of agreements and to promote industrial peace through faithful performance by the parties, collective agreements affecting interstate commerce should be enforceable in the Federal courts. Our amendment would provide for suits by unions as legal entities and against unions as legal entities in the Federal courts in disputes affecting commerce.

Thus collective bargaining contracts were made "equally binding and enforceable on both parties." Id., p. 15. As stated in the House Report, supra, p. 6, the new provision "makes labor organizations equally responsible with employers for contract violations and provides for suit by either against the other in the United States district courts." To repeat, the Senate Report, supra, p. 17, summed up the philosophy of § 301 as follows: "Statutory recognition of the collective agreement as a valid, binding, and enforceable contract is a logical and necessary step. It will promote a higher degree of responsibility upon the parties to such agreements, and will thereby promote industrial peace."

Plainly the agreement to arbitrate grievance disputes is the *quid pro quo* for an agreement not to strike. Viewed in this light, the legislation does more than confer jurisdiction in the federal courts over labor organizations. It expresses a federal policy that federal courts should enforce these agreements on behalf of or against labor organizations and that industrial peace can be best obtained only in that way.

To be sure, there is a great medley of ideas reflected in the hearings, reports, and debates on this Act. Yet, to repeat, the entire tenor of the history indicates that the agreement to arbitrate grievance disputes was considered as *quid pro quo* of a no-strike agreement. And when in the House the debate narrowed to the question whether § 301 was more than jurisdictional, it became abundantly clear that the purpose of the section was to provide the necessary legal remedies. Section 302 of the House bill, the substantial equivalent of the present § 301, was being described by Mr. Hartley, the sponsor of the bill in the House.

Mr. Barden. Mr. Chairman, I take this time for the purpose of asking the Chairman a question, and in asking the question I want it understood that it is intended to make a part of the record that may hereafter be referred to as history of the legislation.

It is my understanding that section 302, the section dealing with equal responsibility under collective bargaining contracts in strike actions and proceedings in district courts contemplates not only the ordinary lawsuits for damages but also such other remedial proceedings, both legal and equitable, as might be appropriate in the circumstances; in other words, proceedings could, for example, be brought by the employers, the labor organizations, or interested individual employees under the Declaratory Judgments Act in order to secure declarations from the Court of legal rights under the contract.

Mr. Hartley. The interpretation the gentleman has just given of that section is absolutely correct.

93 Cong. Rec. 3656–3657.

It seems, therefore, clear to us that Congress adopted a policy which placed sanctions behind agreements to arbitrate grievance disputes, by implication rejecting the common-law rule, discussed in Red Cross Line v. Atlantic Fruit Co., 264 U.S. 109, against enforcement of executory agreements to arbitrate. We would undercut the Act and defeat its policy if we read § 301 narrowly as only conferring jurisdiction over labor organizations.

The question then is, what is the substantive law to be applied in suits under § 301 (a)? We conclude that the substantive law to apply in suits under § 301 (a) is federal law, which the courts must fashion from the policy of our national labor laws. See Mendelsohn, Enforceability of Arbitration Agreements Under Taft-Hartley Section 301, 66 Yale L. J. 167. The Labor Management Relations Act expressly furnishes some substantive law. It points out what the parties may or may not do in certain situations. Other problems will lie in the penumbra of express statutory mandates. Some will lack express statutory sanction but will be solved by looking at the policy of the legislation and fashioning a remedy that will effectuate that policy. The range of judicial inventiveness will be determined by the nature of the problem. See Board of Commissioners v. United States, 308 U.S. 343, 351. Federal interpretation of the federal law will govern, not state law. Cf. Jerome v. United States, 318 U.S. 101, 104. But state law, if compatible with the purpose of § 301, may be resorted to in order to find the rule that will best effectuate the federal policy. See Board of Commissioners v. United States, supra, at 351–352. Any state law applied, however, will be absorbed as federal law and will not be an independent source of private rights.

It is not uncommon for federal courts to fashion federal law where federal rights are concerned. See Clearfield Trust Co. v. United States, 318 U.S. 363, 366–367; National Metropolitan Bank v. United States, 323 U.S. 454. Congress has indicated by § 301 (a) the purpose to follow that course here. There is no constitutional difficulty. Article III, § 2, extends the judicial power to cases "arising under . . . the Laws of the United States. . . ."

The power of Congress to regulate these labor-management controversies under the Commerce Clause is plain. Houston & Texas R. Co. v. United States, 234 U.S. 342; Labor Board v. Jones & Laughlin Corp., 301 U.S. 1. A case or controversy arising under § 301 (a) is, therefore, one within the purview of judicial power as defined in Article III.

The question remains whether jurisdiction to compel arbitration of grievance disputes is withdrawn by the Norris-LaGuardia Act, 47 Stat. 70, 29 U.S.C. § 101. Section 7 of that Act prescribes stiff procedural requirements for issuing an injunction in a labor dispute. The kinds of acts which had given rise to abuse of the power to enjoin are listed in § 4. The failure to arbitrate was not a part and parcel of the abuses against which the Act was aimed. Section 8 of the Norris-LaGuardia Act does, indeed, indicate a congressional policy toward settlement of labor disputes by arbitration, for it denies injunctive relief to any person who has failed to make "every reasonable effort" to settle the dispute by negotiation, mediation, or "voluntary arbitration." Though a literal reading might bring the dispute within the terms of the Act (see Cox, Grievance Arbitration in the Federal Courts, 67 Harv. L. Rev. 591, 602–604), we see no justification in policy for restricting § 301 (a) to damage suits, leaving specific performance of a contract to arbitrate grievance disputes to the inapposite procedural requirements of that Act. Moreover, we held in Virginian R. Co. v. System Federation, 300 U.S. 515, and in Graham v. Brotherhood of Firemen, 338 U.S. 232, 237, that the Norris-LaGuardia Act does not deprive federal courts of jurisdiction to compel compliance with the mandates of the Railway Labor Act. The mandates there involved concerned racial discrimination. Yet those decisions were not based on any peculiarities of the Railway Labor Act. We followed the same course in Syres v. Oil Workers International Union, 350 U.S. 892, which was governed by the National Labor Relations Act. There an injunction was sought against racial discrimination in application of a collective bargaining agreement; and we allowed the injunction to issue. The congressional policy in favor of the enforcement of agreements to arbitrate grievance disputes being clear, there is no reason to submit them to the requirements of § 7 of the Norris-LaGuardia Act.

A question of mootness was raised on oral argument. It appears that since the date of the decision in the Court of Appeals respondent has terminated its operations and has contracted to sell its mill properties. All work in the mill ceased in March, 1957. Some of the grievances, however, ask for back pay for increased workloads; and the collective bargaining agreement provides that "the Board of Arbitration shall have the right to adjust compensation retroactive to the date of the change." Insofar as the grievances sought restoration of workloads and job assignments, the case is, of course, moot. But to the extent that they sought a monetary award, the case is a continuing controversy.

The judgment of the Court of Appeals is reversed and the cause is remanded to that court for proceedings in conformity with this opinion.

Reversed.

MR. JUSTICE BLACK took no part in the consideration or decision of this case.

MR. JUSTICE BURTON, whom MR. JUSTICE HARLAN joins, concurring in the result.

This suit was brought in a United States District Court under § 301 of the Labor Management Relations Act of 1947, . . . seeking specific enforcement of the arbitration provisions of a collective-bargaining contract. The District Court had jurisdiction over the action since it involved an obligation running to a union—a union controversy—and not uniquely personal rights of employees sought to be enforced by a union. Cf. Association of Westinghouse Employees v. Westinghouse Elec. Corp., 348 U.S. 437. Having jurisdiction over the suit, the court was not powerless to fashion an appropriate federal remedy. The power to decree specific performance of a collectively bargained agreement to arbitrate finds its source in § 301 itself, and in a Federal District Court's inherent equitable powers, nurtured by a congressional policy to encourage and enforce labor arbitration in industries affecting commerce.

I do not subscribe to the conclusion of the Court that the substantive law to be applied in a suit under § 301 is federal law. At the same time, I agree with Judge Magruder in International Brotherhood v. W. L. Mead, Inc., 230 F. 2d 576, that some federal rights may necessarily be involved in a § 301 case, and hence that the constitutionality of § 301 can be upheld as a congressional grant to Federal District Courts of what has been called "protective jurisdiction."

MR. JUSTICE FRANKFURTER, dissenting.

The Court has avoided the difficult problems raised by § 301 of the Taft-Hartley Act, . . . by attributing to the section an occult content. This plainly procedural section is transmuted into a mandate to the federal courts to fashion a whole body of substantive federal law appropriate for the complicated and touchy problems raised by collective bargaining. I have set forth in my opinion in Employees v. Weshinghouse Corp. the detailed reasons why I believe that § 301 cannot be so construed, even if constitutional questions cannot be avoided. 348 U.S. 437, 441–449, 452–459. But the Court has a "clear" and contrary conclusion emerge from the "somewhat," to say the least, "cloudy and confusing legislative history." This is more than can be fairly asked even from the alchemy of construction. Since the Court relies on a few isolated statements in the legislative history which do not support its conclusion, however favoringly read, I have deemed it necessary to set forth in an appendix, *post,* p. 485, the entire relevant legislative history of the Taft-Hartley Act and its predecessor, the Case Bill. This legislative history reinforces the natural meaning of the statute as an exclusively procedural provision, affording, that is, an accessible federal forum for suits on agreements between labor organizations and employers, but not enacting federal law for such suits. See also Wollett and Wellington, Federalism and Breach of the Labor Agreement, 7 Stan. L. Rev. 445.

I have also set forth in my opinion in the Westinghouse case an outline of the vast problems that the Court's present decision creates by bringing into conflict state law and federal law, state courts and federal courts. 348 U.S., at 454–455; see also Judge Wyzanski's opinion in Textile Workers Union v. American Thread Co., 113 F. Supp. 137, 140. These problems are not rendered non-existent by disregard of them. It should also be noted that whatever may be a union's *ad hoc* benefit in a particular case, the meaning of collective bargaining for labor does not remotely derive from reliance on the sanction of litigation in the courts. Restrictions made by legislation like the Clayton Act of 1914 ... and the Norris-LaGuardia Act of 1932, ... upon the use of familiar remedies theretofore available in the federal courts, reflected deep fears of the labor movement of the use of such remedies against labor. But a union, like any other combatant engaged in a particular fight, is ready to make an ally of an old enemy, and so we also find unions resorting to the otherwise much excoriated labor injunction. Such intermittent yielding to expediency does not change the fact that judicial intervention is ill-suited to the special characteristics of the arbitration process in labor disputes; nor are the conditions for its effective functioning thereby altered.

> The arbitration is an integral part of the system of self-government. And the system is designed to aid management in its quest for efficiency, to assist union leadership in its participation in the enterprise, and to secure justice for the employees. It is a means of making collective bargaining work and thus preserving private enterprise in a free government. When its works fairly well, it does not need the sanction of the law of contracts or the law of arbitration. It is only when the system breaks down completely that the courts' aid in these respects is invoked. But the courts cannot, by occasional sporadic decision, restore the parties' continuing relationship; and their intervention in such cases may seriously affect the going systems of self-government. When their autonomous sys-

tem breaks down, might not the parties better be left to the usual methods for adjustment of labor disputes rather than to court actions on the contract or on the arbitration award?
Shulman, Reason, Contract, and Law in Labor Relations, 68
Harv. L. Rev. 999, 1024.

These reflections summarized the vast and extraordinarily successful experience of Dean Harry Shulman as labor arbitrator, especially as umpire under the collective-bargaining contract between the Ford Motor Co. and the UAW-CIO. (See his Opinions of the Umpire, Ford Motor Co. and UAW-CIO, 1943–1946, and the review by E. Merrick Dodd in 60 Harv. L. Rev. 486.) Arbitration agreements are for specific terms, generally much shorter than the time required for adjudication of a contested lawsuit through the available stages of trial and appeal. Renegotiation of agreements cannot await the outcome of such litigation; nor can the parties continuing relation await it. Cases under § 301 will probably present unusual rather than representative situations. A "rule" derived from them is more likely to discombobulate than to compose. A "uniform corpus" cannot be expected to evolve, certainly not within a time to serve its assumed function.

The prickly and extensive problems that the supposed grant would create further counsel against a finding that the grant was made. They present hazardous opportunities for friction in the regulation of contracts between employers and unions. They involve the division of power between State and Nation, between state courts and federal courts, including the effective functioning of this Court. Wisdom suggests self-restraint in undertaking to solve these problems unless the Court is clearly directed to do so. Section 301 is not such a direction. The legislative history contains no suggestion that these problems were considered; the terms of the section do not present them.

One word more remains to be said. The earliest declaration of unconstitutionality of an act of Congress—by the Justices on circuit—involved a refusal by the Justices to perform a function imposed upon them by Congress because of the non-judicial nature of that function. Hayburn's Case 2 Dall. 409. Since then, the Court has many times declared legislation unconstitutional because it imposed on the Court powers or functions that were regarded as outside the scope of the "judicial power" lodged in the Court by the Constitution. See, e.g., Marbury v. Madison, 1 Cranch 137; United States v. Ferreira, 13 How. 40; Muskrat v. United States, 219 U.S. 346; Keller v. Potomac Electric Power Co., 261 U.S. 428.

One may fairly generalize from these instances that the Court has deemed itself peculiarly qualified, with due regard to the contrary judgment of Congress, to determine what is meet and fit for the exercise of "judicial power" as authorized by the Constitution. Solicitude and respect for the confines of "judicial power," and the difficult problem of marking those confines, apply equally in construing precisely what duties Congress has cast upon the federal courts, especially when, as in this case, the most that can be said in support of finding a congressional desire to impose these "legislative" duties on the federal courts is that Congress did not mention the problem in the statute and that, insofar as purpose may be gathered from congressional reports and debate, they leave us in the dark.

The Court, however, sees no problem of "judicial power" in casting upon the federal courts, with no guides except "judicial inventiveness," the task of applying a whole industrial code that is as yet in the bosom of the judiciary. There are severe limits on "judicial inventiveness" even for the most imaginative judges. The law is not a "brooding omnipresence in the sky," (Mr. Justice Holmes, dissenting, in Southern Pacific Co. v. Jensen, 244 U.S. 205, 222), and it cannot be drawn from there like nitrogen from the air. These problems created by the Court's interpretation of § 301 cannot be solved by resort to the established canons of construction that enable a court to look through awkward or clumsy expression, or language wanting in precision, to the intent of the legislature. For the vice of the statute here lies in the impossibility of ascertaining, by any reasonable test, that the legislature meant one thing rather than another. . . ." Connally v. General Construction Co., 269 U.S. 385, 394. But the Court makes § 301 a mountain instead of a molehill and, by giving an example of "judicial inventiveness," it thereby solves all the constitutional problems that would otherwise have to be faced.

Even on the Court's attribution to § 301 of a direction to the federal courts to fashion, out of bits and pieces elsewhere to be gathered, a federal common law of labor contracts, it still does not follow that Congress has enacted that an agreement to arbitrate industrial differences be specifically enforceable in the federal courts. On the contrary, the body of relevant federal law precludes such enforcement of arbitration clauses in collective-bargaining agreements.

Prior to 1925, the doctrine that executory agreements to arbitrate any kind of dispute would not be specifically enforced still held sway in the federal courts. See, e.g., Judge Hough's opinion in United States Asphalt Refining Co. v. Trinidad Lake Petroleum Co., 222 F. 1006; Judge Mack's opinion in Atlantic Fruit Co. v. Red Cross Line, 276 F. 319; and Mr. Justice Brandeis' opinion in Red Cross Line v. Atlantic Fruit Co., 264 U.S. 109, 123, 125. Legislation was deemed necessary to assure such power to the federal courts. In 1925, Congress passed the United States Arbitration Act, 9 U.S.C.

§ 1 et seq., making executory agreements to arbitrate specifically enforceable in the federal courts, but explicitly excluding "contracts of employment" of workers engaged in interstate commerce from its scope. Naturally enough, I find rejection, though not explicit, of the availability of the Federal Arbitration Act to enforce arbitration clauses in collective-bargaining agreements in the silent treatment given that Act by the Court's opinion. If an Act that authorizes the federal courts to enforce arbitration provisions in contracts generally, but specifically denies authority to decree that remedy for "contracts of employment," were available, the Court would hardly spin such power out of the empty darkness of § 301. I would make this rejection explicit, recognizing that when Congress passed legislation to enable arbitration agreements to be enforced by the federal courts, it saw fit to exclude this remedy with respect to labor contracts. See Amalgamated Association v. Pennsylvania Greyhound Lines, 192 F. 2d 310; United Electrical, Radio & Machine Workers v. Miller Metal Products, Inc., 215 F. 2d 221; Lincoln Mills v. Textile Workers Union, 230 F. 2d 81; United Steelworkers of America v. Galland-Henning Mfg. Co., 241 F. 2d 323; and the legislative history set forth by the parties in the present cases. Congress heeded the resistance of organized labor, uncompromisingly led in its hostility to this measure by Andrew Furuseth, president of the International Seamen's Union and most powerful voice expressing labor's fear of the use of this remedy against it.

Even though the Court glaringly ignores the Arbitration Act, it does at least recognize the common-law rule against enforcement of executory agreements to arbitrate. It nevertheless enforces the arbitration clause in the collective-bargaining agreements in these cases. It does so because it finds that Congress "by implication" rejected the common-law rule. I would add that the Court, in thus deriving power from the unrevealing words of the Taft-Hartley Act, has also found that Congress "by implication" repealed its own statutory exemption of collective-bargaining agreements in the Arbitration Act, an exemption made as we have seen for well-defined reasons of policy.

The Court of Appeals for the First Circuit, which reached the conclusion that arbitration clauses in collective-bargaining agreements were enforceable under the Arbitration Act, nevertheless found that such clauses would not have been enforceable by virtue of § 301:

> A number of courts have held that § 301 itself is a legislative authorization for decrees of specific performance of arbitration agreements.... We think that is reading too much into the very general language of § 301. The terms and legislative history of § 301 sufficiently demonstrate, in our view, that it was not intended either to create any new remedies or to deny applicable existing

remedies. See H. R. Rep. No. 245, 80th Cong., 1st Sess. 46 (1947); H. R. Rep. No. 510 (Conference Report), 80th Cong., 1st Sess. 42 (1947); 93 Cong. Rec. 3734, 6540 (daily ed. 1947). Arbitration was scarcely mentioned at all in the legislative history. Furthermore, the same practical consideration that militates against judicial overruling of the common law doctrine applies against interpreting § 301 to give that effect. The most that could be read into it would be that it authorizes equitable remedies in general, including decrees for specific performance of an arbitration agreement. Lacking are the procedural specifications needed for administration of the power to compel arbitration.... Thus it seems to us that a firmer statutory basis than § 301 should be found to justify departure from the judicially formulated doctrines with reference to arbitration agreements.
Local 205 v. General Electric Co., 233 F. 2d 85, 96–97.

I would put the conclusion even more strongly because, contrary to the view of the Court of Appeals for the First Circuit, the rule that is departed from "by implication" had not only been "judicially formulated" but had purposefully been congressionally formulated in the Arbitration Act of 1925. And it is being departed from on the tenuous basis of the legislative history of § 301, for which the utmost that can be claimed is that insofar as there was any expectation at all, it was only that conventional remedies, including equitable remedies, would be available. But, of course, as we have seen, "equitable remedies" in the federal courts had traditionally excluded specific performance of arbitration clauses, except as explicitly provided by the 1925 Act. Thus, even assuming that § 301 contains directions for some federal substantive law of labor contracts, I see no justification for translating the vague expectation concerning the remedies to be applied into an overruling of previous federal common law and, more particularly, into the repeal of the previous congressional exemption of collective-bargaining agreements from the class of agreements in which arbitration clauses were to be enforced.

The second ground of my dissent from the Court's action is more fundamental. Since I do not agree with the Court's conclusion that federal substantive law is to govern in actions under § 301, I am forced to consider the serious constitutional question that was adumbrated in the Westinghouse case, 348 U.S., at 449–452, the constitutionality of a grant of jurisdiction to federal courts over contracts that came into being entirely by virtue of state substantive law, a jurisdiction not based on diversity of citizenship, yet one in which a federal court would, as in diversity cases, act in effect merely as another court of the State in which it sits. The scope of allowable federal judicial power that this grant must satisfy is constitutionally described as "Cases, in Law and Equity, arising under this Constitution, the

Laws of the United States, and Treaties made, or which shall be made, under their Authority." Art. III, § 2. While interpretive decisions are legion under general statutory grants of jurisdiction strikingly similar to this constitutional wording, it is generally recognized that the full constitutional power has not been exhausted by these statutes. See, e.g., Mishkin, The Federal "Question" in the District Courts, 53 Col. L. Rev. 157, 160; Shulman and Jaegerman, Some Jurisdictional Limitations on Federal Procedure, 45 Yale L. J. 393, 405, n. 47; Wechsler, Federal Jurisdiction and the Revision of the Judicial Code, 13 Law & Contemp. Prob., 216, 224–225.

Almost without exception, decisions under the general statutory grants have tested jurisdiction in terms of the presence, as an integral part of plaintiff's cause of action, of an issue calling for interpretation or application of federal law. E.g., Gully v. First National Bank, 299 U.S. 109. Although it has sometimes been suggested that the "cause of action" must derive from federal law, see American Well Works Co. v. Layne & Bowler Co., 241 U.S. 257, 260, it has been sufficient that some aspect of federal law is essential to plaintiff's success. Smith v. Kansas City Title & Trust Co., 255 U.S. 180. The litigation-provoking problem has been the degree to which federal law must be in the forefront of the case and not collateral, peripheral or remote.

In a few exceptional cases, arising under special jurisdictional grants, the criteria by which the prominence of the federal question is measured against constitutional requirements have been found satisfied under circumstances suggesting a variant theory of the nature of these requirements. The first, and the leading case in the field, is Osborn v. Bank of the United States, 9 Wheat. 738. There, Chief Justice Marshall sustained federal jurisdiction in a situation—hypothetical in the case before him but presented by the companion case of Bank of the United States v. Planters' Bank, 9 Wheat. 904—involving suit by a federally incorporated bank upon a contract. Despite the assumption that the cause of action and the interpretation of the contract would be governed by state law, the case was found to "arise under the laws of the United States" because the propriety and scope of a federally granted authority to enter into contracts and to litigate might well be challenged. This reasoning was subsequently applied to sustain jurisdiction in actions against federally chartered railroad corporations. Pacific Railroad Removal Cases, 115 U.S. 1. The traditional interpretation of this series of cases is that federal jurisdiction under the "arising" clause of the Constitution, though limited to cases involving potential federal questions, has such flexibility that Congress may confer it whenever there exists in the background some federal proposition that might be challenged, despite the remoteness of the likelihood of actual presentation of such a federal question.

The views expressed in Osborn and the Pacific Railroad Removal Cases were severely restricted in construing general grants of jurisdiction. But the Court later sustained this jurisdictional section of the Bankruptcy Act of 1898:

> The United States district courts shall have jurisdiction of all controversies at law and in equity, as distinguished from proceedings in bankruptcy, between trustees as such and adverse claimants concerning the property acquired or claimed by the trustees, in the same manner and to the same extent only as though bankruptcy proceedings had not been instituted and such controversies had been between the bankrupts and such adverse claimants.
> § 23 (a), as amended, 44 Stat. 664.

Under this provision the trustee could pursue in a federal court a private cause of action arising under and wholly governed by state law. Schumacher v. Beeler, 293 U.S. 367; Williams v. Austrian, 331 U.S. 642 (Chandler Act of 1938, 52 Stat. 840). To be sure, the cases did not discuss the basis of jurisdiction. It has been suggested that they merely represent an extension of the approach of the Osborn case; the trustee's right to sue might be challenged on obviously federal grounds—absence of bankruptcy or irregularity of the trustee's appointment or of the bankruptcy proceedings. National Mutual Ins. Co. v. Tidewater Transfer Co., 337 U.S. 582, 611–613 (Rutledge, J., concurring). So viewed, this type of litigation implicates a potential federal question.

Apparently relying on the extent to which the bankruptcy cases involve only remotely a federal question, Mr. Justice Jackson concluded in National Mutual Insurance Co. v. Tidewater Transfer Co., 337 U.S. 582, that Congress may confer jurisdiction on the District Courts as incidental to its powers under Article I. No attempt was made to reconcile this view with the restrictions of Article III; a majority of the Court recognized that Article III defined the bound of valid jurisdictional legislation and rejected the notion that jurisdictional grants can go outside these limits.

With this background, many theories have been proposed to sustain the constitutional validity of § 301. In Textile Workers Union of America v. American Thread Co., 113 F. Supp. 137, 140, Judge Wyzanski suggested, among other possibilities, that § 301 might be read as containing a direction that controversies affecting interstate commerce should be governed by federal law incorporating state law by reference, and that such controversies would then arise under a valid federal law as required by Article III. Whatever may be said of the assumption regarding the validity of federal jurisdiction under an affirmative declaration by Congress that state law should be applied as federal law by federal courts to contract disputes affecting commerce, we cannot argumentatively legislate for Congress when Congress has failed to legislate. To do so disrespects legislative responsibility and disregards judicial limitations.

Another theory, relying on Osborn and the bankruptcy cases, has been proposed which would achieve results similar to those attainable under Mr. Justice Jackson's view, but which purports to respect the "arising" clause of Article III. See Hart and Wechsler, The Federal Courts and the Federal System, pp. 744–747; Wechsler, Federal Jurisdiction and the Revision of the Judicial Code, 13 Law & Contemp. Prob. 216, 224–225; International Brotherhood v. W. L. Mead, Inc., 230 F. 2d 576. Called "protective jurisdiction," the suggestion is that in any case for which Congress has the constitutional power to prescribe federal rules of decision and thus confer "true" federal question jurisdiction, it may, without so doing, enact a jurisdictional statute, which will provide a federal forum for the application of state statute and decisional law. Analysis of the "protective jurisdiction" theory might also be attempted in terms of the language of Article III— construing "laws" to include jurisdictional statutes where Congress could have legislated substantively in a field. This is but another way of saying that because Congress could have legislated substantively and thereby could give rise to litigation under a statute of the United States, it can provide a federal forum for state-created rights although it chose not to adopt state law as federal law or to originate federal rights.

Surely the truly technical restrictions of Article III are not met or respected by a beguiling phrase that the greater power here must necessarily include the lesser. In the compromise of federal and state interests leading to distribution of jealously guarded judicial power in a federal system, see 13 Cornell L. Q. 499, it is obvious that very different considerations apply to cases involving questions of federal law and those turning solely on state law. It may be that the ambiguity of the phrase "arising under the laws of the United States" leaves room for more than traditional theory could accommodate. But, under the theory of "protective jurisdiction," the "arising under" jurisdiction of the federal courts would be vastly extended. For example, every contract or tort arising out of a contract affecting commerce might be a potential cause of action in the federal courts, even though only state law was involved in the decision of the case. At least in Osborn and the bankruptcy cases, a substantive federal law was present somewhere in the background. See pp. 470–472, supra, and pp. 480–484, infra. But this theory rests on the supposition that Congress could enact substantive federal law to govern the particular case. It was not held in those cases, nor is it clear, that federal law could be held to govern the transactions of all persons who subsequently become bankrupt, or of all suits of a Bank of the United States. See Mishkin, The Federal "Question" in the District Courts, 53 Col. L. Rev. 157, 189.

"Protective jurisdiction," once the label is discarded, cannot be justified under any view of the allowable scope to be given to Article III. "Protective jurisdiction" is a misused label for the statute we are here considering. That rubric is properly descriptive of safeguarding some of the indisputable, staple business of the federal courts. It is a radiation of an existing jurisdiction. See Adams v. United States ex rel. McCann, 317 U.S. 269; 28 U.S.C. § 2283. "Protective jurisdiction" cannot generate an independent source for adjudication outside of the Article III sanctions and what Congress has defined. The theory must have as its sole justification a belief in the inadequacy of state tribunals in determining state law. The Constitution reflects such a belief in the specific situation within which the Diversity Clause was confined. The intention to remedy such supposed defects was exhausted in this provision of Article III. That this "protective" theory was not adopted by Chief Justice Marshall at a time when conditions might have presented more substantial justification strongly suggests its lack of constitutional merit. Moreover, Congress in its consideration of § 301 nowhere suggested dissatisfaction with the ability of state courts to administer state law properly. Its concern was to provide access to the federal courts for easier enforcement of state-created rights.

Another theory also relies on Osborn and the bankruptcy cases as an implicit recognition of the propriety of the exercise of some sort of "protective jurisdiction" by the federal courts. Mishkin, op. cit. supra, 53 Col. L. Rev. 157, 184 et seq. Professor Mishkin tends to view the assertion of such a jurisdiction, in the absence of any exercise of substantive powers, as irreconcilable with the "arising" clause since the case would then arise only under the jurisdictional statute itself, and he is reluctant to find a constitutional basis for the grant of power outside Article III. Professor Mishkin also notes that the only purpose of such a statute would be to insure impartiality to some litigant, an objection inconsistent with Article III's recognition of "protective jurisdiction" only in the specified situation of diverse citizenship. But where Congress has "an articulated and active federal policy regulating a field, the 'arising under' clause of Article III apparently permits the conferring of jurisdiction on the national courts of all cases in the area—including those substantively governed by state law." Id., at 192. In such cases, the protection being offered is not to the suitor, as in diversity cases, but to the "congressional legislative program." Thus he supports § 301: "even though the rules governing collective bargaining agreements continue to be state-fashioned, nonetheless the mode of their application and enforcement may play a very substantial part in the labor-management relations of interstate industry and commerce—an area in which the national government has labored long and hard." Id., at 196.

Insofar as state law governs the case, Professor Mishkin's theory is quite similar to that advanced by Professors Hart and Wechsler and followed by the Court of Appeals for the First Circuit: The substantive power of Congress, although not exercised to govern the particular "case," gives "arising under" jurisdiction to the federal courts despite governing state law. The second "protective jurisdiction" theory has the dubious advantage of limiting incursions on state judicial power to situations in which the State's feelings may have been tempered by early substantive federal invasions.

Professor Mishkin's theory of "protective jurisdiction" may find more constitutional justification if there is not merely an "articulated and active" congressional policy regulating the labor field but also federal rights existing in the interstices of actions under § 301. See Wollett and Wellington, Federalism and Breach of the Labor Agreement, 7 Stan. L. Rev. 445, 475–479. Therefore, before resting on an interpretation of § 301 that would compel a declaration of unconstitutionality, we must, as was stated in Westinghouse, defer to the strong presumption—even as to such technical matters as federal jurisdiction—that Congress legislated in accordance with the Constitution. The difficult nature of the problem of construction to be faced if some federal rights are sought was set forth in Westinghouse, where the constitutional questions were involved only in their bearing on the construction of the statute. Now that the constitutional questions themselves must be faced, the nature of the problem bears repeating.

Legislation must, if possible, be given a meaning that will enable it to survive. This rule of constitutional adjudication is normally invoked to narrow what would otherwise be the natural but constitutionally dubious scope of the language. E.g., United States v. Delaware & Hudson Co., 213 U.S. 366; United States v. Jin Fuey Moy, 241 U.S. 394, 401; United States v. Rumely, 345 U.S. 41. Here the endeavor of some lower courts and of this Court has resulted in adding to the section substantive congressional regulation even though Congress saw fit not to exercise such power or to give the courts any concrete guidance for defining such regulation.

To be sure, the full scope of a substantive regulation is frequently in dispute and must await authoritative determination by courts. Congress declares its purpose imperfectly or partially, and compatible judicial construction completes it. But in this case we start with a provision that is wholly jurisdictional and as such bristles with constitutional problems under Article III. To avoid them, interpolation of substantive regulation has been proposed. From what materials are we to draw a determination that § 301 is something other than what it declares itself? Is the Court justified in creating all the difficult problems of choice within a sphere of delicate policy without any direction from Congress and merely for the sake of giving effect to a provision that seems to deal with a different subject? The somewhat Delphic wisdom of Mr. Justice Cardozo, speaking for the whole Court, pulls us here in the opposite direction: "We think the light is so strong as to flood whatever places in the statute might otherwise be dark. Courts have striven mightily at times to canalize construction along the path of safety. . . . When a statute is reasonably susceptible of two interpretations, they have preferred the meaning that preserves to the meaning that destroys. . . . 'But avoidance of a difficulty will not be pressed to the point of disingenuous evasion.' . . . 'Here the intention of the Congress is revealed too distinctly to permit us to ignore it because of mere misgivings as to power.'" Hopkins Federal Savings & Loan Assn. v. Cleary, 296 U.S. 315, 334–335.

Assuming, however, that we would be justified in pouring substantive content into a merely procedural vehicle, what elements of federal law could reasonably be put into the provisions of § 301? The suggestion that the section permits the federal courts to work out, without more, a federal code governing collective-bargaining contracts must, for reasons that have already been stated, be rejected. Likewise the suggestion that § 301 may be viewed as a congressional authorization to the federal courts to work out a concept of the nature of the collective-bargaining contract, leaving detailed questions of interpretation to state law. See 348 U.S., at 455–459.

Nor will Congress' objective be furthered by an attempt to limit the grant of a federal forum to certain types of actions between unions and employers. It would be difficult to find any basis for, or principles of, selection, either in the terms of § 301 or in considerations relevant to promotion of stability in labor relations. It is true that a fair reading of § 301 in the context of its enactment shows that the suit that Congress primarily contemplated was the suit against a union for strike in violation of contract. From this it might be possible to imply a federal right to bring an action for damages based on such an event. In the interest of mutuality, so close to the heart of Congress, we might in turn find a federal right in the union to sue for a lockout in violation of contract. But neither federal right would be involved in the present cases. Moreover, it bears repetition that Congress chose not to make this the basis of federal law, i.e., it chose not to make such conduct an unfair labor practice.

There is a point, however, at which the search may be ended with less misgiving regarding the propriety of judicial infusion of substantive provisions into § 301. The contribution of federal law might consist in postulating the right of a union, despite its amorphous status as an unincorporated association, to enter into binding collective-bargaining contracts with an employer. The federal courts might also give sanction to this right by refusing to comply with any state law that does not admit that collective bargaining may result in an enforceable contract. It is hard to see what serious federal-state conflicts could arise under this view. At most, a state court might dismiss the action, while a federal court would entertain it. Moreover, such a function of federal law is closely related to the removal of the procedural barriers to suit. Section 301 would be futile if the union's status as a contracting party were not recognized. The statement in § 301 (b) that the acts of the agents of the union are to be regarded as binding upon the union may be used in support of this conclusion. This provision, not confined in its application to suits in the District Court under § 301 (a), was primarily directed to responsibility of the union for its agents' actions in authorizing strikes or committing torts. It can be construed, however, as applicable to the formation of a contract. So applied, it would imply that a union must be regarded as contractually bound by the acts of its agents, which in turn presupposes that the union is capable of contract relations.

Of course, the possibility of a State's law being counter to such a limited federal proposition is hypothetical, and to base an assertion of federal law on such a possibility, one never considered by Congress, is an artifice. And were a State ever to adopt a contrary attitude, its reasons for so doing might be such that Congress would not be willing to disregard them. But these difficulties are inherent in any attempt to expand § 301 substantively to meet constitutional requirements.

Even if this limited federal "right" were read into § 301, a serious constitutional question would still be present. It does elevate the situation to one closely analogous to that presented in Osborn v. Bank of the United States, 9 Wheat. 738. Section 301 would, under this view, imply that a union is to be viewed as a juristic entity for purposes of acquiring contract rights under a collective-bargaining agreement, and that it has the right to enter into such a contract and to sue upon it. This was all that was immediately and expressly involved in the Osborn case, although the historical setting was vastly different, and the juristic entity in that case was completely the creature of federal law, one engaged in carrying out essential governmental functions. Most of these special considerations had disappeared, however, at the time and in the circumstances of the decision of the Pacific Railroad Removal Cases, 115 U.S. 1, see p. 471, supra. There is force in the view that regards the latter as a "sport" and finds that the Court has so viewed it. See Mishkin, 53 Col. L. Rev., at 160, n. 24, citing Gully v. First National Bank, 229 U.S. 109, 113–114 ("Only recently we said after full consideration that the doctrine of the charter cases was to be treated as exceptional, though within their special field there was no thought to disturb them."), and Puerto Rico v. Russell & Co., 288 U.S. 476, 485; see also Mr. Justice Holmes, in Smith v. Kansas City Title & Trust Co., 225 U.S.

180, 214–215 (dissenting opinion). The question is whether we should now so consider it and refuse to apply its holding to the present situation.

I believe that we should not extend the precedents of Osborn and the Pacific Railroad Removal Cases to this case, even though there be some elements of analytical similarity. Osborn, the foundation for the Removal Cases, appears to have been based on premises that today, viewed in the light of the jurisdictional philosophy of Gully v. First National Bank, supra, are subject to criticism. The basic premise was that every case in which a federal question might arise must be capable of being commenced in the federal courts, and when so commenced it might, because jurisdiction must be judged at the outset, be concluded there despite the fact that the federal question was never raised. Marshall's holding was undoubtedly influenced by his fear that the bank might suffer hostile treatment in the state courts that could not be remedied by an appeal on an isolated federal question. There is nothing in Article III that affirmatively supports the view that original jurisdiction over cases involving federal questions must extend to every case in which there is the potentiality of appellate jurisdiction. We also have become familiar with removal procedures that could be adapted to alleviate any remaining fears by providing for removal to a federal court whenever a federal question was raised. In view of these developments, we would not be justified in perpetuating a principle that permits assertion of original federal jurisdiction on the remote possibility of presentation of a federal question. Indeed, Congress, by largely withdrawing the jurisdiction that the Pacific Railroad Removal Cases recognized, and this Court, by refusing to perpetuate it under general grants of jurisdiction, see Gully v. First National Bank, supra, have already done much to recognize the changed atmosphere.

Analysis of the bankruptcy power also reveals a superficial analogy to § 301. The trustee enforces a cause of action acquired under state law by the bankrupt. Federal law merely provides for the appointment of the trustee, vests the cause of action in him, and confers jurisdiction on the federal courts. Section 301 similarly takes the rights and liabilities which under state law are vested distributively in the individual members of a union and vests them in the union for purposes of action in federal courts, wherein the unions are authorized to sue and be sued as an entity. While the authority of the trustee depends on the existence of a bankrupt and on the propriety of the proceedings leading to the trustee's appointment, both of which depend on federal law, there are similar federal propositions that may be essential to an action under § 301. Thus, the validity of the contract may in any case be challenged on the ground that the labor organization negotiating it was not the representative of the employees concerned, a question that has been held to be federal, La Crosse Telephone Corp. v. Wisconsin Employment Relations Board, 336 U.S. 18, or on the ground that subsequent change in the representative status of the union has affected the continued validity of the agreement. Perhaps also the qualifications imposed on a union's right to utilize the facilities of the National Labor Relations Board, dependent on the filing of non-Communist affidavits required by § 9 (h) and the information and reports required by § 9 (f) and (g), might be read as restrictions on the right of the union to sue under § 301, again providing a federal basis for challenge to the union's authority. Consequently, were the bankruptcy cases to be viewed as dependent solely on the background existence of federal questions, there would be little analytical basis for distinguishing actions under § 301. But the bankruptcy decisions may be justified by the scope of the bankruptcy power, which may be deemed to sweep within its scope interests analytically outside the "federal question" category, but sufficiently related to the main purpose of bankruptcy to call for comprehensive treatment. See National Mutual Ins. Co. v. Tidewater Transfer Co., 337 U.S. 582, 652, n. 3 (concurring in part, dissenting in part). Also, although a particular suit may be brought by a trustee in a district other than the one in which the principal proceedings are pending, if all the suits by the trustee, even though in many federal courts, are regarded as one litigation for the collection and apportionment of the bankrupt's property, a particular suit by the trustee, under state law, to recover a specific piece of property might be analogized to the ancillary or pendent jurisdiction cases in which, in the disposition of a cause of action, federal courts may pass on state grounds for recovery that are joined to federal grounds. See Hurn v. Oursler, 289 U.S. 238; Siler v. Louisville & Nashville R. Co., 213 U.S. 175; but see Mishkin, 53 Col. L. Rev. at 194, n. 161.

If there is in the phrase "arising under the laws of the United States" leeway for expansion of our concepts of jurisdiction, the history of Article III suggests that the area is not great and that it will require the presence of some substantial federal interest, one of greater weight and dignity than questionable doubt concerning the effectiveness of state procedure. The bankruptcy cases might possibly be viewed as such an expansion. But even so, not merely convenient judicial administration but the whole purpose of the congressional legislative program—conservation and equitable distribution of the bankrupt's estate in carrying out the constitutional power over bankruptcy—required the availability of federal jurisdiction to avoid expense and delay. Nothing pertaining to § 301 suggests vesting the federal courts with sweeping power under the Commerce Clause comparable to that vested in the federal courts under the bankruptcy power.

In the wise distribution of governmental powers, this Court cannot do what a President sometimes does in returning a bill to Congress. We cannot return this provision to Congress and respectfully request that body to face the responsibility placed upon it by the Constitution to define the jurisdiction of the lower courts with some particularity and not to leave these courts at large. Confronted as I am, I regretfully have no choice. For all the reasons elaborated in this dissent, even reading into § 301 the limited federal rights consistent with the purposes of that section, I am impelled to the view that it is unconstitutional in cases such as the present ones where it provides the sole basis for exercise of jurisdiction by the federal courts.

UNITED STEELWORKERS OF AMERICA V. AMERICAN MANUFACTURING CO.

Supreme Court of the United States, 1960.
363 U.S. 564, 80 S. Ct. 1343, 4 L. Ed. 2d 1403.
(Footnotes Omitted)

Opinion of the Court by MR. JUSTICE DOUGLAS, announced by MR. JUSTICE BRENNAN.

This suit was brought by petitioner union in the District Court to compel arbitration of a "grievance" that petitioner, acting for one Sparks, a union member, had filed with the respondent, Sparks' employer. The employer defended on the ground (1) that Sparks is estopped from making his claim because he had a few days previously settled a workmen's compensation claim against the company on the basis that he was permanently partially disabled, (2) that Sparks is not physically able to do the work, and (3) that this type of dispute is not arbitrable under the collective bargaining agreement in question.

The agreement provided that during its term there would be "no strike," unless the employer refused to abide by a decision of the arbitrator. The agreement sets out a detailed grievance procedure with a provision for arbitration (regarded as the standard form) of all disputes between the parties "as to the meaning, interpretation and application of the provisions of this agreement."

The agreement reserves to the management power to suspend or discharge any employee "for cause." It also contains a provision that the employer will employ and promote employees on the principle of seniority "where ability and efficiency are equal." Sparks left his work due to an injury and while off work brought an action for compensation benefits. The case was settled, Sparks' physician expressing the opinion that the injury had made him 25% "permanently partially disabled." That was on September 9. Two weeks later the union filed a grievance which charged that Sparks was entitled to return to his job by virtue of the seniority provision of the collective bargaining agreement. Respondent refused to arbitrate and this action was brought. The District Court held that Sparks, having accepted the settlement on the basis of permanent partial disability, was estopped to claim any seniority or employment rights and granted the motion for summary judgment. The Court of Appeals affirmed, 264 F. 2d 624, for different reasons. After reviewing the evidence it held that the grievance is "a frivolous, patently baseless one, not subject to arbitration under the collective bargaining agreement." Id., at 628. The case is here on a writ of certiorari. . . .

Section 203 (d) of the Labor Management Relations Act, 1947, . . . states, "Final adjustment by a method agreed upon by the parties is hereby declared to be the desirable method for settlement of grievance disputes arising over the application or interpretation of an existing collective-bargaining agreement. . . ." That policy can be effectuated only if the means chosen by the parties for settlement of their differences under a collective bargaining agreement is given full play.

A state decision that held to the contrary announced a principle that could only have a crippling effect on grievance arbitration. The case was International Assn. of Machinists v. Cutler-Hammer, Inc., 271 App. Div. 917, 67 N. Y. S. 2d 317, aff'd 297 N. Y. 519, 74 N. E. 2d 464. It held that "if the meaning of the provision of the contract sought to be arbitrated is beyond dispute, there cannot be anything to arbitrate and the contract cannot be said to provide for arbitration." 271 App. Div., at 918, 67 N. Y. S. 2d, at 318. The lower courts in the instance case had a like preoccupation with ordinary contract law. The collective agreement requires arbitration of claims that courts might be unwilling to entertain. In the context of the plant or industry the grievance may assume proportions of which judges are ignorant. Yet, the agreement is to submit all grievances to arbitration, not merely those that a court may deem to be meritorious. There is no exception in the "no strike" clause and none therefore should be read into the grievance clause, since one is the *quid pro quo* for the other. The question is not whether in the mind of the court there is equity in the claim. Arbitration is a stabilizing influence only as it serves as a vehicle for handling any and all disputes that arise under the agreement.

The collective agreement calls for the submission of grievances in the categories which it describes, irrespective of whether a court may deem them to be meritorious. In our role of developing a meaningful body of law to govern the interpretation and enforcement of collective bargaining agreements, we think special heed should be given to the context in which collective bargaining agreements are negotiated and the purpose which they are intended to serve. See Lewis v. Benedict Coal Corp., 361 U.S. 459, 468. The function of the court is very limited when the parties have agreed to submit all questions of contract interpretation to the arbitrator. It is confined to ascertaining whether the party seeking arbitration is making a claim which on its face is governed by the contract. Whether the moving party is right or wrong is a question of contract interpretation for the arbitrator. In these circumstances the moving party should not be deprived of the arbitrator's judgment, when it was his judgment and all that it connotes that was bargained for.

The courts, therefore, have no business weighing the merits of the grievance, considering whether there is equity in a particular claim, or determining whether there is particular language in the written instrument which will support the claim. The agreement is to submit all grievances to arbitration, not merely those which the court will deem meritorious. The processing of even frivolous claims may have therapeutic values of which those who are not a part of the plant environment may be quite unaware.

The union claimed in this case that the company had violated a specific provision of the contract. The company took the position that it had not violated that clause. There was, therefore, a dispute between the parties as to "the meaning, interpretation and application" of the collective bargaining agreement. Arbitration should have been ordered. When the judiciary undertakes to determine the merits of a grievance under the guise of interpreting the grievance procedure of collective bargaining agreements, it usurps a function which under that regime is entrusted to the arbitration tribunal.

Reversed.

Mr. Justice Frankfurter concurs in the result.

Mr. Justice Whittaker, believing that the District Court lacked jurisdiction to determine the merits of the claim which the parties had validly agreed to submit to the exclusive jurisdiction of a Board of Arbitrators (Textile Workers v. Lincoln Mills, . . .), concurs in the result of this opinion.

Mr. Justice Black took no part in the consideration or decision of this case.

Mr. Justice Brennan, with whom Mr. Justice Harlan joins, concurring.

While I join the Court's opinions in Nos. 443, 360 and 538, I add a word in Nos. 443 and 360.

In each of these two cases the issue concerns the enforcement of but one promise—the promise to arbitrate in the context of an agreement dealing with a particular subject matter, the industrial relations between employers and employees. Other promises contained in the collective bargaining agreements are beside the point unless, by the very terms of the arbitration promise, they are made relevant to its interpretation. And I emphasize this, for the arbitration promise is itself a contract. The parties are free to make that promise as broad or as narrow as they wish, for there is no compulsion in law requiring them to include any such promises in their agreement. The meaning of the arbitration promise is not to be found simply by reference to the dictionary definitions of the words the parties use, or by reference to the interpretation of commercial arbitration clauses. Words in a collective bargaining agreement, rightly viewed by the Court to be the charter instrument of a system of industrial self-government, like words in a statute, are to be understood only by reference to the background which gave rise to their inclusion. The Court therefore avoids the prescription of inflexible rules for the enforcement of arbitration promises. Guidance is given by identifying the various considerations which a court should take into account when construing a particular clause—considerations of the milieu in which the clause is negotiated and of the national labor policy. It is particularly underscored that the arbitral process in collective bargaining presupposes that the parties wanted the informed judgment of an arbitrator, precisely for the reason that judges cannot provide it. Therefore, a court asked to enforce a promise to arbitrate should ordinarily refrain from involving itself in the interpretation of the substantive provisions of the contract.

To be sure, since arbitration is a creature of contract, a court must always inquire, when a party seeks to invoke its aid to force a reluctant party to the arbitration table, whether the parties have agreed to arbitrate the particular dispute. In this sense, the question of whether a dispute is "arbitrable" is inescapably for the court.

On examining the arbitration clause, the court may conclude that it commits to arbitration any "dispute, difference, disagreement, or controversy of any nature or character." With that finding the court will have exhausted its function, except to order the reluctant party to arbitration. Similarly, although the arbitrator may be empowered only to interpret and apply the contract, the parties may have provided that any dispute as to whether a particular claim is within the arbitration clause is itself for the arbitrator. Again the court, without more, must send any dispute to the arbitrator, for the parties have agreed that the construction of the arbitration promise itself is for the arbitrator, and the reluctant party has breached his promise by refusing to submit the dispute to arbitration.

In *American,* the Court deals with a request to enforce the "standard" form of arbitration clause, one that provides for the arbitration of "[a]ny disputes, misunderstandings, differences or grievances arising between the parties as to the meaning, interpretation and application of this agreement. . . ." Since the arbitration clause itself is part of the agreement, it might be argued that a dispute as to the meaning of that clause is for the arbitrator. But the Court rejects this position, saying that the threshold question, the meaning of the arbitration clause itself, is for the judge unless the parties clearly state to the contrary. However, the Court finds that the meaning of that "standard" clause is simply that the parties have agreed to arbitrate any dispute which the moving party asserts to involve construction of the substantive provisions of the contract, because such a dispute necessarily does involve such a construction.

The issue in the *Warrior* case is essentially no different from that in *American,* that is, it is whether the company agreed to arbitrate a particular grievance. In contrast to *American,* however, the arbitration promise here excludes a particular area from arbitration—"matters which are strictly a function of management." Because the arbitration promise is different, the scope of the court's inquiry may be broader. Here, a court may be required to examine the substantive provisions of the contract to ascertain whether the parties have provided that contracting out shall be a "function of management." If a court may delve into the merits to the extent of inquiring whether the parties have expressly agreed whether or not contracting out was a "function of management," why was it error for the lower court here to evaluate the evidence of bargaining history for the same purpose? Neat logical distinctions do not provide the answer. The Court rightly concludes that appropriate regard for the national labor policy and the special factors relevant to the labor arbitral process, admonish that judicial inquiry into the merits of this grievance should be limited to the search for an explicit provision which brings the grievance under the cover of the exclusion clause since "the exclusion clause is vague and arbitration clause quite broad." The hazard of going further into the merits is amply demonstrated by what the courts below did. On the basis of inconclusive evidence, those courts found that *Warrior* was in no way limited by any implied covenants of good faith and fair dealing from contracting out as it pleased—which would necessarily mean that *Warrior* was free completely to destroy the collective bargaining agreement by contracting out all the work.

The very ambiguity of the *Warrior* exclusion clause suggests that the parties were generally more concerned with having an arbitrator render decisions as to the meaning of the contract than they were in restricting the arbitrator's jurisdiction. The case might of course be otherwise were the arbitration clause very narrow, or the exclusion clause quite specific, for the inference might then be permissible that the parties had manifested a greater interest in confining the arbitrator; the presumption of arbitrability would then not have the same force and the Court would be somewhat freer to examine into the merits.

The Court makes reference to an arbitration clause being the *quid pro quo* for a no-strike clause. I do not understand the Court to mean that the application of the principles announced today depends upon the presence of a no-strike clause in the agreement.

MR. JUSTICE FRANKFURTER joins these observations.

UNITED STEELWORKERS OF AMERICA V. WARRIOR & GULF NAVIGATION CO.

Supreme Court of the United States, 1960.
363 U.S. 574, 80 S. Ct. 1347, 4 L. Ed. 2d 1409.
(Footnotes Omitted)

Opinion of the Court by MR. JUSTICE DOUGLAS, announced by MR. JUSTICE BRENNAN.

Respondent transports steel and steel products by barge and maintains a terminal at Chickasaw, Alabama, where it performs maintenance and repair work on its barges. The employees at that terminal constitute a bargaining unit covered by a collective bargaining agreement negotiated by petitioner union. Respondent between 1956 and 1958 laid off some employees, reducing the bargaining unit from 42 to 23 men. This reduction was due in part to respondent contracting maintenance work, previously done by its employees, to other companies. The latter used respondent's supervisors to lay out the work and hired some of the laid-off employees of respondent (at reduced wages). Some were in fact assigned to work on respondent's barges. A number of employees signed a grievance which petitioner presented to respondent, the grievance reading:

> We are hereby protesting the Company's actions, of arbitrarily and unreasonably contracting out work to other concerns, that could and previously has been performed by Company employees.
> This practice becomes unreasonable, unjust and discriminatory in lieu [sic] of the fact that at present there are a number of employees that have been laid off for about 1 and ½ years or more for allegedly lack of work.
> Confronted with these facts we charge that the Company is in violation of the contract by inducing a partial lock-out, of a number of the employees who would otherwise be working were it not for this unfair practice.

The collective agreement had both a "no strike" and a "no lockout" provision. It also had a grievance procedure which provided in relevant part as follows:

Issues which conflict with any Federal statute in its application as established by Court procedure or matters which are strictly a function of management shall not be subject to arbitration under this section.

Should differences arise between the Company and the Union or its members employed by the Company as to the meaning and application of the provisions of this Agreement, or should any local trouble of any kind arise, there shall be no suspension of work on account of such differences but an earnest effort shall be made to settle such differences immediately in the following manner:

A. For Maintenance Employees:

First, between the aggrieved employees, and the Foreman involved;

Second, between a member or members of the Grievance Committee designed by the Union, and the Foreman and Master Mechanic. . . .

Fifth, if agreement has not been reached the matter shall be referred to an impartial umpire for decision. The parties shall meet to decide on an umpire acceptable to both. If no agreement on selection of an umpire is reached, the parties shall jointly petition the United States Conciliation Service for suggestion of a list of umpires from which selection will be made. The decision of the umpire shall be final.

Settlement of this grievance was not had and respondent refused arbitration. This suit was then commenced by the union to compel it.

The District Court granted respondent's motion to dismiss the complaint. 168 F. Supp. 702. It held after hearing evidence, much of which went to the merits of the grievance, that the agreement did not "confide in an arbitrator the right to review the defendant's business judgment in contracting out work." Id., at 705. It further held that "the contracting out of repair and maintenance work, as well as construction work, is strictly a function of management not limited in any respect by the labor agreement involved here." Ibid. The Court of Appeals affirmed by a divided vote, 269 F. 2d 633, the majority holding that the collective agreement had withdrawn from the grievance procedure "matters which are strictly a function of management" and that contracting out fell in that exception. The case is here on a writ of certiorari. . . .

We held in Textile Workers v. Lincoln Mills . . . that a grievance arbitration provision in a collective agreement could be enforced by reason of § 301 (a) of the Labor Management Relations Act and that the policy to be applied in enforcing this type of arbitration was that reflected in our national labor laws. . . . The present federal policy is to promote industrial stabilization through the collective bargaining agreement. . . . A major factor in achieving industrial peace is the inclusion of a provision for arbitration of grievances in the collective bargaining agreement.

Thus the run of arbitration cases, illustrated by Wilko v. Swan, 346 U.S. 427, becomes irrelevant to our problem. There the choice is between the adjudication of cases or controversies in courts with established procedures or even special statutory safeguards on the one hand and the settlement of them in the more informal arbitration tribunal on the other. In the commercial case, arbitration is the substitute for litigation. Here arbitration is the substitute for industrial strife. Since arbitration of labor disputes has quite different functions from arbitration under an ordinary commercial agreement, the hostility evinced by courts toward arbitration of commercial agreements has no place here. For arbitration of labor disputes under collective bargaining agreements is part and parcel of the collective bargaining process itself.

The collective bargaining agreement states the rights and duties of the parties. It is more than a contract; it is a generalized code to govern a myriad of cases which the draftsmen cannot wholly anticipate. See Shulman, Reason, Contract, and Law in Labor Relations, 68 Harv. L. Rev. 999, 1004–1005. The collective agreement covers the whole employment relationship. It calls into being a new common law—the common law of a particular industry or of a particular plant. As one observer has put it:

> ... [I]t is not unqualifiedly true that a collective-bargaining agreement is simply a document by which the union and employees have imposed upon management limited, express restrictions of its otherwise absolute right to manage the enterprise, so that an employee's claim must fail unless he can point to a specific contract provision upon which the claim is founded. There are too many people, too many problems, too many unforeseeable contingencies to make the words of the contract the exclusive source of rights and duties. One cannot reduce all the rules governing a community like an industrial plant to fifteen or even fifty pages. Within the sphere of collective bargaining, the institutional characteristics and the governmental nature of the collective-bargaining process demand a common law of the shop which implements and furnishes the context of the agreement. We must assume that intelligent negotiators acknowledged so plain a need unless they stated a contrary rule in plain words.

A collective bargaining agreement is an effort to erect a system of industrial self-government. When most parties enter into contractual relationship they do so voluntarily, in the sense that there is no real compulsion to deal with one another, as opposed to dealing with other parties. This is not true of the labor agreement. The choice is generally not between entering or refusing to enter into a relationship, for that in all probability pre-exists the negotiations. Rather it is between having that relationship governed by an agreed-upon rule of law or leaving each and every matter subject to a temporary resolution dependent solely upon the relative strength, at any given moment, of the contending forces. The mature labor agreement may attempt to regulate all aspects of the complicated relationship, from the most crucial to the most minute over an extended period of time. Because of the compulsion to reach agreement and the breadth of the matters covered, as well as the need for a fairly concise and readable instrument, the product of negotiations (the written document) is, in the words of the late Dean Shulman, "a compilation of diverse provisions: some provide objective criteria almost automatically applicable; some provide more or less specific standards which require reason and judgment in their application; and some do little more than leave problems to future consideration with an expression of hope and good faith." Shulman, supra, at 1005. Gaps may be left to be filled in by reference to the practices of the particular industry and of the various shops covered by the agreement. Many of the specific practices which underlie the agreement may be unknown, except in hazy form, even to the negotiators. Courts and arbitration in the context of most commercial contracts are resorted to because there has been a breakdown in the working relationship of the parties; such resort is the unwanted exception. But the grievance machinery under a collective bargaining agreement is at the very heart of the system of industrial self-government. Arbitration is the means of solving the unforeseeable by molding a system of private law for all the problems which may arise and to provide for their solution in a way which will generally accord with the variant needs and desires of the parties. The processing of disputes through the grievance machinery is actually a vehicle by which meaning and content are given to the collective bargaining agreement.

Apart from matters that the parties specifically exclude, all of the questions on which the parties disagree must therefore come within the scope of the grievance and arbitration provisions of the collective agreement. The grievance procedure is, in other words, a part of the continuous collective bargaining process. It, rather than a strike, is the terminal point of a disagreement.

The labor arbitrator performs functions which are not normal to the courts; the considerations which help him fashion judgments may indeed be foreign to the competence of courts.

> A proper conception of the arbitrator's function is basic. He is not a public tribunal imposed upon the parties by superior authority which the parties are obliged to accept. He has no general charter to administer justice for a community which transcends the parties. He is rather part of a system of self-government created by and confined to the parties. . . .
> *Shulman, supra, at 1016.*

The labor arbitrator's source of law is not confined to the express provisions of the contract, as the industrial common law—the practices of the industry and the shop—is equally a part of the collective bargaining agreement although not expressed in it. The labor arbitrator is usually chosen because of the parties' confidence in his knowledge of the common law of the shop and their trust in his personal judgment to bring to bear considerations which are not expressed in the contract as criteria for judgment. The parties expect that his judgment of a particular grievance will reflect not only what the contract says but, insofar as the collective bargaining agreement permits, such factors as the effect upon productivity of a particular result, its consequence to the morale of the shop, his judgment whether tensions will be heightened or diminished. For the parties' objective in using the arbitration process is primarily to further their common goal of uninterrupted production under the agreement, to make the agreement serve their specialized needs. The ablest judge cannot be expected to bring the same experience and competence to bear upon the determination of a grievance, because he cannot be similarly informed.

The Congress, however, has by § 301 of the Labor Management Relations Act, assigned the courts the duty of determining whether the reluctant party has breached his promise to arbitrate. For arbitration is a matter of contract and a party cannot be required to submit to arbitration any dispute which he has not agreed so to submit. Yet, to be consistent with congressional policy in favor of settlement of disputes by the parties through the machinery of arbitration, the judicial inquiry under § 301 must be strictly confined to the question whether the reluctant party did agree to arbitrate the grievance or did agree to give the arbitrator power to make the award he made. An order to arbitrate the particular grievance should not be denied unless it may be said with positive assurance that the arbitration clause is not susceptible of an interpretation that covers the asserted dispute. Doubts should be resolved in favor of coverage.

We do not agree with the lower courts that contracting-out grievances were necessarily excepted from the grievance procedure of this agreement. To be sure, the agreement provides that "matters which are strictly a function of management shall not be subject to arbitration." But it goes on to say that if "differences" arise or if "any local trouble of any kind" arises, the grievance procedure shall be applicable.

Collective bargaining agreements regulate or restrict the exercise of management functions; they do not oust management from the performance of them. Management hires and fires, pays and promotes, supervises and plans. All these are part of its function, and absent a collective bargaining agreement, it may be exercised freely except as limited by public law and by the willingness of employees to work under the particular, unilaterally imposed conditions. A collective bargaining agreement may treat only with certain specific practices, leaving the rest to management but subject to the possibility of work stoppages. When, however, an absolute no-strike clause is included in the agreement, then in a very real sense everything that management does is subject to the agreement, for either management is prohibited or limited in the action it takes, or if not, it is protected from interference by strikes. This comprehensive reach of the collective bargaining agreement does not mean, however, that the language, "strictly a function of management," has no meaning.

"Strictly a function of management" might be thought to refer to any practice of management in which, under particular circumstances prescribed by the agreement, it is permitted to indulge. But if courts, in order to determine arbitrability, were allowed to determine what is permitted and what is not, the arbitration clause would be swallowed up by the exception. Every grievance in a sense involves a claim that management has violated some provision of the agreement.

Accordingly, "strictly a function of management" must be interpreted as referring only to that over which the contract gives management complete control and unfettered discretion. Respondent claims that the contracting out of work falls within this category. Contracting out work is the basis of many grievances; and that type of claim is grist in the mills of the arbitrators. A specific collective bargaining agreement may exclude contracting out from the grievance procedure. Or a written collateral agreement may make clear that contracting out was not a matter for arbitration. In such a case a grievance based solely on contracting out would not be arbitrable. Here, however, there is no such provision. Nor is there any showing that the parties designed the phrase "strictly a function of management" to encompass any and all forms of contracting out. In the absence of any express provision excluding a particular grievance from arbitration, we think only the most forceful evidence of a purpose to exclude the claim from arbitration can prevail, particularly where, as here, the exclusion clause is vague and the arbitration clause quite broad. Since any attempt by a court to infer such a purpose necessarily comprehends the merits, the court should view with suspicion an attempt to persuade it to become entangled in the construction of the substantive provisions of a labor agreement, even through the back door of interpreting the arbitration clause, when the alternative is to utilize the services of an arbitrator.

The grievance alleged that the contracting out was a violation of the collective bargaining agreement. There was, therefore, a dispute "as to the meaning and application of the provisions of this Agreement" which the parties had agreed would be determined by arbitration.

The judiciary sits in these cases to bring into operation an arbitral process which substitutes a regime of peaceful settlement for the older regime of industrial conflict. Whether contracting out in the present case violated the agreement is the question. It is a question for the arbiter, not for the courts.

Reversed.

MR. JUSTICE FRANKFURTER concurs in the result.

MR. JUSTICE BLACK took no part in the consideration or decision of this case.

MR. JUSTICE WHITTAKER, dissenting.

Until today, I have understood it to be the unquestioned law, as this Court has consistently held, that arbitrators are private judges chosen by the parties to decide particular matters specifically submitted; that the contract under which matters are submitted to arbitrators is at once the source and limit of their authority and power; and that their power to decide issues with finality, thus ousting the normal functions of the courts, must rest upon a clear, definitive agreement of the parties, as such powers can never be implied. . . . I believe that the Court today departs from the established principles announced in these decisions.

Here, the employer operates a shop for the normal maintenance of its barges, but it is not equipped to make major repairs, and accordingly the employer has, from the beginning of its operations more than 19 years ago, contracted out its major repair work. During most, if not all, of this time the union has represented the employees in that unit. The District Court found that "[t]hroughout the successive labor agreements between these parties, including the present one . . . [the union] had unsuccessfully sought to negotiate changes in the labor contracts, and particularly during the negotiation of the present labor agreement, . . . which would have limited the right of the [employer] to continue the practice of contracting out such work." 168 F. Supp. 702, 704–705.

The labor agreement involved here provides for arbitration of disputes respecting the interpretation and application of the agreement and, arguably, also some other things. But the first paragraph of the arbitration section says: "[M]atters which are strictly a function of management shall not be subject to arbitration under this section." Although acquiescing for 19 years in the employer's interpretation that contracting out work was "strictly a function of management," and having repeatedly tried—particularly in the negotiation of the agreement involved here—but unsuccessfully, to induce the employer to agree to a covenant that would prohibit it from contracting out work, the union, after having agreed to and signed the contract involved, presented a "grievance" on the ground that the employer's contracting out work, at a time when some employees in the unit were laid off for lack of work, constituted a partial "lockout" of employees in violation of the antilockout provision of the agreement.

Being unable to persuade the employer to agree to cease contracting out work or to agree to arbitrate the "grievance," the union brought this action in the District Court, under § 301 of the Labor Management Relations Act, for a decree compelling the employer to submit the "grievance" to arbitration. The District Court, holding that the contracting out of work was, and over a long course of dealings had been interpreted and understood by the parties to be, "strictly a function of management," and was therefore specifically excluded from arbitration by the terms of the contract, denied the relief prayed, 168 F. Supp. 702. The Court of Appeals affirmed, 269 F. 2d 633, and we granted certiorari. 361 U.S. 912.

The Court now reverses the judgment of the Court of Appeals. It holds that the arbitrator's source of law is "not confined to the express provisions of the contract," that arbitration should be ordered "unless it may be said with positive assurance that the arbitration clause is not susceptible of an interpretation that covers the asserted dispute," that "[d]oubts [of arbitrability] should be resolved in favor of coverage," and that when, as here, "an absolute no-strike clause is included in the agreement then ... everything that management does is subject to [arbitration]." I understand the Court thus to hold that the arbitrators are not confined to the express provisions of the contract, that arbitration is to be ordered unless it may be said with positive assurance that arbitration of a particular dispute is excluded by the contract, that doubts of arbitrability are to be resolved in favor of arbitration, and that when, as here, the contract contains a no-strike clause, everything that management does is subject to arbitration.

This is an entirely new and strange doctrine to me. I suggest, with deference, that it departs from both the contract of the parties and the controlling decisions of this Court. I find nothing in the contract that purports to confer upon arbitrators any such general breadth of private judicial power. The Court cites no legislative or judicial authority that creates for or gives to arbitrators such broad general powers. And I respectfully submit that today's decision cannot be squared with the statement of Judge, later Mr. Justice, Cardozo in *Marchant* that "No one is under duty to resort to these conventional tribunals, however helpful their processes, *except to the extent that he has signified his willingness.* Our own favor or disfavor of the cause of arbitration is not to count as a factor in the appraisal of the thought of others" (emphasis added), 252 N. Y., at 299, 169 N. E., at 391; nor with his statement in that case that "[t]he question is one of intention, to be ascertained by the same tests that are applied to contracts generally." id.; nor with this Court's statement in *Moorman,* "that the intention of the parties to submit their contractual disputes to final determination outside the courts *should be made manifest by plain language*" (emphasis added), 388 U.S., at 462; nor with this Court's statement in *Hensey* that: "To make such [an arbitrator's] certificate conclusive *requires plain language in the contract. It is not to be implied.*" (Emphasis added.) 205 U.S., at 309. "A party is never required to submit to arbitration any question which he has not agreed so to submit, and *contracts providing for arbitration will be carefully construed in order not to force a party to submit to arbitration a question which he did not intend to be submitted.*" (Emphasis added.) Fernandez & Hnos. v. Rickert Rice Mills, supra, 119 F. 2d., at 815.

With respect, I submit that there is nothing in the contract here to indicate that the employer "signified [its] willingness" (Marchant, supra, at 299) to submit to arbitrators whether it must cease contracting out work. Certainly no such intention is "made manifest by plain language" (Moorman, supra, at 462), as the law "requires," because such consent "is not to be implied." (Hensey, supra, at 309.) To the contrary, the parties by their conduct over many years interpreted the contracting out of major repair work to be "strictly a function of management," and if, as the concurring opinion suggests, the words of the contract can "be understood only by reference to the background which gave rise to their inclusion," then the interpretation given by the parties over 19 years to the phrase "matters which are strictly a function of management" should logically have some significance here. By their contract, the parties agreed that "matters which are strictly a function of management shall not be subject to arbitration." The union over the course of many years repeatedly tried to induce the employer to agree to a covenant prohibiting the contracting out of work, but was never successful. The union again made such an effort in negotiating the very contract involved here, and, failing of success, signed the contract, knowing, of course, that it did not contain any such covenant, but that, to the contrary, it contained, just as had the former contracts, a covenant that "matters which are strictly a function of management shall not be subject to arbitration." Does not this show that, instead of signifying a willingness to submit to arbitration the matter of whether the employer might continue to contract out work, the parties fairly agreed to exclude at least that matter from arbitration? Surely it cannot be said that the parties agreed to such a submission by any "plain language." Moorman, supra, at 462, and Hensey, supra, at 309. Does not then the Court's opinion compel the employer "to submit to arbitration [a] question which [it] has not agreed so to submit"? (Fernandez & Hnos., supra, at 815.)

Surely the question whether a particular subject or class of subjects is or is not made arbitrable by a contract is a judicial question, and if, as the concurring opinion suggests, "the court may conclude that [the contract] commits to arbitration any [subject or class of subjects]," it may likewise conclude that the contract does not commit such subject or class of subjects to arbitration, and "[w]ith that finding the court will have exhausted its function" no more nor less by denying arbitration than by ordering it. Here the District Court found, and the Court of Appeals approved its findings, that by the terms of the contract, as interpreted by the parties over 19 years, the contracting out of work was "strictly a function of management" and "not subject to arbitration." That finding, I think, should be accepted here. Acceptance of it requires affirmance of the judgment.

I agree with the Court that courts have no proper concern with the "merits" of claims which by contract the parties have agreed to submit to the exclusive jurisdiction of arbitrators. But the question is one of jurisdiction. Neither may entrench upon the jurisdiction of the other. The test is: Did the parties in their contract "manifest by plain language" (Moorman, supra, at 462) their willingness to submit the issue in controversy to arbitrators? If they did, then the arbitrators have exclusive jurisdiction of it, and the courts, absent fraud or the like, must respect that exclusive jurisdiction and cannot interfere. But if they did not, then the courts must exercise their jurisdiction, when properly invoked, to protect the citizen against the attempted use by arbitrators of pretended powers actually never conferred. That question always is, and from its very nature must be, a judicial one. Such was the question presented to the District Court and the Court of Appeals here. They found the jurisdictional facts, properly applied the settled law to those facts, and correctly decided the case. I would therefore affirm the judgment.

UNITED STEELWORKERS OF AMERICA V. ENTERPRISE WHEEL & CAR CORP.

Supreme Court of the United States, 1960.
363 U.S. 593, 80 S. Ct. 1358, 4 L. Ed. 2d 1424.
(Footnotes Omitted)

Opinion of the Court by MR. JUSTICE DOUGLAS, announced by MR. JUSTICE BRENNAN.

Petitioner union and respondent during the period relevant here had a collective bargaining agreement which provided that any differences "as to the meaning and application" of the agreement should be submitted to arbitration and that the arbitrator's decision "shall be final and binding on the parties." Special provisions were included concerning the suspension and discharge of employees. The agreement stated:

> Should it be determined by the Company or by an arbitrator in accordance
> with the grievance procedure that the employee has been suspended unjustly or

discharged in violation of the provisions of this Agreement, the Company shall reinstate the employee and pay full compensation at the employee's regular rate of pay for the time lost.

The agreement also provided:

> ... It is understood and agreed that neither party will institute *civil suits or legal proceedings* against the other for alleged violation of any of the provisions of this labor contract; instead all disputes will be settled in the manner outlined in this Article III—Adjustment of Grievances.

A group of employees left their jobs in protest against the discharge of one employee. A union official advised them at once to return to work. An official of respondent at their request gave them permission and then rescinded it. The next day they were told they did not have a job any more "until this thing was settled one way or the other."

A grievance was filed; and when respondent finally refused to arbitrate, this suit was brought for specific enforcement of the arbitration provisions of the agreement. The District Court ordered arbitration. The arbitrator found that the discharge of the men was not justified, though their conduct, he said, was improper. In his view the facts warranted at most a suspension of the men for 10 days each. After their discharge and before the arbitration award the collective bargaining agreement had expired. The union, however, continued to represent the workers at the plant. The arbitrator rejected the contention that expiration of the agreement barred reinstatement of the employees. He held that the provision of the agreement above quoted imposed an unconditional obligation on the employer. He awarded reinstatement with back pay, minus pay for a 10-day suspension and such sums as these employees received from other employment.

Respondent refused to comply with the award. Petitioner moved the District Court for enforcement. The District Court directed respondent to comply. 168 F. Supp. 308. The Court of Appeals, while agreeing that the District Court had jurisdiction to enforce an arbitration award under a collective bargaining agreement, held that the failure of the award to specify the amounts to be deducted from the back pay rendered the award unenforceable. That defect, it agreed, could be remedied by requiring the parties to complete the arbitration. It went on to hold, however, that an award for back pay subsequent to the date of termination of the collective bargaining agreement could not be enforced. It also held that the requirement for reinstatement of the discharged employees was likewise unenforceable because the collective bargaining agreement had expired. 269 F. 2d 327. We granted certiorari. ...

The refusal of courts to review the merits of an arbitration award is the proper approach to arbitration under collective bargaining agreements.

The federal policy of settling labor disputes by arbitration would be undermined if courts had the final say on the merits of the awards. As we stated in United Steelworkers of America v. Warrior & Gulf Navigation Co. .... the arbitrators under these collective agreements are indispensable agencies in a continuous collective bargaining process. They sit to settle disputes at the plant level—disputes that require for their solution knowledge of the custom and practices of a particular factory or of a particular industry as reflected in particular agreements.

When an arbitrator is commissioned to interpret and apply the collective bargaining agreement, he is to bring his informed judgment to bear in order to reach a fair solution of a problem. This is especially true when it comes to formulating remedies. There the need is for flexibility in meeting a wide variety of situations. The draftsmen may never have thought of what specific remedy should be awarded to meet a particular contingency. Nevertheless, an arbitrator is confined to interpretation and application of the collective bargaining agreement; he does not sit to dispense his own brand of industrial justice. He may of course look for guidance from many sources, yet his award is legitimate only so long as it draws its essence from the collective bargaining agreement. When the arbitrator's words manifest an infidelity to this obligation, courts have no choice but to refuse enforcement of the award.

The opinion of the arbitrator in this case, as it bears upon the award of back pay beyond the date of the agreement's expiration and reinstatement, is ambiguous. It may be read as based solely upon the arbitrator's view of the requirements of enacted legislation, which would mean that he exceeded the scope of the submission. Or it may be read as embodying a construction of the agreement itself, perhaps with the arbitrator looking to "the law" for help in determining the sense of the agreement. A mere ambiguity in the opinion accompanying an award, which permits the inference that the arbitrator may have exceeded his authority, is not a reason for refusing to enforce the award. Arbitrators have no obligation to the court to give their reasons for an award. To require opinions free of ambiguity may lead arbitrators to play it safe by writing no supporting opinions. This would be undesirable for a well-reasoned opinion tends to engender confidence in the integrity of the process and aids in clarifying the underlying agreement. Moreover, we see no reason to assume that this arbitrator has abused the trust the parties confided in him and has not stayed within the areas marked out for his consideration. It is not apparent that he went beyond the submission. The Court of Appeals' opinion refusing to enforce the reinstatement and partial back pay portions of the award was not based upon any finding that the arbitrator did not premise his award on his construction of the contract. It merely disagreed with the arbitrator's construction of it.

The collective bargaining agreement could have provided that if any of the employees were wrongfully discharged, the remedy would be reinstatement and back pay up to the date they were returned to work. Respondent's major argument seems to be that by applying correct principles of law to the interpretation of the collective bargaining agreement it can be determined that the agreement did not so provide, and that therefore the arbitrator's decision was not based upon the contract. The acceptance of this view would require courts, even under the standard arbitration clause, to review the merits of every construction of the contract. This plenary review by a court of the merits would make meaningless the provisions that the arbitrator's decision is final, for in reality it would almost never be final. This underlines the fundamental error which we have alluded to in United Steelworkers of America v. American Manufacturing Co.... As we there emphasized, the question of interpretation of the collective bargaining agreement is a question for the arbitrator. It is the arbitrator's construction which was bargained for; and so far as the arbitrator's decision concerns construction of the contract, the courts have no business overruling him because their interpretation of the contract is different from his.

We agree with the Court of Appeals that the judgment of the District Court should be modified so that the amounts due the employees may be definitely determined by arbitration. In all other respects we think the judgment of the District Court should be affirmed. Accordingly, we reverse the judgment of the Court of Appeals, except for that modification, and remand the case to the District Court for proceedings in conformity with this opinion.

It is so ordered.

Mr. Justice Frankfurter concurs in the result.

Mr. Justice Black took no part in the consideration or decision of this case.

Mr. Justice Whittaker, dissenting.

Claiming that the employer's discharge on January 18, 1957, of 11 employees violated the provisions of its collective bargaining contract with the employer—covering the period beginning April 5, 1956, and ending April 4, 1957—the union sought and obtained arbitration, under the provisions of the contract, of the issues whether these employees had been discharged in violation of the agreement and, if so, should be ordered reinstated and awarded wages from the time of their wrongful discharge. In August 1957, more than four months after the collective agreement had expired, these issues, by agreement of the parties, were submitted to a single arbitrator, and a hearing was held before him on January 3, 1958. On April 10, 1958, the arbitrator made his award, finding that the 11 employees had been discharged in violation of the agreement and ordering their reinstatement with back pay at their regular rates from a time 10 days after their discharge to the time of reinstatement. Over the employer's objection that the collective agreement and the submission under it did not authorize nor empower the arbitrator to award reinstatement or wages for any period after the date of expiration of the contract (April 4, 1957), the District Court ordered enforcement of the award. The Court of Appeals modified the judgment by eliminating the requirements that the employer reinstate the employees and pay them wages for the period *after* expiration of the collective agreement, and affirmed it in all other respects, 269 F. 2d 327, and we granted certiorari, 361 U.S. 929.

That the propriety of the discharges, under the collective agreement, was arbitrable under the provisions of that agreement, even after its expiration, is not in issue. Nor is there any issue here as to the power of the arbitrator to award reinstatement status and back pay to the discharged employees to the date of expiration of the collective agreement. It is conceded, too, that the collective agreement expired by its terms on April 4, 1957, and was never extended or renewed.

The sole question here is whether the arbitrator exceeded the submission and his powers in awarding reinstatement and back pay for any period after expiration of the collective agreements. Like the Court of Appeals, I think he did. I find nothing in the collective agreement that purports to so authorize. Nor does the Court point to anything in the agreement that purports to do so. Indeed, the union does not contend that there is any such covenant in the contract. Doubtless all rights that accrued to the employees under the collective agreement during its term, and that were made arbitrable by its provisions, could be awarded to them by the arbitrator, even though the period of the agreement had ended. But surely no rights *accrued* to the employees under the agreement after it had expired. Save for the provisions of the collective agreement, and in the absence, as here, of any applicable rule of law or contrary covenant between the employer and the employees, the employer had the legal right to discharge the employees at will. The collective agreement, however, protected them against discharge, for specified reasons, during its continuation. But when that agreement expired, it did not continue to afford rights *in futuro* to the employees —as though still effective and governing. After the agreement expired, the employment status of these 11 employees was terminable at the will of the employer, as the Court of Appeals quite properly held, 269 F. 2d, at 331, and see Meadows v. Radio Industries, 222 F. 2d 347, 349; Atchison, T. & S. F. R. Co. v. Andrews, 211 F. 2d 264, 265; Warden v. Hinds, 163 F. 201, and the announced discharge of these 11 employees then became lawfully effective.

Once the contract expired, no rights continued to accrue under it to the employees. Thereafter they had no contractual right to demand that the employer continue to employ them, and *a fortiori* the arbitrator did not have power to order the employer to do so; nor did the arbitrator have power to order the employer to pay wages to them after the date of termination of the contract, which was also the effective date of their discharges.

The judgment of the Court of Appeals, affirming so much of the award as required reinstatement of the 11 employees to employment status and payment of their wages until expiration of the contract, but not thereafter, seems to me to be indubitably correct, and I would affirm it.

The Torrington decisions

**IN THE MATTER OF ARBITRATION BETWEEN
THE TORRINGTON COMPANY AND UAW-AFL-CIO LOCAL 1645**

Opinion and Decision of Arbitrator Thomas Kennedy, June 25, 1965

The Issue

At the arbitration hearing which was held at the company's plant in Torrington, Connecticut on May 19, 1965 the parties were unable to agree on a statement of the issue. Therefore the arbitrator accepted as the issue to be decided the grievance filed by the union on December 17, 1964 which is as follows:

> Under established contractual past practice, the company is required to grant time off with pay to employees who request it on Election Day in order that they may cast their votes. This contractual practice was violated when the company informed the union that employees would not be granted time off with pay for the purpose of voting on November 3, 1964 and by supervisors' threats that any

employee who left work before the end of his shift on that day for the purpose of voting would be subject to discipline.

Background

On November 1, 1962 the company posted the following bulletin: Voting hours at all voting places in Torrington will be from 6 a.m. until 7 p.m.

Registered Torrington voters will be allowed up to one hour off with pay for the purpose of voting. Any such time off must be arranged in advance with the appropriate supervisor so as to keep the disruption of operations to a minimum.

The right to vote is every citizen's duty as well as his most valuable privilege. Vote for the candidate of your own choice—but vote!!!!

The message in this bulletin was in line with a well-established past practice at this company. For some twenty years or more employees had been given time off with pay on election days, although this benefit was not specifically stated in the labor agreements.

In late 1962 the company decided to change its practice with respect to paying employees for time off to vote. It appears that the company's intention to make this change was stated first in the December issue of the Torrington Company Newsletter. On February 20, 1963 the president of the union wrote to the company asking to be officially informed regarding the company's position on this matter.

On March 8, 1963 the company replied to the union president that it had changed its policy for economic reasons and also because in its opinion conditions had so changed that the time off was no longer necessary to enable employees to vote. The company's letter which dealt also with pay for time lost from work for the purpose of negotiating the collective bargaining agreement ended with the following paragraph.

Since you doubtlessly feel that the question of continuing or discontinuing both of the above past practices is subject to negotiations between the company and the union, I suggest that you consider this as an invitation to so bargain. We will be available at any mutually convenient time for the purpose of such good faith bargaining, or if you prefer, the matters in question may await the contract renegotiations which, presumably, will begin on or about July 27, 1963.

On April 9, 1963 the union filed with the NLRB a charge of unfair labor practices against the company. Among the unfair labor practices claimed by the union was that of "making a unilateral change in its established policy of paid time off for voting for bargaining unit employees." In an amended charge filed on April 29, 1963 and in a second amended charge filed on May 22, 1963 the union continued to include the voting-time issue. However, on June 10, 1963 the union filed a third amended charge in which this issue did not appear. On July 29, 1963 the Acting Regional Director of the NLRB dismissed the charge, as amended.

The old contract between the parties was due to expire on September 27, 1963, so in August the parties began to hold meetings to negotiate a new contract. The first meeting was held evidently on August 14. At that time the company informed the union orally that it did not intend to pay for time off for voting in the future. The union did not present its demands at the first meeting. At a later meeting the union did present a list of demands, including the following:

> Company will allow one hour with pay for Election Day.

By September 26, 1963, the day before the old contract was scheduled to terminate, no agreement had been reached. A number of issues, including time off with pay for voting which the union continued to include in its list of demands, remained in dispute. On that date, September 26, the company presented a written proposal which began as follows:

> The company respectfully proposes that the current collective bargaining agreement and the pension agreement between itself and the union, be extended until September 27, 1966 but with the following amendments.

There followed 22 proposed changes in the contract; none of which made any reference to time off with pay for voting. However, the company's proposal was not acceptable to the union and further negotiations failed to produce an agreement prior to the termination date. On September 27, therefore, the union called the employees out on strike.

Negotiations were continued during the strike and on October 25, 1963 the union made a written proposal to the company. The October 25, 1963 union proposal began as follows:

> The union proposes that the collective bargaining agreement and the pension agreement which expired September 27, 1963 be reinstated with the following amendments.

Among the amendments no reference was made to time off with pay in order to vote on Election Day.

The October 25 proposal did not result in an agreement and the strike continued through the November 1963 Election Day. Some bargaining unit employees worked during the strike but they did not receive paid time off to vote on the November, 1963 Election Day.

The strike continued for 17 weeks until January 18, 1964, at which time the parties reached agreement on the current labor contract which became effective on that date. No language was included in the new contract with respect to time off with pay for voting.

On November 2, 1964 the union issued a flier to its members in which it was stated that "The Torrington Company has again stated that you will *not* be allowed the one hour time off for voting this year." The flier urged the employees to vote. The following day, November 3, 1964, which was Election Day, employees were not given time off with pay to vote.

On December 17, 1964 the union filed the grievance which constitutes the issue in this case. By mutual agreement the grievance was passed directly to the third step of the grievance procedure. However, the parties were unable to reach an agreement on the issue and the union then requested arbitration as provided in Article V of the 1964 labor contract.

Pertinent Contract Clauses

The following clauses in the current labor agreement between the parties, dated January 18, 1964, are applicable to this case:

ARTICLE V, ARBITRATION

Section 1

If a grievance is not settled after it has been processed through the three (3) steps described in Article IV above, and if it is a grievance with respect to the interpretation or application of any provisions in this contract and is not controlled by Section 1 of Article XIV, (Management) it may be submitted to arbitration in the manner herein provided.

Section 3

The arbitrator shall be bound by and must comply with all of the terms of this agreement and he shall have no power to add to, delete from, or modify, in any way, any of the provisions of this agreement. The arbitrator shall not have the authority to determine the right of employees to merit increases. The arbitrator shall have no authority to set or determine wages except as provided by Section 21 of Article VI, Wages.

ARTICLE XIV, MANAGEMENT RIGHTS

Section 1

The management of the company shall have the exclusive rights to determine from time to time the places and products (in Torrington or elsewhere) of manufacture, to sub-contract and to establish the methods and processes of manufacture. The company's right to establish methods and processes of manufacture shall not derogate or diminish any rights of employees otherwise specifically provided by this agreement.

Section 2

The management of the company shall have all other rights of management, including, but not limited to, the direction of the working force, the right to hire, transfer, suspend, promote, retain, discipline or discharge for proper cause, to maintain quality and efficient operations, and to layoff employees because of lack of work or other proper cause: subject only to the specific provisions herein contained dealing with those subject matters.

Discussion

1 Arbitrability

At the outset of the hearing the company raised the question of arbitrability. It argued that the grievance is not arbitrable because the payment for time off for voting was never a matter of contract obligation; the union included this matter in an unfair labor practice charge before the NLRB and later withdrew it; and the matter was negotiated off the table in the last contract negotiations, the union having included it among its demands and later having withdrawn it.

We do not believe that the inclusion of and later the withdrawal of an item from an unfair labor practice charge removes that item from being an arbitrable issue. In fact some items may be withdrawn from a charge for the very reason that they are arbitrable under a contract. Whether the payment for time off for voting was a matter of contract obligation is not clear on the face of it. The same can be said of the statement that the issue was bargained off the table in the recent negotiations. For these reasons we are of the opinion that the issue is arbitrable. The arbitrator must decide whether the payment for time off for voting was a contract obligation and, if so, whether that obligation was bargained off the table in the negotiations which resulted in the current labor agreement.

2 The Substantive Issue

There was no clause which called for the payment of time off for voting in the earlier labor contracts and there is no such clause in the current contract. However, by 1962 this benefit had become a firmly established practice. It had been available to employees for approximately 20 years. We believe that a *benefit* of this nature, continued as it had been without change over a period of so many years, must be considered to have become an implied part of the contract.

We emphasize that it is a *benefit*. We distinguish between a past practice involving a *benefit* of this type and a past practice involving methods of
operation or direction of the working force. In a recent award at the Torrington Company we upheld the company's right to unilaterally change a
method of operation. The latter we believe is a right which management
clearly has under the management clause in this contract in order to promote efficient operation. On the other hand, we do not believe that the
management clause gives to the company the right to discontinue unilaterally a *benefit* which has become an implied part of the contract. In brief,
we conclude that the company did have an obligation under the contract to
continue to pay for time off for voting until such time as it negotiated a
change in the matter. The company recognized its responsibility in this
respect when, in its letter of March 8, 1963, it proposed to the union that
negotiations on the matter be undertaken.

The union's inclusion of this issue in an unfair labor practice charge and
its later withdrawal of it from the charge can have little bearing on this
arbitration decision. The union's inclusion of the issue in the charge did
indicate that it was aware that the company intended to discontinue this
benefit. However, its withdrawal of the issue did not indicate that the
union had accepted the company's right to discontinue it. Likewise, the
union's action did not foreclose its right to bargain about and to arbitrate
this issue. The parties both recognized that it was still a bargainable issue
when they included it in their original demands in August, 1963.

It was the company which introduced the matter of pay for time off for
voting at the first contract negotiations meeting on August 14, 1963. At that
time, the company made it clear that it was insisting on a change in this
practice. The union then followed by including the continuance of such
time off with pay among its demands. These two conflicting demands
evidently remained on the table until September 26.

The company's proposal of September 26, however, in our opinion constituted a significant change in the bargaining position of the parties with
respect to this issue. That proposal suggested that the old agreement "be
extended until September 27, 1966" except for 22 amendments. No mention was made of time off with pay for voting among the 22 amendments.
It may be that the company intended that its earlier oral statement regarding discontinuance of such time off with pay should continue to be considered part of its demands. However, the union had reason to believe that the
September 26 proposal meant that the company was dropping its demand
for a change in this past practice.

The October 25, 1963 proposal of the union also began with the statement that the "collective bargaining Agreement and the Pension Agreement

which expired September 27, 1963 *be reinstated* with the following amendments." There followed then half a dozen or so changes which did not include time off with pay for voting. We believe that the fact that the union did not list this issue among its demands in the October 25 proposal cannot be considered as a withdrawal of the issue by the union and an agreement not to continue this practice. There is no evidence that any union representative ever stated that the union was withdrawing its demand in favor of the company's demand on this issue. In our opinion the company's proposal of September 26 by its failure to mention the company's demand for a change in this practice removed it from the table. Therefore, it was no longer necessary for the union to continue its counterdemand. Thus, by October 25 both parties agreed that the old contract was to be continued except for certain changes among which was *not* a change in the practice of giving time off with pay for voting.

The strike continued following the above proposals and on Election Day in November 1963 the company did not give time off with pay for the purpose of voting to its employees who were still coming to work including some bargaining unit employees. Since no contract was in effect at the time, the company was free to change the employee benefits which had been either stated or implied in the earlier contract. We do not find, however, that the failure to provide the benefit under such conditions affected in any way the bargaining position of the parties. It did not create a precedent under a contract.

We have no evidence that the position of the parties on this issue was changed or that the issue was ever discussed after the exchange of the written proposals of September 26 and October 25. We must conclude, therefore, that the final bargain between the parties did not include an agreement to discontinue the practice of allowing time off with pay for voting—a benefit which had become firmly established by past practice under the old contract. We find, therefore, that the company was in violation of the contract when it refused to pay this benefit to employees on Election Day 1964.

3 Remedy

Prior to the November 1964 Election Day, the employees had been informed that the company would not pay them for time off for voting up to a maximum of one hour, as it had done under prior labor agreements. As a result, most employees did not take the time off, and those who did were not paid for it.

In 1962 and earlier years, when the company did pay this benefit, not all employees asked for and received it. As a result, it is difficult to devise a remedy which will be fair to both parties because we cannot be sure which employees would have claimed and received time off with pay if the company had offered it on Election Day 1964. However, we believe that substantial justice will be achieved if those employees who actually took time off to vote on Election Day 1964 are paid up to the maximum of one hour's pay and if all other employees who received this benefit in 1962 and who were working during the election hours on Election Day 1964 are paid for the same amount of time for 1964 as they were paid in 1962.

Award

1 The issue of whether the company is obliged to grant time off with pay to employees who request it to vote on Election Day is arbitrable.
2 The benefit of time off with pay up to a maximum of one hour for the purpose of voting on Election Day had become a firmly established practice at this company which could be changed by the company only by negotiating it with the union.
3 In the 1963–64 labor negotiations, which culminated in the current labor contract, the parties did *not* reach an agreement to discontinue this practice.
4 The company erred in refusing to grant this benefit to employees on Election Day, November 3, 1964.
5 Employees who took time off to vote on November 3, 1964 shall be paid up to a maximum of one hour and all other employees who worked during the election hours on that Election Day and who were paid this benefit on November 6, 1962 shall be paid for the same amount of time off for Election Day 1964 as they received for Election Day 1962.

TORRINGTON CO. V. METAL PRODUCTS WORKERS

U.S. District Court,
District of Connecticut

Torrington Company v. Metal Products Workers Union, Local 1645,
UAW, AFL-CIO, et al., No. 11044, October 1, 1965

Full Text of Opinion

CLARIE, District Judge:—The plaintiff employer has brought this action to vacate an arbitration award in a labor dispute pursuant to Title 9, § 10 of the United States Arbitration Act. Jurisdiction of this controversy is founded upon § 301 of the Labor Management Relations Act of 1947,

29 U.S.C. § 185. A cross-application has been filed by the defendant unions requesting that the Court confirm the arbitrator's award. The plaintiff employer has also moved to strike the affidavit of the defendants filed with their motion because it contains evidence which is immaterial and irrelevant to the issues and is hence inadmissible.

The current collective bargaining agreement between the parties now in effect, commenced January 18, 1964, and extends to April 20, 1967. There had previously existed an agreement which commenced September 27, 1961, and expired September 27, 1963. The parties agreed that neither of the aforesaid contracts contained any provision granting time off, up to a maximum of one hour with pay, for the purpose of voting on election day. However, the arbitrator did find that this employee benefit had become fairly established by past practice under the old contract and that the current bargaining agreement did not include an agreement to discontinue the practice. For the purpose of adjudicating this question only, the parties agreed not to contest the issue of arbitrability. The plaintiff assented on condition that such action on its part would not prejudice its position, now or in the future, in any other case pending in court or before any arbitrator.

The plaintiff employer concedes that since about 1944, it has permitted its employees who desired time off to vote in state and national elections, the opportunity to take one hour off without loss of pay. At no time was the subject mentioned in any provision of the numerous collective bargaining agreements between the parties. On March 8, 1963, the plaintiff advised the Unions that it had changed its policy for economic reasons and because conditions had so changed "time off" was no longer necessary to enable employees to vote. The employer invited bargaining on the issue or in the alternative suggested that the question might await contract renegotiations which were scheduled to begin on or about July 27, 1963, inasmuch as the old contract was due to expire September 27, 1963.

On April 9, 1963, the Unions filed with the National Labor Relations Board an unfair labor practice charge against the plaintiff. Among other charges was the claim that the employer had made a unilateral change in its established policy of paid time off for voting for bargaining unit employees. Thereafter, the Unions filed amended charges in which the issue did not appear and on July 29, 1963, the Acting Regional Director of the National Labor Relations Board dismissed the claim.

When the old contract expired on September 27, 1963, a strike ensued and continued for seventeen (17) weeks, until January 18, 1964. Prior to the strike, both parties had presented their respective demands at the bargaining table. The plaintiff informed the Unions orally then, that it did not intend to pay for time off for voting in the future and the Unions demanded that the company allow one hour with pay on election day as in the past.

During these negotiations, prior to the strike, the plaintiff employer proposed that the current collective bargaining agreement be extended until September 27, 1966, with twenty-two (22) proposed amendments or changes, none of which referred to the present issue. This proposal was not accepted and the strike commenced. On October 25, 1963, the Unions proposed that the contract which had expired on September 27, 1963, be reinstated with certain amendments, none of which referred to the election day issue; and no agreement resulted. When the new agreement was executed on January 18, 1964, no language was included in the new contract with respect to time off with pay for voting.

On November 2, 1964, just prior to the first election day following the making of the new contract, the Unions notified their members that the plaintiff employer had again stated it would not allow the one hour off for voting. Election day, November 3, 1964, the employees were not given time off to vote.

On December 17, 1964, the Unions filed a grievance setting forth their claims. Grievance procedures were exhausted and arbitration ensued. After formal hearing, the arbitrator held that by 1962 compensable voting time had become a firmly established practice and an implied part of the employment contract. He concluded that the employer could not unilaterally discontinue such a benefit from the contract without first negotiating the change.

When the existing collective bargaining agreement expired on September 27, 1963, and the strike ensued, no agreement whatsoever existed between the parties until January 18, 1964. The new contract contained no mention of the compensable voting time issue. The arbiter took the position in his findings, that since the new agreement did not specifically exclude the benefit, it continued to be an implied part of the labor contract.

The present issue before the Court is simply whether or not the arbitrator exceeded his authority, by going outside the terms of the contract itself to include a benefit which he ruled was implied. If his action did constitute an abuse of the authority conferred upon him, then his decision cannot be sustained and enforced.

> Should his decision or the remedy exceed the bounds of his authority as established by the collective bargaining agreement, that abuse of authority is remediable in an action to vacate the award.
> *Carey v. General Electric Company, 315 F. 2d 499, 508.*

> ... an arbitrator is confined to interpretation and application of the collective bargaining agreement; he does not sit to dispense his own brand of industrial

justice. He may of course look for guidance from many sources, yet his award is legitimate only so long as it draws its essence from the collective bargaining agreement. When the arbitrator's words manifest an infidelity to this obligation, courts have no choice but to refuse enforcement of the award.
Steelworkers v. Enterprise Corp., 363 U.S. 593, 597.

Article V, Sections 3 and 4 of the new contract clearly limit the power and authority of the arbitrator. They provide in part:

Section 3

The arbitrator shall be bound by and must comply with all of the terms of this agreement and he shall have no power to add to, delete from, or modify, in any way, any of the provisions of this agreement. . . .

Section 4

The decision of the arbitrator shall be binding on both parties during the life of this agreement unless the same is contrary, in any way, to law.

The new employment contract was negotiated at the bargaining table and all issues resolved in the agreement of January 18, 1964. Among the controversial issues was this question, whether or not the plaintiff employer would grant time off with pay to those employees who requested time to vote. Throughout the negotiations, the plaintiff employer persistently reiterated its position not to grant this benefit. The contract contains no provision which grants this right. The arbiter took the position that because the practice previously existed, despite the fact that it had become a bargaining issue, since the contract did not spell out that they had agreed to discontinue the practice, it was still an implied part of the contract.

Labor contracts generally affirmatively state the terms which the contracting parties agree to; not what practices they agree to discontinue. This agreement made no provision for "paid voting time" and the arbitrator exceeded and abused his authority when he attempted to read into the agreement this implied contractual relationship.

If the principle of labor arbitration is to be encouraged so as to fulfill the noble purposes for which it was designed, arbitrators must not be permitted unlimited rein to go outside the clear terms of the contract and thus impose their own brand of industrial justice. Such license would place contracting parties in a position where they could never afford to risk agreement that arbitration decide anticipated controversies, which ordinarily arise in the administration of the most carefully worded collective bargaining contracts.

Pursuant to the authority of 9 U.S.C. § 10, this Court finds that the arbitrator's award dated June 25, 1965, relating to "the paid voting time issue" is illegal and invalid on the grounds that the arbitrator exceeded his powers under the arbitration provisions of the collective bargaining agreement dated January 18, 1964, and the award is hereby vacated and set aside.

Defendant's motion to confirm and plaintiff's motion to strike, are denied.

The findings of fact and conclusions of law recited herein, shall be considered as having been made pursuant to Rule 52(a) of the Federal Rules of Civil Procedure.

TORRINGTON CO. V. METAL PRODUCTS WORKERS

U.S. Court of Appeals,
Second Circuit (New York)

The Torrington Company v. Metal Products Workers Union, Local 1645, UAW, AFL-CIO, et al., No. 291, June 22, 1966

Full Text of Opinion

LUMBARD, Chief Judge:—This appeal presents the question whether an arbitrator exceeded his authority under the collective bargaining agreement between The Torrington Company (Torrington) and Metal Products Workers Union Local 1645, UAW, AFL-CIO (the Union), in ruling that the agreement contained an implied provision, based upon prior practice between the parties, that Torrington would allow its employees up to one hour off with pay to vote each election day. The District Court for the District of Connecticut held that "the arbitrator exceeded and abused his authority when he attempted to read into the agreement this implied contractual relationship," and it vacated and set aside the arbitrator's award. We affirm.

In its company newsletter of December 1962, Torrington announced that it was discontinuing its twenty-year policy of permitting employees time off with pay to vote on election days.[1] This policy had been unilaterally instituted by the company and was not a part of the then-existing collective bargaining agreement, which contained an extremely narrow arbitration provision. The Union did not attempt to arbitrate this issue. Rather, on April 9, 1963, it filed a many-faceted complaint with the National Labor Relations Board which included a charge that the unilateral change of election day policy constituted an unfair labor practice.

The Union later dropped this charge, and the Board dismissed the entire complaint on July 29, 1963. In August, the parties began negotiations for

---

[1] Torrington's brief on appeal explains that this decision was made because "in the light of the extension of voting hours and the substitution of voting machines for paper ballots ... it was no longer necessary to permit employees time off to vote."

a new collective bargaining agreement, as the old contract was due to expire September 27, 1963. At the first meeting, Torrington informed the Union that it did not intend to reestablish its paid time off for voting policy. The Union responded by including a contrary provision in its written demands presented at a meeting in August or early September.

At this point, the record is somewhat unclear as to the circumstances surrounding the negotiations. We know that in the written proposals made by Torrington (September 26) and by the Union (October 25), *each* suggested that the old contract be continued with specific amendments, none of which involved the election day policy. We know that a long and costly strike began when the old contract expired on September 27, that some employees worked during the strike, and that those employeees were not given paid time off for the November 1963 elections. And it is conceded by all that the current contract, signed on January 18, 1964, contained, like the old, no mention of paid time off for voting.

When the 1964 elections became imminent, Torrington's understanding of its rights under the new contract was revealed by a union flier to the employees dated November 2, 1964. The Union reported that, "The Torrington Company has again stated that you will *not* be allowed the one hour time off for voting this year." This time, however, the Union was armed with a new weapon, for the new contract contained a much less restrictive arbitration clause.[2] Thus, on December 17, 1964, the Union filed the grievance which underlies this case. When no solution was reached by the parties, application was made to the American Arbitration Association for determination under its Voluntary Labor Arbitration Rules, and the arbitrator was selected by the parties. A hearing was held on May 19, 1965.

In his written decision, the arbitrator first held that the dispute was arbitrable under the new contract's arbitration clause even though the contract contained no express provision for paid time off for voting, a decision which is not challenged. See, e.g., *Steelworkers v. Warrior & Gulf Nav. Co.*, 363 U.S. 574; *Procter & Gamble Independent Union of Port Ivory v. Procter & Gamble Mfg. Co.*, 298 F. 2d 644. Compare *Metal Prods. Workers Union v. The Torrington Co.*, 358 F. 2d 103 (2 Cir., 1966). He then ruled that the benefit of paid time off to vote was a firmly established practice at Torrington, that the company therefore had the burden of changing this policy by negotiating with the Union, and that in the negotiations which culminated in the current bargaining agreement the parties did not agree to terminate this practice. Finding further that this employee benefit was not within management's prerogative under the "management functions" clause of the

---

[2] Omitted.

contract,[3] the arbitrator held that employees who took time off to vote on November 3, 1964, or who worked on that day and had received an election benefit in 1962 must be paid a comparable benefit for Election Day 1964.

The company petitioned to vacate the award. Judge Clarie agreed with the arbitrator that the practice at issue had been long established at Torrington prior to 1963. But he also found that, "Throughout the negotiations [of 1963–1964], the plaintiff employer persistently reiterated its position not to grant this benefit [in the new contract]." Commenting that, "Labor contracts generally affirmatively state the terms which the contracting parties agree to; not what practices they agree to discontinue," Judge Clarie held that the arbitrator had gone outside the terms of the contract and thus had exceeded his authority by reading the election day benefit into the new contract after the parties had negotiated the issue but had made no such provision in that contract.

The essence of the Union's argument on appeal is that, in deciding that the arbitrator exceeded his authority in making this award, the District Court exceeded the scope of its authority and improperly examined the merits of the arbitrator's award. The Union relies on the language in *Steelworkers v. Enterprise Wheel & Car Corp.*, 363 U.S. 593, 596, the third of the famous Steelworkers trilogy in which the Supreme Court outlined the proper role of the judiciary in labor arbitration cases, to the effect that the courts are not "to review the merits of an arbitration award."

I

It is now well settled that a grievance is arbitrable "unless it may be said with positive assurance that the arbitration clause is not susceptible of an interpretation that covers the asserted dispute." *Steelworkers v. Warrior & Gulf Nav. Co.*, 363 U.S. at 582–83.[4] A less settled question is the appropriate scope of judicial review of a specific arbitration award. Although the arbitrator's decision on the merits is final as to questions of law and fact, his authority is contractual in nature and is limited to the powers conferred in

---

[3] Omitted.

[4] It has been argued that this standard should be broadened to render not arbitrable any situation where "a frivolous claim [is made] that a grievance is within the scope of the agreement." Freidin, Discussion of a paper by Sam Kagel, in Arbitration and Public Policy 10, 14 (*Proceedings of the Fourteenth Annual Meeting*, National Academy of Arbitrators 1961). However, while plausible, such a position was not adopted by the Supreme Court, primarily because there is real advantage in sending even frivolous claims to arbitration. Moreover, as a longtime labor arbitrator and member of this court has said, "No great harm is done by applying a liberal rule as to arbitrability, if the court carefully scrutinizes what the arbitrator later decides," Paul R. Hays, *Labor Arbitration, A Dissenting View* 80 (1966).

the collective bargaining agreement.[5]   For this reason, a number of courts have interpreted *Enterprise Wheel* as authorizing review of whether an arbitrator's award exceeded the limits of his contractual authority.   See *H. K. Porter Co. v. United Saw, File & Steel Prods. Workers,* 333 F. 2d 596; *Truck Drivers & Helpers Union Local 784 v. Ulry-Talbert Co.,* 330 F. 2d 562; *I.A.M. v. Hayes Corp.,* 296 F. 2d 238, 242–43.   The precise question seems not to have arisen in this circuit, compare *Local 453 v. Otis Elevator Co.,* 314 F. 2d 25, (2 Cir.), . . . , where the arbitrator's power to settle the dispute was clear, but we have plainly intimated that the arbitrator's authority to render a given award is subject to meaningful review.   *See Carey v. General Elec. Co.,* 315 F. 2d 499, 508 (2 Cir. 1963).   We agree with *Carey* that this is an appropriate question for judicial review.

Torrington contends that the arbitrator exceeded his authority in this case by "adding" the election day bonus to the terms of the January 1964 agreement.   However, the arbitrator held that such a provision was implied by the prior practice of the parties.   In some cases, it may be appropriate exercise of an arbitrator's authority to resolve ambiguities in the scope of a collective bargaining agreement on the basis of prior practice, since no agreement can reduce all aspects of the labor-management relationship to writing.   However, while courts should be wary of rejecting the arbitrator's interpretation of the implications of the parties' prior practice, the mandate that the arbitrator stay within the confines of the collective bargaining agreement . . . requires a reviewing court to pass upon whether the agreement authorizes the arbitrator to expand its express terms on the basis of the parties' prior practice.   Therefore, we hold the question of an arbitrator's authority is subject to judicial review, and that the arbitrator's decision that he has authority should not be accepted where the reviewing court can clearly perceive that he has derived that authority from sources outside the collective bargaining agreement at issue.   See *Textile Workers Union v. American Thread Co.,* 291 F. 2d 894.[6]

---

[5] Omitted.

[6] Of course, it can be argued that our decision authorizes an impermissible review of the "merits" in a case where the principal issue was whether the arbitrator should find an implied substantive obligation in the contract, see Meltzer, *The Supreme Court, Arbitrability, and Collective Bargaining,* 28 U. Chi. L. Rev. 464, 484–85 (1961), but we think this position is contrary to *Enterprise Wheel.* . . .   The question of the arbitrator's authority is really one of his contractual jurisdiction, and the courts cannot be expected to place their stamp of approval upon his action without making some examination of his jurisdiction to act.   As stated above, we think more exhaustive judicial review of this question is appropriate after the award has been made than before the award in a suit to compel arbitration; in this way, the court receives the benefit of the arbitrator's interpretive skills as to the matter of his contractual authority.   See *Livingston v. John Wiley & Sons, Inc.,* 313 F. 2d 52, 59 n. 5. . . .

II

Unfortunately, as the dissenting opinion illustrates, agreeing upon these general principles does not make this case any easier. Certain it is that Torrington's policy of paid time off to vote was well established by 1962. On this basis, the arbitrator ruled that the policy must continue during the 1964 agreement because Torrington did not negotiate a contrary policy into that agreement. To bolster his decision, the arbitrator noted that Torrington's written demands of September 26, 1963, constituted the first occasion on which either party did not expressly insist that its election day position be adopted. Therefore, he concluded, it was the company which removed this question "from the table" and the company cannot complain if its policy under the old contract is now continued.

We cannot accept this interpretation of the negotiations. In the first place, as Judge Clarie stated, labor contracts generally state affirmatively what conditions the parties agree to, more specifically, what restraints the parties will place on management's freedom of action. While it may be appropriate to resolve a question never raised during negotiations on the basis of prior practice in the plant or industry, it is quite another thing to assume that the contract confers a specific benefit when that benefit was discussed during negotiations but omitted from the contract.

> ... in entering into a collective agreement, in the negotiations for which as much care and deliberateness were exercised in respect to the omission as to the inclusion of various restraints and obligations, neither party agreed to submit to an arbitrator the question of whether it should be subjected to the very restraint or obligation which in negotiations the parties, by omitting it from the contract, agreed the contract should *not* subject it to.
>
> *Freidin, supra, note 4, at p. 12.*

The arbitrator's primary justification for reading the election day benefit into the 1964 agreement was that such a benefit corresponded to the parties' prior practice. But in this the arbitrator completely ignored the fact that the company had revoked that policy almost ten months earlier by newsletter to the employees in December 1962 and by formal notice to the Union in April 1963. It was within the employer's discretion to make such a change since the narrow arbitration clause in the previous collective bargaining agreement precluded resort to arbitration by the Union.[7] And there was no showing that Torrington's announcement was merely a statement of bargaining position and was not a seriously intended change in policy.

[7] Omitted.

In light of this uncontroverted fact, and bearing in mind that the arbitrator has no jurisdiction to "add to" the 1964 agreement, we do not think it was proper to place the "burden" of securing an express contract provision in the 1964 contract on the company. At the start of negotiations, Torrington announced its intent to *continue* its previous change of election day policy. This was an express invitation to the Union to bargain with respect to this matter. After the Union failed to press for and receive a change in the 1964 agreement, the company was surely justified in applying in November 1964 a policy it had rightfully established in 1952, and had applied in November 1963 (during the strike).

In our opinion, the Union by pressing this grievance has attempted to have "added" to the 1964 agreement a benefit which it did not think sufficiently vital to insist upon during negotiations for the contract which ended a long and costly strike. We find this sufficiently clear from the facts as found by the arbitrator to agree with the district court that the arbitrator exceeded his authority by ruling that such a benefit was implied in the terms of that agreement. As Judge Brown has written for the Fifth Circuit:

> But if full rein is to be given to this device as a means thought best able to achieve industrial peace, it must be enforced with an even hand. That which the parties have committed to the arbiter is for the arbiter alone, not the Court. Courts must assure that. But it is equally important to assure that neither party —through one guise or another—may obtain the intervention of an arbiter when the contract clearly excludes it from the reach of the grievance machinery. *Local Union No. 787, I.U.E. v. Collins Radio Co., 317 F.2d 214, 220.*

Far from having the disruptive effect upon the finality of labor arbitration which results when courts review the "merits" of a particular remedy devised by an arbitrator, we think that the limited review exercised here will stimulate voluntary resort to labor arbitration and thereby strengthen this important aspect of labor-management relations by guaranteeing to the parties to a collective bargaining agreement that they will find in the arbitrator not a "philosopher king" but one who will resolve their disputes within the framework of the agreement which they negotiated.

The judgment is affirmed.

Appendix C

Commentary on judicial review

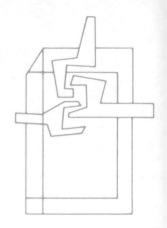

JUDICIAL INTERVENTION IN LABOR ARBITRATION[1]

Benjamin Aaron*

It is now seven years since the United States Supreme Court handed down the decisions in the *Steelworkers Trilogy*, which substantially limited the scope of judicial interference in private labor arbitration. Somewhat surprisingly, federal and state courts rather quickly fell into line with this new policy. For those favoring more active participation in labor arbitration by the judiciary, the past seven years have been lean ones. Whether the next seven will follow Biblical precedent and veer in the opposite direction is not yet clear, although a few faint signs are discernible. This Article will seek to identify those signs and to discuss their possible significance in light of past decisions and will suggest appropriate standards for judicial review of arbitration issues.

* Professor of Law and Director, Institute of Industrial Relations, University of California, Los Angeles.
1 Reprinted from the *Stanford Law Review*, vol. 20, no. 1, November, 1967. Copyright 1967 by the Board of Trustees of the Leland Stanford Junior University.

1 Arbitrability—The Courts' Determination

The one question specifically left for judicial determination by the *Trilogy* decisions is the existence of an agreement to arbitrate, although the Court circumscribed even this area by what is in effect a presumption in favor of arbitrability. The clearest statement appears in *United Steelworkers v. Warrior & Gulf Navigation Company:*

> The Congress . . . has by § 301 . . . assigned the courts the duty of determining whether [in a suit to compel arbitration] the reluctant party has breached his promise to arbitrate. For arbitration is a matter of contract and a party cannot be required to submit to arbitration any dispute which he has not agreed so to submit. Yet . . . the judicial inquiry under § 301 must be strictly confined to the question whether the reluctant party did agree to arbitrate the grievance. . . . An order to arbitrate the particular grievance should not be denied unless it may be said with positive assurance that the arbitration clause is not susceptible of an interpretation that covers the asserted dispute. Doubts should be resolved in favor of coverage.

Most courts have interpreted this language to mean that under a "standard" arbitration clause even farfetched claims of contract violation must be submitted to arbitration and that, conversely, an order to arbitrate may be denied only if the claim has been excluded from the coverage of the arbitration clause by express contract language. Several courts, however, have strayed from this easily applied rule and have involved themselves in the merits.

In *Pacific Telephone and Telegraph Company v. Communications Workers,* for example, the company brought suit under section 301 for a declaratory judgment that it had no obligation under its collective-bargaining agreement to arbitrate a grievance arising out of a disciplinary suspension. The agreement included a provision relating to "dismissals," but was silent on the subject of disciplinary suspensions. Despite language in the contract limiting the application of the arbitration provisions "to controversies between the Union and the Company regarding the true intent and meaning of any provision of this Contract, or regarding a claim that either party hereto has not fulfilled a commitment made in this Contract," the court held that the grievance was covered by the provisions. It refused to consider evidence of the bargaining history preceding the collective agreement, relying on the parol evidence rule and on the assumption that all prior understandings must be held merged into the expressions of the written contract.

This decision was reversed by the Court of Appeals for the Ninth Circuit and remanded for a new trial. The appellate court conceded that "the arbitration clause does not on its face fail to include this dispute within its coverage," but held that the parol evidence rule did not preclude examination of the bargaining history to determine its bearing on the issue of arbitrability. "It simply cannot be said," the court declared, "that as to the arbitrability of disciplinary suspension the contract's meaning is plain when the fact is that the contract is silent." Accordingly, it held that the proffered evidence went to the judicial issue of arbitrability, not to the merits, and had been erroneously excluded.

Following remand and a second trial, the Ninth Circuit, affirming the district court, held that the collective agreement, "construed in the light of bargaining history between the parties and the interpretations placed on the contract by the parties," did not obligate the company to arbitrate the grievance. In this second appeal the union did not rely upon the parol evidence rule, but argued that "judicial determination upon the issue of arbitrability may only be had where the answer is disclosed by the express language of the agreement itself or by some collateral writing. If resort to parol evidence is necessary in order to reach the truth ... then the issue must go to arbitration."

Conceding that this approach would be a workable rule of thumb for the courts, the court of appeals nevertheless rejected it because it could not be squared with the judicial function as defined by the Supreme Court. *Warrior & Gulf,* said the Ninth Circuit, did not announce a rule of evidence, but "simply warned that the persuasive power of the evidence must be such that the truth emerges with forceful clarity." Further, the court concluded,

> If the evidence before the Court of purpose to exclude a particular claim from arbitration is not sufficiently forceful, the result is not ... that the arbitrator must search for the truth at greater depth. The result, rather, is that the answer has been found and that the underlying dispute is arbitrable.

With due respect, I submit that the Ninth Circuit was wrong both in its holding and in the dictum quoted immediately above. The holding is unfaithful to the teaching of *Warrior & Gulf* and *United Steelworkers v. American Manufacturing Company* because it involved the court in precisely the sort of exercise that "comprehends the merits" and the "construction of the substantive provisions of a labor agreement"—functions, the Supreme Court said, which are performed better by arbitrators than by courts. The dictum, too, is wrong to the extent that it suggests that by ordering an issue to be arbitrated when the claim of nonarbitrability is not sufficiently forceful to justify denial of such an order, a court thereby precludes the arbitrator from making his own independent judgment on arbitrability. The court itself in its opinion on the first appeal recognized that in cases of this type "a determination upon the merits will affect the question of arbitrability and vice versa." Had arbitration been ordered, and had the arbitrator then concluded on the basis of his "search for the truth at greater depth" that the grievance was not arbitrable, it is most unlikely that his decision would have been vacated for that reason.

The rule laid down by the Supreme Court limiting judicial intervention in issues of arbitrability is, I think, a sound one. Ignoring all the wonderful nonsense of Mr. Justice Douglas' opinions in the *Steelworkers Trilogy* about the unique qualifications and functions of arbitrators, it remains true, in my opinion, that most arbitrators are better qualified than most judges to decide these questions, and that an arbitration offers a better forum than a court for their resolution. Moreover, because arbitration awards are not self-enforcing, they may be subject to limited court review. Just how limited that review should be is, of course, a matter of considerable controversy, and it is to that subject that the remainder of the Article is directed.

2 Judicial Review of Arbitration Awards

The principles governing the function of a court in reviewing arbitration awards are outlined by Mr. Justice Douglas in *United Steelworkers v. Enterprise Wheel & Car Corporation* in perdurably Delphic language:

> The refusal of courts to review the merits of an arbitration award is the proper approach to arbitration under collective bargaining agreements. The federal policy of settling labor disputes by arbitration would be undermined if courts had the final say on the merits of the awards. . . .
>
> When an arbitrator is commissioned to interpret and apply the collective bargaining agreement, he is to bring his informed judgment to bear in order to reach a fair solution of a problem. This is especially true when it comes to formulating remedies. . . . The draftsmen may never have thought of what specific remedy should be awarded to meet a particular contingency. Nevertheless, an arbitrator is confined to interpretation and application of the collective bargaining agreement; he does not sit to dispense his own brand of industrial justice. He may of course look for guidance from many sources, yet his award is legitimate only so long as it draws its essence from the collective bargaining agreement. When the arbitrator's words manifest an infidelity to this obligation, courts have no choice but to refuse enforcement of the award.

Interpreting this remarkable passage and applying it to specific cases is the frustrating task that has confronted courts and commentators.

A Construing the Contract

Many courts and commentators have adopted the no-nonsense approach outlined by Professor Kagel: "If the arbitrator stays within the submission and makes his award on his construction of the contract, then the award must be enforced." This interpretation has the advantages of tidiness and clarity; but it does not resolve problems of the type illustrated in the following hypothetical case.

Suppose an agreement containing a seniority provision that states: "Where skill and physical capacity are substantially equal, seniority shall govern in the following situations only: promotions, downgradings, layoffs, and transfers." Suppose, further, that the consistent practice for the five years immediately preceding the grievance has been to treat seniority as the controlling consideration in the assignment of overtime work, and that the dispute has arisen out of the employer's unilateral abandonment of that practice. Suppose, finally, that the collective-bargaining agreement includes a clause vesting in management the right, among others, to direct the working forces, subject only to qualifications or restrictions set forth elsewhere in the agreement, and another clause expressly forbidding the arbitrator to add to, subtract from, or modify any provision of the agreement.

Now, if the issue submitted to arbitration is whether the company violated the collective-bargaining agreement by discontinuing its practice of assigning overtime work on the basis of seniority, and if the arbitrator answers "Yes," what result will follow if the employer refuses to abide by the award and the union seeks its enforcement in a suit brought under section 301? Professor Kagel's interpretation of Mr. Justice Douglas' imprecise canon is of limited value because it does not indicate whether past practice —or any evidence other than the language of the document itself—is an allowable tool for the arbitrator to use in construing the contract.[2]

How, then, would the teaching of *Enterprise* apply to this case? Presumably, past practice was one of the "many sources" to which the arbitrator could "look for guidance." The words of his award did not "manifest an

---

[2] In an article written some years before the *Trilogy* cases were decided, I discussed this hypothetical case in detail and defended the arbitrator's reliance on consistent past practice as the basis for an award in the union's favor. Aaron, *The Uses of the Past in Arbitration*, in ARBITRATION TODAY, PROCEEDINGS OF THE EIGHTH ANNUAL MEETING, NATIONAL ACADEMY OF ARBITRATORS 1, 3–7 (J. McKelvey ed. 1955). Several years after those decisions, however, Francis A. O'Connell, Jr., in a paper lamenting current practices in arbitration and reflecting his enthusiastic disrespect for a large number of arbitrators, seized upon my hypothetical case as a horrible example of an arbitrator's abuse of authority. O'Connell, *The Labor Arbitrator: Judge or Legislator*, in PROCEEDINGS OF THE EIGHTEENTH ANNUAL MEETING, NATIONAL ACADEMY OF ARBITRATORS 102, 135–36 (D. Jones ed. 1965).

infidelity" to the submission agreement—that is, the award did not exceed the terms of the submission; but did the award "draw its essence from the collective-bargaining agreement"? Assuming that the arbitrator set forth his reasoning in an opinion accompanying the award, that opinion might be read to indicate either that the arbitrator disregarded the language of the agreement and relied only on past practice, or, as I would argue, that the arbitrator thought the parties, by their past practice, had themselves added this particular gloss to the contract language.

B The Shock Reaction

Mr. Justice Douglas has further complicated the picture, however, by stating elsewhere in *Enterprise* that "[a] mere ambiguity in the opinion . . . which permits the inference that the arbitrator may have exceeded his authority, is not a reason for refusing to enforce the award," and that, in any case, "[a]rbitrators have no obligation to the court to give their reasons for an award." In light of the earlier admonition that "courts have no choice but to refuse enforcement" of an award that does not draw its essence from the collective-bargaining agreement, one is forced to conclude that if a court is sufficiently shocked by an arbitrator's decision in a case of the type described above, it can find a basis for refusing to enforce it. The case of *Truck Drivers Union v. Ulry-Talbert Company* presents an example. Here the issue before the arbitrator was the propriety under the collective-bargaining agreement of a discharge for falsifying records of work hours. A provision of the agreement specified a number of grounds, including dishonesty, for discharge. The arbitration clause provided, among other things, that if a discharge grievance were carried to arbitration,

> the arbitration board shall not substitute its judgment for that of the management and shall only reverse the action or decision of the management if it finds that the Company's complaint against the employee is not supported by the facts, and that the management has acted arbitrarily and in bad faith or in violation of the express terms of this Agreement.

Undaunted by this language, the arbitrator found that although the grievant was guilty of "conduct which justified discipline to him as an employee, discharge was an excessive penalty; accordingly, his award reinstated the grievant without back pay (after a layoff of about 3½ months). The company refused to abide by the award, the district court refused to enforce it, and the Court of Appeals for the Eighth Circuit affirmed.

Sometimes, however, a court's shock reaction leads it to ignore the main thrust of the *Enterprise* language. *H. K. Porter Company v. United Saw,*

File & Steel Products Workers, for instance, involved an arbitration over severance pay and pension rights of employees terminated as a result of a plant removal. After successfully suing to compel arbitration, the union obtained an award granting specified pension and life insurance benefits to terminated employees. Its request for severance pay was denied. The company then sought to have the award vacated on the grounds that the arbitrator had "exceeded his authority and the scope of the submission" and that he had "added to, amended and completely disregarded the explicit and unambiguous provisions of the Agreement." Finding that the arbitrator had not exceeded his authority, and expressly relying upon the Supreme Court's admonition in *Enterprise* not to go into the merits, the district court refused to vacate the award and granted the union's motion for enforcement. On appeal, however, the Third Circuit reversed with respect to part of the award.

The eligibility clause in the applicable collective-bargaining agreement provided that an employee had to have reached age 65 and to have completed at least 25 years of continuous service to receive the disputed benefits. The arbitrator, purporting to rely upon past practice of the company and its predecessor, held that employees who at the time they were terminated had completed 25 or more years of service but had not reached age 65, and employees who had reached age 65 but had not completed 25 years of continuous service, were eligible for the benefits. After reviewing the arbitrator's opinion, the Third Circuit held that "[u]nder the circumstances of this case these practices formed a source of guidance to which the Arbitrator was authorized to look," and that he "acted entirely within his competence in granting the pensions based on duration of service." But with respect to the award of benefits to employees who had reached age 65 without having completed 25 years of service the court declared: "A reference to the cases examined by the Arbitrator upon which he bases his authority to deviate from the clear and unambiguous words of the eligibility clause discloses in all twenty cases each employee rendered not less than twenty-five years of total service." Thus, it concluded, the arbitrator's interpretation "neither goes to the essence nor to the application of the collective bargaining agreement."

To me the reasoning of the court of appeals seems wrong. Having first specifically approved past practice that varied from the "clear and unambiguous words of the eligibility clause" as a legitimate source of guidance to the arbitrator, the court then refused to enforce part of his award because it disagreed with his evaluation of the record. Assuming the court to have been correct on the issue of past practice, the arbitrator was at most guilty of making a factual mistake. An arbitrator's decision on the merits "is final as to questions of law and fact." It should make no difference, therefore, whether the mistake involved interpretation of the agreement or of past practice, when both are legitimate sources of guidance to the arbitrator. To paraphrase a memorable concurrence by Justice Stewart in *Jacobellis v. Ohio,* I shall not attempt to define the kind of arbitration decision I understand to be properly denied enforcement because it does not draw its essence from the collective-bargaining agreement; and perhaps I could never succeed in intelligibly doing so. But I know it when I see it, and the decision involved in this case is not that.

C   The Torrington Case—Unwarranted Extension of Judicial Review

In *Torrington Company v. Metal Products Workers* the court's understandable shock at the arbitrator's award served as a springboard for an unwarranted extension of judicial power of review. The case involved a 20-year-old policy, unilaterally instituted by the company and not included in the collective-bargaining agreement, of granting employees paid time off for voting. In December 1962, the company unilaterally announced discontinuance of this policy. The union did not challenge the company's action through the grievance procedure, which contained an extremely narrow arbitration provision, but in April 1963, it filed an unfair-labor-practice charge against the company, which it subsequently withdrew. Negotiations for a new contract began in August 1963. At the outset, the company announced its intention not to reestablish the policy of paid time off for voting, and the union presented a written demand to the contrary. When the old agreement expired in September, the union struck; the new agreement, executed in January 1964, contained no provision for paid time off for voting. Nonstrikers were not given paid time off for voting, during the strike, in the November 1963 elections, nor was paid time off given for voting in the November 1964 elections. The union later grieved over the company's refusal to reestablish the practice, and an arbitrator held that the company could not abandon it unilaterally. The company's suit to vacate the award was successful in the district court and the Second Circuit affirmed by a divided vote.

Given the bargaining history set forth above, it is difficult to understand how the arbitrator could have reached the decision he did. Assuming for the purposes of discussion that his decision was wrong, however, the question remains whether the district court acted properly in setting it aside. Clearly, mere disagreement with the award on the merits would not justify judicial reversal; but the district court held "that the arbitrator had gone outside the terms of the contract and thus had exceeded his authority by reading the election day benefit into the new contract after the parties had negotiated the issue but had made no such provision in that contract."

In affirming the decision below, the Second Circuit went somewhat beyond the narrow issue of the case. Most of the opinion by Chief Judge Lumbard, speaking for the majority, is devoted to a discussion of the legitimate scope of judicial review of arbitration awards. It is plain that he dislikes the limited role of the judiciary in these matters and is laboring to expand it without doing violence to the rulings of the Supreme Court. "[T]he arbitrator's decision on the merits," he believes, "is final as to questions of law and fact, [but] his authority is contractual in nature and is limited to the powers conferred in the collective bargaining agreement." Conceding that it may be appropriate in some instances for the arbitrator to "resolve ambiguities in the scope of the collective bargaining agreement" on the basis of past practice, he insists nevertheless that "the mandate that the arbitrator stay within the confines of the collective bargaining agreement ... requires a reviewing court to pass upon whether the agreement authorizes the arbitrator to expand its express terms on the basis of the parties' prior practice." And it follows, he says, "that the question of an arbitrator's authority is subject to judicial review, and that the arbitrator's decision that he has authority should not be accepted where the reviewing court can clearly perceive that he has derived that authority from sources outside the collective agreement at issue."

Turning to the arbitrator's decision, Judge Lumbard finds that the arbitrator misread the bargaining history previously recited and improperly "added" to the terms of the collective agreement by placing upon the company the burden of securing the union's consent to the abandonment of the preexisting policy. Then, addressing himself to a wider audience than the litigants, he concludes:

> [W]e think that the limited [sic] review exercised here will stimulate voluntary resort to labor arbitration and thereby strengthen this important aspect of labor-management relations by guaranteeing to the parties ... that they will find in the arbitrator not a "philosopher king" but one who will resolve their disputes within the framework of the agreement which they negotiated.

Supporters of labor arbitration may well wonder whether, with such friends in high places, they lack for enemies. In deposing the "philosopher kings"—the arbitrators—Judge Lumbard seems to be attempting to reinstate the courts as Platonic guardians, as in the good old days of the *Cutler-Hammer* doctrine,[3] which the Supreme Court expressly disparaged in

---

[3] *See* International Ass'n of Machinists v. Cutler-Hammer, Inc., 271 App. Div. 917, 67 N.Y.S.2d 317, *aff'd*, 297 N.Y. 519, 74 N.E.2d 464 (1947). This case held, "If the meaning of the provision of the contract sought to be arbitrated is beyond dispute, there cannot be anything to arbitrate and the contract cannot be said to provide for arbitration." 271 App. Div. at 918, 67 N.Y.S.2d at 318.

American Manufacturing.   Of course, *Cutler-Hammer* is associated with judicial determinations of arbitrability, and Judge Lumbard was careful to point out this distinction in *Torrington,* echoing the comment of his judicial colleague, Paul R. Hays, that "no great harm is done by applying a liberal rule as to arbitrability, if the court carefully scrutinizes what the arbitrator later decides."

Judge Lumbard, like Judge Hays, relies upon the supposed distinction, utterly baffling to me, between the arbitrator's "jurisdiction" and his "authority," a distinction enunciated earlier by the Second Circuit in *Carey v. General Electric Company.*   I had always supposed that "jurisdiction" meant power, which, in the case of arbitrator and court alike, includes the power to decide wrongly; as Judge Lumbard concedes, the arbitrator's decision on the merits is final as to questions of law and fact.   But Judge Lumbard has attached a string to this concession, and he jerks it back by saying, in effect: Jurisdiction is one thing, but authority is quite another; and although we must be wary of restricting the arbitrator's jurisdiction to hear a case, we may determine for ourselves whether the authority for his decision on the merits was derived from sources outside the collective agreement.

Although this approach contains some self-limiting features, it seems considerably more expansive than what the Supreme Court had in mind. Implicit in Judge Lumbard's opinion is the assumption that the court must always review not only the arbitrator's decision, but also his accompanying opinion and the collective-bargaining agreement.   But that assumption appears to contradict the teaching of the *Trilogy,* for if the arbitrator's decision sets forth all the necessary jurisdictional facts, the issue submitted by the parties, and the award, and if the award purports to be based on the agreement and is precisely responsive to the issue submitted, then the reviewing court is logically precluded from analyzing the arbitrator's reasoning as set forth in his accompanying opinion.   Judge Lumbard's approach would also present problems if the parties had previously agreed, in order to save time and money, that the arbitrator would render a decision without opinion.   What would have happened in *Torrington,* for example, if the issue submitted had been whether the company was entitled, without the union's consent, to discontinue the prior practice of granting paid time off to vote, and the arbitrator had simply answered "No," without any explanation?

A similar problem would be presented by a case involving the interpretation of a contractual provision in which the arbitrator's opinion indicated that he had misread the provision and thus had rendered a manifestly incorrect award.   Would this be a simple "mistake of fact," which the court has no power to correct; or would it be, rather, a violation of the prohibition against "adding to, deleting from, or modifying, in any way" any of the provisions of the agreement, and therefore subject to judicial reversal?

On the merits of the particular dispute between the parties in *Torrington,* I much prefer the conclusion of the court to that of the arbitrator. But in upholding the district court's reversal of the award, Judge Lumbard goes much too far and, indeed, deeply undercuts the law of the *Trilogy.*

3 Establishing a Standard for Judicial Review

The argument thus far might appear to suggest that the courts are bound to enforce any arbitration award, however it may outrage their sense of propriety or fairness, so long as the award does not plainly exceed the terms of the submission agreement. This is not necessarily so, but even if it were, the result would not be as bad as some have alleged.

Among the critics of the labor arbitration system as it now exists, Judge Hays is perhaps the most prominent. In his recent book he contends, among other things, that only a "handful" of arbitrators possess "the knowledge, training, skill, and character to make them good judges and therefore good arbitrators"; the remainder, who decide "literally thousands of cases every year," are "wholly unfitted for their jobs" and lack "the requisite knowledge, training, skill, intelligence, and character." Judge Hays offers no empirical evidence to support these sensational charges and would be hard put to do so. To be sure, there are some dishonest and incompetent arbitrators, just as there are dishonest and incompetent lawyers and judges, but the widespread use of arbitration suggests that most employers and unions do not share the view that the overwhelming number of arbitrators are knaves or fools.

An agreement to arbitrate is the product of negotiation. It can be, and sometimes is, hedged with various qualifications, which may range from a requirement that all disputed issues of arbitrability be adjudicated by a court, rather than by an arbitrator, to outright exclusion of a number of issues from arbitration. In this way the parties can protect themselves, if they so desire, from the hazards of incompetent and unfair awards. There are also other protections. A party dissatisfied with an award can always seek to undo its effect at the next negotiation, and in the rare but not-unheard-of situation in which both sides are dissatisfied with an award, they may mutually agree to disregard it. Moreover, if either party is dissatisfied with the approach an ad hoc arbitrator takes to a given type of problem, it can insist that the matter be submitted to someone else. Under these circumstances, automatic judicial enforcement of an award not plainly in violation of the terms of submission results simply in holding the parties to their original agreement to accept the award as the final and binding determination of the grievance.

Nevertheless, many will agree with Professor Bernard D. Meltzer that it is "questionable to require courts to rubberstamp the awards of private decision makers when the courts are convinced that there is no rational basis in the agreement for the award they are asked to enforce." Perhaps not so many will share his conviction that it is wrong to ask the courts "to exercise their powers while they are denied any responsibility for scrutinizing the results they are to enforce"; yet his prediction that this "unique attempt to shrivel judicial responsibility in enforcing arbitration awards is likely to fail because it runs against the grain of judicial tradition" may well be accurate.

Professor Meltzer proposes that the standard for judicial review of arbitration awards be the same as that used by the federal courts in reviewing a master's findings—that is, findings should be respected unless manifestly erroneous. The award would be enforced unless clearly lacking a "rational basis in the agreement read in the light of the common law of the plant where appropriate." To the question whether this standard would permit too great a judicial "penetration" into the arbitration process, one is tempted to respond that the likely judicial penetration would not be sufficient to constitute a rape. Yet such a standard is not entirely safe, largely because of the flexibility of the phrase "lacking a rational basis in the agreement." Even as modified by the words "read in the light of the common law of the plant where appropriate," the standard might provide too ready an access to a review of the merits by the judicial activist.

Professor Meltzer argues that his proposal is based on the same premise as that underlying the recent amendment to the Railway Labor Act,[4] which

---

[4] 45 U.S.C.A. § 153 (Supp. 1966), *amending* 45 U.S.C. § 153 (1964). In its report on the amendments to the judicial-review provisions of the Act, 45 U.S.C. § 153 First (p), (q) (1964), the Senate Subcommittee on Labor stated in part: "[B]ecause the National Railroad Adjustment Board has been characterized as an arbitration tribunal by the courts, the grounds for review should be limited to those grounds commonly provided for review of arbitration awards. . . .

"The committee gave consideration to a proposal that the bill be amended to include as a ground for setting aside an award 'arbitrariness or capriciousness' on the part of the Board . . . [but] declined to adopt such an amendment out of concern that . . . [it] might be regarded as an invitation to the courts to treat any award with which the court disagreed as being arbitrary or capricious. This was done on the assumption that a Federal court would have the power to decline to enforce an award which was actually and indisputedly without foundation in reason or fact, and the committee intends that, under this bill, the courts will have that power." S. Rep. No. 1201, 89th Cong., 2d Sess. 3 (1966).

now provides that findings and orders of any division of the National Railroad Adjustment Board

> shall be conclusive on the parties, except that the order of the division may be set aside, in whole or in part, or remanded to the division, for failure of the division to comply with the requirements of this chapter, for failure of the order to conform, or confine itself, to matters within the scope of the division's jurisdiction, or for fraud or corruption by a member of the division making the order.

An adaptation of this language as an amendment to section 301 of the Labor-Management Relations Act would seem preferable to the language proposed by Professor Meltzer. Such an amendment would accomplish the same result he intends and would have the additional advantage of applying the same standards of judicial review to both arbitration awards under the Labor-Management Relations Act and adjustment-board awards under the Railway Labor Act.

4   Tangential Problems in Judicial Review

In *Textile Workers Union v. Lincoln Mills* Mr. Justice Douglas indicated that in fashioning a federal law of labor arbitration the Court would be guided by existing federal laws where applicable, and would rely for solutions to problems not so covered upon compatible state laws and "judicial inventiveness." Of the types of problems for which guidance may be sought from these various sources, four merit brief attention.

The first type is created by an award that, although faithful to the submission and based upon the collective-bargaining agreement, requires one or both parties to violate the law. *Glendale Manufacturing Company v. Local 520, International Ladies' Garment Workers' Union* is a frequently cited example of such a case. Here the arbitrator's award required the company to bargain over an interim wage increase with a union that was decertified a few days after the award was issued. The Court of Appeals for the Fourth Circuit correctly refused to enforce the award, but sensibly referred the matter back to the arbitrator with the suggestion that he "order the employer to negotiate the wage question with the employees directly or with any properly constituted committee or representative of the employees."[5]

---

[5] 283 F.2d at 940. The question of an arbitrator's responsibility when an award warranted by the agreement would, in his judgment, be repugnant to an applicable federal or state statute or rule of public policy is beyond the scope of this Article. *See generally* Address by Professor Meltzer, *supra* note 48; Smith & Jones, *The Supreme Court and Labor Dispute Arbitration: The Emerging Federal Law,* 63 MICH. L. REV. 751, 804 (1965).

A related problem may arise when the NLRB is asked to rule upon an unfair-labor-practice charge, the substance of which has already been the subject of an arbitration award. The Board's familiar *Spielberg* doctrine, that it will honor an arbitration award when "the proceedings appear to have been fair and regular, all parties had agreed to be bound, and the decision of the arbitration panel is not clearly repugnant to the purposes and policies of the Act," is designed to deal with this kind of case and harmonizes well with the standards of judicial review recommended in this Article.

Of course, on some issues submitted initially to arbitration the Board must have the last word.[6] This "is not to say that independently of a Board proceeding involving the issue opportunity for judicial review of the award would or should be provided." But when the issue has arisen before it, the Board has not hesitated to assert its exclusive power to prevent unfair labor practices, even when this necessitated disregard of an arbitration award. Thus a recent suggestion that "the major problem in this area is the reluctance of the . . . Board to prevent attenuation of its powers by a blind and placid acceptance of arbitration as an alternative, rather than subordinate, forum" seems unjustified.

A third problem, also closely related to the first, concerns judicial enforcement of an award alleged to be contrary to public policy. If the developing law were to follow the decisions of some state courts, it would permit courts to refuse enforcement on that ground.[7] Allowing the judiciary to determine "public policy" on an ad hoc basis in proceedings to enforce or vacate arbi-

---

[6] *See, e.g.,* Carey v. Westinghouse Elec. Corp., 375 U.S. 261 (1964). The Court, in reversing a lower court's refusal to compel arbitration in a dispute involving mixed questions of work assignment (a matter of contract interpretation) and representation (controlled by the National Labor Relations Act), stated: "Should the Board disagree with the arbiter, by ruling, for example, that the employees involved in the controversy are members of one bargaining unit or another, the Board's ruling would, of course, take precedence. . . ." *Id.* at 272. The Court stated that the same result would follow in "[a]rbitral awards construing a seniority provision (*Carey v. General Electric Co.*, 315 F.2d 499, 509–10 [1963]), or awards concerning unfair labor practices [citing Lodge 1021, International Ass'n of Machinists, 116 N.L.R.B. 645 (1956); Monsanto Chem. Co., 97 N.L.R.B. 517 (1951)]. . . ." *Id.*

[7] *See, e.g.,* Black v. Cutter Laboratories, 43 Cal. 2d 788, 278 P.2d 905 (1955), *cert. dismissed with opinion,* 351 U.S. 292 (1956) (refusal to sustain award reinstating Communist employee); Avco Corp. v. Preteska, 22 Conn. Supp. 475, 174 A.2d 684 (Super. Ct. 1961) (refusal to sustain award reinstating employee discharged for gambling on premises); Public Util. Constr. & Gas Appliance Workers v. Public Serv. Elec. & Gas Co., 26 N.J. 145, 139 A.2d 1 (1958) (refusal to enforce agreement to arbitrate discharge of employees who sabotaged employer during a strike); Western Union Tel. Co. v. American Communications Ass'n, 299 N.Y. 177, 86 N.E.2d 162 (1949) (refusal to sustain award setting aside disciplinary suspension of telegraph employees who refused to handle messages emanating from a struck company).

tration awards seems a questionable practice. The suggestion of Professors Russell Smith and Dallas Jones that "orthodox limitations on judicial review should be invoked ... in 'public policy discharge' cases, at least in the absense of an enforceable statute giving the employer the absolute right to discharge for the kind of offense involved," is a wiser approach. This appears to be the course that federal law is taking.[8]

The final problem concerns judicial enforcement of an arbitration award in the face of a claim that one of the parties was denied procedural due process. The only question, of course, is whether the alleged denial of due process was serious enough to have affected the outcome. It can scarcely be doubted that an award should not be enforced if the proceedings were procedurally defective to a material degree, and this has been the general rule under federal and state law. For example, in the recent case of *Harvey Aluminum, Inc. v. United Steelworkers* the federal district court vacated and remanded the case for rehearing by the same arbitrator because the latter had refused to hear an important rebuttal witness.

At the same time it is important to remember that labor dispute arbitration, although adversary in character, is something more than a battle; ideally, at least, it is a cooperative effort by the parties and the arbitrator to develop a workable solution to the problem presented by the grievance within the framework for decision established by the parties.[9] Thus procedures must be allowed to remain flexible, which is one reason why rules of evidence as applied in court proceedings do not prevail in arbitration hearings. Courts should be reluctant, therefore, to set aside awards simply because the arbitration proceeding was conducted informally, and a failure to follow conventional procedures should not in itself be grounds for vacating an award.

---

[8] *See, e.g.,* Local 453, Int'l Union of Elec. Workers v. Otis Elevator Co., 314 F.2d 25 (2d Cir.), *cert. denied,* 373 U.S. 949 (1963), in which the court enforced an award reinstating an employee discharged for gambling on company property, even though it observed that "when [federal] public policy is sought to be interposed as a bar to enforcement of an arbitration award, a court must evaluate its asserted content." 314 F.2d at 29; Jenkins Bros. v. Local 5623, United Steelworkers, 341 F.2d 987 (2d Cir. 1965), *aff'g per curiam* 230 F. Supp. 871 (D. Conn. 1964), *cert. denied,* 382 U.S. 819 (1965), in which the Second Circuit upheld, on the authority of *Otis,* a lower court's order dismissing a motion for an injunction against the holding of an arbitration hearing on a grievance involving discharge of an employee for gambling.

[9] Of course, the framework for decision may be as narrow and rigid as the parties wish to make it, and if the arbitrator exceeds either the substantive or procedural limits laid down by the parties, his award, if challenged on that ground, should not be enforced. The point is, however, that parties do not generally set tight restrictions, and the courts should not do so after the fact.

Conclusion

The foregoing suggested standards for review would maintain the institution of labor dispute arbitration practically as it exists today—that is, as an admittedly imperfect and improvable but obviously viable and widely accepted means for the peaceful solution of grievances arising under collective-bargaining agreements. These standards would invest the courts with responsibility for doing a little more than simply rubberstamping the decisions of arbitrators; but they would not go so far as to permit the courts to substitute their judgments for those of arbitrators selected by the parties. They certainly would not guarantee the competence or integrity of arbitrators, but then, competence and integrity can be guaranteed only when men have become angels, in which event the problem will have become moot.

THE NAME OF THE GAME IS DECISION— SOME REFLECTIONS ON "ARBITRABILITY" AND "AUTHORITY" IN LABOR ARBITRATION[1]

Edgar A. Jones, Jr.*

It is quite unlikely that adverse judicial rulings, even at the level of the Supreme Court, could reverse the widespread acceptance of voluntary arbitration as the only feasible alternative to industrial strife during the terms of collective bargaining agreements.[2] Nonetheless, it is desirable to make clear the buffer zones that insulate arbitral discretion from judicial and administrative interposition. Three cases—*Torrington Company v. Metal Products Workers Local 1645* in the Second Circuit, *Dallas Typographical Union v. A. H. Belo Corporation* in the Fifth Circuit, and the *Cloverleaf*

---

* Professor of Law, University of California, Los Angeles.
[1] Reprinted from July, 1968, issue of the *Texas Law Review*.
[2] *See* D. Jones & R. Smith, *The Impact of the Emerging Federal Law of Grievance Arbitration on Judges, Arbitrators, and Parties*, 52 VA. L. REV. 831, *passim*. (1966), *Management and Labor Appraisals and Criticisms of the Arbitration Process: A Report with Comments*, 62 MICH. L. REV. 1115 (1964). The initial Jones-Smith survey disclosed that only 5% of the management respondents preferred litigation or economic self-help to arbitrating grievances. *Id.* at 1116–17. A majority of them, however, felt they should attempt to strengthen contractual provisions "to safeguard management prerogatives and reduce the risks of arbitral excesses." 52 VA. L. REV. at 889. Professors Jones and Smith (Dallas and Russell, that is) suggest that dissolution of the *Lincoln Mills* federal common law would, if anything, be apt to strengthen rather than weaken adherence to arbitration, certainly on the part of management respondents to their surveys. Judging from the nature of their responses, the union respondents generally are, and foreseeably will continue to remain, satisfied with resort to arbitration. *See id.* at 889–96.

Dairy matter before the Labor Board—well illustrate that judicial and administrative pressure on the b rders of these buffer zones is not apt to lessen.

In the process of settling labor disputes, the name of the game has always been *Decision*. The movable pieces most recently in vogue in its playing are the ideas clustering about the concepts of "arbitrability" and "authority." Before analyzing the cases it may be well to sketch briefly the rules and conditions under which the game is currently supposed to be played.

I

When the parties to collective bargaining agreements argue the issue of "arbitrability" among themselves or before courts or arbitrators, the focal point of contention is whether they may reasonably be said to have conferred contractual "authority" upon the arbitral tribunal to resolve any dispute at all between them, this particular class of disputes, or, in the isolation of the unusual, this individual grievance. Questions of "arbitrability" may be put either to a court or to an arbitrator by a party denying any contractual obligations to submit a particular issue to final and binding arbitration. It is undoubtedly true today that most questions whether a dispute is arbitrable under an agreement are submitted to arbitrators without judicial intervention,[3] and, more often than not, at the same time that the issue on the merits is put before them. Of course the submission to an arbitrator is backstopped by the prospect (some regard it as the specter) of resort to the courts for the enforcement of the obligation to arbitrate. Inevitably, judicial attitudes and doctrines have influenced the dispositions by arbitrators of issues of arbitrability. Since the Supreme Court's decision in *Textile Workers Union v. Lincoln Mills* in 1957, a rather complex set of concepts has been evolving by which are governed both the obligation to arbitrate and the allocation of decisional function among the courts, the National Labor Relations Board, and arbitrators.

Among its several opinions on the subject the Supreme Court has declared that grievances are not to be ordered to arbitration which are "so plainly unreasonable that the subject matter of the dispute must be regarded as nonarbitrable because it can be seen in advance that no award to the Union could receive judicial sanction." That observation clearly

---

[3] There are 150–175 judicial decisions per year involving labor arbitrations, in contrast to about 10,000–15,000 arbitration decisions a year. *See* Jones, *The Schizophrenic World of Labor Arbitration and Mr. Q. Vadis, Arbitrator,* n. 12 and accompanying text, in Sw. Legal Foundation 14th Inst. on Lab. Law (1968).

implies a qualitative judicial review after the arbitrator has rendered his award to determine if it is deserving of "sanction." But in the *Steelworkers Trilogy* opinions the Court was generally so sweeping in its attribution of exclusive competence to arbitrators and the arbitral process that Justice Douglas evidently felt the counterpoint necessity in *Enterprise Wheel & Car* to add judicial palliative to arbitral panegyric by cautioning that

> an arbitrator is confined to interpretation and application of the collective bar-gaining agreements; *he does not sit to dispense his own brand of industrial justice*. He may of course look for guidance from many sources, yet *his award is legitimate only so long as it draws its essence* from the collective bargaining agreement. When the arbitrator's words manifest an infidelity to this obligation, courts have no choice but to refuse enforcement of the award.

Justice Douglas' pronouncement can now be seen to have foreshadowed retrospective analysis by courts of the "authority" of an arbitrator to do what he did in his award. But the Court in the *Trilogy* proceeded to admonish the trial court that a "mere ambiguity" in the arbitrator's opinion "which permits the inference that the arbitrator may have exceeded his authority, is not a reason for refusing to enforce the award." The company's "major argument" in *Enterprise Wheel & Car* was that "correct principles of law" applied to the interpretation of the agreement demon-strated that the agreement did not provide what the arbitrator concluded that it did, so that, therefore, the arbitrator's decision was not based on the contract. The Court flatly rejected that reasoning with the key observation that: "This plenary review by a court of the merits would make meaning-less the provisions that the arbitrator's decision is final, for in reality it would almost never be final." The Court then reemphasized its order of the day as promulgated throughout the three *Steelworkers Cases:*

> It is the arbitrator's construction which was bargained for; and so far as the arbi-trator's decision concerns construction of the contract, the courts have no busi-ness overruling him because their interpretation of the contract is different from his.

As one panel of the Second Circuit has recently succinctly observed of the court-arbitrator relationship. "[T]he rule is that unless the parties expressly exclude a matter, the court will conclude that they intended to submit it to arbitration." Despite the clarity of that formulation of what a lower court must deem arbitrable, there are courts from time to time that still apparently find it terribly difficult to swallow hard but silently in the face of reasoning or results with which the judges disagree. The reversal instinct seems to well up irresistibly on occasion, despite the manifest com-mand of a principle that must certainly be regarded as obvious by now.

Judicial interposition on the merits, then, utilizes either of two entry points to dispose of a grievance allegedly subject to exclusive disposition by an arbitrator. The first is anterior to an arbitral hearing. It asks whether the matter is "arbitrable": Have the parties contractually committed themselves to arbitrate this specific kind of dispute? The second opportunity occurs after the arbitrator has heard the matter and issued his award. Comes now the outraged loser seeking justice before This Honorable Court. The court's question in that context: Did the parties contractually clothe their arbitrator with the "authority" to do this kind of thing to one of them? There have always been courts willing, even eager, to analyze the merits and conclude that no negotiator in his right mind could possibly have intended to open this matter for decision by anyone, other than, perhaps, This Honorable Court.

Vigorous judicial intrusiveness on the merits was the basis of the doctrine of arbitrability announced in *Machinists Local 402 v. Cutler-Hammer, Incorporated*—a doctrine that was expressly disapproved by the Supreme Court in *United Steelworkers of America v. American Manufacturing Company* as "a principle that could only have a crippling effect on grievance arbitration." The prescriptions of the Court, together with a candid reflection on the occupational difficulty of judges in submitting to them, were recently well summarized by a federal district court. "While the temptation is strong to construe the agreements for the parties, a task for which lawyers and judges are supposedly especially trained, and to resolve the dispute, judicial discipline precludes this," District Judge Thompson declared with a certain air of resignation.

> In the so called trilogy of labor arbitration opinions, the Supreme Court has defined guidelines to our decision here. In summary, (1) the means chosen by the parties for settlement of their differences under a collective bargaining agreement should be given full play; (2) grievances should be arbitrated regardless of whether a Court deems them meritorious; (3) the function of the Court is limited to ascertaining whether the party seeking arbitration is making a claim which on its face is governed by the contract; (4) a party may not be required to submit to arbitration a dispute which he has not agreed so to submit, and the meaning of the arbitration clause itself is for the Court unless the parties clearly state to the contrary; (5) doubts should be resolved in favor of arbitration and a dispute should not be excluded unless the parties clearly so provided; (6) exceptions to a general arbitration clause are strictly construed and must specifically cover the particular dispute in question; and (7) a Court should be chary about embarking upon an interpretation of the substantive provisions of a labor agreement under the guise of interpreting the arbitration clause.

This is no small task. But the judge and the lawyer who are, as Judge Thompson observed, especially trained to construe agreements, are also, at a more basic level of temperament and judgmatical habit, professionally expected to have the capacity to respect the integrity of private methods of settling disputes. Judicial forbearance, the withholding rather than the laying on of judicial hands, is what judicial temperament must counsel in these cases if it is to be respected as adjudicative competence.

The fundamental reason for requiring courts to abstain from interposing to oust arbitration except in the clearest of cases is the paramount necessity to avoid external tampering with the machinery of industrial self-government lest the will to govern, which is to say, bargain, be enervated. Vital to the operation of that machinery is the need for rapid resolution of labor disputes by an individual to whose judgment the parties have chosen to submit, thereby avoiding enmeshing in litigation—and exacerbating—what typically are highly charged, often personally colored issues.

II

In *Torrington,* the Second Circuit in 1966 affirmed a district court that had set aside an arbitrator's award. The arbitrator, interpreting past practice and the negotiation history of the parties, had concluded that the company had violated the contract when it had unilaterally withdrawn a benefit during the term of the collective agreement. The arbitrator had concluded, in essence, that an agreement by accretion had occurred when, from 1944 until 1963, the employer had consistently allowed up to an hour of compensated time to vote in state and national elections. The agreement by accretion, he concluded, could only be altered by negotiation.

Prior to entering the 1963 contract under which the arbitration took place, the employer had announced its intention to discontinue the voting practice and had suggested that the matter be incorporated in the forthcoming contract negotiations. Thereafter it submitted twenty-two proposals for contract changes. But no mention was made in them of the voting question. As a capper, the previous agreement had had a stringent arbitration clause that would undoubtedly have supported the company's unilateral discontinuance of the past practice. The clause had stated bluntly that, "The Company's decision will stand and will not be over-ruled by any arbitrator unless the arbitrator can find that the Company misinterpreted or violated the express terms of the agreement." But in the new agreement under which the arbitration had taken place, that sentence had been deleted.

After an extended bargaining strike of sixteen weeks the new agreement was executed in which, again, there was no reference to paid voting time. In place of the stringent arbitration clause was a considerably diluted provision that was obviously the product of compromise. It set up a three-step grievance procedure, short of arbitration, through which might be taken "any dispute or question in regard to wages, hours and working conditions, *or* in regard to the interpretation or application of the provision of the agreement." That funnel was certainly broad enough to scoop up any dispute in the plant whatsoever. But at the arbitration end of the grievance procedure the connective "and" replaced the alternative "or" thusly: "If a grievance is not settled after it has been processed through the three (3) steps described ... *and* if it is a grievance with respect to the interpretation or application of any provisions in the contract *and* is not controlled" by the strictures of the management-prerogative article contained elsewhere in the agreement, it could be arbitrated.

No doubt each of us might have his own view of the merits of an arbitral award that concluded that the vote pay had become integrated in the agreement through accretion and could not unilaterally be removed simply by assertion. But this was a rather complicated case. There had been a long strike. The previously airtight arbitration provision had been considerably ventilated by compromise. There had been a lot of milling around in the negotiations and enough track marks had been laid down by the backing and filling of the parties to obliterate any assured path to a conclusion one way or the other on the vote pay issue. The arbitrator made no egregiously erroneous award; arguably wrong, perhaps, but arguably correct, certainly.

Yet the award was vacated in the district court and the Second Circuit affirmed. The reasoning of the court of appeals is replete with miscellaneous non sequiturs. The court conceded that the arbitrator's decision on the merits in general is final as to questions of law and fact. But the court then took the position that the arbitrator's decision was not final on the particular question of "law" that he actually decided—the import of past practice to the collective agreement. Thus the court concluded that it had to "pass upon whether the agreement authorizes the arbitrator to *expand its express terms* on the basis of the parties' prior practice," even though, in general, a court "should be wary of rejecting the arbitrator's interpretation of the implications of the parties' prior practice." To be "wary" meant that the reviewing court must reject the arbitrator's affirmation of authority when the court "can clearly perceive that [the arbitrator] has derived that authority from sources outside the collective agreement at issue." But recall that the question before the arbitrator and court was: Had the past practice become so imbedded in the agreement that it could only be altered, amended, or modified by mutual agreement?

Stop right there, the *Torrington* court would say. While past practice may properly resolve a question never raised in negotiations, "It is quite another thing to assume that the contract confers a specific benefit when that benefit was discussed during negotiations but omitted from the contract." But once again it must be recalled that the question was whether the benefit had already become part of the fabric of agreement, prior to its discussion in the 1963 negotiations. If so, the benefit surely could not be deleted solely by unilateral assertion. It would have to be cut out by agreement.

Perhaps the court's analytical difficulty may be traced to an unwillingness to accept past practice as amendatory of a written collective agreement. That view, however, has no legal basis. It is elemental contract law that the conduct of the contracting parties after execution of a written agreement can effectively amend that agreement. Whether the amendatory conduct has occurred becomes a matter of proof. If in fact it has occurred, it is inferable that the party economically disadvantaged by the amendment has in one way or another recouped that disadvantage by securing some other kind of concession or advantage in the course of collective bargaining. It may be that the benefit sought by Torrington in this case was the extra-contractual one of a community image as a civic-minded employer. Torrington's motivation is not relevant, however. Whatever it may have been, a bilateral commitment had resulted.

Labor-management agreements do not become static memorials once reduced to writing. They are an important part, but nonetheless only a part, of the active process of effectuating a constructive working relationship between the parties. Thus "past practice"—a course of action knowingly adopted and accepted by the parties over a significant period of time—is important in the interpretation of a collective agreement. This is true even though the language of the agreement may point in a different direction than do the actions of the parties after its execution. The focus is not on prior ambiguous language; it is the later amendatory conduct that is significant. Whether legal theory would require construing the later conduct to amend the old contract or to create a new provision instead, the parties clearly have given concrete expression to their intent in the context of the constantly evolving give-and-take that is collective bargaining.[4] That this

---

[4] A word, said Holmes, "is the skin of a living thought" that "may vary greatly in color and content according to the circumstances and the time in which it is used." Towne v. Eisener, 245 U.S. 418, 425 (1918). That aphorism is peculiarly appropriate to a consideration of the intent of parties to a collective bargaining agreement. Coloration may be drawn from conduct as well as terminology. Even language that by its clear terms is subject to only one interpretation can be effectively amended, even repealed, by a course of contrary interpretation indulged in by the parties over a significant period of time. The actions of the parties subsequent to the execution of the agreement are often far more revealing of consensual intent than are quite explicit contract terms that are not acted upon.

kind of objectively manifested intent ought to be regarded as binding upon a party who has knowingly embraced it is the compelling rational basis of the past practice principle.

An arbitrator confronted with "past practice" circumstances should not flout the intent of the parties. Nor should the employer (or the union) assert that management (or the union) only "tolerated" the deviational conduct, as if somehow one "tolerates" something that one does not intend to allow. The point is that the intent to "tolerate," evidenced over an extended period of time, becomes the mutual intent to alter, amend, or modify.

In *Torrington* the employer, after all, could have effectively reversed the past practice, had he prevailed in the negotiations on this point, by inserting a provision like the following, which is sufficiently common in usage to have acquired the shorthand reference of "zipper clause":

> This agreement concludes all collective bargaining between the parties during its term. It constitutes the sole agreement between the parties. It supersedes all prior agreements, undertakings and practices, oral or written, express or implied.

Comparable language would have extinguished the vote benefit which, by mutual conduct, the parties had previously incorporated as one of the bilateral, albeit unwritten, contractual commitments of their collective bargaining agreement. The employer could have insisted upon a zipper clause in the course of its bargaining, but manifestly it did not, since the final agreement did not contain such a provision. What an odd view of bargaining it would be that sanctioned a unilateral dissolution of a mutually adopted obligation merely because the party dissolving the obligation had asserted during negotiations that the obligation was onerous!

In support of its displacement of the arbitrator's informed judgment, the *Torrington* court cited the Supreme Court's *Enterprise Wheel & Car* mandate to arbitrators to draw the "essence" of their awards from the collective agreement. The court emphasized the company's right to a "meaningful review." The Second Circuit relied on Judge Paul Hays' negative rationale that, "No great harm is done by applying a liberal rule as to arbitrability, if the Court *carefully scrutinizes* what the arbitrator later decides." It is the duty of courts, said the Second Circuit, to enforce "the mandate that the arbitrator *stay within the confines*" of the collective agreement. This "mandate" warrants an "exhaustive judicial review."

Each court has its embarrassing decisions (not to mention each arbitrator) and their usual significance is simply to teach in pages like these and stand guard duty as silent reminders to their uncomfortable authors. But *Torrington* is something else again. It has a basic warp that is hazardous to the collective bargaining process and that must be identified and rejected lest its progeny proliferate through uncritical adherence to precedent. Central to the court's justification for ousting the arbitrator's judgment is its assertion of a broad power of review quite clearly denied to courts by the Supreme Court in *Enterprise Wheel & Car*. Recall that the Court rejected the company's argument that the arbitrator's decision was not based on the contract because "by applying correct principles of law to the interpretation of the collective bargaining agreement it [could] be determined that the agreement did not ... provide" what the arbitrator held that it did. The Court wasted no words on that contention, and its statement just as effectively disposes of the *Torrington* reasoning. "The acceptance of this view," said the Court,

> would require courts, even under the standard arbitration clause, to review the merits of every construction of the contract. This plenary review by a court of the merits would make meaningless the provisions that the arbitrator's decision is final, for in reality it would almost never be final.

In contrast, the *Torrington* court quite evidently conceives of arbitration as merely an intermediate step on the path to justice. "The question of the arbitrator's authority is really one of his contractual jurisdiction," the Second Circuit reasoned, and "we think more exhaustive judicial review of this question is appropriate after the award has been made than before." Why is this? "[I]n this way," the court answers, "the Court receives the benefit of the arbitrator's interpretive skills as to the matter of his contractual authority." The court may indeed receive that benefit, but it is clear enough that the parties would not under the *Torrington* reasoning. Yet, that benefit was precisely their bargain. Thus the *Torrington* court conceives the role of the arbitrator as that of a mere advisor in the interpretation of the collective agreement, as a kind of expert witness, one whose judgment may or may not be influential on the final decision maker, the reviewing court. Yet surely it is impossible to restrict the judicial inquiry into the existence of "contractual authority" so that it does not overreach into a weighing of the merits reserved for arbitral judgment. Especially is this so in the tangled bargaining circumstances of a *Torrington*. The *Torrington* reasoning would thus upend the Supreme Court's arbitration rationales based on the need to protect the arbitrator's judgment from displacement by judges uninformed about the processes of collective bargaining.

It is interesting to speculate how the *Torrington* court would have responded to the Labor Board's recent decision in *Gravenslund Operating Company*, had that case arisen in the Second Circuit and been brought before it for enforcement of the Board's order. For fifteen years an unorganized employer had paid a Christmas bonus according to an established formula. Then a union organized it in the spring; a collective agreement was negotiated in the summer and executed in November. But no mention was made at the bargaining table of the Christmas bonus. After the agreement was executed, and without consulting with the union, the employer announced to the employees that it could not afford to pay the bonus that year. The union asserted a contract violation, but it filed refusal-to-bargain charges rather than resorting to the grievance procedure and arbitration. Two years after the refusal of the employer to pay the Christmas bonus the Board's decision issued, holding that there was indeed a breach of the statutory duty to bargain in good faith. Because of the consistency of the annual Christmas bonus payments, the Board majority held that the "employees had the right to expect and rely upon the continuation of these bonuses as part of their wages." The Board observed the failure either to discuss the subject in negotiations or to adopt an express contractual provision conferring the right on the employer to take the unilateral action it did. This meant to the Board that the employer had the duty to bargain about its decision to discontinue.

In *Gravenslund* the withdrawal of the benefit had come after the collective agreement was executed; in *Torrington* the employer had announced its intent to withdraw the benefit at the outset of negotiations. In each case the later agreement was silent on the subject of the benefit. This difference has no contractual significance, however, since in each instance there was a contractually binding mutual intent that was manifested by adherence to a past practice; it had ripened through common acceptance over a significant period of time into an integral though unwritten part of the bilateral agreement. Of course, the unwritten provision could have been removed by a reversal of the past practice—acquiescence by the union in the employer's abrogation of it. But once the union had refused to accede to its removal, the provision's contractual status would be the same as that of any express provision that is attacked by one party during negotiations but that later turns up unaltered in the new agreement. It remains as binding after the attack as before. In the case of a past practice, therefore, it would take express language to negate the practice.

Thus the Board is on sound ground in regarding the fifteen-year bonus as negotiable and not unilaterally removable. Of course it is one thing to say that the parties must bargain on the matter. But what if they bargain to impasse? Can the employer then refuse payment? By hypothesis, if he did so, he would thereby violate the contract. That prospect should require the Board to confront the contractual issue that remains unresolved by its decision. This is certainly a major reason why Board Member Gerald

Brown dissented, once again urging the Board to hold in abeyance these cases impregnated with contractual issues, requiring the parties to exhaust their contractual grievance procedures before being allowed to invoke the Board's intervention. No material contractual loose ends should remain untied when the Board asserts its undoubted jurisdiction. This after all is the requisite of informed decisional prudence; it is not a matter of jurisdictional power and therefore needs no defensive over-reaction by an administrative agency jealous of its prerogatives.

The major judicial front on which the allocation of jurisdiction between courts and arbitrators was fought out a decade ago between fight-minded labor and management bargainers was that of prehearing "arbitrability." The decisive engagement finally occurred in 1960 before the Supreme Court and, as we have seen, was won by proponents of wider uses of arbitration and a drastically constricted court jurisdiction in labor dispute cases. Thus it was possible by 1964 to observe that "the courts universally purported to avoid reviewing the merits of an arbitrator's award." Nonetheless, as might be expected, there is recurrent skirmish activity observable on that front.

But the main action in courts who still would take hold of the merits appears now to have shifted to postaward review—the "authority" issue. Thus the *Torrington* court conceded it to be "well settled" that a grievance must be held arbitrable by a court "unless it may be said with positive assurance that the arbitration clause is not susceptible of an interpretation that covers the asserted dispute." But a "less settled question" to it was "the appropriate scope of judicial review of a specific arbitration award."

Yet how could that question possibly now be regarded as unsettled? Postaward intrusion into the merits of the collective bargaining dispute simply comes later in the time sequence; it is certainly no less invidious than the preaward ouster of the exercise of arbitral judgment. Vigorous preaward judicial scrutiny of "arbitrability" was the device fashioned in *Cutler-Hammer* (and disapproved in *Enterprise Wheel & Car*) to checkmate the prospect of an unfettered arbitrator disposing of a dispute on the merits. Ironically, of course, the only reason that a *Cutler-Hammer* court felt constrained to invent the prehearing "arbitrability" checkmate was because it had long since become settled doctrine that courts were foreclosed to enter into the realm of the merits once the arbitrator had been there. His award was nonreviewable for alleged errors of law or fact. Thus the *Torrington* reasoning simply upends history with its assertion that postaward reviewability is a "less settled question."

It is hardly surprising that some courts have felt that postaward "authority" was a better checkmate than prehearing "arbitrability." Initially, one could defer safely to the vagaries of arbitral judgment so long as after an award was made, a dissatisfied party could be saved by the reviewing court from the intemperateness and obtuseness of the person whom both parties had selected to arbitrate their dispute, but whose deplorable lack of judgment has now become so transparently evident to one of them. The problem for a court like *Torrington,* however, is that the "authority" reversal rationale is simply outdated. Its rejection was implicit in the disapproval by the Supreme Court of the *Cutler-Hammer* "arbitrability" reasoning. Moreover, the Court, as if anticipating a later judicial effort to switch from "arbitrability" to "authority" in order to get access to the merits, bluntly emphasized in *Enterprise Wheel & Car* that,

> The refusal of courts to review the merits of an arbitration award is the proper approach to arbitration under collective bargaining agreements. The federal policy of settling labor disputes by arbitration would be undermined if courts had the final say on the merits of the awards.

What could be more settled?

III

The appropriate scope of judicial review certainly appeared settled to the Fifth Circuit in the *Dallas Morning News* case. Circuit Judge John R. Brown revelled in the ecclesiastics of the newspaper composing room, in each of which there is a "chapel" with its own "hell box" immediately at hand. But he was by no means diverted from the realities of the bargaining situation involved. The chapel chairman and his assistant had gotten into a heated argument with the composing room foreman about whether a retired ITU man was entitled to slip up on the extra board and occupy a regular situation the following week. The climax was indeed worthy of the setting. The chapel chairman not only refused to remove the man's name from the printed proof sheet but also, according to the record, reared back and with a mighty oath hurled the printing form into the hell box to be melted into oblivion.

What a magnificent scene! It certainly impressed the federal district judge. Two less impressionable arbitrators had reinstated both men, in separate cases, reasoning that the charges of insubordination ought not be sustained since the men were actually engaged, not in an employment assignment, but in processing a grievance. But, as recounted by Judge Brown,

> Proving again that the infusion of judicial enthusiasm for arbitration in labor relations does not always keep the judiciary out of the act, both parties sought

the aid of the Court and neither is happy with the outcome. . . . On motions of summary judgment, the District Court, performing a Solomonic role, declined to deny enforcement as such, denied enforcement of the back pay award, dismissed the Employer's complaint, but declared that if the two discharged employees extended an appropriate written apology to the Employer, he would order reinstatement as to the future.

The Fifth Circuit reversed and remanded, directing that the arbitral award of reinstatement with back pay be enforced. The employer had inveighed against the arbitrators having undertaken to dispense their own brand (or brands) of industrial justice, putting great stress on the reasoning in *Torrington*. But the Fifth Circuit would have none of it and needed little space to say why.

> That decision seems to us to carry its own caveat. Couched as it is in terms of whether the bargaining agreement *"authorizes* the arbitrator to expend its express terms on the basis of the parties' prior practice," we think it has to be very carefully confined lest, under the guise of the arbitrator not having "authority" to arrive at his ill-founded conclusions of law or fact, or both, the reviewing-enforcing court takes over the arbitrator's function.

If the exercise of arbitral discretion is to be preserved against an onslaught of bargainers disappointed by particular awards—an insulation that must be made the norm—the courts are going to have to exercise a degree of self-discipline and rigor of analysis lamentably absent in *Torrington*, but manifested in the *Dallas Morning News* case. As Judge Brown observed in the latter,

> [W]e must take guard that . . . we do not succumb to the temptation to decide the merits of this controversy, not because of a difference with fact findings, but because we differ with what sound legal principles would compel from such fact findings.

As the Fifth Circuit recognized, it is no small matter of self-discipline for a judge who perceives what he believes to be error nonetheless to adhere to his "narrowly circumscribed function" in the review of arbitral awards. Principle requires that a judge refrain from taking hold of the award to correct its supposed error of fact or law. It should be a spur to the conscientious judge to exercise his doctrinally required self-effacement to observe how thoroughly wrongheaded about collective bargaining a Texas federal district court and a New York federal court of appeals can be in responding to moments of insight that each obviously felt to be lucid, even inspired.

IV

The inquiry into arbitrability, once launched in a court, often involves two distinct stages, first judicial, and then, arbitral. Most arbitrability issues are submitted directly to arbitrators without resort to a court. They require no special lens to view them other than that normally used by the arbitrator. But what of the situation when arbitration is initially resisted by one of the parties on the ground that the dispute is nonarbitrable, and arbitration is then ordered by a court or directed by the Labor Board? Does the order to arbitrate preclude a later holding by the arbitrator that the matter is not arbitrable?

Some courts have mistakenly thought so. Thus the Ninth Circuit has observed,

> [I]f the evidence before the court of purpose to exclude a particular claim from arbitration is not sufficiently forceful, the result is not . . . that the arbitrator must search for the truth at greater depth. The result, rather, is that the answer has been found and that the underlying dispute is arbitrable.

That observation misconceives what customarily happens after a court has ordered a party to arbitrate. It is not that the arbitrator plumbs the greater depth. It is rather that his search is focused altogether differently and is conducted by different means and for different purposes. He may well look at and listen to the same evidence as the judge. But he seeks and he hears echoes and nuances that are foreign to the courtroom.

The Supreme Court's consistent rationale has been that courts should refrain from adjudicating contractual issues more properly resolvable by arbitrators. This is because an arbitrator's "informed judgment" is different in composition from that of a judge's. "The ablest judge cannot be expected to bring the same experience and competence to bear upon the determination of a grievance, because he cannot be similarly informed." It would be curious indeed were the Court to hold that an arbitrator is precluded from exercising his expert judgment on the susceptibility to arbitral resolution of a particular dispute solely because a judge—drawing on a less informed sphere of judgment, insight and experience—had ordered the parties to submit their dispute to an arbitrator.

Yet the reasoning of an Illinois district court indicates how little one can take for granted in the area of judicial-arbitral interaction. That court had first ordered arbitration to proceed in a dispute over reemployment rights after a situs change, even though production at the new site was not commenced until after the contract had expired. At the same time, the court had ruled expressly that the question of arbitrability could be examined anew by the arbitrator.   After the district court's order was set aside by the Seventh Circuit, the Supreme Court reinstated the order in a one-sentence per curiam opinion that simply cited *John Wiley & Sons v. Livingston*.   On remand, however, the district court inexplicably reversed itself, reasoning that the Supreme Court had placed the responsibility for determining arbitrability solely on the district courts.   Those courts cannot "abdicate" that duty, it declared, nor can arbitrators be allowed to "second guess" the courts. This is so, the court warned, because there would otherwise be serious disruption in the proper allocation of function and responsibility between courts and arbitrators as formulated by the Supreme Court in *Wiley*. Curiously, the *Wiley* language that "the arbitrator would ordinarily remain free to reconsider the ground covered by the court insofar as it bore on the merits of the dispute," was taken by the court to relate only to questions of "procedural," and not to those of "substantive" arbitrability.   This is reminiscent of the turnabout we have earlier observed relative to "arbitrability" and "authority"; here, "substantive" issues were recognized as exclusive arbitral preserves long before *Wiley* identified procedural issues to be so.   *Sic transit lex!*

One would have thought it clear enough that an arbitrator does not "redetermine" the issue of arbitrability in these cases.   His is not a "second guess."   If it is a guess, it is a guess of first instance in its own proper sphere of judgment.   The first guess, the court's, is whether contract law indicates a legally cognizable agreement to engage in arbitration.   The Supreme Court has rigorously circumscribed that inquiry, as we have seen.   The second guess in point of sequence is actually a first guess in terms of function.   The arbitrator ascertains whether, in terms not of "law" but of the collective bargaining between the specific parties, this dispute ought properly to be resolved through arbitration.

The only question that a court must answer on the issue of arbitrability is whether the parties have manifested their intention that the grievance shall be submitted to decision through arbitration.   The court, confronted with a refusal to arbitrate, is called upon only to determine whether there is a contractual obligation to submit to arbitration the kind of claim made.   It is certainly not called upon, indeed it is expressly forbidden, to determine "substantive arbitrability"—which may be accurately translated as "the merits."   Substantive arbitrability involves the ascertainment of what is intended or what is just in the circumstances of collective bargaining between the parties.   In performing its assigned role, the court must, as Judge Thompson candidly acknowledged, resist the occupational temptation to decide the controversy. It must instead "be chary about embarking upon an interpretation of the substantive provisions . . . under the guise of interpreting the arbitration clause."

Courts must also be chary of interpreting or applying the procedural provisions of an agreement, especially if they cannot be resolved without touching the merits of the dispute. Most courts today will refer such questions even when they feel that it may be possible to isolate the procedural issue from the substantive. There is sound cause for that forbearance. First and foremost, there is the Shylock reality. It is well nigh impossible to excise a procedural question without materially—often drastically—altering the components of the substantive issue. Secondly, it is impossible (not just "well nigh" so) to have only a smidgeon of adjudication and still preserve the crucial necessity that grievances shall be resolved in as brief a timespan as possible. Structurally, the judicial apparatus involves a sequence of demand and notice, followed by a certain amount of formulaic huffing and puffing, before a court can properly arrive at the issue before it. The hazard of judicial receptivity to invitations to weigh justifications for refusals to arbitrate, under whatever contractual concept the refusals be rationalized, is that of inflicting *rigor mortis* on the grievance procedure; and instability and strife would be inevitable in frustrated gropings for relief. Avoidance of industrial breakdown is a prime goal of national labor policy. The prospect of such a breakdown alone should be enough to warrant judicial forbearance in construing collective bargaining agreements brought before the courts by refusals either to submit to arbitration or to abide by an arbitrator's decision.

"The courts therefore have no business weighing the merits of the grievance," the Supreme Court has admonished the judiciary,

> considering whether there is equity in a particular claim, or determining whether there is particular language in the written instrument which will support the claim. The agreement is to submit all grievances to arbitration, not merely those which the courts will deem meritorious.

V

One cannot consider puzzles of "arbitrability" and "authority" without also reflecting on the relationship of arbitration to the Labor Board. It is clear that either the Board or an arbitrator may dispose of a dispute before it without being forestalled by a court holding that jurisdiction properly belongs to the other. The Supreme Court in *Carey v. Westinghouse Electric Corporation, NLRB v. C & C Plywood Corporation,* and *NLRB v.*

Acme Industrial Company[5] has also established the sensible proposition that the Labor Board has the final say in disputes brought to it after an arbitrator has issued an award on the same facts. The Board-arbitrator relationship has also been defined by the Board's basic policy (with a certain amount of institutional deviation in specific cases) of "channelizing" disputes to arbitration, a kind of arbitrability allocation that makes good sense on the part of the Board. It tends to ameliorate disputes. And it helps cut the caseload overburdening (and overhanging) the Board. It is also apparent that the parties still retain the option to arbitrate rather than invoke either Board or court jurisdiction, so long as the Board's aid is not sought by a disaffected employee charging a statutory violation by either or both of the parties to the collective agreement. In the latter instance, it is clear that the Board should not be precluded from jurisdiction of the dispute by an express contractual preference for arbitration in the agreement.

A Arbitral Declaratory Relief

One major area of Board-arbitration—and, for that matter, of court-arbitration—interaction has not yet even opened up. In any refusal-to-bargain case that arises during the term of a collective bargaining agreement, thought should be given to the possibility of using arbitration as a form of declaratory relief. The party (typically the employer) to an agreement who wishes to launch an apparent change in working conditions could submit the contemplated change to arbitration for an advisory opinion on whether the proposal "changes" the agreement. Use of such declaratory opinions is bound to come and would be helpful. A recent study of the refusal-to-disclose cases reveals that considerable grief and many months of indecision and litigation can be saved in most cases if arbitral declaratory relief is available. If a party proceeds in a manner contractually sanctioned or even compelled by an arbitrator's award interpreting the collective agreement, the party's action is hardly apt to be held to constitute a section 8(a)(5) or 8(b)(3) violation.

---

[5] 385 U.S. 432 (1967). For an extensive analysis of the formulation of national labor policy in a specific narrowly defined pattern of problems, illustrative of the planning needed for effective interaction among courts, the Labor Board, and arbitrators, see my series of three articles in successive issues of the current volume of the *University of Pennsylvania Law Review: Blind Man's Bluff and the NOW-Problems of Apocrypha, Inc., and Local 711—Discovery Procedures in Collective Bargaining Disputes,* 116 U. PA. L. REV. 571 (1968); *The Accretion of Federal Power in Labor Arbitration—The Example of Arbitral Discovery,* 116 U. PA. L. REV. 755 (1968); *The Labor Board, the Courts and Arbitration—A Feasibility Study of Tribunal Interaction in Grievable Refusals to Disclose,* 116 U. PA. L. REV.—(1968) [hereinafter cited as *Feasibility Study*].

Aside from use in solving problems of possible Labor Act violations, there is interesting potential for arbitral declaratory relief generally, as for instance, in obtaining arbitral rulings *prior* to an employer's action rather than after it in discipline cases, promotions, jurisdictional disputes, subcontracting, and the like, where preaction declaratory awards might save employer monies and employee dislocation. But innovation is not the accustomed technique of courts. *General Foam Company v. IMW District 50* presents a good example of the kind of stultifying reasoning that could impede the development of arbitral declaratory relief. The contract involved in that case had a broad arbitration clause. Another contractual provision dealt with wildcat strikes and limited grievances in regard to these strikes to the issues of whether a disciplined employee "participated" in or was "responsible" for an "unauthorized" strike. The union requested th at the employer withhold the imposition of discipline on the charged individuals until the question of their personal responsibility or participation had been resolved. When the employer refused, the union sought to have that issue itself arbitrated. On motion to compel arbitration, the district court held the issue not to be arbitrable. The court concluded that the restrictive wildcat provision precluded arbitration of anything other than responsibility or participation. By no means was that conclusion compelled by any "plain" meaning. An interesting issue of suitable collective bargaining function was posed, and should not have been withheld from the arbitrator.

This was an innovative idea on the part of the union that deserved a closer look. The effect of the court's decision was to impose on the individual employee affected the economic burden of unemployment pending a determination of his guilt or innocence. Of course, the employer may have been concerned about the continuing unsettling presence of some blatant ringleaders or fearful about either creating an unhealthy atmosphere of condonation of the unauthorized activity, or of later being told that it had waived disciplinary rights in this or in other and later cases. These would all be legitimate concerns to be carefully assessed by an arbitrator in the circumstances of the particular case. There was no need for the court to prevent the issue being heard. An arbitrator should have had the opportunity to consider whether the case was a proper one in which to apply the interlocking arbitral provisions in a way that would both preserve the economic interests of the employer and avoid the full impact of the dispute being imposed on the individual employee. Unlike an act of moral turpitude or an act of serious affront to the employment relationship, a strike may be contractually sanctioned, even statutorily protected, and a wildcat strike can itself become transformed into a protected one precluding termination if the employer overreacts to it. Mistakes are made. After all, it is not uncommon even in the feline world for wildcats upon closer and less agitated examination to turn out to have been no more than somebody's restless alley cat.

B The Board's Reasoning in Cloverleaf

Surely the option of arbitral declaratory relief would often—even usually —be preferable to invoking the aid of the Labor Board, as the Board's action (or lack of it) in the *Cloverleaf Dairy* case well illustrates. In that case, the Board had before it a charge of violation by the employer's unilateral action of a provision of the collective bargaining agreement. The agreement contained an arbitration provision covering the alleged contractual violation. The trial examiner found as fact that the bargaining environment was aptly describable in terms that had been used in the Board's earlier *Crown Zellerbach* case: "a peaceful and what appears to be a wholly salutary employer-employee relationship."

The unilateral action had occurred on March 21, 1962. The union waited to do anything, of record at least, until filing its section 8(a)(5) charge on August 17, 1962. There was then a time lag of four months during which the complaint did not issue. The time lag may possibly have been due to a decision in the regional office to await the outcome of settlement negotiations between the parties, or to that office's efforts to nudge (but not shove) the parties into arbitration, as is the "channelizing" policy of the Board. In any event, the complaint issued on December 7, 1962, and the matter then proceeded relatively briskly to hearing on February 13 and 14, 1963, and to the issuance of the trial examiner's intermediate report on April 1, 1963.

At that point, Board proceedings and arbitration (had it been elected) were on somewhat the same time scale. Of course, at that point, also, an arbitral award would have been final and binding, not reviewable on the merits by any court except under rarely occurring circumstances (or before the *Torrington* panel in the Second Circuit).

But comes now the Board. The trial examiner's recommended order had issued on April 1, 1963. On July 30, 1963, the Board ordered the record reopened and it remanded the proceeding to the regional director for further hearing. It directed him to receive further evidence relevant to the disposition of a like issue in an earlier arbitral award under the parties' prior contract; matters relating to precontract negotiations in the case at hand; the intended scope of specific contract provisions; and whether the union had waived its right to bargain about the employer's action or had agreed "to submit such action to arbitration."

The trial examiner reopened the hearing on August 19, 1963, and took evidence. He reviewed an arbitral award that arose under the parties' 1959 contract, concluding that this earlier dispute, although concerning the same contractual provisions involved in the current dispute under the 1961 contract, was "clearly different" since the disputes were distinguishable. He found that both in the 1959 and 1961 negotiations "the Union strove to have written into the agreements provisions which, in effect, would have prohibited the employer from making any change in working conditions, or even using 'new types of equipment,' unless the Union approved." The union had also proposed to bar subcontracting "without the written consent of the Union." The employer "flatly" refused to yield to the demands on both occasions. The trial examiner further remarked that no party offered evidence bearing directly on the "scope" of the contractual provisions in issue. As to waiver and arbitration, no new evidence was adduced other than a union spokesman insisting that neither in the 1959 nor in the 1961 negotiations did the union concede that the employer had the authority to subcontract out work.

In his supplemental intermediate report the trial examiner, having had the parties before him for three days of hearing, reiterated his view that the bargaining setting was like that described in *Crown Zellerbach.* He conceded the NLRB General Counsel's assertions that the union had neither waived its right to bargain nor acquiesced in the employer's action, that the union had not sought arbitration, and that the Board undoubtedly had power under section 10(c) to prevent unfair labor practices despite the arbitration clause. Even so, he concluded that a "remedial collective bargaining order" was not appropriate. Accordingly, citing *Crown Zellerbach,* he again recommended that the complaint be dismissed in its entirety and observed:

> If the Board wishes to reverse its clearly stated policy in the cited case of not "policing collective-bargaining agreements," where "the parties have failed to utilize the contractual procedures established for bargaining concerning the interpretation and administration of their contract," and where there is a"background of peaceful and what appears to be a wholly salutary employer-employee relationship," then such reversal is within the province of the Board, not of the Trial Examiner.

Comes now the Board . . . again. Almost a year later, on June 30, 1964, it rejected the trial examiner's recommended "channelizing" of the dispute. Instead of promptly sending this union back to the grievance procedure, and therefore educating untold other unions and employers in like manner, it took hold and kept hold. In musty embrace it held on to this dispute for two years. Then it decided that the employer had violated section 8(a)(5) by its unilateral action in subcontracting.

The Labor Board's reasoning demonstrates the difference between the statutory standards it administers and the contractual ones to which arbitrators are responsive. Its analysis of the 1959 and 1961 bargaining efforts of the union to get a contractual curb on subcontracting indicated that the Board's concern was with whether the union had "waived" its statutory right to bargain. It plucked from the record of the reopened hearing supportive testimony that had been discounted by the trial examiner as "some evidence that at least in the 1959 negotiations the employer spokesman countered the union proposal by stating that such provisions [as had been advanced by the union to bar subcontracting] were unnecessary, the Union being fully protected by [another provision]." To the Board, the remark of the employer spokesman in 1959 became an assurance binding the employer, despite the fact that the union once again made the same proposal in 1961. Of the union's 1961 proposal the Board said it "was not pressed," and excusably so because of the employer's 1959 "assurance of protection." Its conclusion then was as follows:

> The fact that the Union attempted unsuccessfully to include in its contracts [for 1959 and 1961] a statement of its statutory right to bargain about changes in working conditions, coupled with a provision giving it a veto over institution of any such changes, is not evidence that the Union waived its statutory right to advance notice and opportunity to bargain about such changes. All that can be inferred from the negotiating history is that the Union has failed to achieve a contractual veto over subcontracting changes.

An arbitrator would have no direct concern about "waiver" or of "statutory right." His concern would be to reconstruct the parties' mutual intent so far as possible in the circumstances. In this case, it would seem likely that an arbitrator would have upheld the company action against the contractual challenge of the union because of the negotiation history. But the record is too scant, of course, to reach any assured conclusion.

The crucial point, in any event, is that the criteria are different. The Board has an added component in its equation—statutory policy—that is either absent or, if present, results in a markedly different concern for the arbitrator. The Board's statutory policy is both affirmative—to encourage certain kinds of conduct—and negative—to preclude other kinds. Its view of the private interests involved is not like that of an arbitrator. As to statutory policy, the arbitrator's concern, if he entertains it at all, is more apt to be for assurance that no statutory proscription is violated in the circumstances. But it must be observed that arbitrators are so desirous of effectuating the mutual intent of the parties that many of them at this point in the relationship between the Labor Board and arbitration will not take cognizance of statutory proscriptions if to do so would frustrate a clearly evidenced intention of the parties. Of course, the problem is entirely altered when an ambiguous situation comes under scrutiny. Statutory policies, affirmative as well as negative, provide a reasonable basis for finding an intent of the parties to abide by the policy rather than to violate it. But, once again, the arbitrator's search is for the mutual intent of the parties, not the propriety of their conduct as measured by statutory concepts.

This Board-arbitrator difference of function is a very basic one. It tells us much of value in formulating a sound division of responsibility between Board and arbitrator in terms of sequential, *not* concurrent jurisdiction. The arbitrator should be left free to construe the parties' intent as the first-instance tribunal. At that stage of their dispute, the only proper focus for his inquiry and their evidence is the reconstruction of their intent. Furthermore, that is the only needful focus at that point as far as the Board is concerned. The Board, after all, is not commissioned as an inquisitional tribunal to extirpate all evil, actual and suspect. Only after the arbitrator has reconstructed the parties' intent is it proper for the Board to allow itself to be summoned into action. Prior to that reconstruction the matter remains contractually irresolute. If there is conduct that might appear to be violative of the Act, the probabilities are that it will typically be rectified in arbitration as a contract violation, eliminating any need for the Board to intervene and thereby saving the resources of the Board for considering hard-core violations. This is so irrespective of how any particular arbitrator may conceive his duty to apply statutory policy. It is a bourgeois reality (fortunately) that most of us, if a choice is required, will elect to comply with a law rather than to violate it. It ought not surprise us, therefore, to find that collective bargainers have that inclination and, having it, are apt to write provisions intended to be in compliance with the law. It is reasonable thus to expect arbitration to winnow out most problems that could be construed by the Board to be statutory violations. Seeking and finding the parties' intent, the arbitrator will thus be apt to bar conduct which is offensive to the Act. But, it must be repeated, this is actually a function of coincidence. A social propensity to do the "right" or lawful thing makes likely the finding by an arbitrator of the parties' "right" or lawful intent in these circumstances.

Reliance on first-instance arbitration, as the Board ordered in *Crown Zellerbach* but erroneously countermanded in *Cloverleaf,* would thus tend to leave the Board free to deal more expeditiously with conduct that is the result of bad faith or blithe ignorance. The Board would then be reacting to a contractual "given," that is: Given that this conduct was contractually intended by both parties, does it constitute a pattern of action that should be held to violate the Act? An added benefit of this arbitrator-Board sequence would be that the Board, if it finds a violation, might fashion its remedy more responsively to the actual circumstances of the parties.

In *Cloverleaf*, of course, the Board rejected the trial examiner's repeated recommendation of that sequence. Was there some other overbalancing industrial reality that may have prompted it to do so?

Quite typically, the contract in that case subjected to arbitration only those disputes concerning "the interpretation or application of the terms of this Agreement." But, said the Board ingenuously, that is not what this complaint is about. It is about the denial to the union of a statutory right to be informed and consulted in advance so the union can bargain about changes in working conditions "in respects *not covered by the contract*." But how do we (or the Board) know the changes are *"not covered by the contract"*? Why, because analysis of the negotiations and the contractual provisions shows that the parties did not intend to cover this conduct contractually. But analysis by whom? Who is supposed to construe the parties' intent?

The Board reasoned that the conduct was not covered by the contract and, therefore, the union had a statutory right to bargain about it. That made the dispute "basically a disagreement over statutory rather than contractual obligations" so that

> the disposition of the controversy is quite clearly within the competency of the Board, and not of an arbitrator who would be without authority to grant the Union the particular redress it seeks and for which we provide . . . in our remedial order.

But this rationalization collapses when one question is asked: Why should the Board be so concerned to demonstrate here that it is really not interpreting the contract? The answer is simple. If the employer bargained for and got the right to subcontract in the circumstances involved in the case, and then did what he had a contractual right to do, how could it possibly be said that he acted "unilaterally" when he had done no more than what he had a bilaterally negotiated contractual right to do? Section 8(a)(5) cases of "unilateral" action all turn on a finding of whether the employer had a contractual right to do what he did. There can be no statutory question until the contractual one has been resolved. The statutory "right" is nonexistent unless and until a contractual right is found *not* to exist. *Cloverleaf*, then, was not the kind of situation of which it could be said, as the Court put it in *C & C Plywood*, that the Labor Board

> has not construed a labor agreement to determine the extent of the contractual rights. . . . It has done no more than merely enforce a statutory right. . . . *Thus*, the Board, in necessarily construing a labor agreement to decide this unfair labor practice case, has not exceeded the jurisdiction laid out for it by Congress.

That is a telegraphic *"thus."* The Court was cautioning the Board not to stray unnecessarily beyond the statutory compound in which it deals with industrial delinquents. The Board's procedures are ill suited and unadaptable to the world of established collective bargaining, peaceful but tough, economically aggrandizing but lawful.

Contemplate now what the Board did in *Cloverleaf*. It bailed out a union that had been unable to obtain a contractual advantage through bargaining in 1959 or 1961, or in an earlier arbitration in 1961 under the 1959 agreement. The union euchred the Board into a statutory reversal of the employer's subcontract and compelled Cloverleaf Dairy to give back pay to employees displaced two years earlier.

What initially may have prompted the union to file its charge with the Board instead of filing a grievance is unclear. It could be that in the five months that had elapsed between the employer's action and the filing of the charge, a negotiated time limit had run, barring the union's resort to arbitration. But no evidence of that appears. If it had "slept on its rights" to the dismay of its laid-off members, perhaps it might have sought to recoup prestige by filing the charge. If instead it had been deceived by the employer's delaying tactics, and could show that it had been led unsuspectingly down the path by an employer who then slammed the gate shut, arbitrators would have had little difficulty brushing aside that employer's lament of limitation. Indeed, it is precisely because an arbitrator *can* cut through this kind of lament that under section 301 and *Wiley*, the deception question is committed to an arbitrator rather than a court. Thus whether the union erred or was bilked, the trial examiner's recommendation to arbitrate could still have been effectuated properly and protectively back in April, 1963. By tolerating that degree of casualness about the grievance procedure the Board ill serves industrial relations. Surely one would not want to think that the union felt that it had a better chance to reap an unwarranted harvest before a gullible Board than before a skeptical arbitrator.

There is another aspect to this examination of the Board's exercise of institutional expertise in the *Cloverleaf* case. The Board observed, one would have to say somewhat naively, that an arbitrator in 1961 had prevented the union from gaining in arbitration what it had failed to obtain in negotiation. For that is really the import of what happened in 1961, as one gets it from the Board's own account. The arbitrator in 1961 (under the 1959 contract) had determined that the employer's conduct was not barred by the agreement. The Board solemnly concluded from the outcome of the 1961 arbitration that,

> [I]t is highly conjectural that arbitration in this case, even if resorted to by the Union, could have effectively disposed of the basic issue in this case—whether Respondent acted lawfully in engaging in the unilateral actions to which the instant complaint is addressed.

There are enough reasoning circularities in that conclusion to wire up a swinging mobile! "Effectively disposed of"? It would surely have been "effectively disposed of" had the second arbitrator concluded that the employer had a *bilateral* power conferred to act as it did. Labeling the act "unilateral" doesn't alter its consensual nature. The "basic issue" is not converted into a statutory one simply by saying it is. A contractual answer in these allegedly "unilateral" cases is required to tell us if next we must reckon a statutory question. The Board can hardly acknowledge a bilaterally created contractual power that authorizes the employer to perform certain acts, but conclude that the employer exercised it "unilaterally," which is to say, wrongfully.

But then, its reasoning in *Cloverleaf* is not particularly reassuring in this regard. Indeed, with a perfectly straight and earnest face the Board observes that,

> [I]f we are to accept Respondent's premise that the 1961 dispute and the instant one are "precisely the same," it would follow that resort to arbitration would have been futile on the issue of Respondent's right to act unilaterally. For, as interpreted by the arbitrator, the contract neither covers this type of dispute nor provides any remedy for it.

The first sentence is true enough. But it says far more than the writer intended. It is true that it would normally be futile for the union to importune a second arbitrator—once a first had already ruled against it on the same issue—to find that the agreement precludes the employer's action. But the second sentence states a conclusion that doesn't remotely follow from the first. Quite the converse; as interpreted by the arbitrator the conduct in dispute was certainly "covered" by the contract, which is to say, was allowable. That is, it was until the Board had finished with its "interpretation."

There is one final non sequitur in this Labor Board opinion, an opinion that must certainly be regarded as something of a minor epic in the history of non sequiturs. The Board insisted (and this is a thought that runs throughout a number of its opinions in this area) that,

> It is quite clear that the Board is not precluded from resolving an unfair labor practice issue, which may call for appropriate relief under the Act, simply because as an incident to such violation it may be necessary to construe the scope of a contract which an arbitrator is also empowered to construe.

Having thus asserted its statutory power, the Board added a final and somewhat regal conclusion.

> Nor in our view is the situation presented by this case such as to move us in the exercise of our discretion to withhold our own remedial processes in deference to the arbitration processes the parties have agreed upon for the settlement of contract disputes.

Indeed, the Board rejected the trial examiner's dismissal recommendation on the ground that to do so here "would be an unwarranted abuse of our statutory responsibilities."

Certainly section 10(a) provides that "[t]his power shall not be affected by any other means of adjustment or prevention that has been or may be established by agreement, law, or otherwise." But the Board's reliance, indeed its repeated insistence, on this undoubted "power" misses the point implicit in the phrase, "appropriate relief under the Act." That point is not *power;* it is *prudence.* The Labor Board really should no longer feel compelled to defend its manliness in the bruising arena of industrial combat. Unlike the thirties and early forties, everyone concedes (even if some oppose) its power today. In fact, on balance the Labor Board is widely regarded, and properly so, as by far the most effective federal regulatory agency that came out of the New Deal era. The quality of the recurrent political attack upon it emphasizes that reality repeatedly. It has three decades behind it, and more ahead so long as it functions faithful to its history of realistic, effective administration. It must constantly generate and then apply administrative expertise, not simply exercise its statutory muscle.

How did the Board's handling of the *Cloverleaf* case affect the relationship of the bargaining parties? Without a doubt it exacerbated it. The Board took a healable lesion and made of it an open wound, a chronic source of irritation thenceforth to those parties. The federal apparatus is simply too formidable to achieve the immediate first-aid, send-them-back-to-duty treatment that is needed and available in practically all labor disputes arising under collective agreements. Unfortunately, the Board appears in this case not unlike a surgeon who sees the glint of steel in every minor malfunction.

In addition to being a classic of question-begging reasoning, the Board's decision and analysis is an odd manifestation of the kind of *Cutler-Hammer* displacement of arbitration on the merits that was disapproved specifically by the Supreme Court in 1960 in the *Steelworker Cases* and was by no means countenanced on the part of the Labor Board by the Court in *Acme Industrial* and *C & C Plywood*.

Finally, just what were the "remedial processes" that the Board in *Cloverleaf* was moved not to withhold? What did it actually do? First, of course, a major characteristic of the Board's "remedial processes" is the consumption of time. The trial examiner pointed it in the right direction a short four months after the dispute had ripened to the point of issuance of a complaint. But the Board didn't see it his way. After a lapse of another thirteen months, what did the Board add that an arbitrator couldn't have added a year and a half earlier? For one thing, it added the prospect of close judicial review of its own decision on the merits, although *Cloverleaf* itself was not appealed. An arbitrator's award would not normally have added that dimension of review except under rather extreme circumstances. When review of a Board decision does occur, and it occurs in almost half of the Board's orders, it typically adds another thirteen months to the dispute. The average in the Board's refusal-to-disclose cases runs twenty-nine months to get a court of appeals enforcement order; it takes seventeen months to get a Board order.

In the meantime, the specifics of the Board's order were: First, ordering the employer, "upon request of the union ... to restore the *status quo ante*," in addition to ordering the employer to cease and desist from refusing to bargain with the union by "unilaterally subcontracting" unit work, as well as from engaging in a string of generally described acts violative of sections 8(a)(1), (2), (3), and (5); second, ordering the employer, upon request of the union, to bargain about subcontracting unit work; third, upon request of the union, ordering the employer to offer to reestablish the same or equivalent milk routes for five named employees; fourth, ordering the employer to preserve its payroll records so that lost earnings could be computed by Board agents; fifth, requiring the employer to post a notice saying that it will do all the things it was ordered to do and will refrain henceforth from doing the things it was ordered not to do; lastly, requiring the employer to notify the regional director within ten days of what steps it has taken to comply with the provisions of its order.

Of these orders, the Board declared that one of its reasons for not deferring to arbitration was that issuing such orders would not be "within the competency" of an arbitrator. It is somewhat difficult, however, to see what is all that remedially unique about its order that could not be accomplished by an arbitrator. After all—and it is vital to remember—the Board's order is no more self-executing than is the arbitrator's. A court must enforce either, and it is the contempt power of the court that assures compliance. Both the Board and an arbitrator would have to respond anew to a fresh charge of violation arising out of later acts relative to subcontracting. Even the Board's "eat-crow" notice, required to be posted by the employer on his bulletin boards, is a remedial device not unknown to arbitration and certainly within its competence. An order to preserve payroll records, were it to appear needed, is manifestly within the "powers" of an arbitrator.

This is a case, I repeat, that well illustrates the winnowing potential of arbitration relative to the Board's coping with the rising tide of charged statutory violations. The odds are high that an arbitrator would have upheld the company had the trial examiner's repeated recommendation that the matter be returned to the parties for arbitration prevailed. Arbitration would have determined the absence of any "unilateral" act, contractually viewed. Thus there could have been no statutory issue so long as the Board is deemed or regards itself as bound by an arbitrator's contractual finding not itself involving any matter of statutory interpretation or supervening statutory or constitutional policy. Surely in that situation the Board has no business setting aside an arbitrator's affirmance of an existent contractual intent. It is one thing to acknowledge the necessity for the Board to interpret an uninterpreted contract in order to resolve a statutory question. It is quite another to condone the Board thrusting aside a prior arbitral interpretation in order, actually, to create the precise conditions within which it can only then conclude that there is a statutory violation. The latter would be countenancing strawman reasoning *par excellence!*

Had the arbitrator in *Cloverleaf* upheld the union, however, he would many months earlier have ordered effective relief. Furthermore, if there were unusual circumstances that indicated that the employer's action constituted an attack upon the integrity of the bargaining unit, the fact that the union had prevailed in the arbitration would certainly not have prevented it from also filing section 8(a)(1), (2), (3), and (5) unfair labor practice charges to invoke governmental condemnation of the wrongful activities and secure Board remedies then appropriate. The point is, however, those circumstances were not even hinted at in *Cloverleaf.*

VI

In our customary pragmatic way, we are working out an important structure of interactive decision-making in the resolution of labor disputes. As a voluntary tribunal of considerable functional utility and widespread usage, those who administer it being chosen jointly by the disputants, arbitration is being integrated with federal and state courts and the National Labor Relations Board. That integration to a very considerable extent is being accomplished by thousands of decisions of hundreds of labor arbitrators in disputes in which the parties seek neither judicial nor administrative intervention before or after the fact of their joint and willing submission to arbitration. At the same time, labor arbitrators are themselves observably sensitive to the evolution of judicial and administrative concepts of public policy that may have import in the disposition of the disputes which they are called upon to resolve.

It is inevitable that courts and the Labor Board will repeatedly experience the urge to reverse when confronted with the supposed procedural or substantive gaffs of an arbitrator. But even assuming that the judicial lens focuses accurately on supposed arbitral error, it is a mark of professional competence that the urge to reverse be steadfastly resisted. In the evolution of this interactive decisional structure it is far more important that the lines of responsibility based on institutional competence be established and maintained than what may be regarded as an error be corrected. There is the further consideration, after all—shifting the lens from the judicial to the arbitral—that the arbitrator's award may actually not be a mistake. And, in any event, a truly disadvantaged party can fashion his own remedy at the bargaining table.

In the final analysis, collective bargaining is a voluntary system of checks and balances that generates its own methods of adjustment, including the form and extent that its grievance procedures will take. It is preferable that the tribunal of the parties should be left almost entirely free to develop its own procedural and substantive responses to the needs of the bargainers. Arbitration is readily subject to the parties' will in recurrent negotiations and is not impaled on the cumbersome timespan that afflicts proceedings before both the courts and the Labor Board. To determine and then to enforce the parties' voluntarily undertaken commitment to submit disputes to arbitration, but no more, is all that should be expected of the courts (or by them) in those infrequent instances when their aid is invoked. As for the Labor Board, were it consistently to "channelize" grievances to arbitration, and to honor the contractual determinations of arbitrators rather than unnecessarily superimposing its own, its statutory jurisdiction would not only remain unimpaired—it would be reinforced. And the national labor policy would be the better served.

Selected
bibliography

For reader convenience the bibliography of selected references on arbitration is divided into the following ten categories:

1 Books
2 Articles in periodicals and journals
3 Law review articles
4 Articles on state and international arbitration practices
5 Symposia and conferences on arbitration
6 Proceedings of the National Academy of Arbitrators
7 Standard arbitration reporting services
8 Special references for the arbitrator
9 Arbitration bibliographies
10 Dissertations on arbitration

Books

Aaron, Benjamin (ed.): *Dispute Settlement Procedures in Five Western Countries,* UCLA, Institute of Industrial Relations, 1969.

Abersold, John R., and Wayne E. Howard: *Cases in Labor Relation: An Arbitration Experience,* Prentice-Hall, Inc., Englewood Cliffs, N.J., 1967.

Beatty, Marion: *Labor-Management Arbitration Manual,* Eppler, New York, 1960.

Bernstein, Irving: *Arbitration of Wages,* University of California Press, Berkeley, Calif., 1954.

Bernstein, Merton C.: *Private Dispute Settlement,* The Free Press, New York, 1968.

Bogardus, J. F.: *Industrial Arbitration in the Book and Job Printing Industry of New York City,* University of Pennsylvania Press, Philadelphia, 1934.

Brandt, Floyd S., and Carroll R. Daugherty: *Conflict and Cooperation—Cases in Labor Management Behavior,* R. D. Irwin, Homewood, Ill., 1967.

Braun, Kurt: *Labor Disputes and Their Settlement,* The Johns Hopkins Press, Baltimore, 1955.

Chandler, Margaret K.: *Management Rights and Union Interests,* McGraw-Hill Book Company, New York, 1964.

Ching, Cyrus Stuart: *Review and Reflections, A Half Century of Labor Relations,* B. C. Forbes, New York, 1953.

Copelof, Maxwell: *Management-Union Arbitration: A Record of Cases, Methods, Decisions,* Harper & Row, Publishers, Incorporated, New York, 1948.

Cox, Archibald: *Law and the National Labor Policy,* UCLA Institute of Industrial Relations, Los Angeles, 1960.

Cox, Archibald, and Derek Bok: *Cases and Materials on Labor Law,* 6th ed., The Foundation Press, Brooklyn, 1965.

Elkouri, Frank, and Edna A. Elkouri: *How Arbitration Works,* BNA, Inc., Washington, D.C., 1960.

Elliott, Shelden D.: *Arbitration Awards, Opinions and Problems,* New York University School of Law, New York, 1968.

Elliott, S. D.: *Materials and Cases on Arbitration,* vol. 1, The Foundation Press, Inc., Mineola, N.Y., 1968.

Essentials of Labor Arbitration, a Handbook for the Guidance of Management, Commerce and Industry Association of New York, 1967.

Fleming, R. W.: *The Labor Arbitration Process,* The University of Illinois Press, Urbana, Ill., 1965.

Gregory, Charles O.: *Labor and Law,* W. W. Norton & Company, Inc., New York, 1961.

Hays, Paul Raymond: *Labor Arbitration: A Dissenting View,* Yale University Press, New Haven, Conn., 1966.

How to Minimize the Arbitration Risk, Personnel Journal, Swarthmore, Pennsylvania, 1962.

Jones, D. L.: *Arbitration and Industrial Discipline,* Bureau of Industrial Relations, Ann Arbor, Mich., 1961.

Kagel, Sam: *Anatomy of a Labor Arbitration,* BNA, Inc., Washington, D.C., 1961.

Katz, Milton: *The Relevance of International Adjudication,* Harvard University Press, Cambridge, Mass., 1968.

Kellor, Frances: *Arbitration in Action,* Harper & Row, Publishers, Incorporated, New York, 1941.

Kellor, F.: *American Arbitration,* Harper & Row, Publishers, Incorporated, New York, 1948.

Kennedy, Thomas: *Effective Labor Arbitration: The Impartial Chairmanship of the Full-Fashioned Hosiery Industry,* University of Pennsylvania Press, Philadelphia, 1948.

Kuhn, Alfred: *Arbitration in Transit,* University of Pennsylvania Press, Philadelphia, 1952.

Kuhn, James W.: *Bargaining in Grievance Settlement,* Columbia University Press, New York, 1961.

Lapp, John A.: *How to Handle Labor Grievances,* National Foreman's Institute, Inc., New York, 1945.

Lapp, J. A.: *Labor Arbitration: Principles and Procedures,* National Foreman's Institute, Inc., New York, 1942.

Mabry, Bevars D.: *Cases in Labor Relations and Collective Bargaining,* The Ronald Press Company, New York, 1966.

Morgan, Rita: *Arbitration in the Men's Clothing Industry in New York City,* Teachers College, Columbia University, New York, 1940.

Phelps, Orme: *Discipline and Discharge in the Unionized Firm,* University of California Press, Berkeley, Calif., 1959.

Schoen, Sterling H., and Raymond L. Hilgert: *Cases in Collective Bargaining and Industrial Relations: A Decisional Approach,* R. D. Irwin, Homewood, Ill., 1969.

Shulman, Harry, and Neil W. Chamberlain: *Cases on Labor Relations,* The Foundation Press, Inc., Brooklyn, 1949.

Siegel, Boaz: *Proving Your Arbitration Case,* BNA, Inc., Washington, D.C., 1961.

Stessin, Lawrence: *Employee Discipline,* BNA, Inc., Washington, D.C., 1960.

Stessin, L.: *The Practice of Personnel in Industrial Relations: A Casebook,* Pitman Publishing Corporation, New York, 1964.

Stone, Morris: *Managerial Freedom and Job Security,* Harper & Row, Publishers, Incorporated, New York, 1964. (From cases of the American Arbitration Association)

Stone, M.: *Labor-Management Contracts at Work* (An Analysis of Awards Reported by the American Arbitration Association), Harper & Row, Publishers, Incorporated, New York, 1961.

Stone, M.: *Labor Grievances and Decisions,* Harper & Row, Publishers, Incorporated, New York, 1965.

Sturges, Wesley A.: *Cases on Arbitration Law,* Matthew Bender & Co., Albany, New York, 1953.

Tracy, Estelle R. (ed.): *Arbitration Cases in Public Employment,* American Arbitration Association, 1969.

Trotta, Maurice S.: *Labor Arbitration: Principles, Practices, Issues,* Simmons-Boardman Publishing Corporation, New York, 1961.

Updegraff, Clarence M., and W. McCoy: *Arbitration of Labor Disputes,* 2d ed., BNA, Inc., Washington, D. C., 1961.

U.S. Department of Labor, *A Guide to Industrial Relations in the U.S., No. 19 Voluntary Arbitration,* Bureau of Labor Statistics, December, 1956.

Witte, Edwin E.: *Historical Survey of Labor Arbitration,* University of Pennsylvania Press, Philadelphia, 1952.

Woods, H. D. (ed.): *Patterns of Industrial Dispute Settlement in Five Canadian Industries,* McGill University, Industrial Relations Center, Montreal, 1958.

Articles in Periodicals and Journals

Aaron, Benjamin: "Labor Arbitration and Its Critics," *Labor Law Journal,* vol. 10, no. 9, September, 1959, pp. 605–610.

Aaron, B.: "The State of Labor Relations Law, A Double Arbitration Standard," *Monthly Labor Review,* vol. 89, no. 12, December, 1966, pp. 1387–1388.

Aaron, B.: "The Use of Arbitration on the West Coast," *Monthly Labor Review,* vol. 82, no. 5, May 1959, pp. 543–546.

Abernethy, B. R.: "An Arbitrator Speaks to the Parties on Presentation of a Case," *Arbitration Journal,* vol. 12, no. 1, 1957, pp. 3–13.

Baer, W. E.: "Precedent Value of Arbitration Awards," *Personnel Journal,* vol. 45, September, 1966, pp. 484–488.

Bailer, Lloyd H.: "The Discipline Issue in Arbitration: Individual Differences and Shop Practices," *Labor Law Journal,* vol. 15, no. 9, September, 1964, pp. 567–570.

Bain, Trevor: "Arbitration: An Alternative to Crisis Bargaining," *Arbitration Journal,* vol. 23, no. 2, 1968, pp. 103–109.

Bangs, John R., and Frank K. Fraser: "The Impact of the Courts on Arbitration and the Right to Manage," *California Management Review,* vol. 51, Summer, 1963, pp. 51–60.

Beatty, Marion: "Arbitration of Unfair Labor Practice Disputes," *Arbitration Journal,* vol. 14, no. 4, 1959, pp. 180–191.

Berger, Harriet: "The Grievance Process in the Philadelphia Public Service," *Industrial and Labor Relations Review,* vol. 13, no. 4, July, 1960, pp. 568–580.

Bernstein, Irving: "Recent Legislative Developments Affecting Mediation and Arbitration," *Industrial and Labor Relations Review,* vol. 1, no. 3, April, 1948, pp. 406–420.

Bloch, Howard R.: "Arbitration as a Tool for Settling a Major Industrial Dispute," *Personnel Journal,* vol. 48, February, 1969, pp. 92–101.

Bloch, Richard I.: "The NLRB and Arbitration: Is the Board's Expanding Jurisdiction Justified?" *Labor Law Journal,* vol. 19, no. 10, October, 1968, pp. 640–662.

Bodle, George E.: "New Techniques and Remedies in the Grievance and Arbitration Process," *Proceedings of the Fifteenth Annual Institute on Labor Law,* The Southwestern Legal Foundation, 1969, pp. 199–229.

Brown, Howard J.: "Some Comments on Arbitration in the Newspaper Industry," *Journalism Quarterly,* vol. 34, 1957, pp. 19–30.

Burstein, Herbert: "The U.S. Arbitration Act: A Re-evaluation," *Labor Law Journal,* vol. 9, no. 7, July, 1958, pp. 511–520.

Cahn, Sidney L.: "One Way to Reduce the Cost of Arbitration," *Labor Law Journal,* vol. 10, no. 9, September, 1959, pp. 611–614.

Clark, S. G., Jr.: "Interplay between the LMRA and Arbitration: Concurrent Unfair Labor Practices and Grievances," *Labor Law Journal,* vol. 16, no. 7, July, 1965, pp. 412–422.

Coulson, Robert, "Experiments in Labor Arbitration," *Labor Law Journal,* vol. 17, no. 5, May, 1966, pp. 259–265.

Coulson, R.: "Labor Arbitration: The Insecure Profession?" *Labor Law Journal,* vol. 18, no. 6, June, 1967, pp. 336–343.

Coulson, R.: "Spring Checkup on Labor Arbitration Procedure," *Labor Law Journal,* vol. 16, no. 5, May, 1965, pp. 259–265.

Cushman, Bernard: "Voluntary Arbitration of New Contract Terms—A Forum in Search of a Dispute," *Labor Law Journal,* vol. 16, no. 12, December 1965, pp. 765–777.

Cushman, Kenneth M.: "Arbitration and State Law," *Arbitration Journal,* vol. 23, no. 3, 1968, pp. 162–174.

Davey, Harold W.: "Hazards in Labor Arbitration," *Industrial and Labor Relations Review,* vol. 1, no. 3, April, 1948, pp. 386–405.

Davey, H. W.: "Labor Arbitration: A Current Appraisal," *Industrial and Labor Relations Review,* vol. 9, no. 1, October, 1955, pp. 85–94.

Davey, H. W.: "The Arbitrator Views the Industrial Engineer," *California Management Review,* vol. 7, no. 1, Fall, 1964, pp. 23–30.

Davey, H. W.: "The Arbitrator Speaks on Discharge and Discipline," *Arbitration Journal,* vol. 17, no. 2, 1962, pp. 97–104.

Davis, Pearce: "Arbitration of Work Rules Disputes," *Arbitration Journal,* vol. 16, no. 2, 1961, pp. 51–60.

Daykin, Walter: "Arbitration of Work Rules Disputes," *Arbitration Journal,* vol. 18, no. 1, 1963, pp. 36–45.

DeVyver, Frank T.: "Labor Arbitration after 25 Years," *Southern Economic Journal,* vol. 28, January, 1962, pp. 235–245.

Doyle, C. T.: "Past Practice as a Standard in Arbitration," *Personnel,* vol. 39, May, 1962, pp. 66–69.

Doyle, C. T.: "Precedent Values of Labor Arbitration Awards," *Personnel Journal,* vol. 42, February, 1963, pp. 66–69.

Eaton, William: "Labor Arbitration in the San Francisco Bay Area," *Arbitration Journal,* vol. 22, no. 2, 1967, pp. 93–113.

Edelman, Milton, and Irving Kovarsky: "Featherbedding: Law and Arbitration," *Labor Law Journal,* vol. 10, no. 4, April, 1959, pp. 233–246.

Elson, Alex: "The Supreme Court and the 'Private' World of Arbitration," *Arbitration Journal,* vol. 18, no. 2, 1963, pp. 65–76.

Feldacker, Bruce: "Processing Grievances When Bargaining Units Are Combined: Conflict with Doctrine of Exclusive Representation?" *Labor Law Journal,* vol. 18, no. 11, November, 1967, pp. 649–664.

Fisher, Robert W.: "Arbitration in Discharge Cases," *Monthly Labor Review,* vol. 19, no. 10, October, 1968, pp. 1–5.

Fisher, R. W.: "How Garnisheed Workers Fare Under Arbitration," *Monthly Labor Review,* vol. 90, no. 5, May, 1967, pp. 1–6.

Fleming, Robben W.: "The Changing Duty to Bargain," *Labor Law Journal,* vol. 14, no. 4, April, 1963, pp. 297–312.

Foster, Howard G.: "Disloyalty to the Employer," *Arbitration Journal,* vol. 20, no. 3, 1965, pp. 157–167.

Givry, J. De, and J. Schregle: "The Role of the Third Party in the Settlement of Grievances at the Plant Level," *International Labour Review,* vol. 97, no. 4, April, 1968, pp. 333–350.

Glick, Leslie Alan: "Bias, Fraud, Misconduct and Partiality of the Arbitrator," *Arbitration Journal,* vol. 22, no. 3, 1967, pp. 161–172.

Goldberg, Arthur J.: "A Supreme Court Justice Looks at Arbitration," *Arbitration Journal,* vol. 20, no. 1, 1965, pp. 13–19.

Gross, James A.: "Value Judgments in the Decisions of Labor Arbitrators," *Industrial and Labor Relations Review,* vol. 21, no. 1, October, 1967, pp. 55–72.

Hageman, Carl H.: "The Pros and Cons of Labor Arbitration," *Personnel,* vol. 37, May/June, 1960, pp. 27–35.

Handsaker, Morrison: "Arbitration of Discipline Cases," *Personnel Journal,* vol. 46, March, 1967, pp. 153–156.

Handsaker, M.: "Grievance Arbitration and Mediated Settlements," *Labor Law Journal,* vol. 17, no. 10, October, 1966, pp. 579–583.

Harris, Philip: "Arbitration and the Selection and Retention of Supervisors," *Personnel Journal,* vol. 46, April, 1967, pp. 231–237.

Harris, P.: "Labor Arbitration and Technological Innovation," *Labor Law Journal,* vol. 17, no. 11, November, 1966, pp. 664–670.

Harris, P.: "The Arbitration Process and the Disciplining of Supervisors," *Labor Law Journal,* vol. 16, no. 11, November, 1965, pp. 679–684.

Heimbach, William: "Cooperation and Arbitration in the Federal Service," *Monthly Labor Review,* vol. 89, no. 6, June, 1966, p. 614.

Hennigan, W. K.: "Arbitration: A Dangerous Game," *Personnel Administration,* vol. 30, November, 1967, pp. 52–54.

Herzog, Paul M. and Morris Stone: "Voluntary Labor Arbitration in the United States," *International Labour Review,* vol. 82, October, 1960, pp. 301–326.

Howard, Wayne E.: "Criteria of Ability," *Arbitration Journal,* vol. 13, no. 4, 1958, pp. 179–196.

Howard, W. E.: "The Interpretation of Ability by Labor-Management Arbitrators," *Arbitration Journal,* vol. 14, no. 3, 1959, pp. 117–132.

Howard, W. E.: "Seniority Rights and Trial Periods," *Arbitration Journal,* vol. 15, no. 2, 1960, pp. 51–64.

Howlett, Robert G.: "State Labor Relations Boards and Arbitrators," *Labor Law Journal,* vol. 17, no. 1, January, 1966, pp. 27–35.

Howlett, Robert G.: "Arbitration in the Public Sector," *Proceedings of the Fifteenth Annual Institute on Labor Law,* The Southwestern Legal Foundation, 1969, pp. 231–275.

Isaacson, William J.: "Labor Arbitration in State Courts," *Arbitration Journal,* vol. 12, no. 4, 1957, pp. 179–190.

Jensen, Vernon H.: "Dispute Settlement in the New York Longshore Industry," *Industrial and Labor Relations Review,* vol. 10, no. 4, July, 1957, pp. 588–608.

Johnson, Fred H.: "Contrasts in the Role of the Arbitrator and of the Mediator," *Labor Law Journal,* vol. 9, no. 10, October, 1958, pp. 769–776.

Jones, E. A.: "Arbitration and the Dilemma of Possible Error," *Labor Law Journal,* vol. 11, no. 11, November, 1960, pp. 1023–1030.

Jones, E. A., Jr.: "The Schizophrenic World of Labor Arbitration and Mr. Q. Vadis, Arbitrator," *Proceedings of the Fourteenth Annual Institute on Labor Law,* The Southwestern Legal Foundation, 1968, pp. 251–302.

Justin, Jules J.: "Arbitration under the Labor Contract—Its Nature, Function and Use," American Management Association, 1951.

Justin, Jules J.: "How to Preserve Management's Rights under the Labor Contract," *Labor Law Journal,* vol. 11, no. 3, March, 1960, pp. 189–215.

Kennedy, Van Dusen: "Arbitration in the San Francisco Hotel and Restaurant Industries," *Wharton School of Finance,* University of Pennsylvania Press, Philadelphia, 1952.

Killingsworth, Charles C.: "Grievance Adjudication in Public Employment," *Arbitration Journal,* vol. 13, no. 1, 1958, pp. 3–15.

Krislov, Joseph and Jacob Schmulowitz: "Grievance Arbitration in State and Local Government Units," *Arbitration Journal,* vol. 18, no. 3, 1963, pp. 171–178.

Lafferty, Linda E.: "Conflict of Medical Evidence in Labor Arbitration," *Arbitration Journal,* vol. 23, no. 3, 1968, pp. 175–183.

Leahy, William H.: "Arbitration, Union Stewards, and Wildcat Strikes," *Arbitration Journal,* vol. 24, no. 1, 1969, pp. 50–58.

Leonard, John W.: "Discipline for Off-the-Job Activities," *Monthly Labor Review,* vol. 91, no. 10, October, 1968, pp. 5–11.

Lockwood, David: "Arbitration in Industrial Conflict," *British Journal of Sociology,* vol. 6, December, 1955, pp. 335–347.

Loomis, Walter P., Jr., and Joseph Herman: "Management's Reserved Rights and the NLRB—An Employer's View," *Labor Law Journal,* vol. 19, no. 11, November, 1968, pp. 695–724.

Luskin, Bert L.: "Arbitration Comes of Age," *Third Annual Arbitration Conference,* University of Massachusetts, Labor Relations and Research Center, 1967.

Matthews, Herb: "Employer Initiated Grievances in the Collective Bargaining Contract: A Friendly View," *Labor Law Journal,* vol. 18, no. 6, June, 1967, pp. 360–368.

McDermott, Thomas J.: "Arbitrability: The Courts versus the Arbitrator," *Arbitration Journal,* vol. 23, no. 1, 1968, pp. 18–38.

McDermott, Thomas J.: "Enforcing No-strike Provisions via Arbitration," *Labor Law Journal,* vol. 18, no. 10, October, 1967, pp. 579–587.

McCulloch, Frank W.: "Past, Present and Future Remedies under Section 8 (a) (5) of the NLRA," *Labor Law Journal,* vol. 19, no. 3, March, 1968, pp. 131–142.

McKelvey, Jean T.: "Fact Finding in Public Employment Disputes: Promise or Illusion?" *Industrial and Labor Relations Review,* vol. 22, no. 4, July, 1969, pp. 528–543.

McLaughlin, Richard P.: "Custom and Past Practice in Labor Arbitration," *Arbitration Journal,* vol. 18, no. 4, 1963, pp. 205–228.

Meyers, Frederic: "The Task of the Labor Arbitrator," *Personnel Administration,* vol. 22, November/December, 1959, pp. 24–30.

Miller, Richard V.: "Arbitration of Reopened Wage Disputes," *Arbitration Journal,* vol. 22, no. 1, 1967, pp. 24–30.

Moore, Ernestine, and James Nix: "Arbitration Provisions in Collective Agreements," *Monthly Labor Review,* vol. 76, no. 3, March, 1953, pp. 261–266.

Morgan, C. Baird, Jr.: "Adequacy of Collective Bargaining in Resolving the Problem of Job Security and Technological Change," *Labor Law Journal,* vol. 16, no. 2, Fall, 1965, pp. 87–99.

Morvant, R. H.: "The Nature of Industrial Arbitration," *Labor Law Journal,* vol. 12, no. 11, November, 1961, pp. 1042–1052.

Myers, Morris L.: "Duplication of Arbitration with Other Litigation," *Labor Law Journal,* vol. 18, no. 2, February, 1967, pp. 103–111.

Northrup, Herbert R., and Richard L. Rowan: "Arbitration and Collective Bargaining—An Analysis of State Experience," *Labor Law Journal,* vol. 14, no. 2, February, 1963, pp. 178–191.

Northrup, Herbert R., and Mark L. Kahn: "Railroad Grievance Machinery: A Critical Analysis," *Industrial and Labor Relations Review,* vol. 5, no. 3, April, 1952, pp. 365–382.

Northrup, H. R., and M. Kahn: "Railroad Grievance Machinery: A Critical Analysis II," *Industrial and Labor Relations Review,* vol. 5, no. 4, July, 1952, pp. 540–559.

Piccoli, J. George: "Ground Rules of Successful Arbitration, *Personnel,* vol. 35, July/August, 1958, pp. 77–85.

Platt, Harry H.: "The Arbitration Process in the Settlement of Labor Disputes," *Journal of the American Judicature Society,* vol. 31, August, 1947, pp. 54–60.

Plaut, Frank: "Arbitrability under the Standard Labor Arbitration Clause," *Arbitration Journal,* vol. 14, no. 2, 1959, pp. 51–72.

Porter, Arthur R. Jr.: "The Irony of Arbitration," *Labor Law Journal,* vol. 15, no. 11, November, 1964, pp. 691–695.

Pragan, Otto: "Grievance Procedures in the Federal Service," *Monthly Labor Review,* vol. 89, no. 6, June, 1966, p. 609.

Prasow, Paul, and Edward Peters: "Semantic Aspects of Collective Bargaining," *ETC.: A Review of General Semantics,* vol. 25, no. 3, September, 1968, pp. 283–298.

Prasow, P., and E. Peters: "The Development of Judicial Arbitration in Labor Management Disputes," *California Management Review,* vol. 9, Spring, 1967, pp. 7–16.

Prasow, P., and E. Peters: "New Perspectives on Management's Reserved Rights," *Labor Law Journal,* vol. 18, no. 1, January, 1967, pp. 3–14.

Prasow, P.: "Reducing the Risks of Labor Arbitration," *California Management Review,* vol. 1, no. 3, Spring, 1959, pp. 39–46.

Prasow, P.: "Preventive Mediation: A Technique to Improve Industrial Relations," *Labor Law Journal,* vol. 1, no. 11, August, 1950, pp. 866–868.

Repas, Bob: "Grievance Procedures without Arbitration," *Industrial and Labor Relations Review,* vol. 20, no. 3, April, 1967, pp. 381–390.

Roberts, Benjamin C.: "Arbitration and Security Risk Disputes," *Arbitration Journal,* vol. 10, no. 1, 1955, pp. 13–30.

Roberts, Benjamin C., and G. Allan Dash, Jr.: "How to Get Better Results from Labor-Management Arbitration," *Arbitration Journal,* vol. 22, no. 1, 1967, pp. 1–23.

Rose, George: "Do the Requirements of Due Process Protect the Rights of Employes under Arbitration Procedures?" *Labor Law Journal,* vol. 16, no. 1, January, 1965, pp. 44–57.

Ross, Arthur M.: "The Well-Aged Arbitration Case," *Industrial and Labor Relations Review,* vol. 11, no. 2, January, 1958, pp. 262–271.

Sarnoff, Bernard: "Arbitration, Not NLRB Intervention," *Labor Law Journal,* vol. 18, no. 10, October, 1967, pp. 602–631.

Satter, Robert: "Principles of Arbitration in Wage Rate Disputes," *Industrial and Labor Relations Review,* vol. 1, no. 3, April, 1948, pp. 363–385.

Schubert, Robert C.: "Arbitration and Damage Claims for Violation of the No-strike Clause," *Labor Law Journal,* vol. 16, no. 12, December, 1965, pp. 751–764.

Seitz, Peter, and George Moskowitz: "The Arbitrator's Responsibility for Public Policy," *Arbitration Journal,* vol. 19, no. 1, 1964, pp. 23–44.

Seitz, Peter: Comment on "Value Judgments in the Decisions of Labor Arbitrators," *Industrial and Labor Relations Review,* vol. 21, no. 3, April, 1968, pp. 427–432.

Selby, Rose, and Maurice L. Cunningham: "Grievance Procedures in Major Contracts" and "Processing of Grievances," *Monthly Labor Review,* vol. 87, no. 10, October, 1964, pp. 1125–1130, vol. 87, no. 11, November, 1964, pp. 1269–1272.

Seligson, Harry: "Minority Group Employees, Discipline and the Arbitrator," *Labor Law Journal,* vol. 19, no. 9, September, 1968, pp. 544–554.

Seward, Ralph T.: "Arbitration and the Functions of Management, *Industrial and Labor Relations Review,* vol. 16, no. 2, January, 1963, pp. 235–239.

Shore, R. P.: "Conceptions of the Arbitrator's Role," *Journal of Applied Psychology,* vol. 50, April, 1966, pp. 172–178.

Shutkin, Joseph J.: "Preventive Arbitration—A Path to Perpetual Labor Peace and Prosperity," *Labor Law Journal,* vol. 19, no. 9, September, 1968, pp. 539–543.

Sirefman, Josef: "Rights without Remedies in Labor Arbitration," *Arbitration Journal,* vol. 18, no. 1, 1963, pp. 17–35.

Snyder, Franklin B.: "What Has the Supreme Court Done to Arbitration?" *Labor Law Journal,* vol. 12, no. 2, February, 1961, pp. 93–98.

Stark, Arthur (Executive Secretary, New York State Board of Mediation): "Factfinding in Labor Disputes," *Labor Law Journal,* vol. 3, no. 12, December, 1952, pp. 846–871.

Stein, Bruno: "Loyalty and Security Cases in Arbitration," *Industrial and Labor Relations Review,* vol. 17, no. 1, October, 1963, pp. 96–113.

Stevens, C. M.: "Analytics of Voluntary Arbitration Contract Disputes," *Industrial Relations,* vol. 7, no. 1, October, 1967, pp. 68–79.

Straus, Donald B.: "Labor Arbitration and Its Critics," *Arbitration Journal,* vol. 20, no. 4, 1965, pp. 197–211.

Sussman, Arthur: "Work Discipline versus Private Life: An Analysis of Arbitration Cases," *Industrial and Labor Relations Research,* vol. 10, no. 1, 1964, pp. 3–12.

Teele, John W.: "The Thought Processes of the Arbitrator," *Arbitration Journal,* vol. 17, no. 2, 1962, pp. 85–96.

Teele, J. W.: "But No Back Pay is Awarded," *Arbitration Journal,* vol. 19, no. 2, 1964, pp. 103–112.

Thomas, W. C.: "Preparing for Arbitration: A Do-It-Yourself Technique," *Personnel,* vol. 44, November, 1967, pp. 47–50.

Tobias, Paul H.: "In Defense of Creeping Legalism in Arbitration," *Industrial and Labor Relations Review,* vol. 13, no. 4, July, 1960, pp. 596–607.

United States Department of Labor: "Significant Decisions in Labor Cases," *Monthly Labor Review,* vol. 83, no. 8, August, 1960, pp. 853–857.

Van de Water, John R.: "Growth of Third-Party Power in the Settlement of Industrial Disputes," *Labor Law Journal,* vol. 12, no. 12, December, 1961, pp. 1135–1160.

Waks, Jay W.: "Arbitrator, Labor Board, or Both?" *Monthly Labor Review,* vol. 91, no. 12, December, 1968, pp. 1–5.

Waks, J. W.: "The 'Dual Jurisdiction' Problem in Labor Arbitration: A Research Report," *Arbitration Journal,* vol. 23, no. 4, 1968, pp. 201–227.

Wallen, Saul: "Arbitrators and Judges: Dispelling the Hays Haze," *California Management Review,* vol. 9, April, 1967, pp. 17–24.

Warns, Carl A.: "Arbitration and the Law," *Arbitration Journal,* vol. 15, no. 1, 1960, pp. 3–16.

Warren, Edgar L., and Irving Bernstein: "A Profile of Labor Arbitration," *Industrial and Labor Relations Review,* vol. 4, no. 2, January, 1951, pp. 200–222.

Wortman, Max S., and Fred Luthans: "Arbitration in a Changing Era," *Labor Law Journal,* vol. 15, no. 5, May, 1964, pp. 309–315.

Wyle, Benjamin: "Labor Arbitration and the Concept of Exclusive Representation," *Labor Law Journal,* vol. 17, no. 10, October, 1966, pp. 604–620.

Yagoda, Louis: "The Discipline Issue in Arbitration: Employer Rules," *Labor Law Journal,* vol. 15, no. 10, September, 1964, pp. 571–576.

Young, Dallas M.: "Fifty Years of Arbitration in Cleveland Transit," *Monthly Labor Review,* vol. 83, no. 5, May, 1960, pp. 464–471.

Law Review Articles

Aaron, Benjamin: "Some Procedural Problems in Arbitration," *Vanderbilt Law Review,* vol. 10, 1957, p. 733.

Aaron, Benjamin: "Arbitration in the Federal Courts: Aftermath of the Trilogy," *UCLA Law Review,* vol. 9, no. 2, March, 1962, p. 360.

Aaron, B.: "Judicial Intervention in Labor Arbitration, *Stanford Law Review,* vol. 20, 1967, p. 41.

Banta, William F.: "Labor Obligations of Successor Employers," *George Washington Law Review,* vol. 36, 1967, p. 215.

Bernstein, Merton: "Nudging and Shoving All Parties to a Jurisdictional Dispute into Arbitration: The Dubious Procedure of National Steel," *Harvard Law Review,* vol. 78, 1965, p. 784.

Bernstein, Merton C., and E. A. Jones, Jr.: "Jurisdictional Dispute Arbitration: The Jostling Professors," *UCLA Law Review,* vol. 14, 1966, p. 347.

Brinckerhoff, Clarke W.: "Judicial Review of Labor Arbitration Awards after the Trilogy," *Cornell Law Review,* vol. 53, 1967, p. 136.

Burstein, Herbert: "Labor Arbitration—A New Theology," *Villanova Law Review,* vol. 10, 1965, p. 287.

Cohen, Seymour: "NLRB—Poacher on the Arbitral Domain," *ABA Journal,* vol. 55, May, 1969, p. 437.

Cox, Archibald: "Some Lawyers' Problems in Grievance Arbitration," *Minnesota Law Review,* vol. 40, 1955, p. 41.

Cox, A.: "Reflections upon Labor Arbitration," *Harvard Law Review,* vol. 72, 1959, p. 1482.

Cox, A.: "Grievance Arbitration in the Federal Courts," *Harvard Law Review,* vol. 67, 1954, p. 591.

Crumbley, Alex: "A Union Obligation to Arbitrate a Member's Grievance," *Georgia State Bar Journal,* vol. 3, 1967, p. 340.

Cushman, Bernard: "Arbitration and the Duty to Bargain," *Wisconsin Law Review,* vol. 3, 1967, p. 612.

Davey, Harold W.: "The Supreme Court and Arbitration: The Musings of an Arbitrator," *Notre Dame Lawyer,* vol. 36, 1961, p. 138.

Davey, Harold W.: "Restructuring Grievance Arbitration Procedures: Some Modest Proposals," *Iowa Law Review,* vol. 54, Feb., 1969, p. 560.

De Silva, J. Thomas: "Arbitration Law: The Role of the Court on a Petition to Compel Arbitration [Posner v. Grunwald-Max Inc. (Cal) 363 P 2d 313]," *Southern California Law Review,* vol. 35, 1961, p. 52.

Diamond, Abraham A.: "The Process of Arbitration," *Chicago Bar Record,* vol. 46, 1964, p. 73.

Domke, Martin: "Arbitration," *New York University Law Review,* vol. 31, 1956, p. 577.

Feldesman, William: "Another Approach to Strikes: Inducements to Voluntary Arbitration," *George Washington Law Review,* vol. 33, 1964, p. 457.

Finley, Joseph E.: "Labor Arbitration: The Quest for Industrial Justice," *Western Reserve Law Review,* vol. 18, 1967, p. 1091.

Fleming, Robben Wright: "Arbitrators and Arbitrability," *Washington University Law Quarterly,* vol. 1962, 1962, p. 201.

Fleming, R. W.: "Arbitrators and the Remedy Power," *Virginia Law Review,* vol. 48, 1962, p. 1199.

Fleming, R. W.: "Labor Arbitration Process 1943–1963," *Kentucky Law Journal,* vol. 52, 1964, p. 817.

Fleming, R. W.: "The Labor Court Idea," *Michigan Law Review,* vol. 65, 1967, p. 1551.

Fleming, R. W.: "Problems of Procedural Regularity in Labor Arbitration," *Washington University Law Quarterly,* vol. 1961, 1961, p. 221.

Fleming, R. W.: "Reflections on the Nature of Labor Arbitration," *Michigan Law Review,* vol. 61, 1963, p. 1245.

Fleming, R. W.: "Some Observations on Contract Grievances before Courts and Arbitrators," *Stanford Law Review,* vol. 15, 1963, p. 595.

Fleming, R. W.: "Some Problems of Due Process and Fair Procedure in Labor Arbitration," *Stanford Law Review,* vol. 13, 1961, p. 235.

Fleming, R. W.: "Some Problems of Evidence before the Labor Arbitrator," *Michigan Law Review,* vol. 60, 1961, p. 133.

Freidin, Jesse, and Francis J. Ulman: "Arbitration and the National War Labor Board," *Harvard Law Review,* vol. 58, 1945, p. 309.

Fuller, Lon L.: "Collective Bargaining and the Arbitrator," *Wisconsin Law Review,* vol. 1963, 1963, p. 3.

Getman, J. G.: "Debate over the Caliber of Arbitrators: Judge Hays and His Critics," *Indiana Law Journal,* vol. 44, Winter, 1969, p. 182.

Gitelman, Morton: "The Evolution of Labor Arbitration,"*DePaul Law Review,* vol. 9, 1960, p. 181.

Graev, Lawrence G.: "Judicial Enforcement of Arbitration Awards: Employer's Neutrality Obligation Pending NLRB Certification Election Suspends Collectively Bargained Duty to Arbitrate," *George Washington Law Review,* vol. 36, 1968, p. 462.

Gregory, Charles O.: "Enforcement of Collective Agreements by Arbitration," *Virginia Law Review,* vol. 48, 1962, p. 883.

Gregory, C. O.: "Arbitration of Grievances under Collective Labor Agreements," *Georgia Law Review,* vol. 1, 1966, p. 20.

Hafen, Bruce C.: Note: "A Study of Labor Arbitration: The Values and the Risks of the Rule of Law," *Utah Law Review,* vol. 1967, 1967, p. 223.

Hays, Paul: "The Future of Labor Arbitration," *Yale Law Journal,* vol. 74, 1965, p. 1019.

Heiner, S. Phillip: "Express Exclusions from Arbitration–Accommodating the Consensual of the Nonconsensual," *Georgia Law Review,* vol. 1, 1967, p. 363.

Jones, Dallas L., and Russell A. Smith: "Management and Labor Appraisals and Criticisms of the Arbitration Process: A Report with Comments," *Michigan Law Review,* vol. 62, 1964, pp. 1115–1156.

Jones, Edgar A. Jr.: "The Accretion of Federal Power in Labor Arbitration–The Example of Arbitral Discovery," *University of Pennsylvania Law Review,* vol. 116, 1968, p. 830.

Jones, E. A., Jr.: "An Arbitral Answer to a Judicial Dilemma: The Carey Decision and Trilateral Arbitration of Jurisdictional Disputes," *UCLA Law Review,* vol. 11, 1964, p. 327.

Jones, E. A., Jr.: "Autobiography of a Decision: The Function of Innovation in Labor Arbitration and the National Steel Orders of Joinder and Interpleader," *UCLA Law Review*, vol. 10, 1963, p. 987.

Jones, E. A., Jr.: "Blind Man's Bluff and the 'Now' Problems of Apocrypha, Inc. and Local 711–Discovery Procedures in Collective Bargaining Disputes," *University of Pennsylvania Law Review*, vol. 116, 1968, p. 571.

Jones, E. A., Jr.: "Evidentiary Concepts in Labor Arbitration: Some Modern Variations on Ancient Legal Themes," *UCLA Law Review*, vol. 13, 1966, p. 1241.

Jones, E. A., Jr.: "The Labor Board, the Courts, and Arbitration–A Feasibility Study of Tribunal Interaction in Grievance Refusals to Disclose," *University of Pennsylvania Law Review*, vol. 116, 1968, p. 1185.

Jones, E. A., Jr.: "The Name of the Game Is Decision–Some Reflections on 'Arbitrability' and 'Authority' in Labor Arbitration," *Texas Law Review*, vol. 46, 1968, p. 865.

Jones, E. A., Jr.: "On Nudging and Shoving the National Steel Arbitration into a Dubious Procedure," *Harvard Law Review*, vol. 79, 1965, p. 327.

Jones, E. A., Jr.: "Power and Prudence in the Arbitration of Labor Disputes: A Venture in Some Hypotheses," *UCLA Law Review*, vol. 11, 1964, p. 675.

Jones, E. A., Jr.: "A Sequel in the Evolution of the Trilateral Arbitration of Jurisdictional Labor Disputes–The Supreme Court's Gift to Embattled Employers, *UCLA Law Review*, vol. 15, 1968, p. 877.

Jones, F. E., Jr.: "Nature of the Courts 'Jurisdiction' in Statutory Arbitration Post Awarded Motions," *California Law Review*, vol. 46, 1958, p. 411.

Kovarsky, Irving: "Labor Arbitration and Federal Pre-emption: The Overruling of Black vs. Cutter Laboratories, *Minnesota Law Review*, vol. 47, 1963, p. 531.

Kovarsky, Irving: "Individual Suits and Arbitration," *Howard Law Journal*, vol. 12, 1966, 213.

Martin, Donald J.: "Comment: The Polygraph and Labor Arbitration," *Syracuse Law Review*, vol. 19, Spring, 1968, p. 684.

Mendelsohn, Leonard T.: "Arbitration: A Review and Perspective, 1966," *Journal of the State Bar of California*, vol. 41, 1966, p. 494.

Meltzer, Bernard: "Ruminations about Ideology, Law and Labor Arbitration," *University of Chicago Law Review*, vol. 34, 1967, p. 546.

Meltzer, B.: "The Supreme Court, Arbitrability, and Collective Bargaining," *University of Chicago Law Review*, vol. 28, 1961, p. 464.

Meyer, Walter: "Enforcement of Arbitrators' Labor Injunctions in the Federal Courts," *Howard Law Journal*, vol. 7, 1961, p. 17.

Mueller, Robert J.: "The Role of the Wisconsin Employment [Relation] Board Arbitrator," *Wisconsin Law Review*, vol. 1963, 1963, p. 47.

Pirsig, Maynard E.: "The Minnesota Uniform Arbitration Act and the Lincoln Mills Case," *Minnesota Law Review*, vol. 42, 1958, p. 333.

Platt, H. H., and R. A. Levitt: "Practical Problems in Handling of Grievance and Arbitration Matters: The Relationship between Arbitration and Title VII of the Civil Rights Act of 1964," *Georgia Law Review*, vol. 54, Winter, 1969, p. 560.

Ringer, James M.: "Legality and Propriety of Agreements to Arbitrate Major and Minor Disputes in Public Employment," *Cornell Law Review*, vol. 54, 1968, p. 129.

Rothschild, Donald P.: "Arbitration and the NLRB, An Examination of Preferences and Prejudices and Their Relevance," *Ohio State Law Journal,* vol. 28, 1967, p. 195.

Rubenstein, Jerome S.: "Some Thoughts on Arbitration," *Marquette Law Review,* vol. 49, 1966, p. 695.

Sarpy, Leon, "Arbitration as a Means of Reducing Court Congestion," *Notre Dame Lawyer,* vol. 41, 1965, p. 182.

Shulman, Harry: "Reason, Contract and Law in Labor Relations," *Harvard Law Review,* vol. 68, 1955, p. 999.

Smith, Russell A., and Dallas L. Jones: "The Supreme Court and Labor Dispute Arbitration: The Emerging Federal Law," *Michigan Law Review,* vol. 63, 1965, p. 751.

Smith, R. A., and D. L. Jones: "The Impact of the Emerging Federal Law of Grievance Arbitration on Judges, Arbitrators, and Parties," *Virginia Law Review,* vol. 52, 1966, p. 831.

Sturges, W. A.: "Common-Law and Statutory Arbitration: Problems Arising from Their Co-existence," *Minnesota Law Review,* vol. 46, 1962, p. 819.

Taylor, George W.: "Voluntary Arbitration of Labor Disputes," *Michigan Law Review,* vol. 49, 1951, p. 787.

Tighe, William R., Jr.: "The Successor Employer and His Duty to Arbitrate under the Collective Bargaining Agreement of the Predecessor: The Progeny of John Wiley and Sons v. Livingston," *University of Pittsburgh Law Review,* vol. 29, 1967, p. 276.

Wallen, Saul: "Recent Supreme Court Decisions on Arbitration: An Arbitrator's View," *West Virginia Law Review,* vol. 63, 1961, p. 295.

Weiler, P. C.: "Role of the Labor Arbitrator: Alternative Versions," *University of Toronto Law Journal,* vol. 19, 1969, p. 16.

Weiss, Leo: "Labor Arbitration in the Federal Courts," *George Washington Law Review,* vol. 30, 1961, p. 285.

Wellington, Harry: "Judge Magruder and the Labor Contract," *Harvard Law Review,* vol. 72, 1959, p. 1268.

Youngdahl, James E.: "Awarding Interest in Labor Arbitration Cases," *Kentucky Law Journal,* vol. 54, 1966, p. 717.

"Admissibility of Parol Evidence in Judicial Determination of Arbitrability," *Michigan Law Review,* vol. 63, 1965, p. 1274.

"Circumventing Norris-LaGuardia with Arbitration Clauses," *Notre Dame Lawyer,* vol. 44, Feb., 1969, p. 31.

"Federal Arbitration Act and Application of the 'Separability Doctrine' in Federal Courts," *Duke Law Journal,* vol. 1968, 1968, p. 588.

"John Wiley and Sons v. Livingston, Survival of Arbitration Rights and Procedural Arbitrability," *Northwestern University Law Review,* vol. 60, 1965, p. 224.

"Judicial Enforcement of Labor Arbitrators' Awards," *University of Pennsylvania Law Review,* vol. 114, 1966, p. 1050.

"Judicial Review of Labor Arbitration Awards Which Rely on the Practices of the Parties," *Michigan Law Review,* vol. 65, 1967, p. 1647.

"Labor Law: Duty of Employer to Arbitrate with Union Representing Employees of Purchased Company," *Columbia Law Review,* vol. 66, 1966, p. 967.

"Some Problems Relating to Judicial Protection of the Right to Have Arbitration

Agreements Enforced under Subsection 301 (a) of the Taft-Hartley Act," *Columbia Law Review,* vol. 59, 1959, p. 153.
"The Supreme Court Speaks on Labor Arbitration–Exeunt the Courts," *Stanford Law Review,* vol. 13, 1961, p. 635.

Articles on State and International Arbitration Practices

Albritton, A. Dallas, Jr.: "Florida Arbitration Law," *Florida Bar Journal,* vol. 31, 1957, pp. 121–128.
Carrington, Paul: "The General Arbitration Statute of Texas," *Southwestern Law Journal,* vol. 20, March, 1966, pp. 21–62.
Craig, Alton W.: "Arbitration of Labor-Management Disputes in Canada," *Labor Law Journal,* vol. 12, no. 11, November, 1961, pp. 1053–1068.
Ehrlich, Leon: "Labor Arbitration in Pennsylvania," *Temple Law Quarterly,* vol. 24, October, 1950, pp. 107–136.
Feldman, Eddy S.: "Arbitration Law in California: Private Tribunals for Private Government," *Southern California Law Review,* vol. 30, no. 4, July, 1957, pp. 375–500.
Feldman, E. S.: "Arbitration Modernized–The New California Arbitration Act," *Southern California Law Review,* vol. 34, Summer, 1961, pp. 413–444.
Flexner, Jean Atherton: "Arbitration of Labor Disputes in Great Britain," *Industrial and Labor Relations Review,* vol. 1, no. 3, April, 1948, pp. 421–430.
Goldman, Alvin L.: "A Proposed Arbitration Act for Kentucky," *Arbitration Journal,* vol. 22, no. 4, 1967, pp. 193–221.
Gratch, Alan S.: "Grievance Settlement Machinery in England: Comparative Survey of the Arbitration Machinery as It Functions in the U. S. and in Three Major Industries in Great Britain," *Labor Law Journal,* vol. 12, no. 9, September, 1961, pp. 861–870.
Handsaker, Morrison, and Marjorie L. Handsaker: "Arbitration in Great Britain," *Industrial Relations,* vol. 1, no. 1, October, 1961, pp. 117–136.
Jagadeesh, T. K.: "Industrial Adjudication and Arbitration Procedure," *Industrial Relations,* vol. 15, no. 1, Calcutta, 1963, pp. 15–24.
"Judicial Arbitration in New York," *Saint John's Law Review,* vol. 36, December, 1961, pp. 110–126.
Kagel, Sam: "Application of the California Arbitration Statute," *California Law Review,* vol. 38, no. 5, December, 1950, pp. 799–829.
"Labor Arbitration in New Jersey," *Rutgers Law Review,* vol. 14, 1959, pp. 143–184.
Mantica, Margit: "Arbitration in Ancient Egypt," *Arbitration Journal,* vol. 12, no. 3, 1957, pp. 155–163.
Moran, Robert D.: "State Subsidized Arbitration: The Massachusetts Experience," *Labor Law Journal,* vol. 19, no. 10, October, 1968, pp. 628–639.
"The New York Arbitration Law," *Arbitration Journal,* vol. 18, no. 3, 1963, pp. 132–146.
"An Outline of Procedure under New York Arbitration Law," *Arbitration Journal,* vol. 20, no. 2, 1965, pp. 73–96.
Rosenzweig, Stefan: "International Arbitration as Viewed by a Student of Labor Arbitration," *Arbitration Journal,* vol. 20, no. 4, 1965, pp. 212–222.
Ross, M. H.: "Arbitration in North Carolina," *North Carolina Law Review,* vol. 29, June, 1951, pp. 460–472.

Sullivan, A. M.: "The Brehon, Ireland's Ancient Arbitrator," *Arbitration Journal,* vol. 11, no. 1, 1956, pp. 32–39.

Symposia and Conferences on Arbitration

"An Appraisal of Labor Arbitration," *Industrial and Labor Relations Review,* vol. 8, no. 1, October, 1954, pp. 49–89.

"Management Rights and Labor Arbitration: A Symposium," *Industrial and Labor Relations Review,* vol. 16, no. 2, January, 1963, pp. 183–253.

"Advanced Arbitration Seminar," *Labor Law Journal,* vol. 15, no. 9, September, 1964, pp. 577–621.

"Current Problems in Labor Relations and Arbitration," *New York State School of Industrial Relations,* 1954.

New York University Annual Conference on Labor (Published yearly since 1948. Each volume usually contains a series of articles on arbitration based upon lectures delivered during the Annual Conference on Labor conducted by the New York University Institute of Labor Relations), Matthew Bender, New York and BNA, Inc. Washington, D.C.

New York University Law Review, "Labor Arbitration," 37, May 1962, pp. 359–484.

"Book Review Symposium: Labor Arbitration Series," *Stanford Law Review,* vol. 5, July, 1953, pp. 846–889.

"Book Review Symposium: Labor Arbitration," *Stanford Law Review,* vol. 19, Fall, 1967, pp. 671–722.

Vanderbilt Law Review, vol. 10, no. 4, June, 1957. (Entire issue on arbitration)

Proceedings of the National Academy of Arbitrators

National Academy of Arbitrators, *Proceedings of Annual Meetings,* BNA, Inc. Washington, D.C. (These volumes constitute one of the richest collection of source material on labor arbitration in the United States and abroad. The articles are based upon papers read at the Annual Academy Meetings. The volumes also contain as appendices excellent reports of various Academy committees.)

The Profession of Labor Arbitration (Cumulative selection of addresses at first seven annual meetings, 1948 through 1954), Jean T. McKelvey, (ed.)

Arbitration Today, 1955, 8th Annual Meeting, Jean T. McKelvey, (ed.)

Management Rights and the Arbitration Process, 1956, 9th Annual Meeting, Jean T. McKelvey, (ed.)

Critical Issues in Labor Arbitration, 1957, 10th Annual Meeting, Jean T. McKelvey, (ed.)

The Arbitrator and the Parties, 1958, 11th Annual Meeting, Jean T. McKelvey, (ed.)

Arbitration and the Law, 1959, 12th Annual Meeting, Jean T. McKelvey, (ed.)

Challenges to Arbitration, 1960, 13th Annual Meeting, Jean T. McKelvey, (ed.)

Arbitration and Public Policy, 1961, 14th Annual Meeting, Spencer D. Pollard, (ed.)

Collective Bargaining and the Arbitrator's Role, 1962, 15th Annual Meeting, Mark L. Kahn, (ed.)

Labor Arbitration and Industrial Change, 1963, 16th Annual Meeting, Mark L. Kahn, (ed.)

Labor Arbitration—Perspectives and Problems, 1964, 17th Annual Meeting, Mark L. Kahn, (ed.)

Proceedings of the Eighteenth Annual Meeting of the National Academy of Arbitrators, 1965, 18th Annual Meeting, Dallas L. Jones, (ed.)

Problems of Proof in Arbitration, 1966, 19th Annual Meeting, Dallas L. Jones, (ed.)

The Arbitrator, the NLRB, and the Courts, 1967, 20th Annual Meeting, Dallas L. Jones, (ed.)

Developments in American and Foreign Arbitration, 1968, 21st Annual Meeting, Charles M. Rehmus, (ed.)

Arbitration and Social Change, 1969, 22nd Annual Meeting, Gerald G. Somers, (ed.).

Standard Arbitration Reporting Services

Labor Arbitration Reports (Contains full text of selected arbitration awards and opinions, reports of fact-finding boards, and Court decisions on labor arbitration—bound volumes published every six months), Bureau of National Affairs, Inc., Washington, D. C.

Labor Arbitration Awards (A full text reporter of labor arbitration awards and opinions rendered in the United States—bound volumes published periodically), Commerce Clearing House, Inc., Chicago, Ill.

American Labor Arbitration (Contains full text of selected arbitration awards and opinions rendered in the United States), Prentice-Hall, Inc., Englewood Cliffs, N. J.

Special References for the Arbitrator

These government publications represent a compilation of significant and varied collective agreement clauses, arranged in related categories, and accompanied by an analysis of the purpose and background of each category.

Arbitration Procedures, U.S. Department of Labor (Major Collective Bargaining Agreements), Bulletin No. 1425-6, Washington, D. C., 1966.

Grievance Procedures, U.S. Department of Labor (Major Collective Bargaining Agreements), Bulletin No. 1425-1, Washington, D. C., 1964.

Arbitration Bibliographies

American Arbitration Association: *Arbitration Bibliography* (A comprehensive list of books, pamphlets, articles and unpublished manuscripts on arbitration), New York, N.Y., 1954.

Jensen, Vernon H., and Harold Ross: *Bibliography of Dispute Settlement by Third Parties,* New York State School of Industrial Relations, Cornell University, 1955.

Burns, Robert K.: *Collective Bargaining and Arbitration: The Case of the Daily Newspaper,* Ph.D., University of Chicago, 1943.

Dissertations on Arbitration

Cordell, J. W.: *The Arbitration of Seniority Disputes: Standards and Decision Patterns,* Ph.D., Claremont Graduate School, 1965.

Gadon, Herman: *Arbitration and the Meaning of the Collective Bargaining Agreement,* Ph.D., M.I.T., 1953.

Harris, Philip: *An Analysis of Selected Arbitration Awards as They Affect Management's Control over the Supervisor in the Organization,* Ph.D., New York University, 1964.

Heliker, George B., *Grievance Arbitration in the Automobile Industry: A Comparative Analysis of the History and Results in the Big Three,* Ph.D., University of Michigan, 1954.

Prasow, Paul: *An Examination of the Role of Arbitration Principles in an Emerging Industrial Jurisprudence,* Ph.D., University of Southern California, 1948.

Stessin, Lawrence: *Employee Discipline and the Arbitration Process,* Ph.D., New York University, 1959.

Wiggins, Ronald Luther: *Arbitration of Industrial Engineering Cases,* Ph.D., UCLA, 1965.

Young, Stanley J.: *Grievance Arbitration in the Anthracite Industry,* Ph.D., University of Pennsylvania, 1956.

Case Index

Name Index

415

Subject Index

419

γ